Oracle Database Exadata Cloud Service: A Beginner's Guide

Brian Spendolini

Mc
Graw
Hill
Education

New York   Chicago   San Francisco
Athens   London   Madrid   Mexico City
Milan   New Delhi   Singapore   Sydney   Toronto

Library of Congress Cataloging-in-Publication Data

Names: Spendolini, Brian, author.
Title: Oracle Database Exadata Cloud Service : a beginner's guide / Brian
  Spendolini.
Description: New York : McGraw-Hill Education, [2019] | Includes index.
Identifiers: LCCN 2018043758 | ISBN 9781260120875 (alk. paper)
Subjects: LCSH: Cloud computing. | Database management. | Oracle (Computer
  file)
Classification: LCC QA76.585 .S64 2019 | DDC 004.67/82—dc23 LC record available at
https://lccn.loc.gov/2018043758

McGraw-Hill Education books are available at special quantity discounts to use as premiums and sales promotions, or for use in corporate training programs. To contact a representative, please visit the Contact Us pages at www.mhprofessional.com.

Oracle Database Exadata Cloud Service: A Beginner's Guide

1 2 3 4 5 6 QVS 22 21 20 19 18

ISBN   978-1-260-12087-5
MHID   1-260-12087-2

Sponsoring Editor	**Technical Editor**	**Production Supervisor**
Lisa McClain	Jeffrey Cowen	James Kussow
Editorial Supervisor	**Copy Editor**	**Composition**
Janet Walden	Lisa Theobald	Cenveo Publisher Services
Project Manager	**Proofreader**	**Illustration**
Ishan Chaudhary,	Lisa McCoy	Cenveo Publisher Services
Cenveo® Publisher Services	**Indexer**	**Art Director, Cover**
Acquisitions Coordinator	Karin Arrigoni	Jeff Weeks
Claire Yee		

This book is dedicated to my wife, Jenny. The immeasurable amount of wisdom and countless life lessons she has imparted upon me continue to shape and guide my path through life, with the most important one being, "Just Relax."

About the Author

Brian Spendolini is currently the product manager of Oracle's Exadata Cloud Service and previously served as a product manager for the Oracle Enterprise Database Cloud Service (DBCS). Brian started Oracle back in 2000 when there were no camera phones and has been in multiple roles and positions, from sales to support. He lives with his family on the west side of a volcano.

About the Technical Editor

Jeffrey Cowen is an Oracle Cloud Infrastructure Certified Associate with more than 18 years of IT experience, 10 years of which have been working with Exadata. He has been working with Exadata since its inception, specializing in the Exadata Cloud Service since it was released in the Oracle Public Cloud. At Oracle, Jeffrey is considered an expert in the Exadata Cloud Service and has delivered many successful proofs of concept, demonstrating to customers the power of Exadata in the Cloud.

Contents at a Glance

1   The Oracle Database Exadata Cloud Service   1

2   Creating an Oracle Database Exadata Cloud Service   9

3   The Exadata Cloud Service UI   57

4   Exadata Cloud Services Tooling and CLIs   101

5   Smart Scans and Storage Indexes   147

6   Compression Techniques   171

7   Exadata Resource Management   197

8   Exadata Smart Flash Cache   227

9   Managing and Monitoring the Exadata Cloud Service   239

10   Migrating to the Exadata Cloud Service   269

    Index   321

Contents

Introduction   xi
Acknowledgments   xii

1 The Oracle Database Exadata Cloud Service **1**
What Have We Here?   2
    Exadata in the Cloud   3
A Tale of Two Data Centers   3
Exadata Cloud Service Shapes   4
    X5 Exadata Cloud Service   4
    X6 Exadata Cloud Service   5
    X7 Exadata Cloud Service   6
    Virtualized?   6
Database Options   7
Exadata in a Cloud Environment   8
Summary   8

2 Creating an Oracle Database Exadata Cloud Service **9**
On-Premises Exadata Database Machine Setup   10
    On-Premises Physical Setup   10
    Setting Up the Software   12
    Securing the Platform   13
Creating the Exadata Cloud Service   15
    Creating the Exadata Cloud Service in OCI-C   15
    Creating the Exadata Cloud Service in OCI   35
Summary   56

3 The Exadata Cloud Service UI **57**
The ExaCS UI in Oracle Cloud Infrastructure Classic   58
    Modifying the ExaCS   58
    Deploying Database Features on the ExaCS   73

The ExaCS UI in OCI 87
    The Service Details Page 88
Summary 99

4 Exadata Cloud Services Tooling and CLIs **101**
Setting Up Your Local Environment 102
The Exadata Cloud Service REST Services 102
    REST Services in OCI-C 104
    REST Services in OCI 110
    Configure the OCI CLI 111
    Using the OCI CLI 115
The Exadata Cloud Service CLIs 121
    Connecting to Your Exadata Cloud Service 121
    Using dbaasapi Tooling 126
    Using dbaascli Tooling 129
    Patching a Database Using exadbcpatchmulti 135
The Database Backup CLI 137
    Working with Backups Using the bkup CLI 145
    Database Recovery Using the bkup CLI 146
Summary 146

5 Smart Scans and Storage Indexes **147**
The Exadata Database Machine Architecture 148
    Hardware Components 149
    Software Components 150
Query Offloading 152
Using Smart Scans with an Exadata Cloud Service 154
    Setting Up Your Environment 154
Using Smart Scans 159
Storage Indexes 165
Summary 170

6 Compression Techniques **171**
Data Blocks, Extents, and Segments 172
    Data Blocks 173
    Extents 176
    Segments 176
Oracle Advanced Row Compression 179
    Using Advanced Row Compression 179
Hybrid Columnar Compression Overview 182
Using Hybrid Columnar Compression 184
    Warehouse Compression 184
    Archive Compression 185
    Examples of HCC Use 185
    HCC Performance 189

DBMS_COMPRESSION 193
Compression Tips 196
Summary 196

7 Exadata Resource Management **197**
I/O Resource Manager 198
    Configuring IORM in ExaCS 199
Database Resource Manager 203
    Resource Consumer Groups 204
    Resource Plan Directives 204
    Resource Plans 204
    Putting It All Together 204
Database Resource Manager and Multitenancy 206
Configuring DBRM in the Exadata Cloud Service 207
    Prerequisites for Using Resource Manager with a CDB 207
    Creating a CDB Resource Plan 208
    Seeing DBRM in Action 214
    Intra-Database Resource Manager 218
    Changing Plans Using DBMS_SCHEDULER 224
Instance Caging 224
Summary 226

8 Exadata Smart Flash Cache **227**
The Rise of Flash 228
    Exadata and Flash 229
Exadata Smart Flash Cache 229
    When the Flash Cache Is Used 229
    WriteThrough and WriteBack 230
    Exadata Smart Flash Logging 231
    Creating the Flash Cache and Flash Grid Disks 233
    Columnar Flash Caching and Storage Server In-Memory Cache 236
    The CELL_FLASH_CACHE Storage Clause 236
Summary 237

9 Managing and Monitoring the Exadata Cloud Service **239**
11g Database Control and Enterprise Manager Express 240
    Database Control 240
    Enterprise Manager Express 243
SQL Developer 246
    Connecting to an Exadata Cloud Service with SQL Developer 246
    Managing the Database with the DBA Panel 250
Enterprise Manager Cloud Control 13cR2 251
    Configure the Hybrid Gateway 251
ExaCLI 259
    Using ExaCLI 261
    ExaCLI Examples 263
Summary 268

10 Migrating to the Exadata Cloud Service **269**
     TDE Location 270
     Data Pump 270
          Schema Export and Import 270
          Full Transportable Export and Import 273
     RMAN 277
          Creating a Stage Directory 278
          Recovering the Database 281
     Transportable Tablespaces 285
          Moving a Single Tablespace 285
          Cross-Platform Transportable Tablespaces Using Backup Sets 290
     Pluggable Databases 293
          PDB Unplug/Plug in 293
          Non-CDB to a PDB 296
          Remote Clone a PDB or Non-CDB 304
          Remote Clone a PDB 311
     TDE, 18c, and PDBs 314
          Isolated Mode 315
     Summary 320

Index **321**

Introduction

The Exadata Database Machine has traditionally been a hardware-only service, purchased and placed in your data center for you to manage, from top to bottom. With the Exadata Cloud Service, Oracle brings the power of the Exadata into anyone's hands with a few simple clicks, simplifying a once lengthy and time-consuming process into a single web page.

The book starts with creating the Exadata Cloud Service and the components that go into its creation. From networking to security, we cover the steps to create a full Exadata in the Oracle Cloud. Next, you'll create your first database on the service. Choose a version, backup strategy, and type, and in no time you'll have a fully functioning database in the Cloud.

The next section covers all the cloud-based tooling, the "special sauce" of the Exadata Cloud Service. Use the tooling via REST services or from the command line; the book covers how to use each method and the functions within.

The next chapters of the book cover what makes an Exadata an Exadata. We start with query offloading—how the Exadata Database Machine removes the database I/O bottleneck. The compression chapter covers Hybrid Columnar Compression, the built-in compression method that improves compression ratios up to 30 times.

The resource management chapter covers the various levels in which we can control how the service and databases within act. We can assign CPU power, memory, processes, and priority at multiple levels to enable different workloads to be on a single platform.

We end the book with how to manage the Exadata Cloud Service, as well as how to move existing databases to the service. Examples and code show you how you can move on-premises databases to the Exadata Cloud Service. You'll learn how you can move multiple versions, PDBs, non-CDBs, and platform transitions (endianness) in the final chapter.

Code Available Online

All code examples in the book are available on the Downloads & Resources tab of the book page at www.oraclepressbooks.com.

Acknowledgments

I'd like to thank the Exadata PM team under Ashish Ray at Oracle. They have been integral in the development of this book.

CHAPTER 1

The Oracle Database Exadata Cloud Service

I n 2000, when I started working at Oracle, the company's tag line was "The Internet Changes Everything." Now it's all about the cloud. The move to the cloud has been accelerating faster than any trend I have seen in the enterprise technology community. So what's driving the change? How we work, do business, develop applications, and demand information is fueling the movement. With just about everyone having computers in their pocket these days, we have access to information and services 24/7 around the world. Our need for information and services is helping to drive the move to cloud systems, which are highly available and accessible anywhere, to anyone, at any time. And as hardware is aging and data centers become more expensive, the cloud is a logical step for the enterprise to reduce costs and modernize processes.

The Oracle Cloud Infrastructure (OCI) is Oracle's solution to the enterprise cloud question, bringing the ability to have secure private networks, encrypted communications, and the best-performing databases and bare metal servers. And speaking of the best-performing database platform, the Exadata Cloud Service is the platform on which Oracle runs best, as seen in thousands of on-premises customers (and cloud customers), and it provides a cloud experience that anyone can use.

What Have We Here?

This book will guide you through creating and setting up the Oracle Database Exadata Cloud Service, or ExaCS for short. It covers the various ways you can create and deploy ExaCS and how you can move your data and connect your applications to this service. A few chapters also discuss what you can do with the service once it's up and running. What this book isn't going to do is provide a deep exploration into the inner workings of an Exadata Database Machine. Many excellent books have already been written about this, and attempting to go into that level of detail in a beginner book isn't necessary. Also, because those books' authors have done such a good job, attempting to replicate them would be futile!

So why an introductory book on an engineered system that traditionally was set up, maintained, and used by very experienced people? A few reasons. First, is me. As the product manager of the service, I have a unique perspective. I try to talk with as many customers who purchase the service as I can to see how they are using it and understand their experience with an Exadata Database Machine. In many of these scenarios, the customer purchasing and using the ExaCS has never been exposed to Exadata. They come to this service after hearing from marketing and word of mouth that the Exadata Database Machine is the best platform on which to run an Oracle database. But when handed the keys, they don't really know how to start or what features are available to them. That's why this book has come into being. The cloud has brought technology to the masses in ways never seen before, and I hope to offer some helpful information about it in this book.

One of the main goals of any cloud, especially the Oracle Cloud, is to make what was once complex or out of the reach to many users easy. With our smart phones, sharing and taking pictures that look great is as easy as touching the screen—the software takes care of the rest. White balance, focusing, exposure—all settings we previously had to keep in mind when composing a picture are pushed into the background, automatically set based on what the software deems to be the best for that particular situation. Taking a landscape photo of a beach in Hawaii? The phone will adjust the exposure from the bright sun. Taking a portrait of a spouse or child? Now the phone can blur the background, isolating the subject.

The Oracle Cloud seeks to replicate this ease of use. You can now create Java application servers and Oracle databases with an OS and all the storage needed in as little as 20 minutes.

Not only that, you can do it simply by answering a few questions in the user interface. Think back, previous to this, the steps you needed to perform to get a similar system up and running:

1. Find or procure hardware.
2. Place the hardware in the data center.
3. Set up networking.
4. Get the Linux or Windows admin to install and configure the operating system.
5. Download or stage the software of the particular product you want to use.
6. Get a DBA to install and configure the database or application server.

As you can see, it was a very lengthy process with multiple actors. To paraphrase a line from a popular movie, "What if I told you that you could have an Oracle database up and running in 20 minutes." This is the promise of the Oracle Cloud.

Exadata in the Cloud

This now brings us to the Exadata Database Machine. We've mentioned the steps once required to configure an Oracle database or Java application server. Add the complexity of an engineered system. Once the Exadata shows up at your data center, it has to sit a while to acclimate to the temperature. Then you start the process of plugging it in. Now this isn't a "grab a power strip and you're done" kind of thing. Each rack has two preinstalled power distribution units, not to mention that if the data center does not have enough power, you could inadvertently cause a brownout. And even before plugging it in, you have to consider weight requirements of the data center floor, temperature, and humidity settings, as well as ventilation and air conditioning specifications.

With Exadata Cloud Service, you can have a service up and running in as little as 2 hours—hardware prepped, networking set up, OS installed and ready for a database to be created. How long does it take to get a database created on the service? Around 30 minutes. ExaCS truly brings the cloud to a complex system, making it accessible to anyone with a web browser.

A Tale of Two Data Centers

ExaCS is available in both types of Oracle Cloud data centers. Let's start with the Oracle Cloud Infrastructure Classic (OCI-C) data centers, where it appeared first. The OCI-C data centers, also referred to as OPC or Oracle Public Cloud, are located across the world with four locations having ExaCS: Chicago, Illinois, and Ashburn, Virginia, in the United States; Slough/London in the United Kingdom; and Amsterdam in the Netherlands. These data centers also house our Platform as a Service (PaaS) and Infrastructure as a Service (IaaS) cloud products. These include application server services such as Java and Node.js, Integration services such as Process Cloud, Integration Cloud, and Oracle SOA Suite, as well as Business Intelligence (BI) and Data Visualization Cloud Services. All of these services can easily be integrated or attached to the ExaCS as the backend database. The OPC data centers have been online for more than three years now and are expanding into other regions. The OPC data centers have X5, X6, and X7 Exadata Cloud Services, which are discussed later in this chapter.

The other type of cloud data center is Oracle Cloud Infrastructure. OCI data centers offer bare metal servers, fully software-defined networks, high-performance infrastructure services, and at least three availability zones in each region. They are also home to Oracle's new Autonomous services. These data centers are located in Phoenix, Arizona, and Ashburn, Virginia, in the United

States; London in the UK; and in Frankfurt, Germany. They promote bare metal servers with fast NVM Express (NVMe) storage and a flat or Clos network. ExaCS is available in all OCI regions in each of the availability domains with X6 and X7 Exadata Cloud Services.

Exadata Cloud Service Shapes

When choosing the ExaCS, you have many options based upon your computing and storage needs. The service offers a quarter, half, or full rack. Each of these services offers different CPU and storage options. The shapes comprise the following hardware components:

	Base System	Quarter	Half	Full
Database Compute Nodes	2	2	4	8
Storage Servers	3	3	6	12

Let's look at computing power first. As mentioned, the OPC data centers have X5, X6, and X7 Exadata Cloud Services, with the OCI data centers having X6 and X7.

X5 Exadata Cloud Service

The X5 shapes start with a maximum of 34 per-database compute nodes, up to 272 for a full rack shape. The following table describes the OCPU counts for each shape:

	X5 Quarter	X5 Half	X5 Full
Maximum CPU Count	68	136	272

Next is storage. The X5 option contains less storage and memory than the X6, with half the storage and a third of the memory. Although this sounds suboptimal, many workloads fit with no issues with these lower-resourced X5s.

The next table shows the storage and memory options for the X5 shapes. Each X5 database compute node has 240GB of RAM. This table also includes the total flash capacity on an ExaCS.

	X5 Quarter	X5 Half	X5 Full
Total Memory	480GB	960GB	1920GB
Usable Storage	42TB	84TB	168TB
Flash Capacity	19.2TB	38.4TB	76.8TB

The usable storage number is a bit misleading: it gives you the usable storage amount before you split the disks for backup, recovery, and sparse cloning. The next table will give you the true counts for the maximum database size on an X5. Storage can be broken down a few ways, depending on the options you choose. While creating your service, you can pick whether you want local backups (backups on the Exadata Storage Servers) and cloud backups, or just cloud backups. You can choose also to have some of the disk reserved for sparse cloning. Here are the storage breakdowns:

- **Cloud backups only** 80 percent data, 20 percent recovery
- **Cloud and local backups** 40 percent data, 60 percent recovery

- **Cloud backups only and sparse cloning**   60 percent data, 20 percent recovery, 20 percent sparse
- **Local and cloud backups with sparse cloning**   35 percent data, 50 percent recovery, 15 percent sparse

Using these ratios, you can determine the maximum size of the data disks for database data file storage:

	X5 Quarter	X5 Half	X5 Full
Cloud Backups Only (80% data, 20% recovery)	33.6TB Data 8.4TB Recovery	67.2TB Data 16.8TB Recovery	134.4TB Data 33.6TB Recovery
Cloud and Local Backups (40% data, 60% recovery)	16.8TB Data 25.2TB Recovery	33.6TB Data 50.4TB Recovery	67.2TB Data 100.8TB Recovery
Cloud Backups and Sparse Cloning (60% Data, 20% Recovery, 20% Sparse)	25.2TB Data 8.4TB Recovery 8.4TB Sparse	50.4TB Data 16.8TB Recovery 16.8TB Sparse	100.8TB Data 33.6TB Recovery 33.6TB Sparse
Local and Cloud Backups with Sparse Cloning (35% Data, 50% Recovery, 15% Sparse)	14.7TB Data 21.0TB Recovery 6.3TB Sparse	29.4TB Data 42.0TB Recovery 12.6TB Sparse	58.8TB Data 84TB Recovery 25.2TB Sparse

X6 Exadata Cloud Service

The maximum X6 CPU counts for each shape are shown here:

	X6 Quarter	X6 Half	X6 Full
Maximum CPU Count	84	168	336

An X6 offers three times more memory and double the storage compared to an X5. The following table shows the storage, flash capacity, and memory contained in each of the shapes. In this case, the X6 has 720GB of RAM per database compute node.

	X6 Quarter	X6 Half	X6 Full
Total Memory	1440GB	2880GB	5760GB
Usable Storage	85.4TB	170.9TB	341.7TB
Flash Capacity	38.4TB	76.8TB	153.6TB

And here's a breakdown of disk sizes for the X6:

	X6 Quarter	X6 Half	X6 Full
Cloud Backups Only (80% Data, 20% Recovery)	67.2TB Data 16.8TB Recovery	134.4TB Data 33.6TB Recovery	268.8TB Data 67.2TB Recovery
Cloud and Local Backups (40% Data, 60% Recovery)	33.6TB Data 50.4TB Recovery	67.2TB Data 100.8TB Recovery	134.4TB Data 201.6TB Recovery
Cloud Backups and Sparse Cloning (60% Data, 20% Recovery, 20% Sparse)	50.4TB Data 16.8TB Recovery 16.8TB Sparse	100.8TB Data 33.6TB Recovery 33.6TB Sparse	201.6TB Data 67.2TB Recovery 67.2TB Sparse
Local and Cloud Backups with Sparse Cloning (35% Data, 50% Recovery, 15% Sparse)	29.4TB Data 42.0TB Recovery 12.6TB Sparse	58.8TB Data 84TB Recovery 25.2TB Sparse	117.6TB Data 168.0TB Recovery 50.4TB Sparse

X7 Exadata Cloud Service

The X7 is Oracle's latest version of the Exadata Database Machine. It offers more storage and double the flash of an X6, plus 25-gigabit Ethernet. It also introduces the Base System, a lower-cost option than an X7 quarter rack with less storage and fewer CPUs. The maximum CPU count for the four shapes is as follows:

	X7 Quarter	X7 Half	X7 Full
Maximum CPU Count	92	184	368

Although the memory remains the same per compute node from the X6, storage and flash amount increase:

	X7 Quarter	X7 Half	X7 Full
Total Memory	1440GB	2880GB	5760GB
Usable Storage	106.9TB	213.8TB	427.6TB
Flash Capacity	76.8TB	153.6TB	307.2TB

Here's a breakdown of maximum database sizes for the X7:

	X7 Quarter	X7 Half	X7 Full
Cloud Backups Only (80% Data, 20% Recovery)	85.5TB Data 21.4TB Recovery	171.1TB Data 42.8TB Recovery	342.1TB Data 85.6TB Recovery
Cloud and Local Backups (40% Data, 60% Recovery)	42.8TB Data 64.1TB Recovery	85.5TB Data 128.2TB Recovery	171.1TB Data 256.4TB Recovery
Cloud Backups and Sparse Cloning (60% Data, 20% Recovery, 20% Sparse)	64.1TB Data 21.4TB Recovery 21.4TB Sparse	128.2TB Data 42.8TB Recovery 42.8TB Sparse	256.4TB Data 85.6TB Recovery 85.6 TB Sparse
Local and Cloud Backups with Sparse Cloning (35% Data, 50% Recovery, 15% Sparse)	37.4TB Data 53.5TB Recovery 16TB Sparse	74.8TB Data 107TB Recovery 32TB Sparse	149.6TB Data 214TB Recovery 64TB Sparse

Virtualized?

If you are familiar with the Exadata Database Machine, you may notice that some memory and CPUs are missing from the preceding tables. This is correct, and here is why: ExaCS virtualizes the OS on the database compute nodes. Some of the CPUs and memory are needed to run the hypervisor, thus the missing resources. Now you may ask, "Wait a minute. It's virtualized?" Yes, but the overhead is quite small and not noticeable in day-to-day workloads and operations. The OS is virtualized for a few reasons as well. First, it enables Oracle to perform maintenance independent of the running operating system. It also allows for scaling or bursting of CPUs, dynamically adding or removing them with zero downtime. Lastly, it enables customers to create multiple VM clusters on their Exadata Cloud Service isolating workloads and groups of users, all getting dedicated Exadata resources.

Database Options

One of the advantages of ExaCS is that the subscription price includes just about every database option available. This is a change in the licensing modes Oracle usually uses, where customers pick and choose what they want to use, similar to a menu. Although pricing and licensing will not be discussed in this book, it's important to point out that the ability to use options that may have been out of a customer's budget is a tremendous benefit to customers moving to the cloud. Although I'll discuss how to implement and use some of these options later in the book, I'll go over a few details now regarding what is available with the service. With the flex pricing model, all Enterprise Edition features such as Virtual Private Database (VPD) and Flashback database are included as well as the following:

- Multitenant
- Partitioning
- Real Application Testing
- Advanced compression
- Advanced security
- Label security
- Database Vault
- Online Analytical Processing (OLAP)
- Advanced analytics
- Spatial and Graph
- Diagnostics Pack
- Tuning Pack
- Database Lifecycle Management Pack
- Data Masking and Subsetting Pack
- Cloud Management Pack for Oracle Database
- Real Application Clusters (RAC)
- Database In-Memory
- Active Data Guard

You also get all the Exadata Database Machine innovations. This is what separates traditional commodity hardware from Exadata. Some of these innovations are Smart Scan, Smart Flash Cache, I/O Resource Manager (IORM), Hybrid Columnar Compression (HCC), and storage indexes. Later chapters of this book will discuss these innovations and how they work, with examples that will hopefully give you ideas about how they can work for you and your workloads.

The other pricing model is called Bring Your Own License. In this model, if you have Enterprise Edition Database licenses shelved on premises, you can bring those to the Exadata Cloud Service. Also, any options you have shelved can be used as well.

You also get some free options with this pricing model: Transparent Database Encryption, Data Masking and Subsetting Pack, Diagnostics and Tuning Packs, and Real Application Testing.

In addition, the high availability of the Exadata hardware system itself includes many redundant components such as power supplies, storage nodes, and networking. If a particular component were to fail, a backup will pick up the load until the primary is replaced. In the cloud, you don't have to worry about replacing it; data center operations see the part failure, schedule a repair/replace time, and perform the maintenance—and all of this is usually transparent to you and the workload running on the Exadata Cloud Service.

Exadata in a Cloud Environment

If you have done any research on the Exadata Cloud or you follow Oracle's marketing, you may have come across the Exadata Cloud at Customer. In this model, Oracle will deliver an Exadata Database Machine to your data center, wire it up, turn it on, and "cloudify" it, making it act just as the cloud service does. The advantage here is that if you have sensitive data, regional data restrictions, or you like having the hardware where you can see it, the Exadata Cloud at Customer is an option. It acts just like the cloud service; all the user interfaces, functionality, and ease of use are retained. While this book is based on the Exadata Cloud Service, many of the UI flows and the core Exadata functionality will be relevant to Exadata Cloud at Customer.

Whether you chose the cloud service or the at Customer model, we can apply use cases across both. One of the use cases for Exadata is consolidation. The service enables you to deploy multiple Oracle databases on a single service. The space on the database compute nodes can hold about 12 to 14 Oracle homes comfortably on an X5/X6 and over 50 on an X7. You can also deploy a mix of Oracle versions—choose from 11.2.0.4, 12.1.0.2, 12.2.0.1, or 18c with a 12.2 or 18c Grid Infrastructure. This mix of versions enables a consolidation of multiple databases deployed across multiple pieces of hardware in the enterprise to be placed on one highly available service. The multitenant option of the 12c and 18c databases further add to the consolidation story, with the ability to have multiple pluggable databases under a single container database.

Existing on-premises Exadata Database Machine customers also look to the cloud service as a disaster recovery platform. With Active Data Guard, the cloud has become an offsite DR platform that can be utilized for development and testing until the need to switch over. This enables enterprises to regain some of the computing power and space used for test and development on premises and shift it to the cloud.

Combining data movement services to a single database can create a secure cloud data warehouse for reporting and analytics. Using such cloud services as the GoldenGate; Data Integration Platform Cloud; or an extract, transform, and load (ETL) tool, you can move large amounts of data into a single cloud database running on the Exadata Cloud Service for a secure unified reporting platform.

The last use case centers on the platform itself. Again, being the product manager of the service, I get to interact with many customers who are using the service. One of the most popular use cases I see is the moving of the Oracle E-Business Suite to the cloud. This is not a decision to be taken lightly, because some companies store all their financial data in these databases. Such a move mainly stems from aging hardware and the cost to keep it up and running.

Summary

So, back to the question posed in the beginning of this chapter: What have we here? Who is it for? This book is a roadmap, a guide, a workbook for those who have access to an ExaCS service with little or no previous Exadata Database Machine experience. Over half of the customers who have purchased the system have no experience with Exadata, and this book will serve as a companion, getting them through the creation of the service and their first database. This book will give you ideas on how to use this service to speed up database workloads and create a highly available, secure platform for your data.

CHAPTER 2

Creating an Oracle Database Exadata Cloud Service

A s mentioned in the previous chapter, the cloud is all about speed: the ability to create a service or database within minutes and hours rather than days or months, and the ability to be agile, to change how we work day-to-day with these new tools brought to us by the cloud. This chapter discusses how to create an Exadata Cloud Service and a starter database.

On-Premises Exadata Database Machine Setup

Each on-premises Exadata Database Machine is built according to the customer's specific requirements at a factory in Oregon. A customer may want extra memory, extra storage cells for more database storage, or more compute nodes for higher availability and more processing power. On the pricelist, as it stands today, is the X7, Oracle's newest offering. (To view the pricelist, use your favorite search engine and look up "Oracle Engineered Systems Price List.")

Oracle offers a few variations of the on-premises Exadata: the X7-8 and X7-2. The X7-8 uses large-scale, eight-socket symmetric multiprocessing (SMP) servers instead of the two-socket servers used in X7-2. The X7-8 can also hold about four times more memory than the X7-2. The additional processors and memory on the X7-8 create a platform well suited for high-end OLTP workloads and in-memory workloads.

Another configuration option with the X7-2 and X7-8 involves storage: you can choose between Extreme Flash (EF) or High Capacity (HC). With the EF option, each storage server contains eight 6.4TB F640 PCI flash drives, offering 51.2TB of raw flash capacity. The HC storage server comprises twelve 10TB Serial Attached SCSI (SAS) disk drives with 120TB total raw disk capacity per storage server. It also contains four F640 NVM Express (NVMe) PCIe cards with a total raw capacity of 25.6TB of flash memory. The flash memory on the HC servers is used differently from the flash memory in the EF storage servers where it is configured as Exadata Smart Flash Cache—a cache in front of the disks. The storage servers consist of memory, CPU, and the two choices of disk (EF or HC).

So, with all these specifications, what are the configurations of the Exadata Cloud Service? The cloud offers, as mentioned previously, a mix of X5s, X6s, and X7s. All the cloud configurations are the -2 models with high-capacity storage servers. This offers the greatest flexibility while providing shapes that meet the broadest customer needs.

On-Premises Physical Setup

After you have chosen the configuration you want to use on-premises, Oracle builds it and ships it to your data center. The process of setting up the Exadata in your data center is a lengthy one that starts with the unboxing.

NOTE
I was curious whether, seeing unboxing videos of new electronics is popular on the Net, anyone had ever created an "unboxing my Exadata" video. Sadly, there are no Exadata unboxing videos. I'll add that to my "to-do" list.

The Oracle Exadata Database Machine documentation provides a detailed section on the unboxing or unpacking process. The documentation even includes a picture, as shown in Figure 2-1. (I find it humorous that, with all the specialty tools included in the shipping container, a No. 2 Phillips screwdriver is not included.)

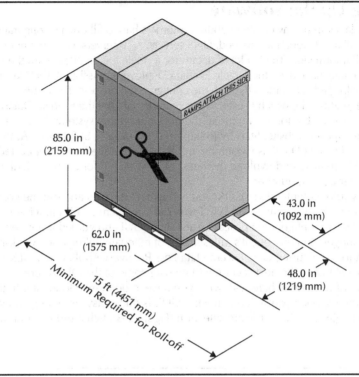

85.0 in
(2159 mm)

43.0 in
(1092 mm)

62.0 in
(1575 mm)

48.0 in
(1219 mm)

15 ft (4451 mm)
Minimum Required for Roll-off

FIGURE 2-1.   *Unpacking the Exadata Database Machine. Who even owns scissors that big?*

After you've unpacked the machine, you need to roll it onto the data center floor. The floor and space in the data center must adhere to specific requirements: The floor must be able to support more than 2100 pounds, and the unit has specific power requirements for the power distribution units (PDUs). Each rack has two PDUs and specific power plugs are used depending on your country's configuration (Figure 2-2).

After you plug in the Exadata, but before you power it on, you need to let the Exadata acclimate to the temperature of the data center. This will enable any humidity or moisture to leave the hardware before the power on.

FIGURE 2-2.   *Low-voltage, three-phase PDU power connector for North America*

Setting Up the Software

When Exadata was first available in 2008, customers had to fill out a Configuration Worksheet that contained all the IP addresses needed, DNS servers, NTP servers, compute node hostnames, and storage cell information. That's a lot of details for a single file. In 2012, with the release of the X3 Exadata, Oracle introduced the Oracle Exadata Deployment Assistant (OEDA). This application offers a GUI to help guide customers through the configuration process. The result is the Oracle Exadata Rack configuration file, which is used to create and configure the Exadata Database Machine.

OEDA is available for just about all the major operating systems. You can download it from the Oracle Support website. Start by looking up "MOS Note 888828.1." At the bottom of this note, titled "Exadata Database Machine and Exadata Storage Server Supported Versions (Doc ID 888828.1)," are links to download the latest OEDA version for each particular OS—the download itself is under a patch number.

Once you've downloaded OEDA, you can extract the files and run the config.sh on Linux, macOS, or UNIX; or, on Microsoft Windows, run config.cmd. This launches OEDA, and you are ready to start the configuration process. The OEDA GUI and guided input helps you streamline the Exadata configuration process; it's miles ahead of manually filling out a worksheet. You can also use OEDA for configuring Oracle Zero Data Loss Recovery Appliance (ZDLRA) and the Oracle SPARC SuperCluster. The next section will go over some of the OEDA screens so you can compare the amount of work done here with what you have to do in the cloud later in this chapter.

The process, once you've launched the GUI, is quite easy, assuming you know the values to enter. You begin with the hardware selection (Figure 2-3). What did you purchase?

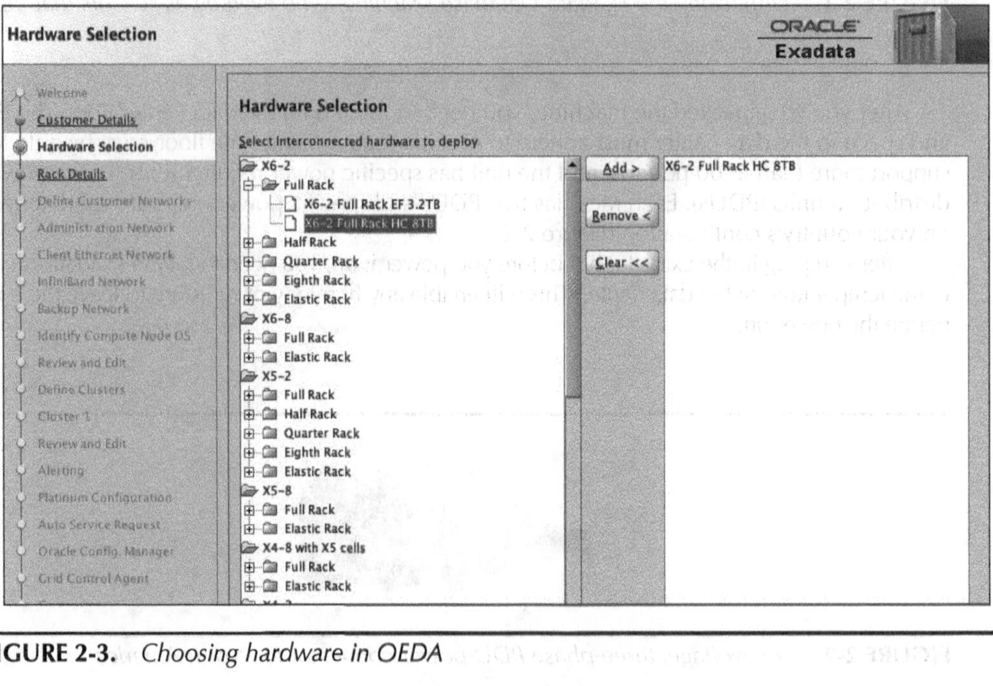

FIGURE 2-3. *Choosing hardware in OEDA*

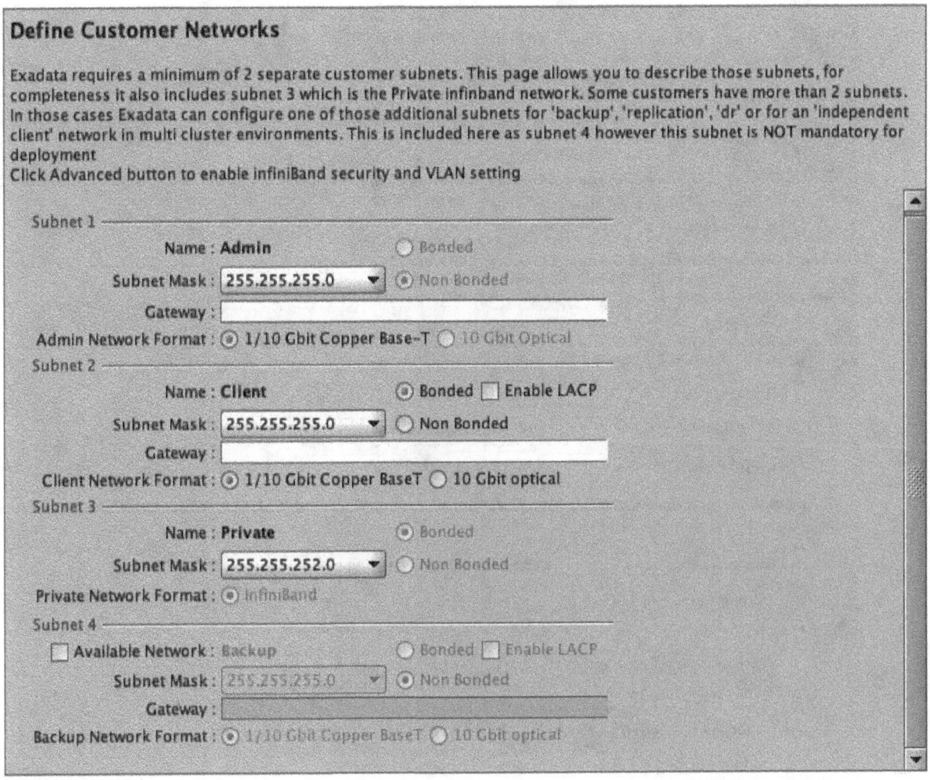

Define Customer Networks

Exadata requires a minimum of 2 separate customer subnets. This page allows you to describe those subnets, for completeness it also includes subnet 3 which is the Private infinband network. Some customers have more than 2 subnets. In those cases Exadata can configure one of those additional subnets for 'backup', 'replication', 'dr' or for an 'independent client' network in multi cluster environments. This is included here as subnet 4 however this subnet is NOT mandatory for deployment
Click Advanced button to enable infiniBand security and VLAN setting

Subnet 1
Name : **Admin**   ○ Bonded
Subnet Mask : 255.255.255.0 ▼   ◉ Non Bonded
Gateway :
Admin Network Format : ◉ 1/10 Gbit Copper Base-T ○ 10 Gbit Optical
Subnet 2
Name : **Client**   ◉ Bonded ☐ Enable LACP
Subnet Mask : 255.255.255.0 ▼   ○ Non Bonded
Gateway :
Client Network Format : ◉ 1/10 Gbit Copper BaseT ○ 10 Gbit optical
Subnet 3
Name : **Private**   ◉ Bonded
Subnet Mask : 255.255.252.0 ▼   ○ Non Bonded
Private Network Format : ◉ InfiniBand
Subnet 4
☐ Available Network : Backup   ○ Bonded ☐ Enable LACP
Subnet Mask : 255.255.255.0 ▼   ◉ Non Bonded
Gateway :
Backup Network Format : ◉ 1/10 Gbit Copper BaseT ○ 10 Gbit optical

FIGURE 2-4.   *Configuring the Exadata networks*

Next up is the network configuration (Figure 2-4). OEDA will guide you through configuring the network of the data center, the admin and client networks, the InfiniBand Network of the Exadata rack, and the backup network for database backups.

Next, you'll configure the database node clusters (Figure 2-5). Here you can define users, software locations, the starter database, and Automatic Storage Management (ASM) disk group layouts.

Once OEDA is completed, it will return a configuration XML file and an HTML file (Figure 2-6) with the values you entered for review. You can now start configuring the Exadata Database Machine.

Securing the Platform

You should now have a running Exadata Database Machine (if all went well), but you need to keep it secure at multiple levels so that you do not allow unauthorized access to the OS, database, or storage cells.

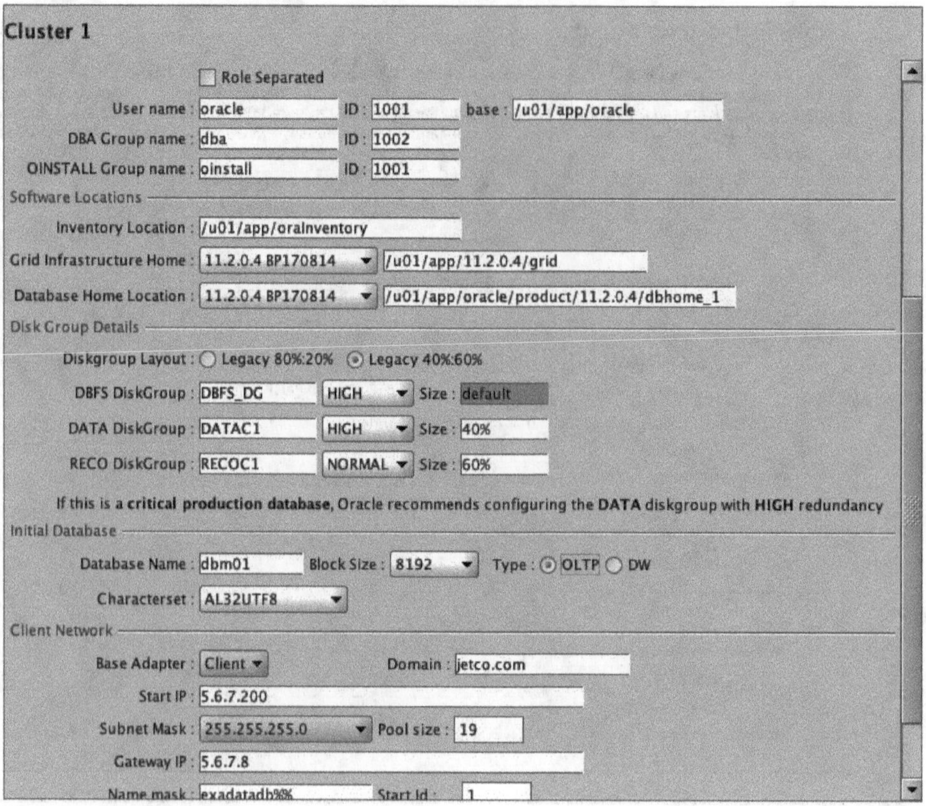

Cluster 1

☐ Role Separated

User name : oracle   ID : 1001   base : /u01/app/oracle
DBA Group name : dba   ID : 1002
OINSTALL Group name : oinstall   ID : 1001

Software Locations
Inventory Location : /u01/app/oraInventory
Grid Infrastructure Home : 11.2.0.4 BP170814 ▼ /u01/app/11.2.0.4/grid
Database Home Location : 11.2.0.4 BP170814 ▼ /u01/app/oracle/product/11.2.0.4/dbhome_1

Disk Group Details
Diskgroup Layout : ○ Legacy 80%:20% ● Legacy 40%:60%
DBFS DiskGroup : DBFS_DG   HIGH ▼ Size : default
DATA DiskGroup : DATAC1   HIGH ▼ Size : 40%
RECO DiskGroup : RECOC1   NORMAL ▼ Size : 60%

If this is **a critical production database**, Oracle recommends configuring the **DATA** diskgroup with **HIGH** redundancy

Initial Database
Database Name : dbm01   Block Size : 8192 ▼   Type : ● OLTP ○ DW
Characterset : AL32UTF8 ▼

Client Network
Base Adapter : Client ▼   Domain : jetco.com
Start IP : 5.6.7.200
Subnet Mask : 255.255.255.0 ▼ Pool size : 19
Gateway IP : 5.6.7.8
Name mask : exadatadb%% Start Id : 1

FIGURE 2-5. *Configuring the cluster*

NOTE
The following is not a comprehensive list, but more of an overview. If you are securing an actual on-premises Exadata, follow the documentation and your company's best practices.

You need to configure four levels of security with an Exadata Database Machine: network, database compute node, storage cell, and backups. Each level has specific guidelines you need to follow for your intranet as well as your particular corporate standards. Oracle provides best practices in their documentation to help with this process.

TIP
Remember that you have to keep the physical machine secure. Keep the rack door locked and monitor data center access.

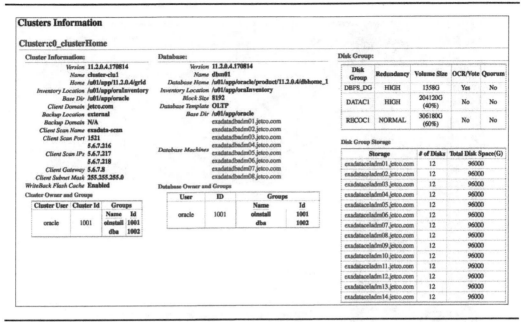

Clusters Information

Cluster:c0_clusterHome

Cluster Information:

Version	11.2.0.4.170814
Name	cluster-clu1
Home	/u01/app/11.2.0.4/grid
Inventory Location	/u01/app/oraInventory
Base Dir	/u01/app/oracle
Client Domain	jetco.com
Backup Location	external
Backup Domain	N/A
Client Scan Name	exadata-scan
Client Scan Port	1521
	5.6.7.216
Client Scan IPz	5.6.7.217
	5.6.7.218
Client Gateway	5.6.7.8
Client Subnet Mask	255.255.255.0
WriteBack Flash Cache	Enabled

Cluster Owner and Groups

Cluster User	Cluster Id	Groups	
		Name	Id
oracle	1001	oinstall	1001
		dba	1002

Database:

Version	11.2.0.4.170814
Name	dbm01
Database Home	/u01/app/oracle/product/11.2.0.4/dbhome_1
Inventory Location	/u01/app/oraInventory
Block Size	8192
Database Template	OLTP
Base Dir	/u01/app/oracle
	exadatadbadm01.jetco.com
	exadatadbadm02.jetco.com
	exadatadbadm03.jetco.com
	exadatadbadm04.jetco.com
Database Machines	exadatadbadm05.jetco.com
	exadatadbadm06.jetco.com
	exadatadbadm07.jetco.com
	exadatadbadm08.jetco.com

Database Owner and Groups

User	ID	Groups	
		Name	Id
oracle	1001	oinstall	1001
		dba	1002

Disk Group:

Disk Group	Redundancy	Volume Size	OCR/Vote	Quorum
DBFS_DG	HIGH	1358G	Yes	No
DATAC1	HIGH	204120G (40%)	No	No
RECOC1	NORMAL	306180G (60%)	No	No

Disk Group Storage

Storage	# of Disks	Total Disk Space(G)
exadataceladm01.jetco.com	12	96000
exadataceladm02.jetco.com	12	96000
exadataceladm03.jetco.com	12	96000
exadataceladm04.jetco.com	12	96000
exadataceladm05.jetco.com	12	96000
exadataceladm06.jetco.com	12	96000
exadataceladm07.jetco.com	12	96000
exadataceladm08.jetco.com	12	96000
exadataceladm09.jetco.com	12	96000
exadataceladm10.jetco.com	12	96000
exadataceladm11.jetco.com	12	96000
exadataceladm12.jetco.com	12	96000
exadataceladm13.jetco.com	12	96000
exadataceladm14.jetco.com	12	96000

FIGURE 2-6.   *The OEDA configuration HTML file*

Creating the Exadata Cloud Service

This section outlines the steps to create an Exadata Cloud Service, which are similar to setup in some aspects, but simplified with fewer steps. At this time, Oracle provides the Exadata Cloud Service within its two types of Cloud Data Centers, as mentioned in Chapter 1, and both are discussed throughout this and the following chapters.

I'm making a big assumption for the following two sections: I'm assuming you have or can get access to all the services and modules we will be using to create the services. If that's not the case, you will need to work with the person who has access to the networking pieces to create the Exadata Cloud Service (ExaCS).

Creating the Exadata Cloud Service in OCI-C

Let's start by creating ExaCS in the Oracle Cloud Infrastructure Classic (OCI-C). After purchasing the Oracle Cloud Service, you will receive an e-mail asking you to activate your account. Once it's activated, you log in to the cloud account (Figure 2-7) with your username and password. Once you've logged in, you will be presented with the Oracle Cloud Services Dashboard.

NOTE
If you forget about the e-mail or have deleted it, you can access your service via cloud.oracle.com. On cloud.oracle.com, click Sign In in the top section of the page. On the next page, set the select list to Cloud Account with Identity Service and enter your Cloud Account Name (Identity Domain) in the text box. Then click the blue My Services button.

FIGURE 2-7.   *Logging into the cloud account*

Here you also may or may not see the Exadata tile (the clickable tile). If you do not see it, there should be a Customize Dashboard tile or a Customize Dashboard button in the upper-right corner (Figure 2-8).

Click the tile or button to open a modal window. In the Customize Dashboard modal, click the Show button next to the Exadata service, and click Show next to any other services you want to show (Figure 2-9). Close the modal when you're done.

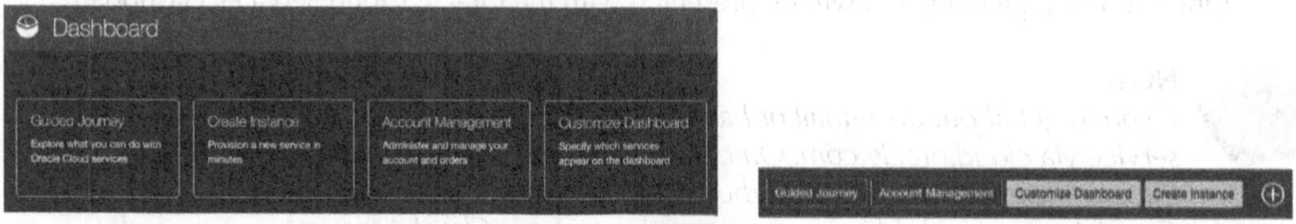

FIGURE 2-8.   *Customize Dashboard tile (left) and button*

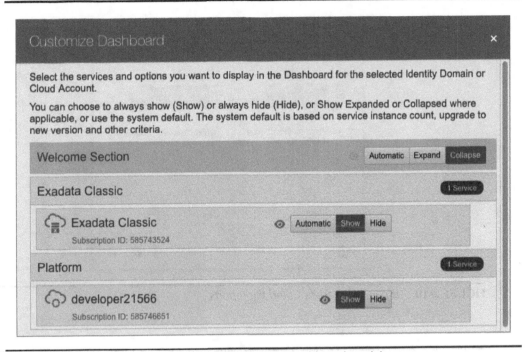

FIGURE 2-9.   *Showing services from the Customize Dashboard modal*

Now that you can see the Exadata tile on the dashboard, let's look at the features it contains. Start by clicking the plus icon to expand the tile—this will show reports that inhabit this section (Figure 2-10).

Click the gear icon at the bottom right to open a modal where you can select up to four billing metrics/reports to display on the tile when it's expanded (Figure 2-11).

After you select some metrics or leave it as is, close the modal (click Done or Cancel) and look back at the Exadata tile. Click the pop-out menu icon to see four choices: View Details, Open Service Console, View Account Usage Details, and Maintenance and Service Requests:

- **View Details**   Shows a page where you can not only view the details of your Exadata Cloud Service but also more importantly, start the creation process.

- **Open Service Console**   Opens the Database as a Service creation page, which is used for creating databases not only on your Exadata Cloud Service but also for the Platform as a Service (PaaS) product for general-purpose databases.

- **View Account Usage Details**   Shows the accounts area of the cloud UI. Here you can view the usage patterns of the cloud account, approve additional purchased orders, and see who the account administrators are.

- **Maintenance and Service Requests**   Shows all service requests you have logged against this account as well as maintenance notifications.

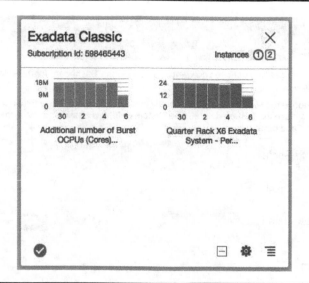

FIGURE 2-10. *Expanded Exadata Cloud tile reports*

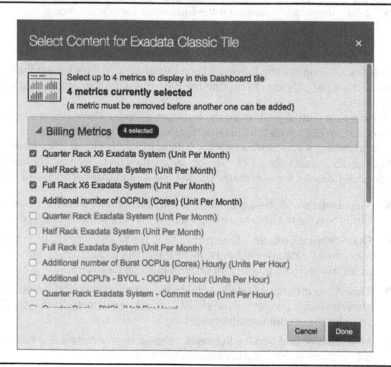

FIGURE 2-11. *Billing Metrics selection modal*

Now it's time to start the service instance creation process. First, though, if this service uses IP networks, you will need to create these. If your service does not use IP networks, you can skip the next section.

Creating IP Networks

To create an IP network, go to the Compute Classic tile on the dashboard and from the pop-up menu, choose the Open Service Console (Figure 2-12).

At the top of the next page, click the Network tab (Figure 2-13). On this page you will create two IP networks: one for the client traffic and a second for the backup traffic. Before you create any IP networks, however, make sure that where the IP networks are being created is at the same data center location where you want the Exadata Cloud Service to be located. Figure 2-14 shows the site location of the data center you are currently using. To change the site, click the Site drop-down and a Site Selector modal opens (Figure 2-15).

Choose the data center where you want the IP networks created—this should be the same site where the Exadata Cloud Service will be created. Click OK.

Along the left side of the Compute Classic Network tab in the dashboard, choose IP Networks. Click the Create IP Network button at the upper right of the page (Figure 2-16).

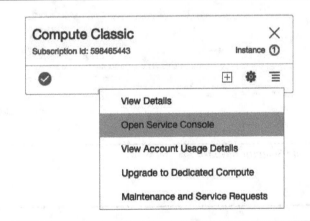

FIGURE 2-12. *Choose the Compute Classic Service Console.*

FIGURE 2-13. *Click the Network tab*

FIGURE 2-14. *Site selector*

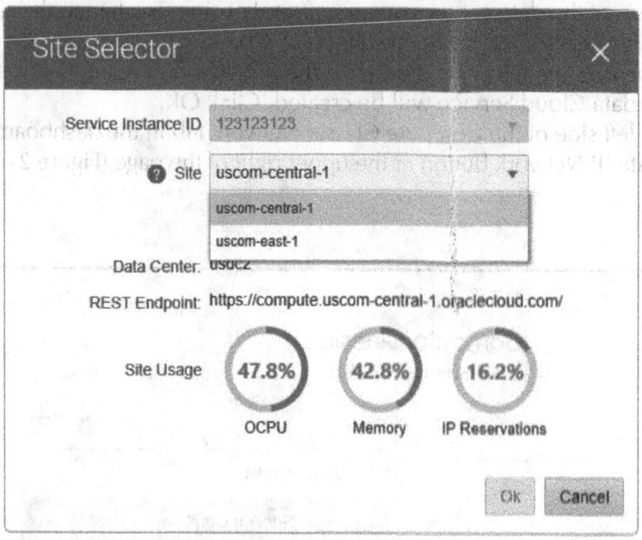

FIGURE 2-15. *Site Selector modal*

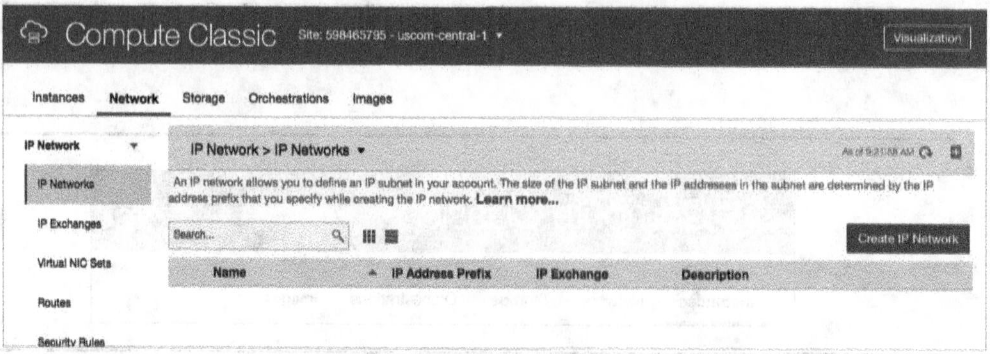

FIGURE 2-16. *Click the Create IP Network button*

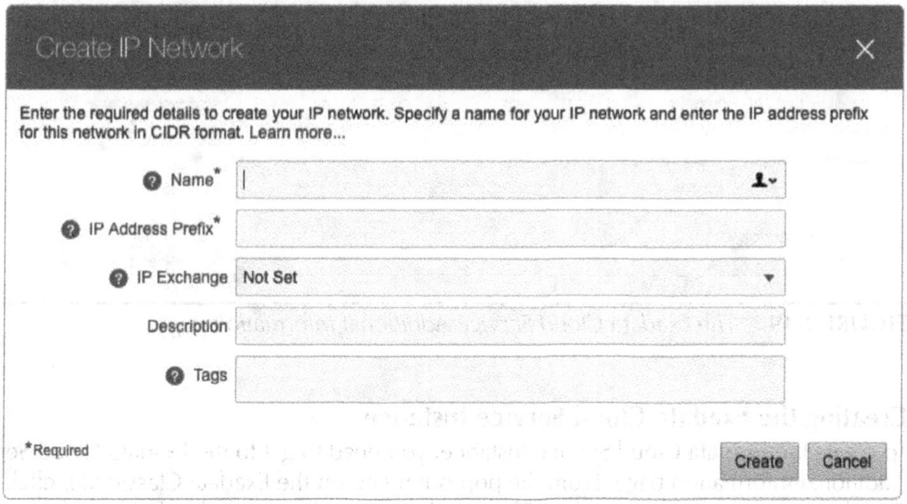

FIGURE 2-17. *Naming the network and creating a CIDR block*

In the Create IP Network modal (Figure 2-17), name your network and assign it a CIDR block. For this example, we'll name the network client-network and assign it a CIDR block (IP range) of 10.10.0.0/20. (You may assign any CIDR block you want.) For now, all you need to fill out in this modal are these two fields. Click Create when you're done.

Perform the exact same steps for the backup network, except name the backup network backup-network and assign it a CIDR block of 10.11.0.0/20. (You may assign any CIDR block you want.) Click Create.

You now have our two IP networks created for your Exadata Cloud Service (Figure 2-18). When you're done, return to the Cloud Services dashboard.

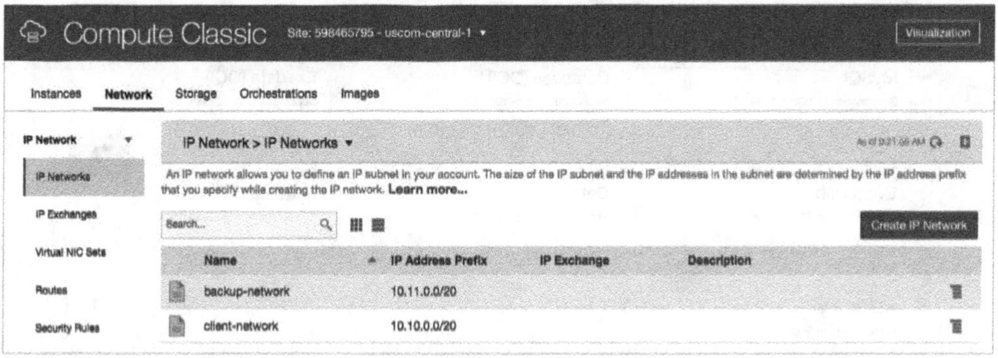

FIGURE 2-18. *Created IP networks in the dashboard*

FIGURE 2-19. *The Exadata Cloud Service Additional Information page*

Creating the Exadata Cloud Service Instance

To create the Exadata Cloud Service instance, you need to get to the Exadata Cloud Service Additional Information page. From the pop-out menu on the Exadata Classic tile, click the View Details option; or click the Exadata Classic title itself in the tile on the dashboard.

On the Additional Information page, click the Create Service Instance button at the lower right (Figure 2-19).

You can also click the Create Instance button at the upper right of the dashboard to open the Create Instance modal. Here you can quickly create an instance of many cloud services. To create an ExaCS instance, find the Exadata Classic mini tile and click Create (Figure 2-20). Either method will get you to the Create Service Instance page, where you can create the Exadata Cloud Service.

Instance Details   Your Instance Details page will look similar to the top screenshot in Figure 2-21 if IP networks are enabled or the bottom screenshot if they are not enabled. As you fill out this page, the differences will be pointed out.

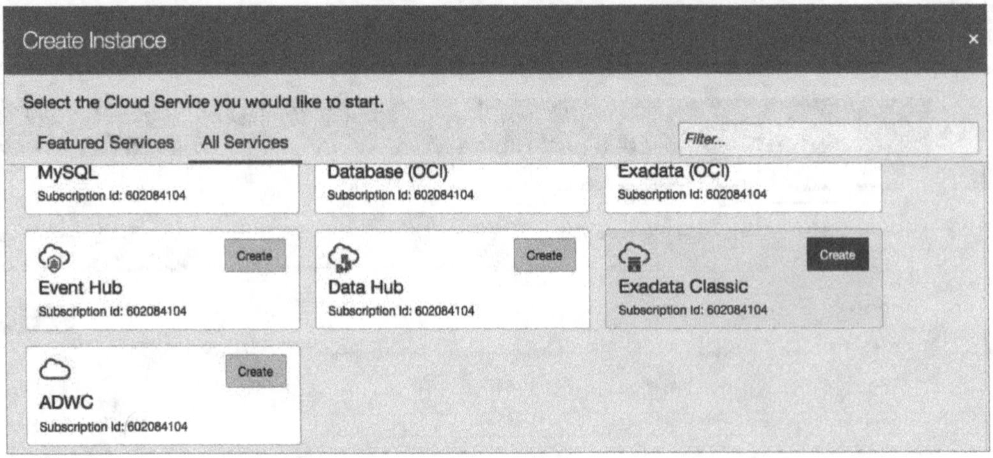

FIGURE 2-20. *Create Instance modal*

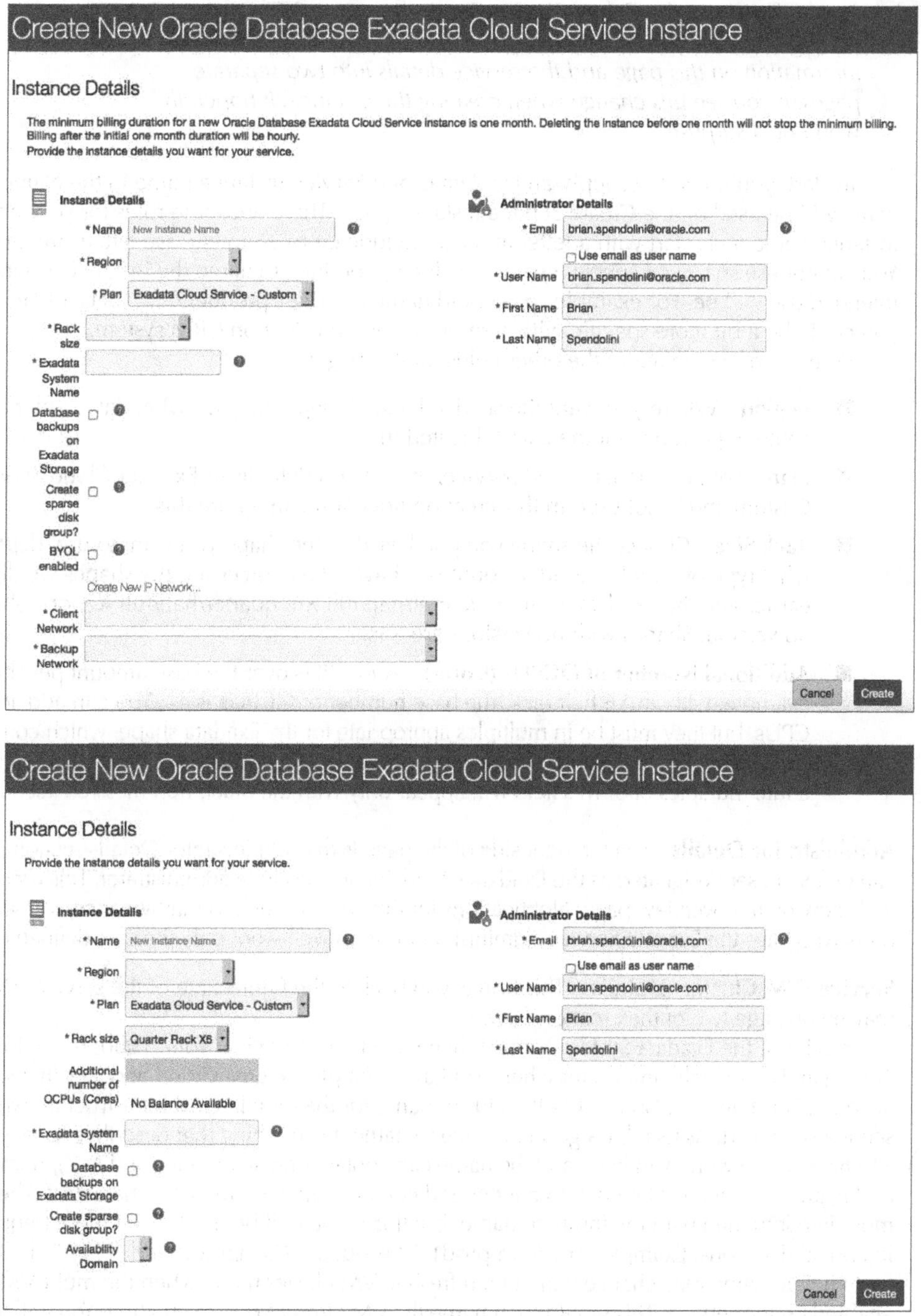

FIGURE 2-21. *Instance Details page with IP networks, top, and without IP networks, bottom*

NOTE
As of this writing, the Create Exadata Service pages in OCI-C were undergoing changes. I submitted the UI mock-ups and split the admin information on this page and the service details into two separate pages. If you see this change when creating the instance, it hopefully won't be a surprise.

To start, you'll need to supply an Exadata Cloud Service instance name in the Name field. This name will be used on the Create Service Instance page. There are some rules for your name: The instance name must start with a letter and can include up to 25 lowercase letters and numbers. You cannot use spaces or special characters. It's a good idea to name the instance around what its intended use will be. For example, you could name this one "production," "uat," or "testdev," or you could be a bit more specific with "crmprod" for a production CRM system.

Here's information about the other fields on this page:

- **Region**   Where you want the service located, depending on what data center and data center type you want the ExaCS located in.

- **Plan**   For an Exadata Cloud Service, this always defaults to Exadata Cloud Service – Custom and is not used in this creation flow. You can ignore this.

- **Rack Size**   Choose the shape you purchased or the shape you want to use, depending on what type of Oracle Cloud account you have. The choices are the shapes we discussed earlier and the Exadata version: quarter/half/full X6, quarter/half/full X7, or a shape with no version. Shapes with no versions are X5s.

- **Additional Number of OCPUs (Cores)**   Add CPUs over the base amount per shape. For example, with an X6 half rack, the base number of OCPUs is 44. You can add additional CPUs, but they must be in multiples appropriate for the Exadata shape, which corresponds to the number of DB compute nodes. So for a quarter, multiples of 2; a half, multiples of 4; and a full, multiples of 8. This field will appear only with the older, non-metered account types.

Administrator Details   On the right side of the page is the Administrator Details section, where you can define a user designated as the Exadata Cloud Service instance administrator. This user's details will show on the overview page. Notifications for this service, such as maintenance, are sent out to users who have the Exadata Service Administrator role as well—not only the user defined here.

Service (VM Cluster) Details   This brings you back to the future state of the service. This section may be on page two of the creation flow.

You'll use the Exadata System Name when you create and view your database deployments. This again is especially important when you have multiple Exadata Cloud Services in a single account. This name is also used as the cluster name for the Oracle Grid Infrastructure when the service is created. As usual, it's good practice to name it something that describes its use. You have 11 characters to work with here, and the name can contain only letters (a–z and A–Z), numerals (0–9), and hyphens (-); it must begin with a letter and contain a maximum of 11 characters. There's a bit more freedom than with the instance name, but this name will be used much more frequently and in critical decisions. Examples are "crm-prod1," "test-uat," "CRMprod," and "HR1." The Exadata System field name may change with a UI refresh to VM cluster name when the multi-VM option is enabled on the service. This would then name the VM cluster you are creating. You will also have the option of creating this initial VM cluster with a set number of OCPUs, memory, Exadata storage, and local storage for Oracle homes.

The Database Backups On Exadata Storage checkbox is a very important selection. Here you decide if you want to use local backups or just cloud backups. This choice cannot be easily changed after instance creation, so do not take this selection lightly. One guiding decision for local backups is how you are going to use this ExaCS. Do you need to have lightning-fast recovery at the expense of less database data file space? For production deployments, the answer is usually yes. You can sacrifice database data file space for the ability to recover in case of an emergency.

With a test, development, or user acceptance testing (UAT) system, recovering from a cloud backup may be fast enough to allow for more database data file storage on that particular instance. Again, this is a decision that needs to be carefully considered so that you utilize the space correctly.

The next checkbox, Create Sparse Disk Group, has a similar effect; it will reduce the amount of recovery and database data file space for the ability to create snapshots and clones. Depending on the usage of the system and your needs, you can decide whether or not to choose this option. Refer to Chapter 1 to see how the grid disks can be split out and sized per Exadata version.

You may also see a checkbox for BYOL. This sets up your service to use the BYOL (bring your own licensing) licensing model when you use shelved licenses that you have on premises for this Exadata Cloud Service instance.

Selecting the Oversubscribe checkbox lets you oversubscribe the OCPUs on your service, essentially using them twice for VM clusters. For example, if you have a base count of 20 OCPUs, oversubscription would enable you to use 40 OCPUs for VM clusters. There are two rules, though: First, the largest VM cluster cannot exceed the total number of physical OCPUs available. In this example, even if oversubscribed, you can not create a VM larger than 20 OCPUs. The second rule is that the total number of OCPUs used across all VM clusters cannot be greater than two times the physical limit. So, in this example, you cannot have more than 40 OCPUs used across all VM clusters.

Last on this page are the networking details for IP network–enabled Exadata Cloud Service accounts. Here you will select the client network you created from the Client Network list and the Backup Network you created from the Backup Network list—pretty simple if you named the networks Client and Backup.

Again, depending on the version and location of your Exadata Cloud Service, the ability to create an initial VM cluster may also be available. You would start by supplying the number of OCPUs each node of the VM cluster would use. Next is memory, and like OCPUs, the memory is set for each node. If you used 100GB, 100GB would be used on each node. Exadata Storage is the amount of DATA, RECO, and SPRSE disk the VM cluster has access to. Last is Local Storage: this is the storage amount that /u02 will have on each node. This mount point is used for Oracle homes. Each home takes up about 15 to 20GB, so size accordingly.

Once you're done with this page, click Create. You'll see a Confirmation modal (Figure 2-22), where you click Create to confirm that you want to create the Exadata Cloud Service instance.

This will redirect you to the Service Instances overview page. You will not see your instance here unless you change the report filter from Active to All (Figure 2-23).

Back on the Service dashboard, you will see a small number "1" in an orange box in the Exadata tile. This indicates that a service is being created.

Depending on the shape you chose, the service instance will be ready to create the first database in as little as two hours. That's a metric you can compare to the first section of this book—from weeks and months to the first database created, to only two hours!

Creating the Starter Database

Once the Exadata Cloud Service instance is created, you will receive an e-mail stating it is ready to use. Log in to the account just as you did before, but you will notice a small number "1" with a

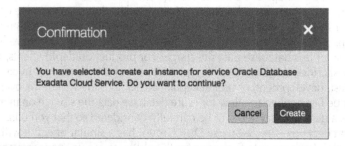

FIGURE 2-22.   *The Confirmation modal*

Service Instances

No instances yet.

Create Service Instance   Show:Active ▼

Active

Inactive

All

FIGURE 2-23.   *Change the report filter on the Exadata Service details page*

green circle around it on the Exadata tile in the dashboard. This indicates you have one running instance of the cloud service (Figure 2-24).

To start the database creation process, you need to get back to the Database as a Service console. Remember that you can click the pop-out menu in the Exadata tile and select Open Service Console. There is also a hidden, quicker method: click the green circled 1 and that will bring you directly to the Database as a Service console (DBCS). You can use either method to get to that page.

On the DBCS console page, you may see the Welcome to Oracle Database Cloud Service! page (Figure 2-25) if no existing databases were created. This page is shared with the PaaS DBCS product. If you see the Welcome page, click the yellow Go To Console button.

On the DBCS console page, you'll see a blue Create Service button; if no databases are present, a big arrow will be pointing to it. Click the Create Service button.

NOTE
If you were not patient in waiting for your Exadata Cloud Service instance to create, you can get to this page, but you'll see some errors about not having the correct role and the Create Service button will be disabled.

Instance Page   The first page of the Create Instance wizard is the Instance page, which provides details about the database instance you are about to create (Figure 2-26).

FIGURE 2-24. *Exadata tile indicating service is created*

FIGURE 2-25. *Welcome to Oracle Database Cloud Service! page*

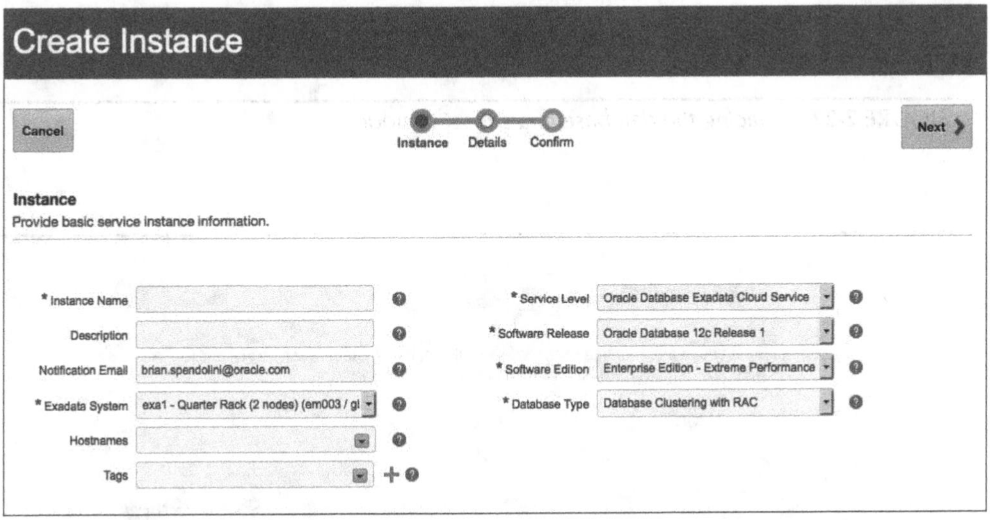

FIGURE 2-26. *The first page of the Create Instance wizard*

The following fields are provided on the left side of the page:

- **Instance Name** Type in a name for the database service instance. This is not the name of the database but a name that will be used in the UI. As usual, there are naming rules: the name must be 50 characters or less; must start with a letter; can contain only letters, numbers, and hyphens; and cannot end with a hyphen. This is the name you will see on the UI, and it's used in REST calls. It is not the name of the database.

- **Description** Enter a description if needed, or leave this blank. The description can be up to 1024 characters in length.

- **Notification Email** This field is used for provisioning status updates. This address will be used to notify when the database has been created or if an error occurred during creation.

- **Exadata System** Here you can select the Exadata System or VM cluster you want to place this database on. If you have access to multiple Exadata Cloud Services or VM clusters, you can see how this field is important in deciding which system to place the database on.

- **Hostnames** You can place this database on a subset of nodes in your cluster. By clicking the down arrow, you can choose to place the database you are about to create on a subset of the available Exadata compute nodes or on all of them (Figure 2-27) by checking the boxes next to the node you want. Not checking any boxes will place the database on all nodes of the Exadata shape.

- **Tags** Click the plus sign to open the Create New Tags modal (Figure 2-28) to create a new tag for this service. You can also use the drop-down list to choose an existing tag.

FIGURE 2-27. *Placing the database in a subset of nodes*

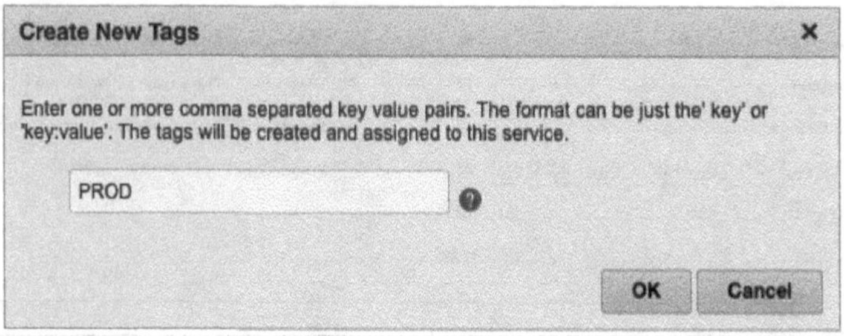

FIGURE 2-28. *Creating a new tag*

On the right side of this page are other options:

- **Service Level**   When creating an Exadata Cloud Service Database, you should set this to Oracle Database Exadata Cloud Service. If you click the select list, you will see options for the DBCS PaaS products. Leave this as Oracle Database Exadata Cloud Service.

- **Software Release**   Choose what database version you want to deploy:
  - Oracle Database 11g Release 2
  - Oracle Database 12c Release 1
  - Oracle Database 12c Release 2
  - Oracle Database 18c

  Depending on which version you select, the grid infrastructure will be different: Selecting 18c will give you an 18c grid infrastructure; selecting 12.2 or earlier will give you a 12.2 grid infrastructure. As Database 19c comes along, we will shift down, with 19c giving a 19c Grid Infrastructure, and 18c and below giving you an 18c Grid Infrastructure.

- **Software Edition**   For the Exadata Cloud Service, the Software Edition will be the Enterprise Edition – Extreme Performance. There are other editions that are used for the Database Cloud Service PaaS offering. The Extreme Performance Edition creates a database with all database options enabled.

- **Database Type**   Here we can select if we want a database just on this Exadata Cloud Service or if we want to automatically create another database on a different Exadata Cloud Service in a different data center utilizing Data Guard.

Once you have selected your options on this page, click Next.

Details Page   The Details page of the Create Database wizard asks for database-level details (Figure 2-29).

NOTE
If you forgot what you chose on the previous page, click the Selection Summary link to the right of the page for a quick check.

Enter information for the following fields in the Database Configuration section:

- **DB Name**   This is the name of your database, and in 12c and 18c, the name of your CDB (Container Database). This name must begin with a letter and can contain only letters and numbers.

- **PDB Name**   If you selected an 11g Release 2 database on the previous page of the wizard, you will not see this field. Used for 12c and 18c databases, in this field you name the first PDB, or pluggable database, created. Although this book will not go over Oracle's Multitenant option, just know you can have multiple PDBs within a single CDB. As for naming the first PDB, you have 30 characters to work with; the name must begin with a letter and can contain only letters and numbers. Do not use a PDB name of an existing PDB on the service.

- **Administration Password**   This is the password that will be used for the users SYS, SYSTEM, and the oracle wallet for Transparent Data Encryption (TDE). The password

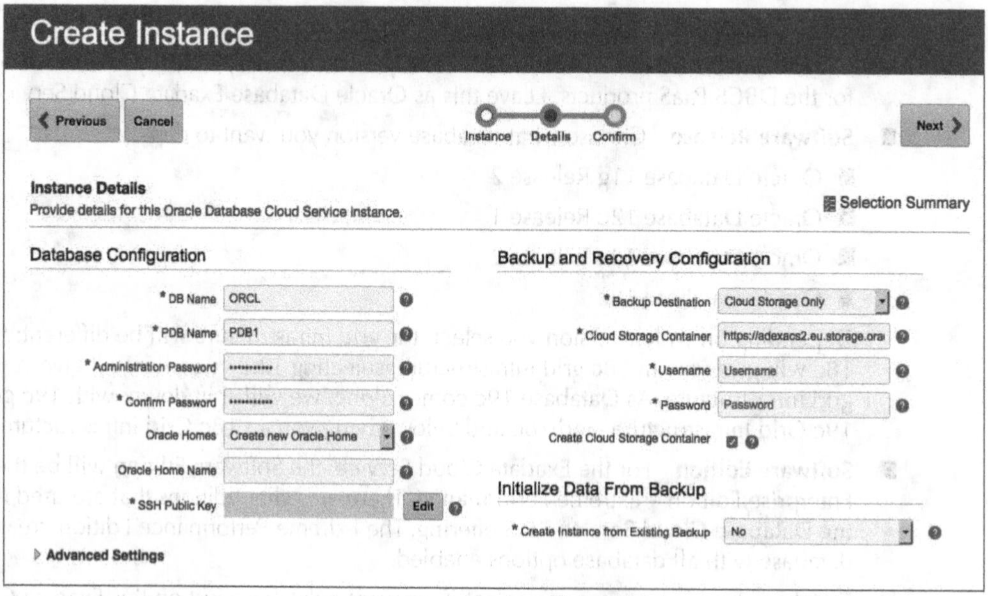

FIGURE 2-29. *The Details page of the Create Database wizard*

must be between 8 and 30 characters with at least one lowercase letter, one uppercase letter, one number, one special character (_, - , #), and no white space character. It must also not contain the following keywords or their reversed form: sys, system, dbsnmp, oracle. When enabled, this will also be the password for the cloud_user when using ExaCLI.

- **Oracle Homes** If you have existing databases on the service, you can select an existing Oracle home, in essence sharing that Oracle home. The service will not create a new home on the DB compute nodes but will use the home you selected, sharing it with another or multiple other databases.

- **Oracle Home Name** If this is your first database or you want to create a new Oracle home, enter in a home name you want to use. If you leave this blank and do not select an existing home, the service will assign the home a pre-created name.

- **SSH Public Key** This field is shown only for your first or starter database on an Exadata Cloud Service. It will use this SSH key for logging on the OS with the oracle and opc users. Clicking the Edit button will bring up the SSH public key for the VM Access modal. Here you have three options:
  - **Key File Name** Use the file browse option of your web browser to find and use a key on your local file system.
  - **Key Value** Copy and paste a public key value into this field.
  - **Create a New Key** Let the system create a key for you and download it to your local file system.

Creating a Key

Creating a key is easy if you want to use your own. If you are using a UNIX, Linux, or macOS–based system, open a terminal and enter the following command:

```
ssh-keygen -b 2048 -t rsa -f myKeyFilename
```

You'll then be asked if you want to use a passphrase with this key, securing it further. Once done, on the file system, in the directory in which you ran this command, you will have two keys. For example, if I ran the following command,

```
ssh-keygen -b 2048 -t rsa -f myExadataCS_Key
```

I would have two files: myExadataCS_Key and myExadataCS_Key.pub. The one without a file extension is the private key and the .pub file is the public key. I would use myExadataCS_Key.pub for creating my service.

If you are using a Windows system, you can use the PuTTYgen program to create a public and private key.

The Advanced Settings section of the console is shown in Figure 2-30. To open this section, click the triangle icon. You'll see four options:

- **Application Type** Sets the database template for the starter database to one of two options: an OLTP template for transactional databases or a data warehouse template. Remember that you can also change the init parameters of the database after creation.

- **Character Set and National Character Set** Leave these at the default settings, AL32UTF8 and AL16UTF16, respectively, unless you have a specific need or are migrating a database over with a specific character set. At some point in this database's life, you might need to store multibyte character sets, but best practice is to start with these UTF choices, so you don't have to do any painful character set migrations.

- **Enable Oracle GoldenGate** Select this checkbox to set this database as a GoldenGate target if you have the GoldenGate Cloud Service. This prepares this database as a target.

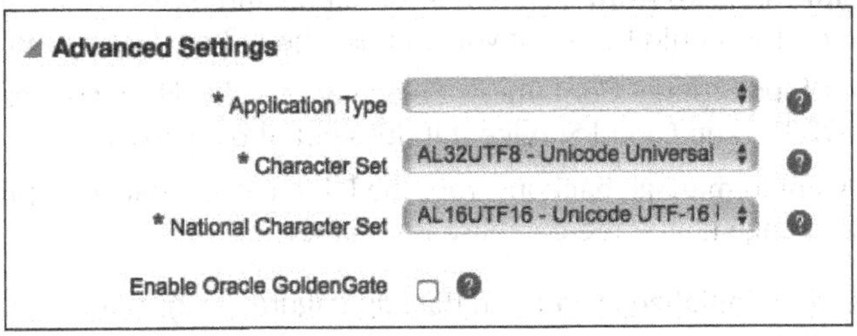

FIGURE 2-30. *Advanced Settings section*

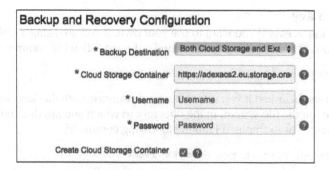

FIGURE 2-31.   *Backup And Recovery Configuration section*

Next, at the upper right of the form, is the Backup And Recovery Configuration section (Figure 2-31).

This section includes the following options:

- **Backup Destination**   The values that appear in this list are based on whether or not you selected the Database Backups On Exadata Storage checkbox on the Create Exadata Cloud Service Instance page. If you selected that checkbox, you can choose Both Cloud Storage And Exadata Storage For Backups, Cloud Storage Only Backups, or None, for no backups at all. If you did not select this checkbox, the Both Cloud Storage And Exadata Storage option will not be present in the select list. If you select None for this field, the other fields in the Backup And Recovery Configuration section will disappear. The None option is useful for temporary databases—perhaps you want to test out a database option or check a query, or it's a test database that just doesn't need backups. If you choose either of the other two options, you'll need to fill out the fields that tell the service where the Database Backup Cloud Service container is located.

- **Cloud Storage Container**   This is the location of your storage container. You can enter the full URL or the short location in the format *instance-id_domain/container*. If, for example, your ID Domain was abc123, then this shortened location would be Storage-abc123/myBackupContainer. The containers can be made via the Storage Service console or via REST services.

- **Username and Password**   Enter the username and password for the user who owns the container. This could be you if you can use the DB Backup Cloud Service.

- **Create Cloud Storage Container**   Selecting this checkbox creates the container for you in the DB Backup Cloud Service if it does not already exist.

  If you want to manage backups from the UI, choose a backup option here, because you cannot change it after the database is created.

The next section, Initialize Data From Backup (Figure 2-32), is another very useful part of the cloud and its tooling.

Here you can create a database and then restore a backup in its place. The origin of the backup you want to use may be from another Exadata Cloud Service database deployment in

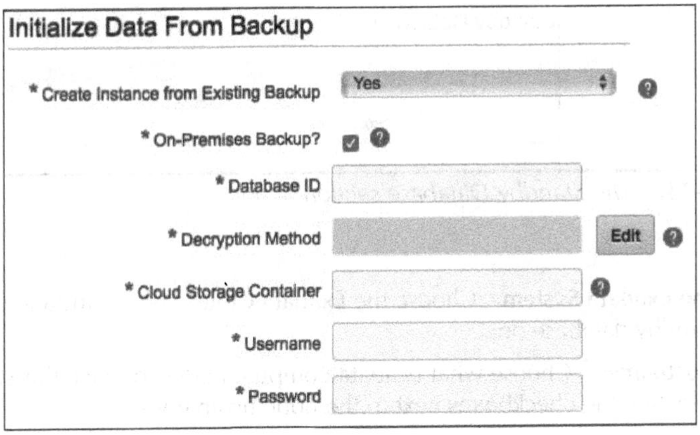

FIGURE 2-32.   *Initialize Data From Backup section*

the same identity domain or from another database that was backed up to cloud storage using Database Backup Cloud Service. That database can be from a cloud database or an on-premises database.

If you choose to use an on-premises backup by selecting the On-Premises Backup? checkbox, you'll need to populate the following fields:

- **Database ID**   This is a unique ID from the origin database. You can get this ID from the origin database by running the following SQL, entering the result in the Database ID field:

  ```
  SQL> select dbid from v$database;
  ```

- **Decryption Method**   Backups in the DB Backup Cloud Service are encrypted, so you need to decrypt it to recover. The field includes an Edit button; click it to choose the method in a pop-up modal. You can decrypt the backup with either the database wallet or a password that was used to encrypt it.

- **Cloud Storage Container, Username, and Password**   These fields are used the same way as those in the the Backup Configuration section, but here you are pointing to the storage container that holds the backup you want to recover from.

If you deselect the On-Premises Backup? checkbox, all the fields will disappear except Source Service Name. Select the database deployment on an Exadata Cloud Service you want to recover from. This is a great option for jumpstarting an on-premises-to-cloud Data Guard/Disaster Recovery implementation.

Next, the Standby Database section on this page is available only if you set the Database Type (refer back to Figure 2-26) to Database Clustering With RAC and Data Guard Standby. This option is available only if you have two Exadata Cloud Services in the same ID domain—that is, two or more provisioned shapes or instances, not multiple database deployments on the same shape or instance. The Standby Database section (Figure 2-33) lets you use the cloud tooling to create a standby database automatically using Data Guard.

Standby Database
* Exadata System
Hostnames

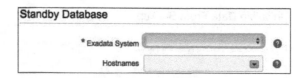

FIGURE 2-33. *The Standby Database section*

- **The Exadata System** Choose the Exadata Cloud Service instance you want to place the standby database on.
- **Hostnames** Choose what Exadata compute nodes to place this standby database on by selecting the checkboxes next to the node hostnames.

Finally, once this page is complete, click the Next button to move on to the Confirmation page.

On the Confirmation page, you can double-check your options to be sure they are correct for your starter database (Figure 2-34). If you're happy with the options, click Create.

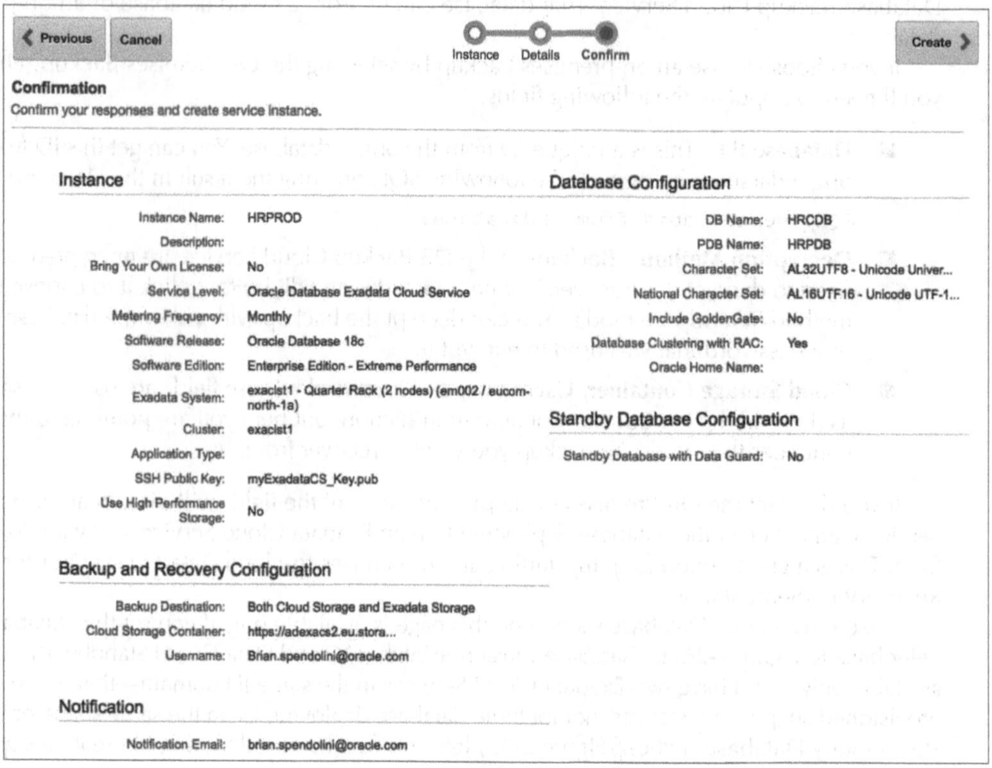

Previous
Cancel
Instance
Details
Confirm
Create
Confirmation
Confirm your responses and create service instance.
Instance
Instance Name: HRPROD
Description:
Bring Your Own License: No
Service Level: Oracle Database Exadata Cloud Service
Metering Frequency: Monthly
Software Release: Oracle Database 18c
Software Edition: Enterprise Edition - Extreme Performance
Exadata System: exacist1 - Quarter Rack (2 nodes) (em002 / eucom-north-1a)
Cluster: exacist1
Application Type:
SSH Public Key: myExadataCS_Key.pub
Use High Performance Storage: No
Database Configuration
DB Name: HRCDB
PDB Name: HRPDB
Character Set: AL32UTF8 - Unicode Univer...
National Character Set: AL16UTF16 - Unicode UTF-1...
Include GoldenGate: No
Database Clustering with RAC: Yes
Oracle Home Name:
Standby Database Configuration
Standby Database with Data Guard: No
Backup and Recovery Configuration
Backup Destination: Both Cloud Storage and Exadata Storage
Cloud Storage Container: https://adexacs2.eu.stora...
Username: Brian.spendolini@oracle.com
Notification
Notification Email: brian.spendolini@oracle.com

FIGURE 2-34. *The database deployment Confirmation page*

HRPROD					
Status:	Creating instance ...	**Submitted On:**	Jul 19, 2018 7:00:45 AM UTC	**OCPUs:**	22.0
Version:	18.0.0.0	**Exadata System:**	exaclst1	**Memory:**	1,440 GB
Edition:	Enterprise Edition - Extr...	**Cluster:**	exaclst1	**Storage:**	96 TB

FIGURE 2-35. *Database deployment status*

DBCS Console Page

Back on the DBCS console page, you can see the status of your database creation (Figure 2-35).

In about 60 minutes, this database and grid infrastructure will be done and available to be used. The summary bar across the top of the page provides a summary of all the resources available. It does not, however, reflect the ratio of data/storage/sparse you selected for the storage number, and that number will not go down as you consume storage on the Exadata Cloud Service—it's informational only.

Creating the Exadata Cloud Service in OCI

To log into the cloud console for Oracle Cloud Infrastructure (OCI), or the bare metal data centers, you start just as you did when logging into OCI-C. Once you're on the Service dashboard, find the Exadata (OCI) tile or add it via the customize option. On the Overview page, click the Open Service Console button at the upper right.

You can use several shortcut URLs to get to the OCI web console as well, depending on what region is your home region:

- https://console.us-phoenix-1.oraclecloud.com/
- https://console.us-ashburn-1.oraclecloud.com/
- https://console.eu-frankfurt-1.oraclecloud.com/
- https://console.uk-london-1.oraclecloud.com/

If you go directly to the console, you have to enter your Cloud Tenant ID (Figure 2-36). Then click the Continue button.

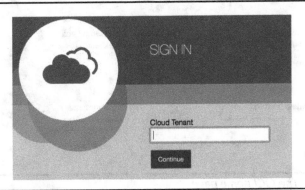

FIGURE 2-36. *Enter your Tenant ID.*

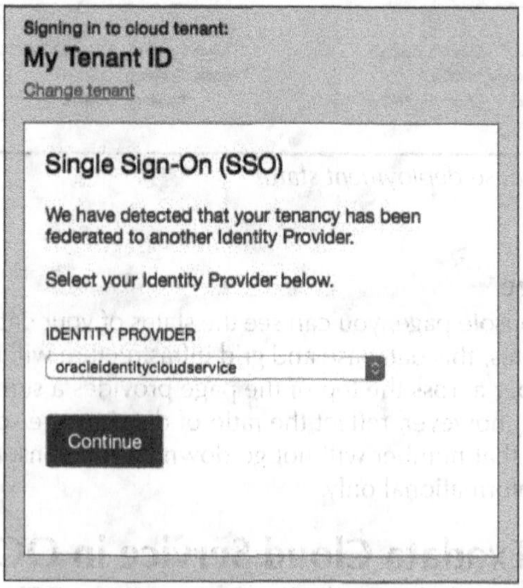

Signing in to cloud tenant:

My Tenant ID

Change tenant

Single Sign-On (SSO)

We have detected that your tenancy has been federated to another Identity Provider.

Select your Identity Provider below.

IDENTITY PROVIDER

oracleidentitycloudservice

Continue

FIGURE 2-37. *The credentials page, Single Sign-On section*

The credentials page (Figure 2-37) displays the Tenant ID. If this is not the Tenant ID you want to use, click the Change Tenant link. After verifying your Tenant ID, click Continue in the Single Sign-On box to open the cloud sign-in page and then back to the OCI web console.

After logging into the OCI console, the home page opens, which looks similar to Figure 2-38. On this page, you can perform various tasks as indicated by the tiles on the page. At the upper-left corner of the page is a pop-out menu with all the components of OCI.

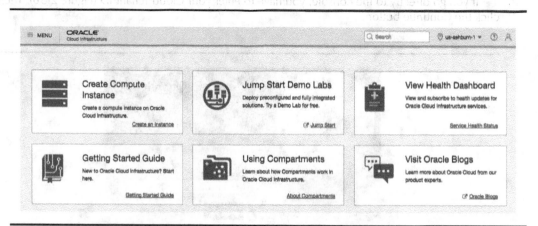

FIGURE 2-38. *The OCI home page*

Notice the region drop-down in the upper-right section of the page; in Figure 2-38, it says us-ashburn-1. Here you can change regions to place resources in either a High Availability or Disaster Recovery mode. For creating your initial Exadata Cloud Service, you would have been granted a service limit or quota in one or multiple availability domains in the same or different regions. Hovering your mouse over the region will display all the regions you have access to. You can also click Manage Region to add or remove region access.

Before we get into creating our Exadata Cloud Service, we need to discuss a few aspects of the OCI interface and functions. Open the pop-out menu at the upper-left corner of the page (Figure 2-39).

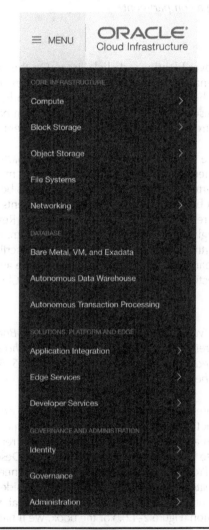

FIGURE 2-39. *The OCI pop-out menu*

Compartments

Displaying 2 Compartments

Create Compartment

RC | My Tenant ID (root) | Description: The root Compartment of the tenancy
| OCID: ...budvwq Show Copy | Created: –
| Authorized: Yes |

C | ManagedCompartmentForPaaS | Description: idcs-e48d50317ad040749417aed9b9f1558f|15427437|Oracle Cloud Ops Internal
| OCID: ...rug23a Show Copy | Created: Mon, 14 May 2018 22:27:41 GMT
| Authorized: Yes |

FIGURE 2-40. *Creating a compartment*

Hover your mouse over Identity and click Users. On the Users Detail page, you'll see a list of all the users in this tenancy. Users in OCI are given access to all the components of OCI via groups and the policies held within those groups. OCI also has compartments that let you organize specific OCI resources and control access to them based on groups and policies. Let's go through the entire process of creating a compartment, user, and group, and a policy for that user.

On the left side of the Users Detail page, click the Compartments link. On the next page, you will see a root compartment: this is the default compartment made for all OCI accounts. Think of it as the top-level compartment, with all other compartments being children of the root. Click the Create Compartment button at the top of the Compartments section (Figure 2-40). Note that compartments can span regions as well as users and groups. Resources such as our Exadata Cloud Service live only in a single region in a single availability domain.

In the Create Compartment modal, you can name and describe the compartment. For now, go ahead and create a compartment, giving it a meaningful name and a quick description. You can also add tags from the Tags section at the lower part of the modal. Click Create when you're through.

NOTE
For our example, we've named the compartment ExaCS_Book for screenshots and for referencing the compartment throughout this book. You do not need to name your compartment ExaCS_Book—in fact, please give it a better name.

Once you have created a compartment, it will be listed on the Compartment Detail page. Next, create a user. Click the Users link from the Links list on the left side of the page. Notice the large Create User button at the top of the section (notice a trend here?). Click the Create User button to open the Create User modal. Enter a Name and a Description (Figure 2-41), and then click the Create button. (You can also add tags to this user if needed.)

Next you need to create a group for this user. On the left side of the page, click the Groups link. Click the Create Group button to open the Create Group modal, where you'll enter a group name and optionally a description (Figure 2-42). For the book, we'll name the group ExaCS_Group.

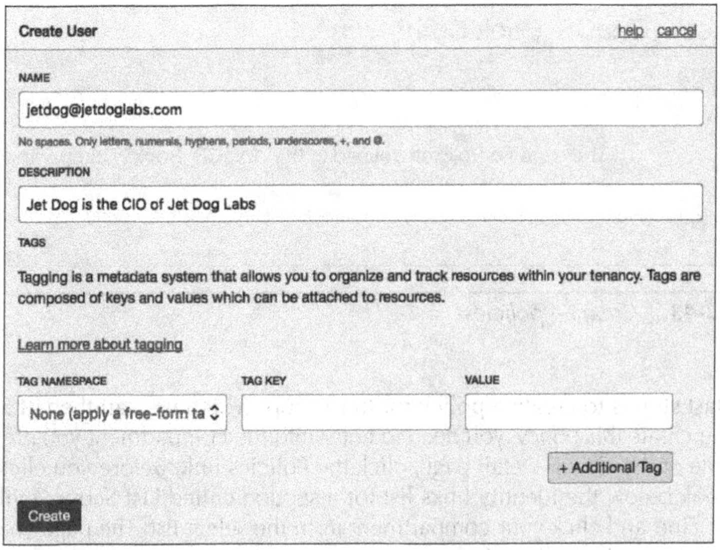

Create User   help cancel

NAME

jetdog@jetdoglabs.com

No spaces. Only letters, numerals, hyphens, periods, underscores, +, and @.

DESCRIPTION

Jet Dog is the CIO of Jet Dog Labs

TAGS

Tagging is a metadata system that allows you to organize and track resources within your tenancy. Tags are composed of keys and values which can be attached to resources.

Learn more about tagging

TAG NAMESPACE   TAG KEY   VALUE

None (apply a free-form ta ↕

                                                                 + Additional Tag

Create

FIGURE 2-41. *Creating a user*

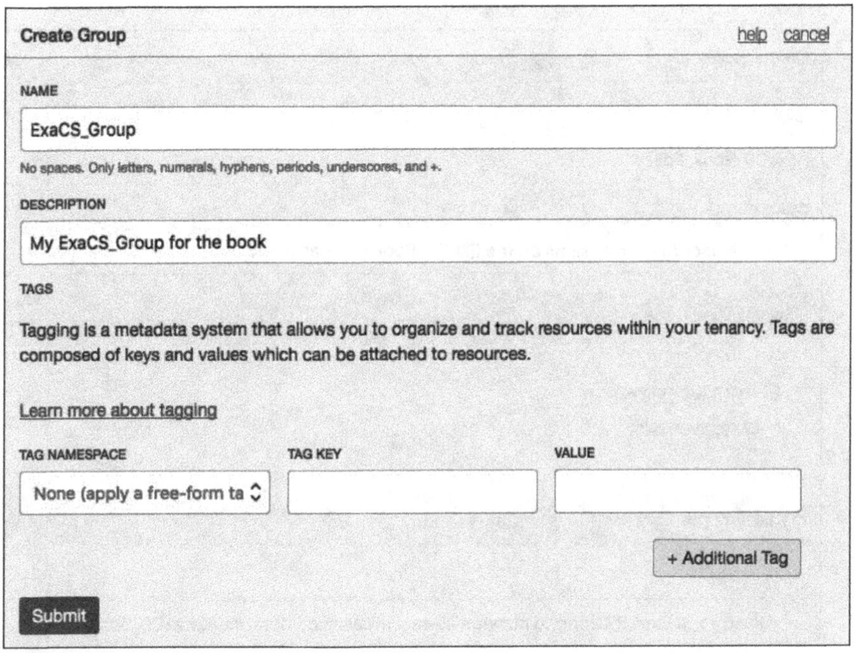

Create Group   help cancel

NAME

ExaCS_Group

No spaces. Only letters, numerals, hyphens, periods, underscores, and +.

DESCRIPTION

My ExaCS_Group for the book

TAGS

Tagging is a metadata system that allows you to organize and track resources within your tenancy. Tags are composed of keys and values which can be attached to resources.

Learn more about tagging

TAG NAMESPACE   TAG KEY   VALUE

None (apply a free-form ta ↕

                                                                 + Additional Tag

Submit

FIGURE 2-42. *Creating a group*

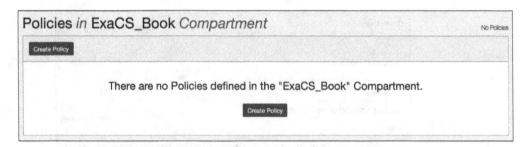

Policies *in* ExaCS_Book *Compartment*   No Policies

Create Policy

There are no Policies defined in the "ExaCS_Book" Compartment.

Create Policy

FIGURE 2-43. *Creating policies*

The last stop is to create a policy for this group, which we can then attach to a user. But before you create this policy, you need to enter into the compartment you previously created. On the left side of the Group Detail page, click the Policies link. Before you click the Create Policy button, look below the Identity links list for a section called List Scope, with a Compartment select list. Find and click your compartment from the select list. The page changes to indicate that you are working with policies in your compartment (in our case, the ExaCS_Book compartment), as shown in Figure 2-43.

Now click the Create Policy button to open the Create Policy modal (Figure 2-44). Enter a name for your policy as well as a description. We'll name ours ExaCS_Book_Policy, and for a

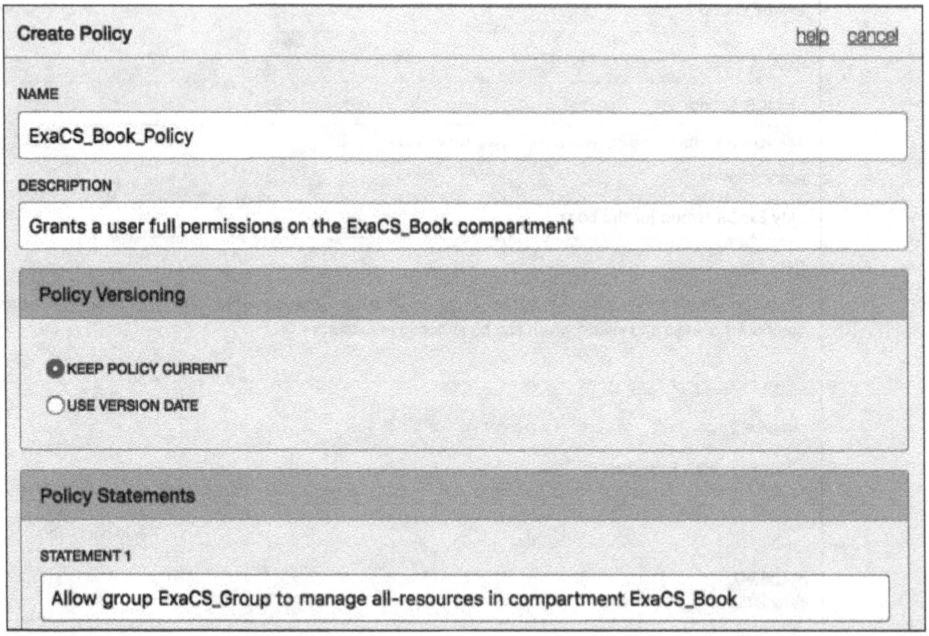

Create Policy   help   cancel

NAME

ExaCS_Book_Policy

DESCRIPTION

Grants a user full permissions on the ExaCS_Book compartment

Policy Versioning

○ KEEP POLICY CURRENT
○ USE VERSION DATE

Policy Statements

STATEMENT 1

Allow group ExaCS_Group to manage all-resources in compartment ExaCS_Book

FIGURE 2-44. *Create Policy modal*

description we can use "Grants a user full permissions on the ExaCS_Book compartment". In the Policy Versioning section, make sure the Keep Policy Current radio button is selected.

The last section in the modal is Policy Statements, which deserves a bit more explanation.

How Policy Statements Work

Policy statements in OCI can be very powerful, but they do take a bit of explanation to understand how to create them. Policies will dictate who or what group has access to what components in an OCI account. You create policies using the following syntax:

```
Allow group <group_name> to <verb> <resource-type> in compartment
<compartment_name>
```

With this format, you can allow, but not deny, access to different resources in a compartment. You can also expand the policy to work above the compartment with the following syntax:

```
Allow group <group_name> to <verb> <resource-type> in tenancy
```

So, when to use which one? Imagine you have a development group and you place them in compartment A. User A will be working with databases in this compartment. User B may be the networking admin for this compartment. User C is a project manager and needs to have access to the database and the networking. You will want to assign these users access to a particular resource, or a set of resources, in this compartment, so you would use the first clause—the "in compartment" clause.

Now imagine that you have a corporate network architect. This person would need to have access to all networking resources across all compartments, a perfect use case for using the "in tenancy" clause.

Let's build a policy for our compartment that will grant access to all the resources in the compartment, but not in the tenancy, using the group we created earlier. Looking at the syntax, we start with

```
Allow group ExaCS_Group
```

Next up is the verb. We can choose from the following verbs for our policy:

- **inspect** Ability to list resources. This verb also restricts access to any confidential information or user-specified metadata that may be part of that resource.
- **read** Similar to the `inspect` verb, but displays user-specified metadata and the actual resource name.
- **use** Includes all the rights of the `read` verb, but also allows for updating resources. The only restriction with updating is if the act of updating acts like a create—in that case, this verb cannot act upon that resource.
- **manage** Gives access to all resources with the ability to create, delete, update, and edit.

We want this group to be able to create, delete, update, and edit, so the `manage` verb would work best for our policy. Continuing to construct the policy, we now have

```
Allow group ExaCS_Group to manage
```

Next are resources. Resources in OCI are divided into family resource types:

- `all-resources`
- `database-family`
- `instance-family`
- `object-family`
- `virtual-network-family`
- `volume-family`

We see that restrictions can happen at very low levels using a resource type within a family. As stated previously, the policy should allow working with all resources, so we can now add to the statement

```
Allow group ExaCS_Group to manage all-resources
```

The last part of the statement is the compartment. The compartment we used was named ExaCS_Book, so to finish our policy statement, we have

```
Allow group ExaCS_Group to manage all-resources in compartment ExaCS_Book
```

Back in the UI, we add this statement to the Policy Statements section of the Create Policy modal (shown in Figure 2-44) and click the Create button. On the Policies page, we can see our newly created policy.

Next, we need to add this policy to the user we created by adding the user to the ExaCS_Group. Remember that we don't explicitly add policies to *users* but to *groups*, and then we add users to those groups so that users inherit the policy effects.

On the left side of the Policies Detail page, in the Identity links list, click Users. On the list, find the user you created in the previous section (Figure 2-41) and click the username. At the lower left, in the Resources links list, click Groups.

Now, in the middle of the page, click the Add User To Group button. In the Add User To Group modal, Groups field, select ExaCS_Group. Then click Add (Figure 2-45).

In summary, we created a compartment, group, and policy. We attached that policy to the group with the policy statement. That statement also enabled us to manage all resources in the compartment we created. Finally, we added a user to that group, which enables that user to manage all resources in that compartment and only that compartment.

FIGURE 2-45. *Adding a user to a group*

OCI Networking

OCI networking is completely software-based. Everything you need to do with the network can be done in the OCI UI (or via REST APIs). Let's get started.

From the pop-out menu on the OCI interface (Figure 2-39), click Networking. The networking home page starts with virtual cloud networks. A virtual cloud network (VCN) is a private (or public) network that is set up by you and controlled by you with security lists. You can choose whether or not you want to expose this network to the public Internet, and who, where, and how access is gained. The VCN consists of subnets, Internet gateways, dynamic routing gateways, routing tables, security lists, service gateways, and Dynamic Host Configuration Protocol (DHCP) options. We will go over most of these components as we build the network for the Exadata Cloud Service.

On the VCN home page, start by creating a VCN. Make sure that you are in the correct compartment by looking at the Compartment select list in the lower right of the page. The current compartment will be selected in the Compartment select list, as shown in Figure 2-46.

You can also check the compartment by looking at the top-middle of the page, where it should say "Virtual Cloud Networks in ExaCS_Book Compartment." It should also indicate that "There are no Virtual Cloud Networks in the 'ExaCS_Book' Compartment." Click the Create Virtual Cloud Network button to start the process.

In the Create Virtual Cloud Network modal (shown in the upcoming Figure 2-47), notice that the Create In Compartment select list has defaulted to our current compartment, ExaCS_Book. You can change it here if you want to as well—for our example, we'll leave it as ExaCS_Book. For Name, we'll use ExaCS Network.

TIP
Naming a VCN is optional but strongly suggested. The default random string of numbers is not very descriptive when, after a year, you need to remember what this VCN is used for. And a good descriptive name is also beneficial for others.

Next are two radio buttons: Create Virtual Cloud Network Only and Create Virtual Cloud Network Plus Related Resources. Make sure Create Virtual Cloud Network Only is selected so that we can create and define all the components of our network.

Next, in the CIDR Block field, we enter a block of IPs in the CIDR notation. For this VCN, we can use the default 10.0.0.0/16 CIDR block.

For DNS Resolution, leave the box checked next to Use DNS Hostnames In This VCN. This will benefit our ExaCS later after creation by giving us a routable hostname on the SCAN listeners. As of this writing, using a custom DNS here will result in many issues with the ExaCS down the road; it's best to use the default DNS.

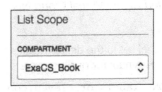

FIGURE 2-46. *Current compartment*

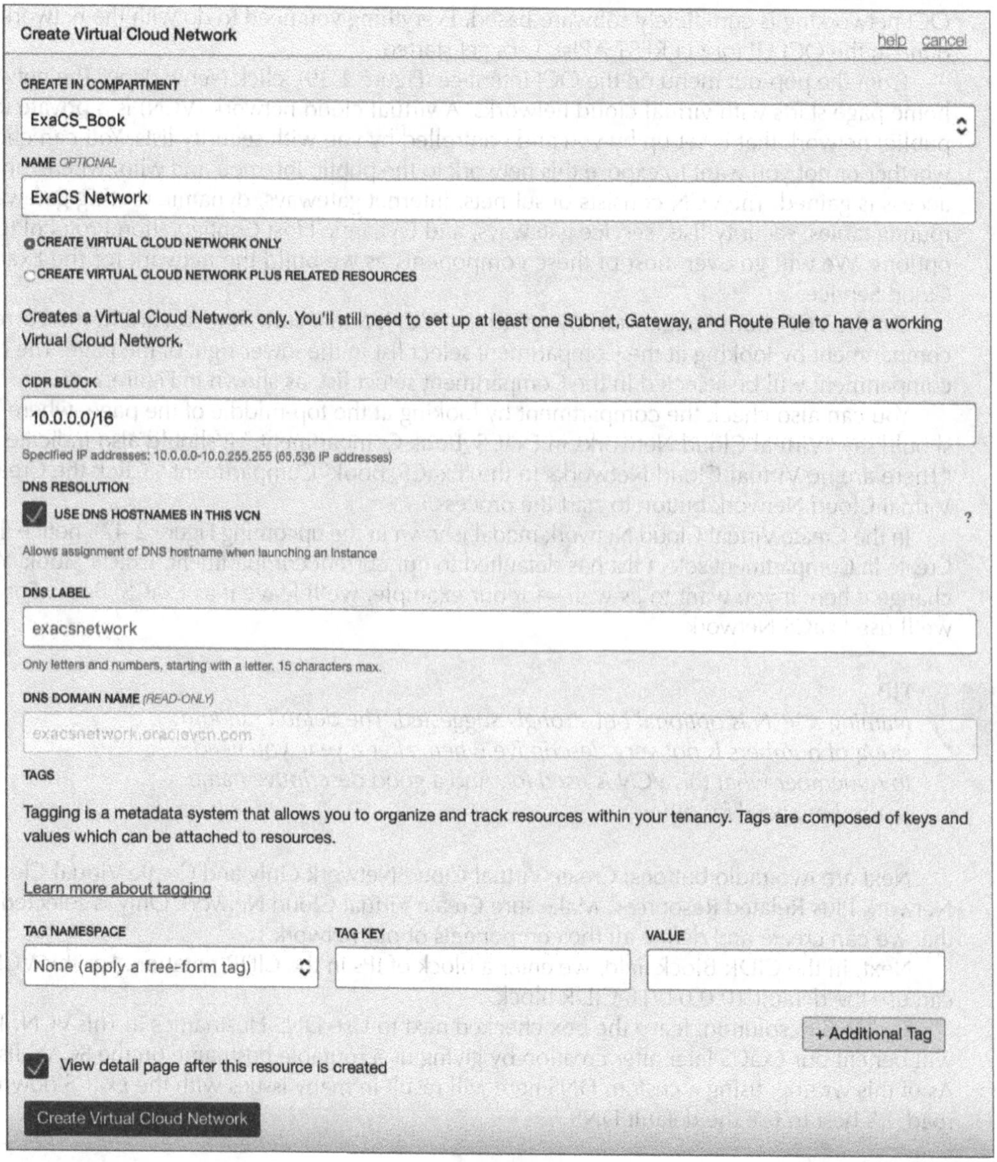

Create Virtual Cloud Network

<help> cancel

CREATE IN COMPARTMENT

ExaCS_Book

NAME *OPTIONAL*

ExaCS Network

○ CREATE VIRTUAL CLOUD NETWORK ONLY
○ CREATE VIRTUAL CLOUD NETWORK PLUS RELATED RESOURCES

Creates a Virtual Cloud Network only. You'll still need to set up at least one Subnet, Gateway, and Route Rule to have a working Virtual Cloud Network.

CIDR BLOCK

10.0.0.0/16

Specified IP addresses: 10.0.0.0-10.0.255.255 (65,536 IP addresses)

DNS RESOLUTION

☑ USE DNS HOSTNAMES IN THIS VCN

Allows assignment of DNS hostname when launching an Instance

DNS LABEL

exacsnetwork

Only letters and numbers, starting with a letter. 15 characters max.

DNS DOMAIN NAME *(READ-ONLY)*

exacsnetwork.oraclevcn.com

TAGS

Tagging is a metadata system that allows you to organize and track resources within your tenancy. Tags are composed of keys and values which can be attached to resources.

Learn more about tagging

TAG NAMESPACE   TAG KEY   VALUE

None (apply a free-form tag)

+ Additional Tag

☑ View detail page after this resource is created

Create Virtual Cloud Network

FIGURE 2-47. *The completed Create Virtual Cloud Network modal*

We can leave the DNS Label set to the default, exacsnetwork, or create our own DNS label. Here is an example of the VCN syntax for our instances:

```
VCN domain name: <VCN DNS label>.oraclevcn.com
Subnet domain name: <subnet DNS label>.<VCN DNS label>.oraclevcn.com
```

If we use exacsnetwork, we would have `exacsnetwork.oraclevcn.com`. In the modal, if you change the DNS label, you will see in real time the DNS Domain Name update with the new label. For now, leave this set to the default.

We can apply tags just as we can on all OCI resources, and we can also go directly to the details page if we keep the option View Detail Page After This Resource Is Created checked. When your modal looks similar to Figure 2-47, click the Create Virtual Cloud Network button.

Now, back in the VCN home page, if the creation of the VCN didn't take you to the details page, click the ExaCS network name in the list of VCNs.

On the ExaCS network VCN details page, you'll see we have an empty network. We need to create two subnets—one for the Exadata Cloud's client network and one for its backup network. Before we do this, though, we need to create some security lists. On the left side of the page, in the Resources links list, click Security Lists.

A security list provides or restricts network access to an instance or multiple instances in a subnet. This means all instances within that subnet will have the security list rules applied. This is an important fact to remember.

On the Security Lists page is one security list: the default security list. We want to create security lists that are specific to the subnets we are creating. Some of the lists we are going to create will be applied across our two subnets, but most will be subnet specific, pertaining only to that particular subnet—for example, SQL*Net traffic. We do not want to globally open up port 1521; we want to be smart about that and open it only on the ExaCS client network and to specific traffic.

To start, click the Create Security List button. The Create Security List modal includes the following fields:

- **Create In Compartment**   We want to create the security list in our ExaCS_Book compartment, so we can leave this set to the default.

- **Security List Name**   Here we can define the name of the list. It's a good idea to name it based on what we think the use will be. Let's name the first one SSH_Access. This list will be used for SSH traffic and open port 22 to either Internet traffic or from a destination we choose.

The next two sections are Allow Rules For Ingress, or incoming traffic rules, and Allow Rules For Egress, or outgoing traffic rules. Let's start in the Allow Rules For Ingress section:

- **Source Type**   We are going to allow traffic from a CIDR block so choose CIDR.

- **Source CIDR**   Enter **0.0.0.0/0** for the Source CIDR. This will allow access from any IP on the Internet, and it's also a mighty insecure way to allow SSH access. We can leave it at 0.0.0.0/0 or we can do better: In a web browser search field, enter **what's my IP**. As long as you don't have an IPv6 address, you should see an IPv4 address. You can then use that IP with /32 appended at the end instead of 0.0.0.0/0 for the source CIDR. We need to get our IP from an external site because the majority of us are behind a NAT router and need to see what the IP address is after we are out on the Internet. Also, this field is named Source CIDR, so we can use a block of IPs here as well. Your company may use a VPN, and all the addresses that end up on the Internet can be defined in a small CIDR block. We can use that in the Source CIDR to allow access.

- **IP Protocol**   Choose TCP.

- **Source Port Range and Destination Port Range**   We want to allow only SSH access, so enter **22** for the Destination Port Range, and leave Source Port Range empty.

- **Stateless checkbox** If you want two-way communication over this port with the source initiating communication, leave the box above Stateless unchecked; not only will the destination be able to access this port, but your instance in OCI can call back over port 22 to the origin IP. If you check this box, the rule is stateless and only ingress traffic will be allowed.

  For SSH, we want a stateless rule. Only IPs defined in the security list should be able to access port 22, and the instance itself should not be calling out on port 22 back to the origin IP. Now, you may be thinking that you might want to use SSH for outgoing traffic on this instance. That's fine, because the instance itself is initiating the communication. For this, we would create an egress rule for port 22, allowing our OCI instance to initiate SSH traffic over port 22.

Once you have defined the ingress rule, click the dark gray box at the upper right in the Egress section. That will remove that empty rule. The modal should look similar to Figure 2-48 (IPs will be different). Click the Create Security List button at the lower left.

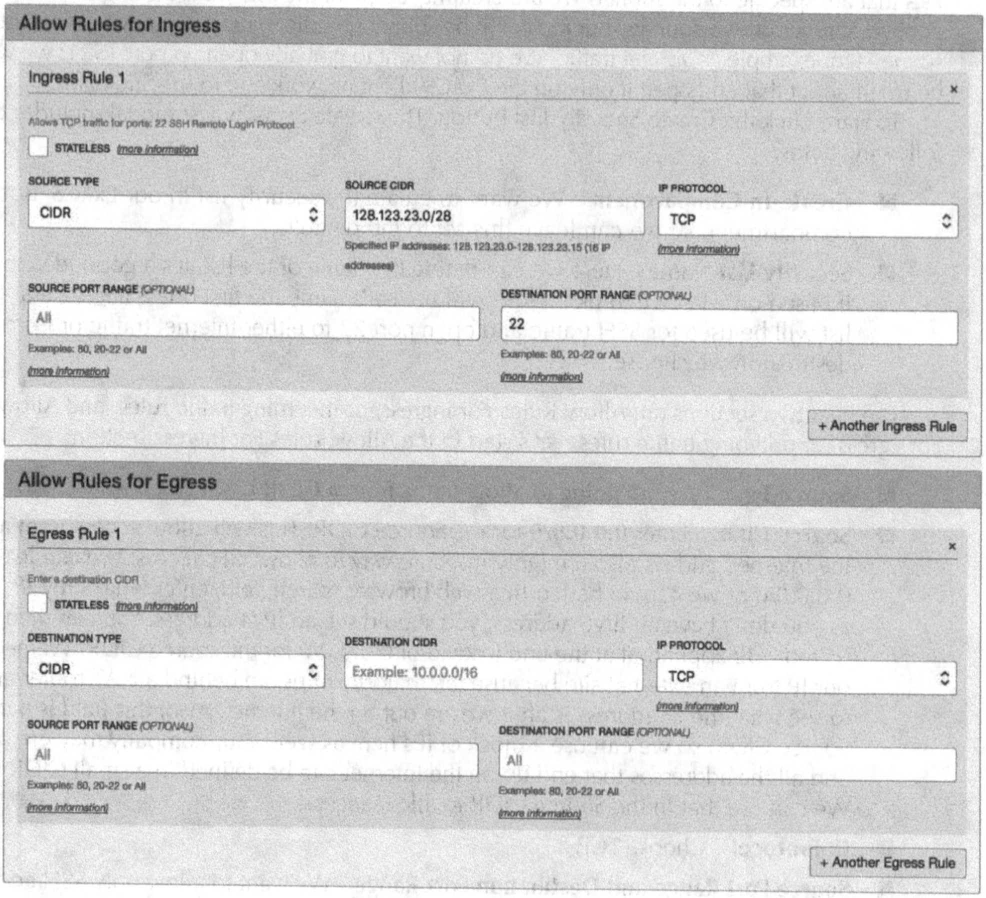

FIGURE 2-48. *Creating ingress rules in the Create Security List modal*

We now need to create a few more security lists. We'll name the security list and then delete both rule defaults in the Create Security List modal. This will create empty security lists that we can define later.

Clicking the Create Security List button and using the Create Security List modal, create the following security lists in the ExacCS_Book compartment:

- SQLNet_Traffic
- Backup_Subnet_Traffic
- Backup_Subnet_Traffic2
- Client_Subnet_Traffic
- Client_Subnet_Traffic2
- JDBC_Traffic
- Admin_Access
- Node_Traffic

NOTE
We are creating many security lists now, because once we create a subnet, we cannot add lists at a later time. It's best to look toward the future and be able to add rules on a subnet level rather than having to use the default list and applying it to the entire VCN. Development knows this is an issue, and by the time this book is published, this restriction may have been lifted.

After you've created the new security lists, we can create our two subnets. On the left side of the VCN details page, in the Resources links list, click Subnets. On the Subnets home page, click the Create Subnet button to open the Create Subnet modal.

The following fields are shown:

- **Name**   This is our client subnet, so enter **Client_Subnet**.
- **Availability Domain**   Each OCI data center or region has three availability domains, all interconnected with very fast networking. Here we will create the subnet where our Exadata Cloud Service quota or service limits are. If this is your first experience with OCI and you have no other instances, choose any of the three availability domains where you have a service limit for an Exadata Cloud Service. For this book, we will be using AD1. The select list will indicate the region short name and then the availability domain number. For our book example, we are in the Phoenix region, so we select PHX-AD-1.
- **CIDR Block**   This is the CIDR block for our subnet. Remember that 10.0.0.0/16 was our VCN CIDR block. Here we can use the same block or create a smaller set of IPs to use. Let's put the client subnet on a smaller set: enter **10.0.1.0/26**. This will give us a range of IPs from 10.0.1.0 to 10.0.1.63 (64 IP addresses). The UI also gives us this exact information.
- **Route Table**   Select the default route table for the VCN.
- **Subnet Access**   Choose from either a private subnet, where no public IPs are assigned, or a public subnet, where public IPs will be assigned. Note that only the compute node will have a public IP address and not the SCAN listener or the VIPs.

- **DNS Label** We briefly discussed DNS resolution when creating the VCN, and we will continue to use it here. This is an open text field, and we can change the domain name of this subnet. The default is clientsubnet.exacsnetwork.oraclevcn.com. By changing the label, the DNS Domain Name field will change as well. For now, leave it at the default.
- **DHCP Options** Select the Default DHCP server.

The last section is the Security Lists section. Click the plus icon to add the following security lists to this subnet along with the default security list:

- Client_Subnet_Traffic
- Client_Subnet_Traffic2
- JDBC_Traffic
- SQLNet_Traffic
- Node_Traffic

This should complete the five-security-list limit on a subnet (Figure 2-49). Once you're done, click the Create button.

Next, we'll create the Backup_Subnet. Because we have already created one, we can do this quickly.

Just as when we created the Client Subnet previously, on the Subnets home page, click the Create Subnet button. Then complete the following fields:

- **Name** Enter **Backup_Subnet**.
- **Availability Domain** Choose PHX-AD-1.

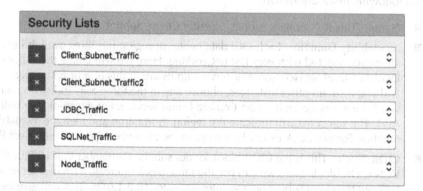

FIGURE 2-49. *Adding five security lists to the Client_Subnet*

- **CIDR Block**   Enter **10.0.2.0/26**, which gives you 64 IP addresses from 10.0.2.0 to 10.0.2.63.
- **Route Table**   Use the default table.
- **Subnet Access**   Choose public or private. Again, we can have two private subnets here, completely isolating the ExaCS in its own VCN.
- **DNS sections**   Leave these set to their default values.
- **DHCP Options**   Choose the default DHCP.
- **Security Lists**   Add the following to the Default Security list:
  - Backup_Subnet_Traffic
  - Backup_Subnet_Traffic2
  - Admin_Access
  - Node_Traffic
  - SSH_Access

Once these lists are added, as we did with the client subnet, click the Create button. We have created our two subnets and they are listed in the Subnets home page.

Now that we have defined our subnets, we need to alter one of the security lists for the Exadata Cloud Service.

On the left of the VCN details page, in the Resources links list, click Security Lists. On the next page, find and click the name for Node_Traffic. Then, on the details page for Node_Traffic, click the Edit All Rules button.

We need to add four ingress and four egress rules. In the Allow Rules For Ingress section, click the +Add Rule button four times. Before we start adding CIDR blocks, click the Stateless box for all four rules. We need to allow traffic between all the nodes in the Client Subnet to be able to talk to each other. Here's how to do this:

- For the first two rules, select CIDR as the Source Type, and for Source CIDR, enter **10.0.1.0/26**.
- For the second rule, change the IP Protocol to ICMP.
- For the last two rules, enter our backup subnet's Source CIDR block, **10.0.2.0/26**.
- Change the fourth rule's IP Protocol to ICMP.
- In the Source Port Range and Destination Port Range text fields for the TCP IP Protocol rules, it should default to **All**.
- For the ICMP IP Protocol rules, again **All** should default in the Type And Code text field.

Your Ingress rules should look like Figure 2-50.

For the egress rules (Allow Rules For Egress section), we'll enter the same information: four rules, two TCP, and two ICMP; All Stateless; and open to All ports. When you're done, the egress rules should look like Figure 2-50 as well.

When you're done entering the rules, click the Save Security Lists Rules button at the lower left. Now we can create our Exadata Cloud Service.

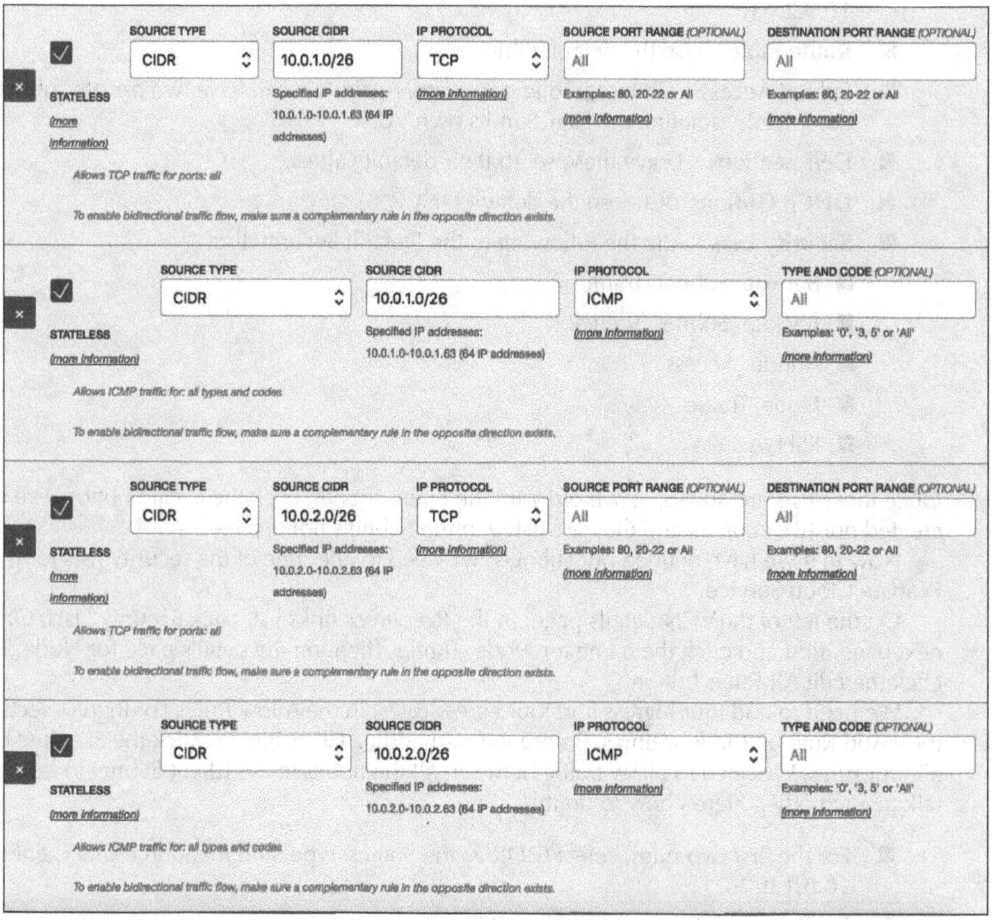

FIGURE 2-50. *Rules for the Node_Traffic security rule*

Creating the Exadata Cloud Service Instance in OCI

To start creating the Exadata Cloud Service, use the pop-out menu and select Bare Metal, VM, and Exadata (Figure 2-51).

We should still be working in the ExaCS_Book compartment, and the DB Systems in ExaCS_Book Compartment page should say, "There are no DB Systems in the 'ExaCS_Book' Compartment."

Click the Launch DB System button to start the process and bring up the Launch DB System modal.

The first section, DB System Information, includes the following fields:

■ **Display Name** Enter **ExaCS_Prod** into the text field.

■ **Availability Domain** Select the same domain that we created our subnet in: PHX-AD-1.

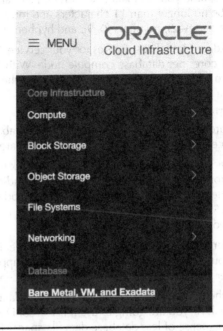

FIGURE 2-51. *Selecting Bare Metal, VM, and Exadata to create a Database*

- **Shape type** Select the Exadata radio button. If the Exadata radio button is not there, use the Bare Metal Machine radio button.
- **Shape** From this select list, choose an Exadata Cloud Service shape (quarter/half/full). We have a few options:
  - Exadata.Quarter1.84
  - Exadata.Quarter2.92
  - Exadata.Half1.168
  - Exadata.Half2.184
  - Exadata.Full1.336
  - Exadata.Full2.368

  The Exadata.SHAPE_NAME1 includes X6s and the Exadata.SHAPE_NAME2 includes X7s, and based on our selection here, the values in the Total Node Count and CPU Core Count fields will alter their values.
- **Total Node Count** This field is informational and indicates how many Exadata compute nodes come with a particular shape.
- **Oracle Database Software Edition** Will default to Enterprise Edition Extreme Performance, giving us the potential to use all the Oracle Database options. This field cannot be changed.

- **Cluster Name** Name your Exadata RAC cluster. Here are the rules for a cluster name: The name can be no longer than 11 characters and must begin with a letter and contain only letters (a–z and A–Z), numbers (0–9), and hyphens (-); the name is not case sensitive.

- **Core Count** Add an initial set of cores for your service. With X6 shapes, we have a minimum of 11 cores per database compute node. With X7, there are no minimums but cores need to be added symmetrically in multiples of the number of compute nodes—for example, 2 for a quarter, 4 for a half, and 8 for a full.

- **License Type** This indicates how you have purchased your service. If you have flex licensing, you are able to use all the options of the database. With BYOL, you need to have shelved licenses on premises to match what you are using in the cloud.

- **SSH Public Key** You have a few options: You can click the Browse button and upload your SSH key from the file system. Or you can drag-and-drop the key file into the Drop SSH Key Files Here... area in the UI. The second method for inputting your keys is to select the Paste SSH Keys radio box, copy the key text, and paste it into the text box that appears when you select the radio button.

- **Data Storage Percentage** You have a few choices here. Do you want to use local backups? Do you want to use Sparse Disk? Select the appropriate boxes in this section. Refer to Chapter 1 to see the storage amounts and percentages based on your selection.

  As outlined in the previous OPC section on local Exadata Storage, a guiding decision for local backups is how you are going to use this ExaCS. Do you need to have lightning-fast recovery at the expense of less database data file space? For production deployments, this choice is usually yes. You can sacrifice database data file space for the ability to recover in the case of an emergency.

In the Advanced Options section, the Disk Redundancy field is always set to High, setting the Exadata storage cells to triple-mirror the data across three cells. This is the default for OPC and OCI. Your selections should look similar to Figure 2-52.

In the Network Information section, we'll use the VCN and subnets we created earlier and assign them to the Exadata:

- **Virtual Cloud Network** Choose the VCN we created, ExaCS Network.
- **Client Subnet** Choose Client_Subnet.
- **Backup Subnet** Choose Backup_Subnet.
- **Hostname Prefix** Enter **exacs**. The value you enter in this field is appended to the Host Domain Name field name in the host and domain URL. This will create a custom hostname for the Exadata Cloud Service compute nodes. In this case, exacs.clientsubnet .exacsnetwork.oraclevcn.com is the host and domain URL.

The Network Information section should look like Figure 2-53.

In the Database Information section, OCI differs from OCI-C in that the Exadata Cloud Service instance creation page is merged with the database creation steps:

- **Database Name** Enter the name of the database in an 11gR2 database and the CDB in a 12c or 18c database. For this database, enter **HRCDB** (or whatever you wish to name the database).

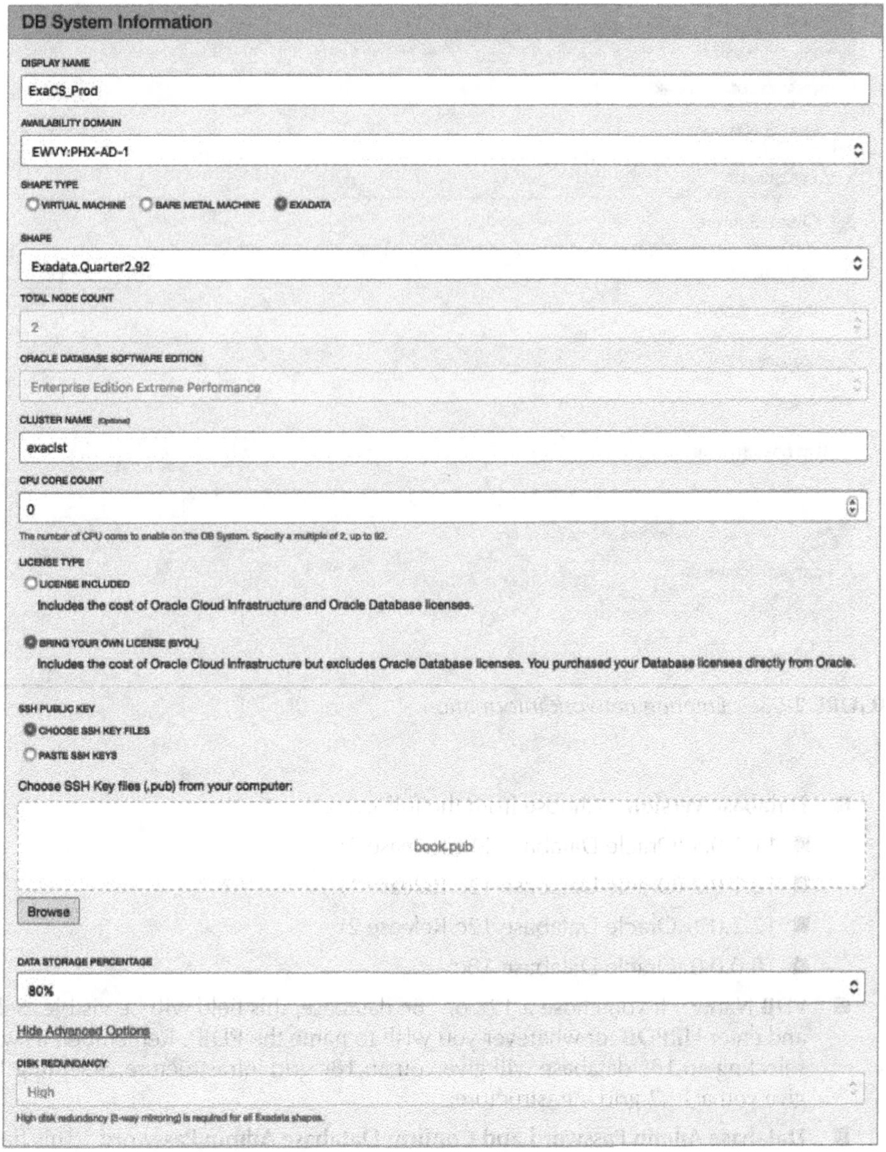

DB System Information

DISPLAY NAME

ExaCS_Prod

AVAILABILITY DOMAIN

EWVY:PHX-AD-1

SHAPE TYPE

○ VIRTUAL MACHINE ○ BARE METAL MACHINE ◉ EXADATA

SHAPE

Exadata.Quarter2.92

TOTAL NODE COUNT

2

ORACLE DATABASE SOFTWARE EDITION

Enterprise Edition Extreme Performance

CLUSTER NAME (Optional)

exaclst

CPU CORE COUNT

0

The number of CPU cores to enable on the DB System. Specify a multiple of 2, up to 92.

LICENSE TYPE

○ LICENSE INCLUDED

Includes the cost of Oracle Cloud Infrastructure and Oracle Database licenses.

◉ BRING YOUR OWN LICENSE (BYOL)

Includes the cost of Oracle Cloud Infrastructure but excludes Oracle Database licenses. You purchased your Database licenses directly from Oracle.

SSH PUBLIC KEY

◉ CHOOSE SSH KEY FILES

○ PASTE SSH KEYS

Choose SSH Key files (.pub) from your computer:

book.pub

Browse

DATA STORAGE PERCENTAGE

80%

Hide Advanced Options

DISK REDUNDANCY

High

High disk redundancy (3-way mirroring) is required for all Exadata shapes.

FIGURE 2-52. *Launch Database System modal, DB System Information*

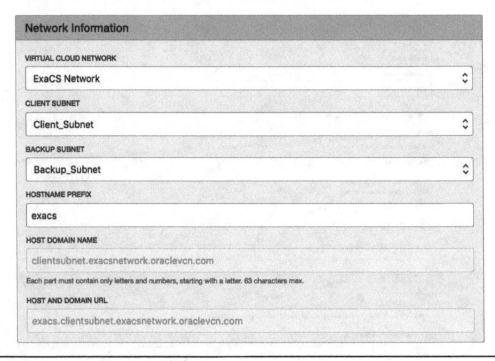

FIGURE 2-53. *Entering network information*

- **Database Version** Choose from the following:
  - 11.2.0.4 (Oracle Database 11g Release 2)
  - 12.1.0.2 (Oracle Database 12c Release 1)
  - 12.2.0.1 (Oracle Database 12c Release 2)
  - 18.0.0.0 (Oracle Database 18c)
- **PDB Name** If you chose a 12c or 18c database, this field will be visible. Select 18.0.0.0 and enter **HRPDB** (or whatever you wish to name the PDB). Remember, as with OCI-C, selecting an 18c database will give you an 18c grid infrastructure. Selecting 12 or 11 will give you a 12.2 grid infrastructure.
- **Database Admin Password and Confirm Database Admin Password** This field has a very specific and stringent set of rules: the password must be 9 to 30 characters in length and contain at least two uppercase, two lowercase, two special (_, #, -), and two numeric characters. Set your password accordingly and enter it into both fields.
- **Database Workload** Choose from two radio buttons:
  - On-Line Transaction Processing (OLTP) (transaction-based database)
  - Decision Support System (DSS) (data warehouse)

■ **Show Advanced Options** Click this link to choose from two more select lists: Character Set and National Character Set. Unless you're migrating a database with a specific existing character set, always use a UTF-based character set.

Once the Database Information section looks like Figure 2-54, click the Launch DB System button to create the Exadata Cloud Service.

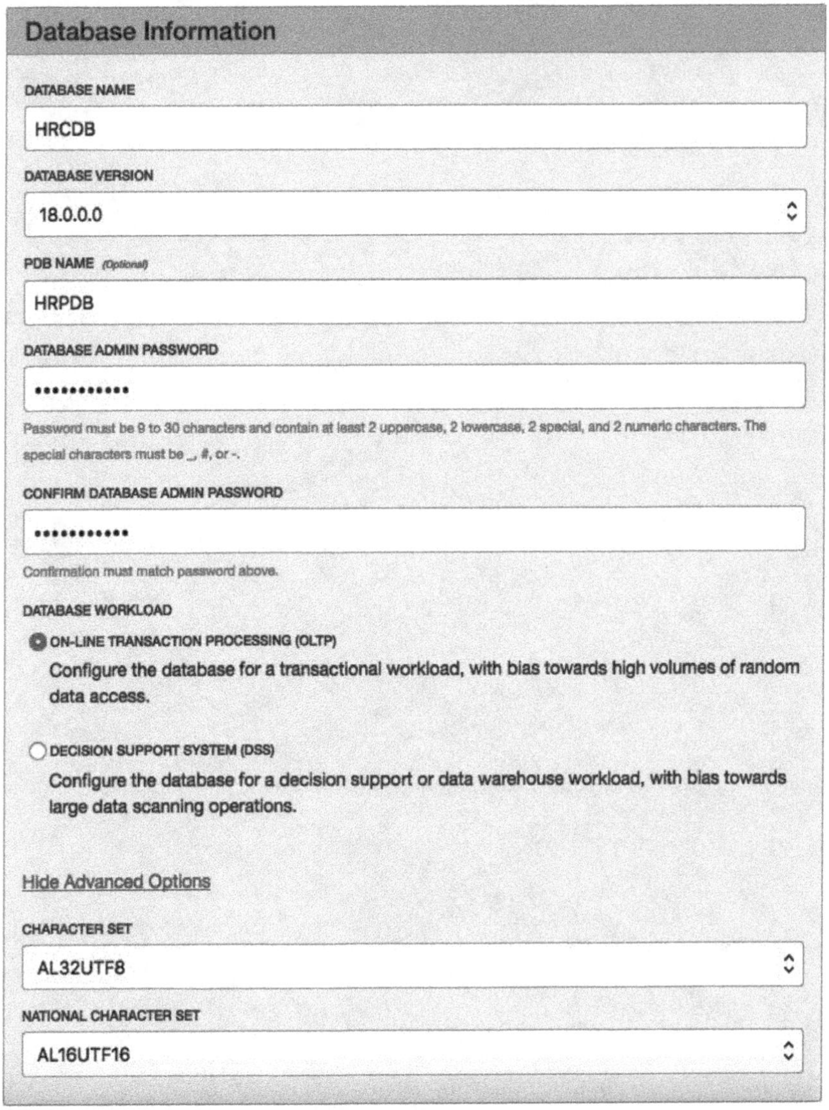

Database Information

DATABASE NAME

> HRCDB

DATABASE VERSION

> 18.0.0.0

PDB NAME *(Optional)*

> HRPDB

DATABASE ADMIN PASSWORD

> ••••••••••

Password must be 9 to 30 characters and contain at least 2 uppercase, 2 lowercase, 2 special, and 2 numeric characters. The special characters must be _, #, or -.

CONFIRM DATABASE ADMIN PASSWORD

> ••••••••••

Confirmation must match password above.

DATABASE WORKLOAD

◉ ON-LINE TRANSACTION PROCESSING (OLTP)

Configure the database for a transactional workload, with bias towards high volumes of random data access.

○ DECISION SUPPORT SYSTEM (DSS)

Configure the database for a decision support or data warehouse workload, with bias towards large data scanning operations.

Hide Advanced Options

CHARACTER SET

> AL32UTF8

NATIONAL CHARACTER SET

> AL16UTF16

FIGURE 2-54. *The Database Information section*

Summary

After reading the steps involved in creating and setting up an on-premises Exadata, you can see why the cloud is as popular as it is. Software-defined networks save you hours of time configuring switches, and with just a few text fields and select lists, you can provision a full rack of an Exadata Database Machine in hours. This speed enables agility when you're starting projects and selecting new hardware (or cloud services) for new database deployments.

CHAPTER 3

The Exadata
Cloud Service UI

N ow that we have created our databases and Exadata Cloud Service, it's time to work with the UI features. The web UI for the Exadata Cloud Service will let us back up, recover, patch and manage the lifecycles of our databases. This chapter will cover both the web UIs for OCI and OCI-C and the various features within each.

The ExaCS UI in Oracle Cloud Infrastructure Classic

To start, let's look at the features and functionality of the UI for the Exadata Cloud Service (ExaCS) in Oracle Cloud Infrastructure Classic (OCI-C). In OCI-C, you can interact with the ExaCS at two or three levels, depending on where your service is provisioned.

From the dashboard, you can alter firewall rules and modify OCPU counts, or go to the Compute Classic section to work with IP networks. From the Database as a Service (DBCS) console, which we used in the last chapter, you can view and alter aspects of the databases deployed to the ExaCS.

Modifying the ExaCS

You can modify aspects of the service itself on the Instance Details page. To get to that page, you start on the service dashboard, the page you see after logging into the Oracle Cloud. Find and click the Exadata Classic tile (Figure 3-1).

On the next page, look for the pop-up menu to the right of the service you want to modify and click it to open the menu options (Figure 3-2).

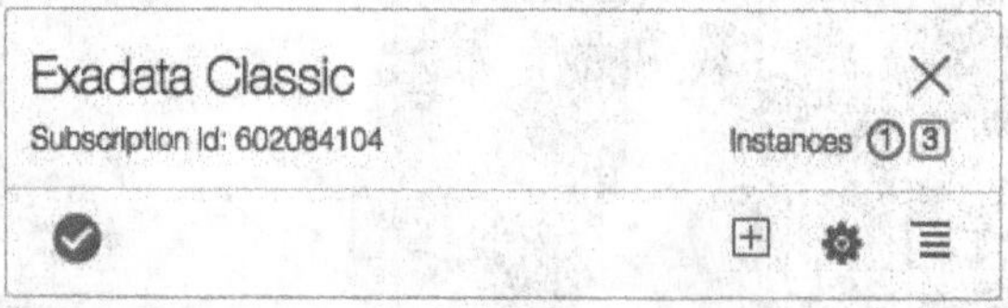

FIGURE 3-1. *Click the Exadata Classic tile.*

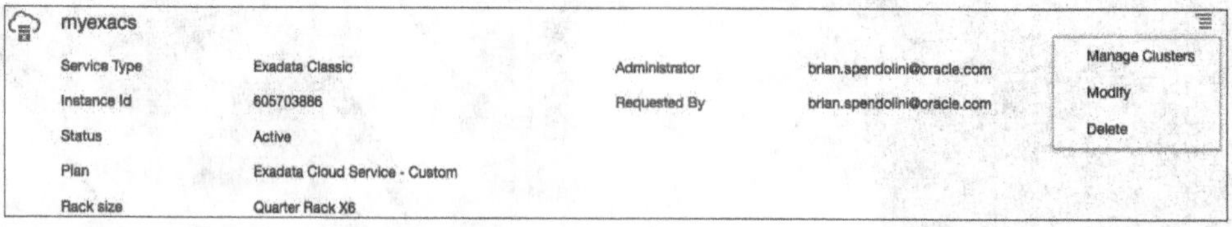

FIGURE 3-2. *The pop-up menu for an Oracle Database ExaCS*

The options available on the pop-up menu depend on where your ExaCS is located and your payment subscription type. If you are in an OCI-C legacy zone with a non-metered account, the options will be Delete, Modify, Create Like, Associate Security Groups, and Manage Security Groups. If you're in an OCI-C availability domain with a universal credits account, the options you will see will be Manage Clusters, Modify, and Delete (as shown in the figure). Let's go over some of these options.

Deleting the Service

Clicking Delete will delete the entire service, including all databases that are deployed. The service will go into a secure erase mode, where it continuously writes 1's and 0's on the disks and flash so that no data can be recovered from them. This process can take 60 or more hours, but new features such as Crypto Erase will speed up the erase time in the future. This option is best used when you're leaving the service permanently or you need to re-create the service but ensure that the data is completely destroyed.

Adding OCPUs

Click the Modify option to add or remove OCPUs from your service. An OCPU is a physical core on the service with two threads per core. The page that opens after you click this option will vary depending on how you have paid for or purchased the service. If you or your company had purchased in a non-metered model, the page would look like Figure 3-3.

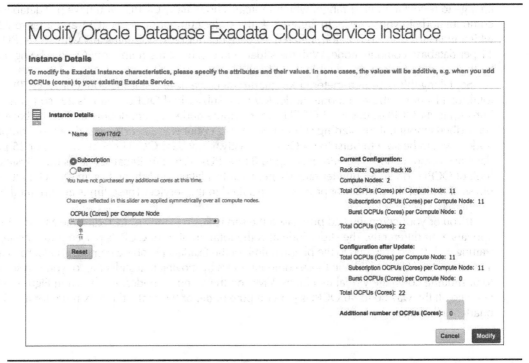

FIGURE 3-3.   *The Modify Oracle Database Exadata Cloud Service Instance Details page*

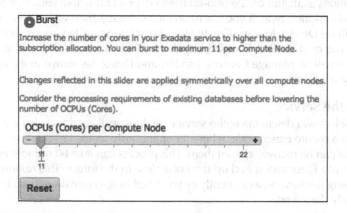

FIGURE 3-4. *The Burst slider*

Notice two radio buttons, Subscription and Burst, under the name of the system. If you had purchased additional OCPUs upon buying the service or after the service was purchased, you can add them here with the slider. This will add those OCPUs to your service permanently.

If you click the Burst radio button, the page changes slightly. Most importantly, the slider will change to reflect a number range, which indicates how many OCPUs you have per database compute node in your ExaCS. In Figure 3-4, the slider numbering starts at 11 and goes to 22, which indicates that this is a non-metered X6 base quarter-rack shape. It starts with 22 OCPUs, or 11 per database compute node. With the slider, you can burst the number of OCPUs being used by the compute nodes up to double the subscribed amount.

So, taking this base non-metered X6 quarter rack, we have a starting count of 22 OCPUs total, or 11 per database compute node. My base subscribed OCPU count is 22, so I can burst up to 44 OCPUs; this is 22 OCPUs per compute node—again, double that of my base subscribed amount. If my starting subscribed OCPU count was 32, or 16 per database compute node, I would be able to burst to 64 OCPUs. Lastly, if my base OCPU count was 50, or 25 per database compute node, I could burst up to 84 OCPUs. Why 84? Because that is the physical limit of OCPUs on an X6 quarter-rack shape. Each Exadata Cloud shape has an OCPU limit—the physical limit of the number of processors installed in the service. These limits are outlined in Chapter 1.

If you or your company had purchased the service using Universal Credits, the Modify Page appears a bit differently. The slider indicates the total number of OCPUs per compute node, starting with 0 and going up to the physical limit of the Exadata Database compute node. You can add all the OCPUs available on those compute nodes by moving that slider bar, or you can set them to 0, shutting down the virtual machines (VMs) on the compute nodes. As shown in Figure 3-5, I can go all the way up to 46 OCPUs per compute node, or 92 total—the maximum for an X7 quarter-rack shape.

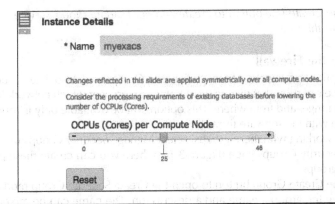

FIGURE 3-5.   *The slider for ExaCS with Universal Credits*

NOTE
The scaling or bursting of OCPUs is done symmetrically, over all the DB compute nodes in your shape, and you must burst or add symmetrically as well. If you are adding to a quarter rack, the number must be in multiples of two, for the two database compute nodes. If you add to a half-rack shape, it needs to be in multiples of four, for the four database compute nodes. If you're using a full rack, it must be in multiples of eight, for the eight database compute nodes. This is very important to remember, because when you're adding to the larger shapes, you could be increasing the amount by eight for every notch of the slider in the UI. This symmetric bursting is set to change in the future, though, giving a bit more flexability.

Once you add or decrease the number of OCPUs, click the Modify button at the lower right of the Service Instance page. The amazing feature of adding OCPUs is that it's done dynamically, with the OS seeing the added CPUs in less than a minute. The database will also see and utilize them.

No downtime is needed because of the virtualization layer used in the ExaCS. There is a Representational State Transfer (REST) API to control bursting as well.

One last important fact to mention is that the service will not automatically burst for you. A user has to add or remove OCPUs manually or have an event trigger the adding of OCPUs via the REST API. This can be considered in two different lights. On one side, why wouldn't you burst automatically? Wouldn't that help when you need the extra horsepower? On the other hand, if it bursts automatically, what happens when a badly written piece of code spikes the system and bursts in the middle of the night? You are now responsible for paying for that bursting period. So, as you can see, this is a double-edged sword, as they say. The best way to be in the middle of this predicament is to script the burst based on events you set.

TIP
Click the Create Like option to create another Exadata Cloud Service similar to this one.

Modifying the Firewall

Our next options go together: Manage Security Groups and Associate Security Groups. Security groups are sets of rules that dictate what traffic can go over which network interface on a particular port or port range, and from where. This option will be available only if your ExaCS is in an OCI-C legacy zone with the software firewall.

To start working with these groups, select Manage Security Groups from the pop-up menu to open the Security Groups page (Figure 3-6), where you can create these groups and the rules within the groups.

Click the Create Group button to open the Create Security Group modal (Figure 3-7), where you can give the group a name and a description. The name can be mixed case but cannot

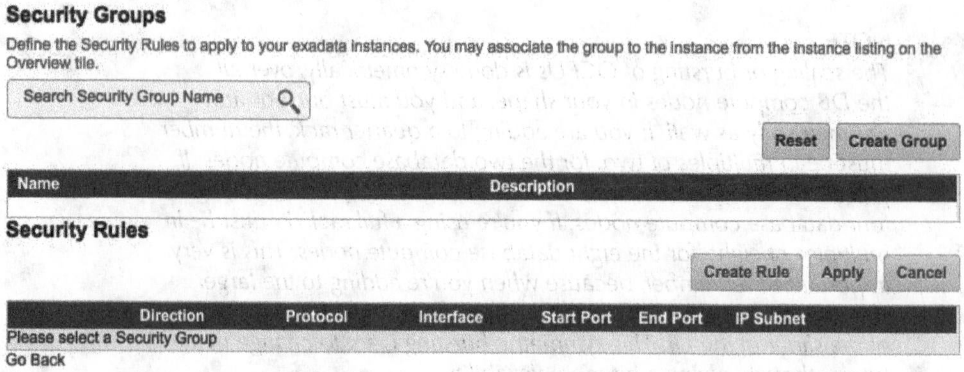

Security Groups

Define the Security Rules to apply to your exadata instances. You may associate the group to the instance from the instance listing on the Overview tile.

Search Security Group Name 🔍

Reset   Create Group

Name	Description

Security Rules

Create Rule   Apply   Cancel

	Direction	Protocol	Interface	Start Port	End Port	IP Subnet
Please select a Security Group						

Go Back

FIGURE 3-6. *Defining security in the Security Groups page*

Create Security Group   ✕

* Name [   ]

Description [   ]

Create   Cancel

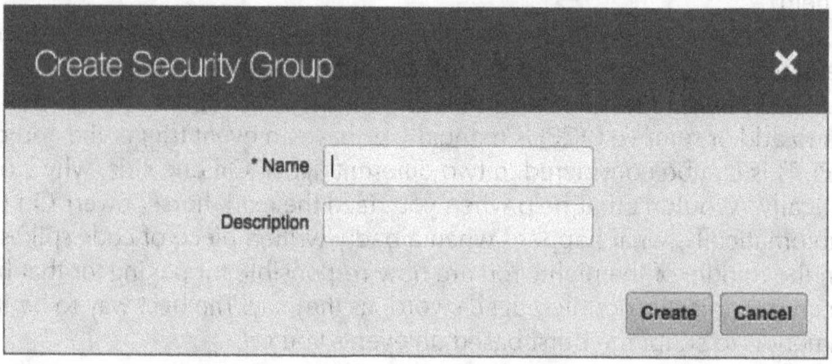

FIGURE 3-7. *Creating a group in the Create Security Group modal*

include any spaces. Once you set the name and description of a group, you are not allowed to change them later, so be sure that you name it correctly and in a descriptive manner. You can create up to five security groups with ten rules in each group; unfortunately, you cannot delete groups at this time. If you need more groups, you can create a service request and ask Oracle to increase this limit. For our example, we use the name SecureShellAccess.

Once you have entered a name and description, click Create. The group name will be displayed on the Security Groups page (Figure 3-6).

Next, you need to add rules. Click the group name you just created in the UI (SecureShellAccess in this example). In the lower part of the section, the Create Rule button is enabled. Click Create Rule to open the Add Security Rule modal (Figure 3-8).

In this modal, you'll select several options:

- **Direction** Choose Inbound for incoming traffic or Outbound for outgoing traffic. The rule we are going to outline in this section is SSH Access, and this is an inbound rule, so choose Inbound.

- **Protocol** Choose from TCP (Transmission Control Protocol) and UDP (User Datagram Protocol). TCP is used for a stateful connection, where the source is usually connected directly to the destination. UDP will not connect directly to the destination, but will send packets. TCP is more reliable for applications such as SSH, HTTPS, and SQL*Net. UDP is used for DNS lookups and online gaming and streaming services. For the SSH connection, choose TCP.

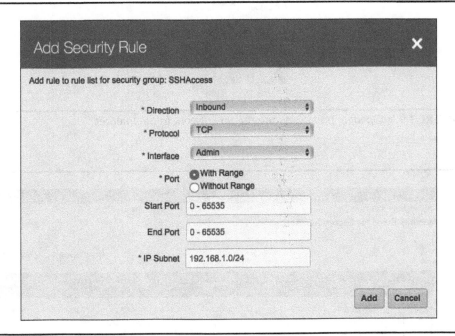

FIGURE 3-8. *The Add Security Rule modal*

■ **Interface** Choose from the networks available for the SSH connection. The options are Admin, Backup, and Client. For SSH, we want to stay off the client network, so the Admin network is probably the best choice here.

■ **Port** SSH runs on port 22, so for Port, select Without Range.

■ **Start Port / End Port** If we needed a range of ports to be opened, we could use the With Range option, using these fields to specify the range.

■ **Port Value** When you select Without Range, this field is displayed. Enter **22**.

■ **IP Subnet** Enter either an individual address or a CIDR block containing a range of IP addresses that are allowed to use this rule and access this port. For access to all IP addresses, enter **0.0.0.0/0**. Note that we will use this subnet address in this example, though it's not a security best practice. You should set this range based upon your company's security rules and policies.

After making your choices in this modal (as shown in Figure 3-9), click Add.

Back on the Security Groups page, click the group you created previously. You will also see the rule you just created in the lower report section (Figure 3-10).

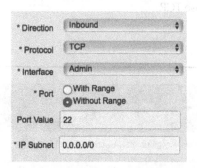

FIGURE 3-9. *Opening port 22 on the Admin network to the Internet*

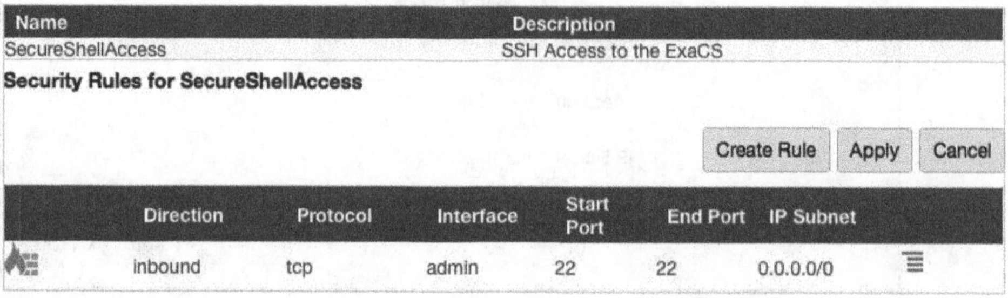

Name	Description
SecureShellAccess	SSH Access to the ExaCS

Security Rules for SecureShellAccess

Create Rule   Apply   Cancel

	Direction	Protocol	Interface	Start Port	End Port	IP Subnet
	inbound	tcp	admin	22	22	0.0.0.0/0

FIGURE 3-10. *The created security rule*

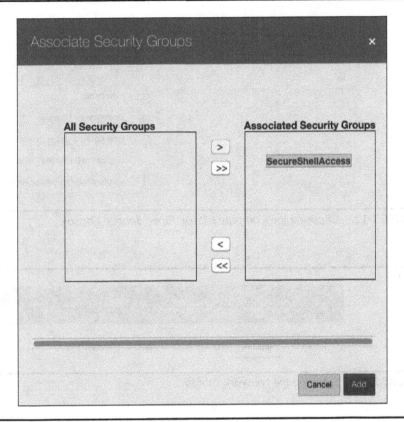

FIGURE 3-11. *Associating security groups*

After you have created a security group and a rule, you can apply or associate this rule with your service. To do this, go back to the Details page (Figure 3-3) of your Oracle Database ExaCS. To reach this page, click the Overview vertical tab in the upper-left of the Security Groups page.

From the pop-up menu to the right of the service details, select Associate Security Groups. The Associate Security Groups modal contains a shuttle, and you should see the SecureShellAccess group on the left side of the shuttle under All Security Groups. By double-clicking the security group or using the shuttle controls, move the SecureShellAccess group from the left to the right under Associated Security Groups, as shown in Figure 3-11.

Click the Add button. That port is now opened on your ExaCS.

Modifying the Firewall in an OCI-C Availability Domain

If you have created an ExaCS in OCI-C in an availability domain, you can alter the firewall rules using Security Lists on the Compute Classic pages for your IP network. To start, click the pop-up menu on the Compute Classic tile in the dashboard and select Open Service Console (Figure 3-12).

On the Compute Classic console page, select the Network subtab (Figure 3-13).

FIGURE 3-12. *Choosing the Compute Classic Open Service Console*

FIGURE 3-13. *Selecting the Network subtab*

Important Note About the Site Selector

Notice the Site selector at the top middle of the Compute Classic console page (Figure 3-14), to the right of the page name. If you are in an OCI-C AD, you may create your resources in two regional locations, or you may have created your resources in a specific location. It's important to ensure that the Site selector is set to the data center and region where your ExaCS is located.

Clicking the Site select list (Figure 3-14) opens the Site Selector modal (Figure 3-15). Use the drop-down to select the region you want to be in. Then click OK.

On the left side of the page, select the Security Rules option, as shown in Figure 3-16.

In the next page, you can see all the security rules that were created for your service. You can choose an existing rule to open that particular protocol or create a new rule by clicking the Create Security Rule button. To open an existing rule, find the rule you want to enable and click the pop-up menu to the right of the rule (Figure 3-17), and then select Update. Once the Create Security Rule modal opens, change the Status select list from Disabled to Enabled (Figure 3-18).

FIGURE 3-14.   *The Site selector*

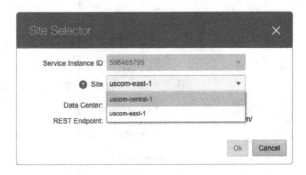

FIGURE 3-15.   *Selecting a region in the Site Selector modal*

To create a rule, again, click the Create Security Rule button to open the Create Security Rule modal (Figure 3-18).

This modal includes the following fields:

- **Name**   For this example, suppose we need to open up VNC, so enter **VNC**.
- **Status**   Set this rule to Enabled and working or to Disabled and blocking access to this port.
- **Type**   Indicates whether this is an inbound (Ingress) or outbound (Egress) rule. Set this to Ingress.
- **Access Control List**   Contains rules that are applied to a specific virtualized Network Interface Card (vNIC). We'll set this on the ExaCS access list. Click the select list to see two lists for your ExaCS: one for the client network and one for the backup network. These lists will be in the format ExadataCloudServiceName_HostName_NetworkName_ACL. Chose either list for an example rule.
- **Security Protocols**   These are preset or predefined application types you can use to set access for specific uses. For example, choosing VNC opens up ports 5900 through 5910, covering all the common VNC ports we usually see when starting a VNC server. You can choose from the pre-created types or create and use your own custom types. These can be displayed and created on the Security Protocols page (accessed via the list of options shown in Figure 3-16). Choose VNC.

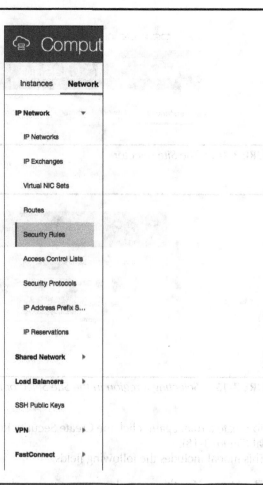

FIGURE 3-16. *Selecting the Security Rules option*

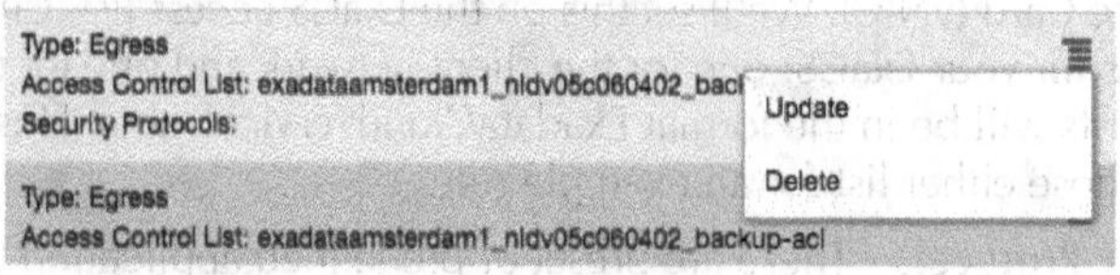

Type: Egress
Access Control List: exadataamsterdam1_nldv05c060402_bacl
Security Protocols:

Update

Delete

Type: Egress
Access Control List: exadataamsterdam1_nldv05c060402_backup-acl

FIGURE 3-17. *Enabling a pre-created rule*

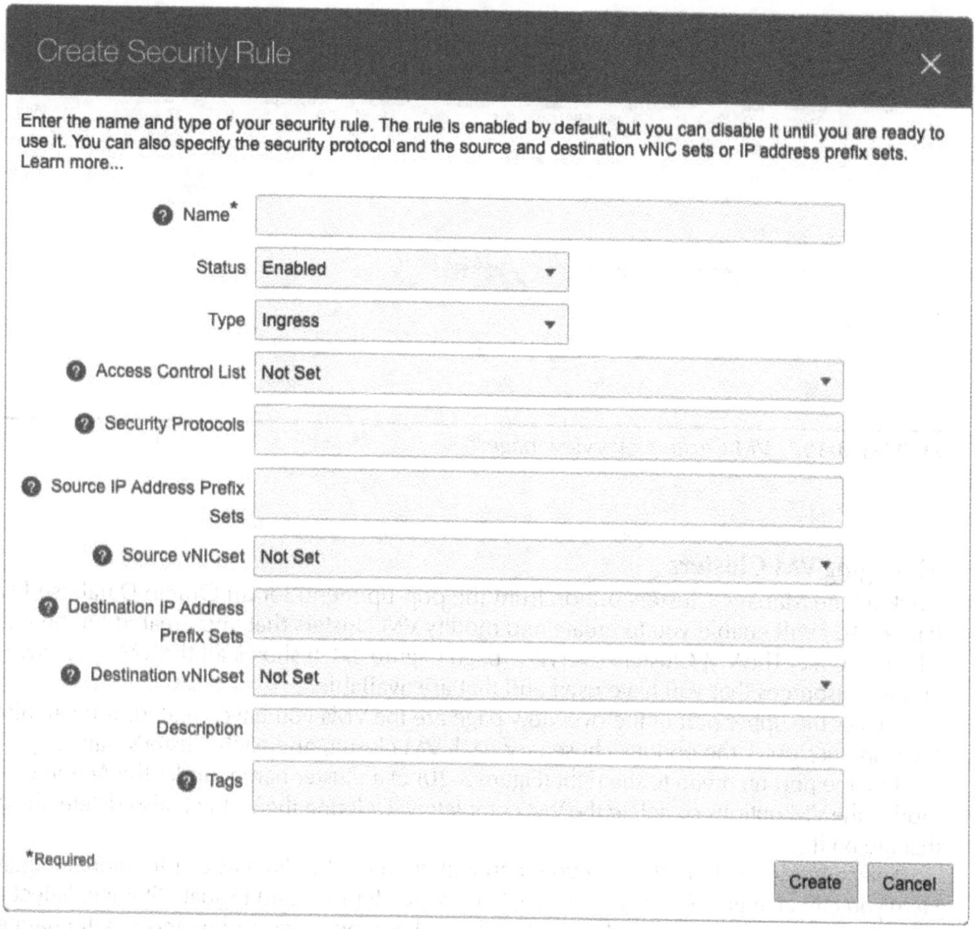

FIGURE 3-18. *The Create Security Rule modal*

- **Source IP Address Prefix Sets** Provide IP ranges where traffic can originate from, locking down this port access to a specific IP or a range of IPs.
- **Source vNICset** Similar to the Source IP Address Prefix Sets, but limits traffic from a particular vNIC in your IP network.
- **Destination IP Address Prefix Sets / Destination vNICset** These act similarly to the Source Sets variants, but this option restricts the traffic to go to a particular vNIC or IP/IP range.
- **Description** Describe your rule.
- **Tags** Add tags.

Once you've created the rule, click Create.

VM Clusters

Instance Name: exaclibs1   Instance Id: 500084672   [Create VM Cluster]

Cluster Name	CPU Cores	Memory (GB)	Exadata Storage (TB)	Local Storage (GB)	Client Network	Backup Network	Exadata Database Backups	Sparse Disk Group	Status	Action
exaclibs1	8	60	4	60			N	N	Provisioned	☰
exaclitwo	8	60	4	60			N	N	Provisioned	☰

Resource Overview

	CPU Cores	Memory (GB)	Exadata Storage (TB)	Local Storage (GB)
Allocated	16	120	8	202
Unallocated	4	360	45	3618
Total	20	480	53	3820

FIGURE 3-19. *VM Clusters overview page*

Managing VM Clusters

Clicking the Manage Clusters option from the pop-up menu for an Oracle Database ExaCS (Figure 3-2) will enable you to create and modify VM clusters that you created on the Exadata Cloud Service. The VM Clusters overview page (Figure 3-19) shows all the VMs you have created and the resources that you have used and that are available.

Across the upper part of the overview page are the VMs you have created. You can also see the resources used, the options chosen for each VM cluster, and each cluster's status.

Use the pop-up menu to the right (Figure 3-20) of a cluster name, under the Action column, to modify the VM options or delete the VM completely. Deleting the VM will also delete all databases that are on it.

Selecting Modify from the pop-up menu will open the Modify VM Cluster modal (Figure 3-21). Here you can change a few parameters: CPU Cores, Memory, and Exadata Storage. Select the radio button next to each option to change its value. Changing cores and memory will change these values across all nodes that this VM is created on.

Instance Name: exaclibs1   Instance Id: 500084672   [Create VM Cluster]

Exadata Database Backups	Sparse Disk Group	Status	Action	
N	N	Provisioned	Modify
N	N	Provisioned	Delete

FIGURE 3-20. *Choosing options from the cluster pop-up menu*

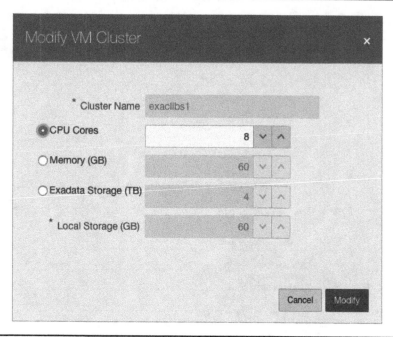

FIGURE 3-21. *The Modify VM Cluster modal*

Back on the VM Clusters overview page, click the Create VM Cluster button to create another VM. A total of eight VMs can be created on an ExaCS regardless of shape but within the resource constraints. Clicking the button opens the Create VM Cluster modal (Figure 3-22). It's similar to creating the initial VM with the same options.

NOTE
A feature called VM Subsetting will be available, but is not at this writing, which enables you to select the nodes this VM will be created on.

The following fields are available on the modal:

- **Cluster Name**   Enter a name for the new cluster.
- **Shape**   This choice may or may not be available in your UI, but it has predefined sizes of VMs (Small, Medium, Large, and Custom). Whether you see it in your UI depends on the version of the cloud software you are using. Later versions have it removed.

The other options can all be set using the resources available on your service: Settings for CPU Cores, Memory (GB), and Local Storage (GB) are done symmetrically across all nodes on which you choose to create the VM. Exadata storage will be used for the DATA, RECO, and SPARSE disk groups, depending on the settings you choose. If you have an Exadata Cloud at

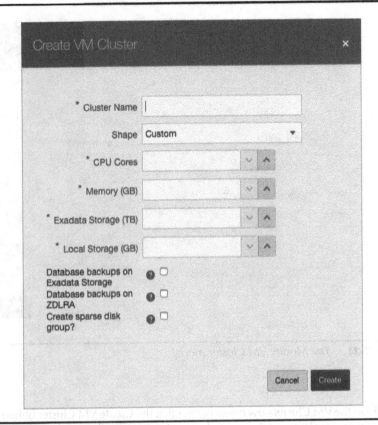

FIGURE 3-22. *Creating a VM cluster*

Customer, you can also back up to a Zero Data Loss Recovery Appliance (ZDLRA). When you are done choosing options, click Create.

NOTE
One of the advantages of multi-VM is the ability to segregate workloads as well as have different Grid Infrastructure and OS versions all running at the same time. You can create an environment where databases start in the development VM and move all the way to the production VM cluster.

Go back to the overview page by clicking the Overview subtab in the upper left.

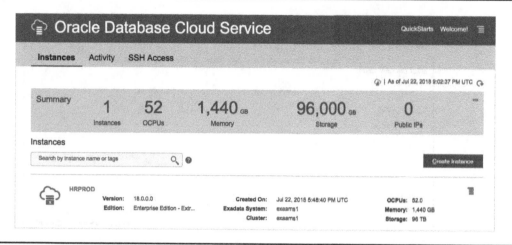

FIGURE 3-23. *Deployed databases on your ExaCS*

Deploying Database Features on the ExaCS

Now let's take a look at the options and features of the Database console for the deployed databases on the ExaCS. While still on the Details page (Figure 3-2), click the Open Service Console button at the upper right. You can also go back to the Dashboard, use the pop-up menu on the Exadata Classic Tile (Figure 3-1) and select Open Service Console.

On the database console page, you'll see all the deployed databases you have on your ExaCS (Figure 3-23). In this console, the database is named HRPROD.

Console Operations

In Chapter 2, we created a service; you should see the name of your created service listed on the console page. To the right of the service name is a pop-up menu. Click the menu to view the options.

EM Console For 12c and 18c databases, choosing this option (Open EM Console) will open EM Express and Database Control for 11g databases. Note that this is not a full version of Enterprise Manager. For the web page to be accessed, you must open the ports in the firewall before using the EM Console option. The port number is usually 5500 through 5510 for EM Express, depending on the version, and 1158 for the 11g Database Console.

SSH Access Choose the SSH Access option to add SSH public keys into the service, in case you lose the original key or want to add more keys. You supply the public key here while using the matching private key to gain access. After choosing this option, the Add New Key modal will open (Figure 3-24).

You have a couple of options for adding a new public key:

- **Upload A New SSH Public Key Value From File** Click the Browse button to use a key stored locally to your computer.
- **Key Value** Click this radio button and then paste a key in the text box.

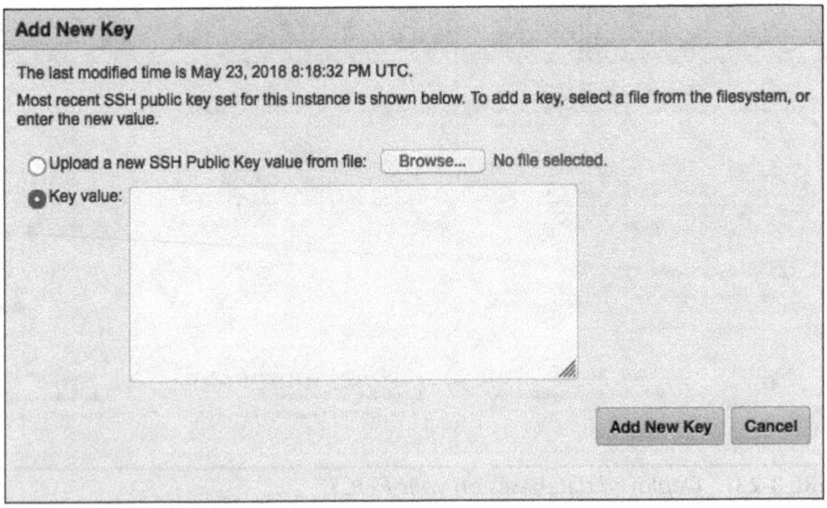

FIGURE 3-24. *The Add New Key modal*

After using either of these methods, click the Add New Key button. The service will quickly go into maintenance mode while the service places that key on all the database compute nodes. After it is done, you can log into the OS of the database compute nodes with the matching private key.

Update Exadata IORM   This option controls Exadata I/O Resource Manager (IORM), which lets you divide I/O resources among multiple databases. You assign shares out to each individual database by using the modal to grant each database a portion of the shares. The values assigned to the databases are between 1 and 32, with 1 being the lowest share. By default, upon creation, all databases are assigned a 1. As you assign a higher share, those databases get their queries prioritized over databases with lower shares. The more important the database, the higher the number of shares.

As an example, let's use an ExaCS with five databases deployed. Upon creation, one share is allocated to each database, thus each database is allocated one out of every five I/Os when IORM is needed for a system that is getting overloaded.

Now let's change the shares of an important database that needs priority. If the share value for one database is changed to 5 from 1, the total number of shares increases to nine (four with 1 share, one with 5 shares). When IORM is needed, the database with a share value of 5 is allocated five out of every nine I/Os. The databases with a share value of 1 are each allocated one out of every nine I/Os, prioritizing the database with a value of 5. IORM also controls priority to the Exadata flash storage on the storage cells. The more shares given to a database, the more flash storage it can use. (We look at IORM in depth in Chapters 7 and 9.)

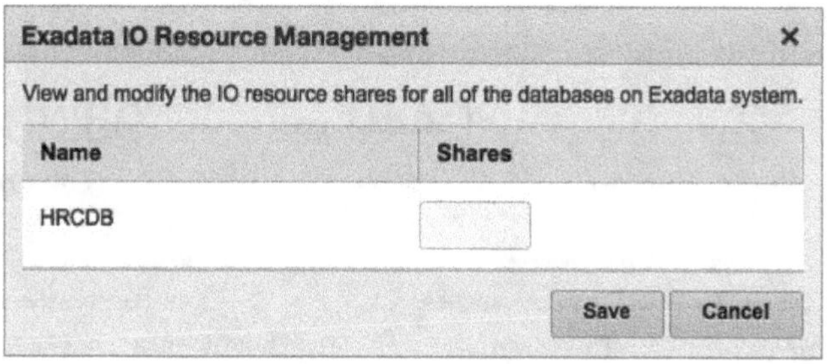

FIGURE 3-25. *Setting share numbers in the Exadata I/O Resource Management modal*

Using the Exadata I/O Resource Management modal (Figure 3-25), you can set the number of shares to each database. The name of the CDB will show in this modal, not the name of the Database Service. In our example, the Service was named HRPROD with the CDB being HRCDB, thus we see HRCDB in figure 3-25. After you set the number of shares, click Save.

Delete Choosing this option will open the Delete Service modal (Figure 3-26) where you can delete the database, with the option of deleting the backups pertaining to this database. Remember that this deletes just the database and not the entire ExaCS.

Individual Database Operations

While still on the database console page, click the title of a database deployment to see the Database Service Details page. The page starts with an Instance Overview (Figure 3-27) in the upper right. This is an overview of the deployed database, not the Exadata Service.

This overview section contains details about the database, such as the version, backup method, the connect string for the SCAN listener, and the character sets. Click Show More to see these additional details. The large resources box at the top of this section contains information such as how many nodes, memory, OCPUs, and storage units this database has access to. Remember that this is a total number and does not reflect consumption.

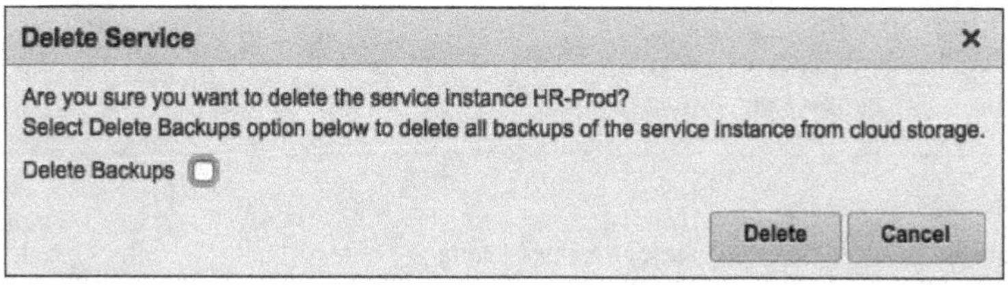

FIGURE 3-26. *Deleting a service and backups*

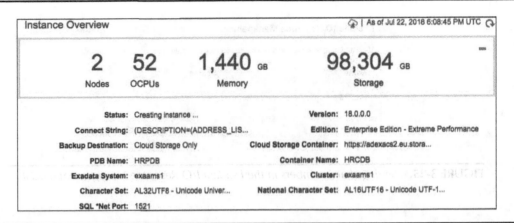

Instance Overview				As of Jul 22, 2018 6:08:45 PM UTC
2 Nodes	**52** OCPUs	**1,440** GB Memory	**98,304** GB Storage	

Status: Creating instance ...		**Version:** 18.0.0.0	
Connect String: (DESCRIPTION=(ADDRESS_LIS...		**Edition:** Enterprise Edition - Extreme Performance	
Backup Destination: Cloud Storage Only		**Cloud Storage Container:** https://adexacs2.eu.stora...	
PDB Name: HRPDB		**Container Name:** HRCDB	
Exadata System: exaams1		**Cluster:** exaams1	
Character Set: AL32UTF8 - Unicode Univer...		**National Character Set:** AL16UTF16 - Unicode UTF-1...	
SQL *Net Port: 1521			

FIGURE 3-27. *Database Instance Overview on the Database Service Details page*

The Resources section (Figure 3-28) shows database compute node–level details. Here you can see the hostname of the compute nodes, the IP addresses of the various network interfaces, the Virtual IPs, the SCAN listener, and the SID of the databases on each node. From the pop-up menu, you can stop, start, or restart the compute node. This does not change the state of the database, but of the entire database compute node or VM cluster. If you stop or restart this compute node/VM cluster, all databases on this compute node/VM cluster will be affected.

Resources

Host Name: nidv05c060402.nldc1.oracl...	**OCPUs:** 26	
SID: HRCDB	**Memory:** 720 GB	
Client IP: 20.20.0.2		
Virtual IP: 20.20.0.3		
Admin IP: 20.20.0.2		
Backup IP: 20.30.0.2		

Host Name: nidv06c060402.nldc1.oracl...	**OCPUs:** 26	
SID: HRCDB	**Memory:** 720 GB	
Client IP: 20.20.0.4		
Virtual IP: 20.20.0.5		
Admin IP: 20.20.0.4		
Backup IP: 20.30.0.3		

Network Information

SCAN IPs:	20.20.0.6,20.20.0.7,20.20.0.8
Client Network:	20.20.0.0/16
Admin Network:	20.20.0.0/16
Backup Network:	20.30.0.0/16

FIGURE 3-28. *The Resources section of the Database Service Details page*

◢ Network Information	
SCAN IPs:	20.20.0.6,20.20.0.7,20.20.0.8
Client Network:	20.20.0.0/16
Admin Network:	20.20.0.0/16
Backup Network:	20.30.0.0/16

FIGURE 3-29. *The Network Information section of the Database Service Details page*

The last section on this page is the Network Information section (Figure 3-29). Here you can see the subnets of the network interfaces as well as the SCAN IP addresses. These subnets are in a CIDR block notation. With ExaCS instances in the OCI-C Availability Domains, the Admin Network is no longer used.

Going back to the very top of the Database Service Details page is a pop-up menu with some service-level options (Figure 3-30).

The first option echoes the previous page, with the ability to open the EM Express (12c+) or Database Control (11g). Same with the second option, SSH Access. You can add public SSH keys to the service with this option just like the previous page.

Choosing Add Tags lets you add appropriate tags to this database. You add and manage the tags through the Manage Tags modal (Figure 3-31). If you added a tag upon creation of the database, this option will not be available, and you can use the details section to manage the tags.

Choosing Replace Database Using Backup enables you to replace the existing running database with a database from the Oracle Database Backup Cloud Service. This is just like the Initialize Data From Backup option you saw during the create process (Chapter 2), except you can do this after the creation of the database. Selecting this option brings up the Replace Database Using Backup modal (Figure 3-32).

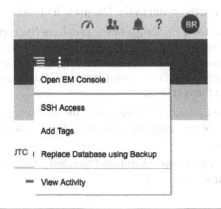

FIGURE 3-30. *The Database Service Details page top-level pop-up menu*

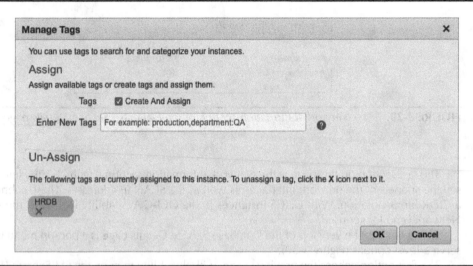

FIGURE 3-31. *Managing tags*

You can refer to the previous chapter for the options in this modal, but here is a quick review:

- **On-Premises Backup?** Select this checkbox if you choose to do just that, use an on-premises backup to recover from. If you uncheck the On-Premises Backup checkbox, all the fields will disappear except a Source Service Name field, where you can select the database deployment on an Exadata Cloud Service you want to recover from.

- **Database ID** This is a unique ID that you can get from the origin database by running the following SQL:

```
SQL> select dbid from v$database;
```

We can then use the result in the Database ID Field.

- **Decryption Method** Backups in the Database Backup Cloud Service are encrypted, so you need to decrypt them to recover. You can decrypt the backup with either the database wallet or a password that was used to encrypt it. Use either the File Browse button to choose Upload Wallet File to use a local wallet on your computer, or paste the RMAN key value into the text field.

- **Cloud Storage Container** These fields are used when the backup is in a cloud container. Enter the URL of the container's location, the username, and the password for an authorized user.

- **Administration Password / Confirm Password** Enter the password used for the sys and system users and confirm it.

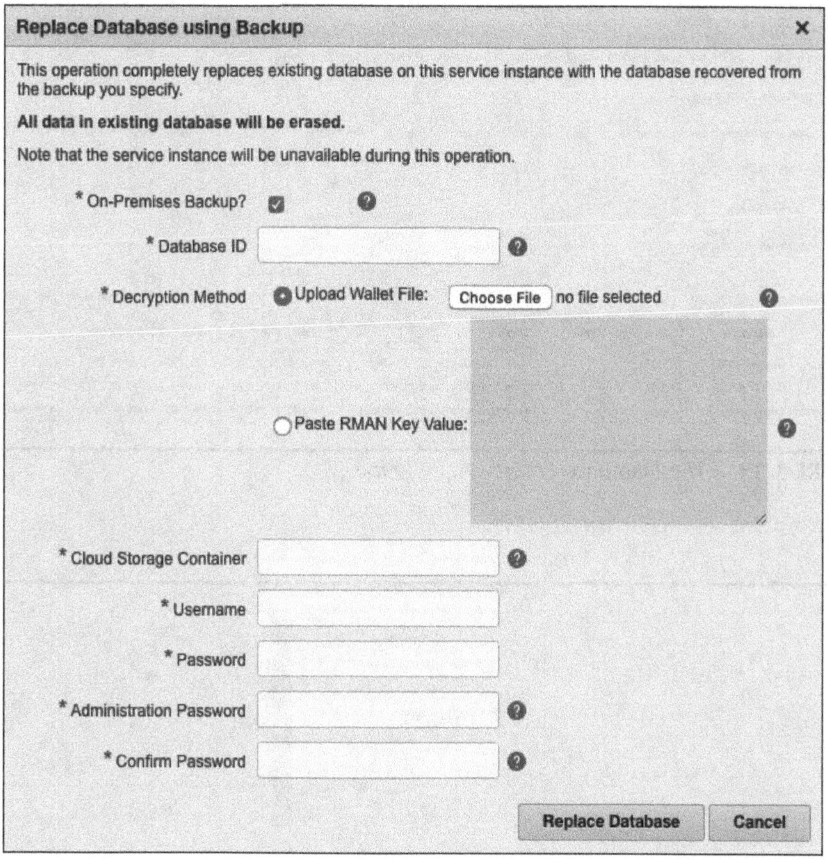

Replace Database using Backup   ✕

This operation completely replaces existing database on this service instance with the database recovered from the backup you specify.

All data in existing database will be erased.

Note that the service instance will be unavailable during this operation.

* On-Premises Backup?   ☑   ❓

* Database ID   [   ] ❓

* Decryption Method   ⦿ Upload Wallet File: [Choose File] no file selected   ❓

⭕ Paste RMAN Key Value: ❓

* Cloud Storage Container   [   ] ❓

* Username   [   ]

* Password   [   ]

* Administration Password   [   ] ❓

* Confirm Password   [   ] ❓

[Replace Database]   [Cancel]

FIGURE 3-32.   *The Replace Database Using Backup modal*

The last option in the pop-up menu at the top of the Database Service Details page is View Activity. Choose this option to open an Activity log, where you can see all the activities that have been performed on the database service, such as backups, snapshots, and patches (Figure 3-33).

Database Backup and Recovery   The Database Service Details page also offers the ability to back up and recover a database. To access this section, click the Administration vertical tab on the left side of the page, as shown in Figure 3-34. Note that this option to back up and recover the database will not be available if you did not set up backups during the initial creation.

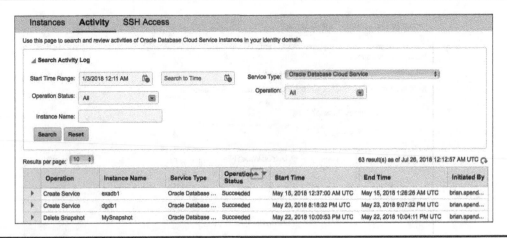

FIGURE 3-33. *The Database Service Activity log*

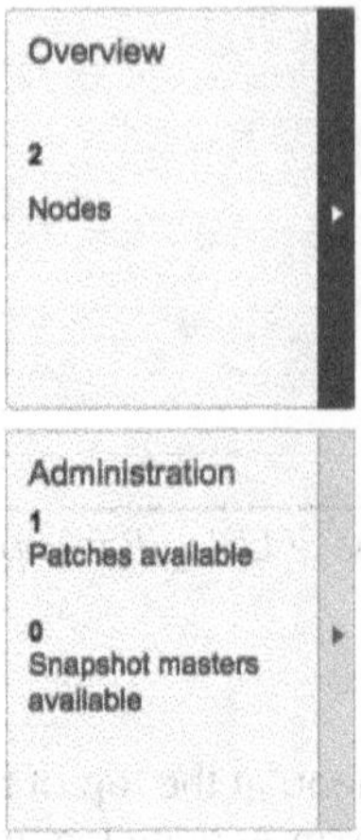

Overview

2
Nodes ▶

Administration

1
Patches available

0
Snapshot masters
available ▶

FIGURE 3-34. *The Administration tab*

On the Backup page, you can take point-in-time backups as well as recover from any previous backup listed (Figure 3-35).

To create a point-in-time backup, click the Backup Now button. In the Backup Now modal, shown in Figure 3-36, is an option to keep this particular backup forever. Selecting Yes will keep this particular backup beyond the default: a periodic full (RMAN level 0) backup and daily incremental backup, with a seven-day cycle between full backups with an overall retention period of 30 days.

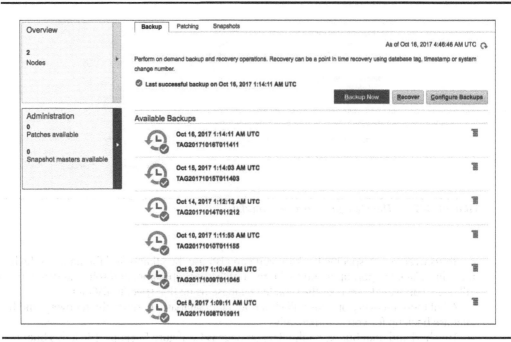

FIGURE 3-35. *The Backup page*

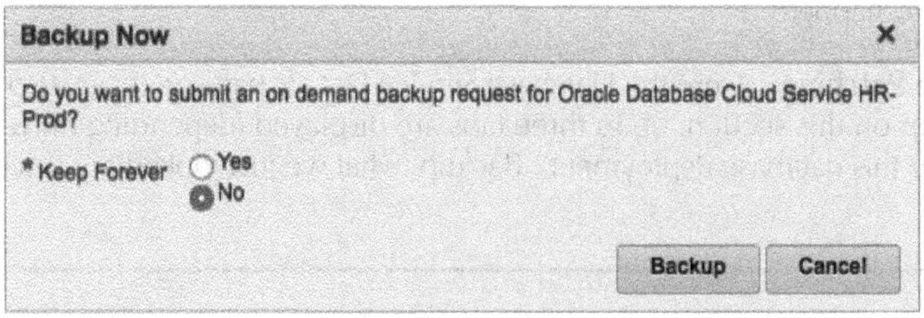

FIGURE 3-36. *Selecting backup options in the Backup Now modal*

On the Backup page, click the Recover button to the right of the Backup Now button to open the Database Recovery modal (Figure 3-37), where you can recover your Oracle Database using three choices: recover from the latest backup that has been taken, recover from a backup at a particular time using the date picker pop-up, or recover from a system change number (SCN). The last two options will restore the database to a specific point in time.

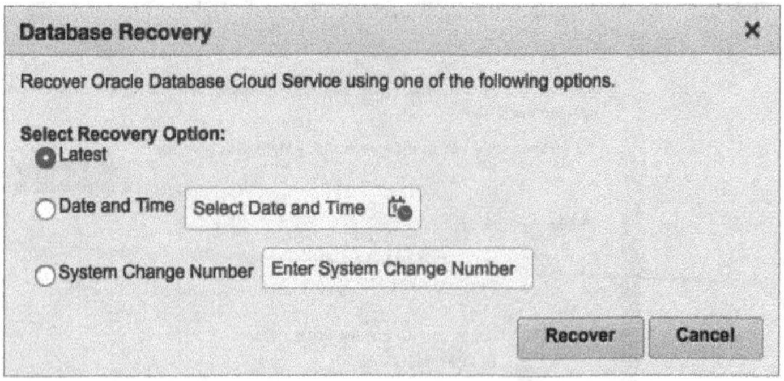

FIGURE 3-37. *The Database Recovery modal*

To recover from a specific backup, you can also use the UI and find the name of the backup in the list. Click the pop-up menu to the right of the backup name, and select Recover. The service will ask if you want to recover the Oracle Database using that specific TAG ID.

All of these recovery options will shut down the database, perform the recovery, and bring the database back up for you automatically.

The third and final button on the Backup page is Configure Backups. Click this button, and the Configure Backups modal opens (Figure 3-38). Here you can change the username and/or password of the container in the Database Backup Cloud Service.

Every few months, the service requires you to change your password. If you were to change the password and not update the backup configuration, backups to the cloud would stop working. Here you can quickly and easily update the password and user if you choose so that backups continue to happen.

Database Patching   From the Database Service Details page, you can also patch your databases. On the top on this section, up to three tabs are displayed (depending on what options you have chosen for this database deployment): Backup (what we just looked at), Patching, and Snapshots.

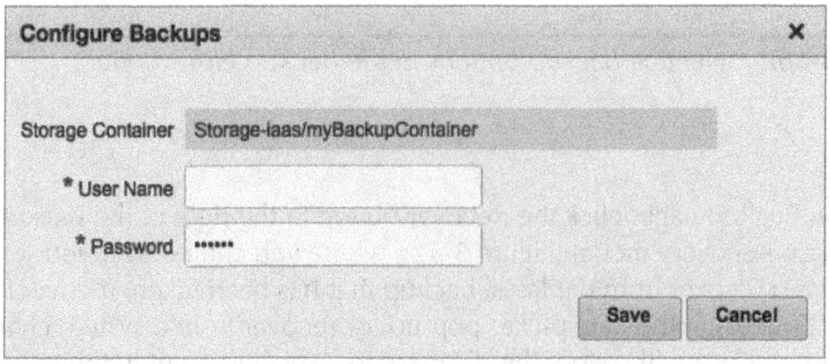

FIGURE 3-38. *The Configure Backups modal*

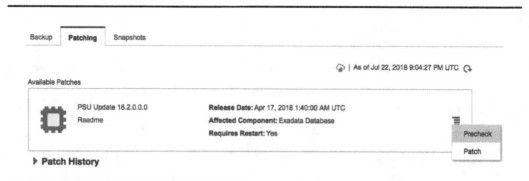

FIGURE 3-39. *Patching a database deployment*

Click the Patching tab to see how you can patch a specific Oracle home using the UI. You can see all the patches available, not only for this particular database deployment but any available Grid Infrastructure (GI) patches as well. These patches are Exadata Bundle Patches and not the regular quarterly updates that a non-engineered system database would use. All patching is done in a rolling fashion, one node at a time, so there is no downtime. Be aware, however, that when patching the GI, all databases on a node will be taken down, but when patching an individual database, only that database will go down, a node at a time.

Starting the patching process begins with clicking the pop-up menu to the right of the patch you want to apply (Figure 3-39). The menu offers two options: Precheck and Patch. Selecting Precheck is just like running precheck with OPatch. The service will check to see if this patch can be applied without issues. If precheck reports errors, you have a few options: You can update the Cloud Tooling, or you can log into the OS and look where the patching log files are (both options are covered in Chapter 4). Patching log files are in the following directory: /var/opt/oracle/log/ *DATABASE_NAME*, with the *DATABASE_NAME* being the name of the SID (11g) or CDB (12c and beyond).

Once precheck gives you the green light (a green checkmark on the UI), you can go ahead and patch the database. To reiterate, this is done in a rolling fashion, with only one node down at a time. Once the patch has been applied, you may roll it back with the Rollback button.

Sparse Cloning and Snapshots   Recall from Chapter 2 that upon creating an Exadata Cloud Service instance, you could add the sparse disk feature. If you selected this option, the Snapshots tab is displayed at the top of the Database Service Details page, as shown in Figure 3-40.

NOTE
Snapshots are available only when using a 12c or later database. This feature will not work with an 11g database.

Open the Snapshots tab and you'll see the Create Snapshot Master button. Click this button to open the Create Snapshot Master modal (Figure 3-41).

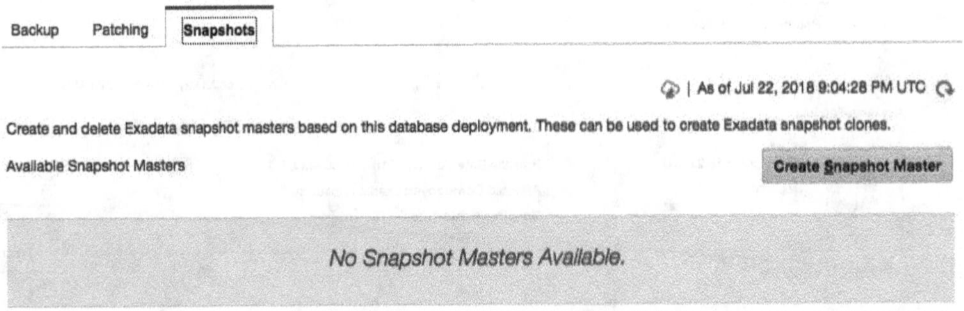

Backup   Patching   Snapshots

☁ | As of Jul 22, 2018 9:04:28 PM UTC ↻

Create and delete Exadata snapshot masters based on this database deployment. These can be used to create Exadata snapshot clones.

Available Snapshot Masters   **Create Snapshot Master**

No Snapshot Masters Available.

FIGURE 3-40. *The Snapshots tab*

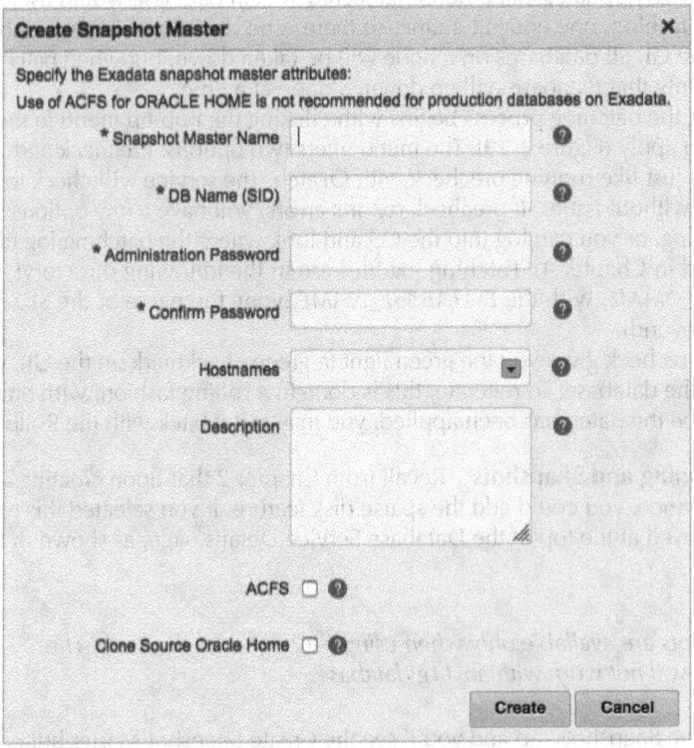

Create Snapshot Master   ✕

Specify the Exadata snapshot master attributes:
Use of ACFS for ORACLE HOME is not recommended for production databases on Exadata.

* Snapshot Master Name   [   ]   ❷

* DB Name (SID)   [   ]   ❷

* Administration Password [   ]   ❷

* Confirm Password   [   ]   ❷

Hostnames   [▼]   ❷

Description   [   ]   ❷

ACFS   ☐ ❷

Clone Source Oracle Home ☐ ❷

                                              Create   **Cancel**

FIGURE 3-41. *Create Snapshot Master modal*

In this modal, you can create a point-in-time snapshot of your database. Once you've created this snapshot, you can create clones from the master. Any changes you make in the clone databases will be recorded in the SPARSE disk group, not in the DATA disk group, thus never modifying the snapshot master and saving space. The clone databases also share the snapshot master's Oracle home.

The following fields are in this modal:

- **Snapshot Master Name**   Use this to name your snapshot.
- **DB Name (SID)**   Name your master snapshot database.
- **Administration Password**   Enter the password for SYS and SYSTEM users.
- **Confirm Password**   Re-enter the password.
- **Hostnames**   As with creating the database, choose what nodes this master snapshot database will be deployed on.
- **Description**   Enter a description for the snapshot.
- **ACFS checkbox**   Select this checkbox and the Oracle home for this master snapshot database will be put on an Oracle ASM Cluster File System (ACFS) mount and not on the local storage to the database compute node. This option should be used only for test and development databases. The performance of the database will be impacted when the Oracle home is on an ACFS mount. This option will save space on the local compute file system.
- **Clone Source Oracle Home checkbox**   Clones the Oracle home the master lives in. This is very useful for E-Business Suite installs where the home may have special patches and customizations.

When you're done, click Create. The database will go into maintenance mode while the snapshot is created.

Once the snapshot is created, you can create a clone. There are couple of ways to do this: Go back to the main Database Console page, find your snapshot, and click the pop-up menu to the right (Figure 3-42). This menu will give you the option to create a clone. Or you can create a clone from the Snapshots tab by choosing the Create Database Clone option from the pop-up menu to the right of the master snapshot (Figure 3-43).

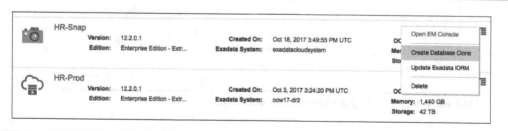

FIGURE 3-42.   *Creating a clone from the DBCS console page*

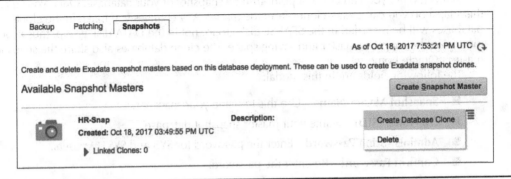

| Backup | Patching | **Snapshots** |

As of Oct 18, 2017 7:53:21 PM UTC ↻

Create and delete Exadata snapshot masters based on this database deployment. These can be used to create Exadata snapshot clones.

Available Snapshot Masters   **Create Snapshot Master**

HR-Snap   Description: Create Database Clone
Created: Oct 18, 2017 03:49:55 PM UTC
▶ Linked Clones: 0   Delete

FIGURE 3-43.   *Creating a clone from a snapshot master on the Snapshots tab*

After you choose to create a clone from the master snapshot, you'll see the Create Service flow (Figure 3-44) that was used to create a database deployment in Chapter 2. On the first page, all you need to do is name the clone database and choose the nodes you want this clone to be created on. Then click Next in the upper right of the page to move to the next page in the flow.

On the Instance Details page (Figure 3-45), fill in the details just as you did when you created your first database in OCI-C. You cannot use the Initialize Data From Backup feature with a clone, however. Enter a name for the database and enter the Administration Password. Then, in the right-hand column, choose whether this database will be backed up and how. Lastly, click the Next button at the upper right. Look over the details on the final page of the flow and click Create; the clone will be created shortly after.

Instance   Snapshot Master Name: HR-Snap
Provide basic service instance information.   Source Instance Name: HR-Snap

* Instance Name	HRClone		* Service Level	Oracle Database Exadata Cloud Service
Description			* Software Release	Oracle Database 12c Release 2
Notification Email	brian.spendolini@oracle.com		* Software Edition	Enterprise Edition - Extreme Performance
* Exadata System	ocw17-dr2 - Quarter Rack (2 nodes)		* Database Type	Database Clustering with RAC
Hostnames				
Tags				

FIGURE 3-44.   *Creating a clone database instance*

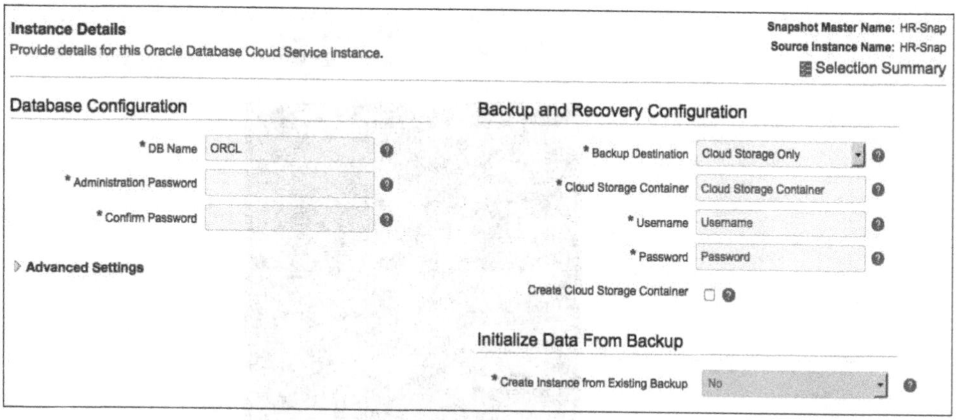

Instance Details
Provide details for this Oracle Database Cloud Service instance.

Snapshot Master Name: HR-Snap
Source Instance Name: HR-Snap
🗟 Selection Summary

Database Configuration

* DB Name ORCL ❓

* Administration Password ❓

* Confirm Password ❓

▷ Advanced Settings

Backup and Recovery Configuration

* Backup Destination Cloud Storage Only ❓

* Cloud Storage Container Cloud Storage Container ❓

* Username Username ❓

* Password Password ❓

Create Cloud Storage Container ☐ ❓

Initialize Data From Backup

* Create Instance from Existing Backup No ❓

FIGURE 3-45. *The Instance Details page for a clone database*

The ExaCS UI in OCI

Let's take a look at the UI for an Exadata Cloud Service created in OCI, starting with the DB Systems page after you log in. We can get to this page by going back to the Dashboard and clicking the Exadata (OCI) tile's title. Now, start by clicking the fly-out menu in the upper-left corner of the OCI homepage (Figure 3-46). Then click the Bare Metal, VM, and Exadata link (Figure 3-47).

On the DB Systems page, you'll see the created Exadata Cloud Service, which we named ExaCS_Prod in Chapter 2. (You may have named it something a bit more meaningful—regardless, you should see it listed on the page.) If you don't see it, remember that you can put resources into compartments in OCI, so your service may be located there. To check, from the Compartment drop-down list on the left side of the page, select the compartment in which you placed the Exadata Cloud Service (Figure 3-48). Also make sure you are in the correct region. You can refer back to Chapter 2 if you need help navigating to this page.

FIGURE 3-46. *Click the fly-out menu.*

FIGURE 3-47. *Choosing the link to launch the DB Systems page*

FIGURE 3-48. *Selecting the compartment with your service*

The Service Details Page

On the DB Systems page are details of your Exadata Cloud Service (Figure 3-49): the software version, the virtual cloud network you used, and the public and private IPs. Click the service name (ExaCS_Prod) to see the service details page.

The details page has three sections that contain buttons, service details, and resources.

Buttons

Let's start by looking at the buttons (Figure 3-50): Scale Up/Down, Add SSH Keys, Apply Tag(s), and Terminate.

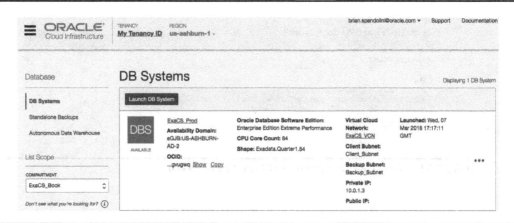

FIGURE 3-49.   *The Exadata Cloud Service details page*

FIGURE 3-50.   *The buttons section*

Clicking Scale Up/Down will launch a modal (Figure 3-51) in which you can scale the OCPUs of this service from zero to the maximum physical OCPUs.

For our X6 quarter-rack shape, we must scale up in multiples of 2, and we can go all the way up to 84. Use the up/down arrows to the right in the text field to change the amount, or type the amount in the field. Then click the Scale Up/Down button to commit the changes. Within seconds, the OCPUs will be added to your service, with the OS and database seeing and being able to utilize them immediately. No downtime or bouncing of the service is needed.

Click Add SSH Keys to open a modal, where you can paste in a new SSH key to be used for your service (Figure 3-52). Then click the Add SSH Keys button.

NOTE
Remember that you must have the matching private key to the public key you paste into this modal. Chapter 2 goes over how to create these keys.

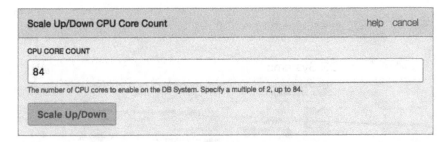

FIGURE 3-51. *The Scale Up/Down CPU Core Count modal*

FIGURE 3-52. *The Add SSH Keys modal*

Click the Apply Tag(s) button to open the modal in which you can apply tags to this resource (Figure 3-53). These tags can help you track resources in this tenancy. Tag keys cannot be changed later, but tag values can be changed. After you've filled in the tag information, click Apply Tag(s).

Click the Terminate button to delete your Exadata Cloud Service. Note that this will delete the entire service, including all deployed databases and any files you have on the OS, and it will shred the backend storage cells by writing 1's and 0's over all the disks.

CAUTION
Exercise caution when using the Terminate button.

DB System Information: Service Details

The information area for the service (Figure 3-54) shows vital information about the Exadata Cloud Service, especially details regarding external connectivity.

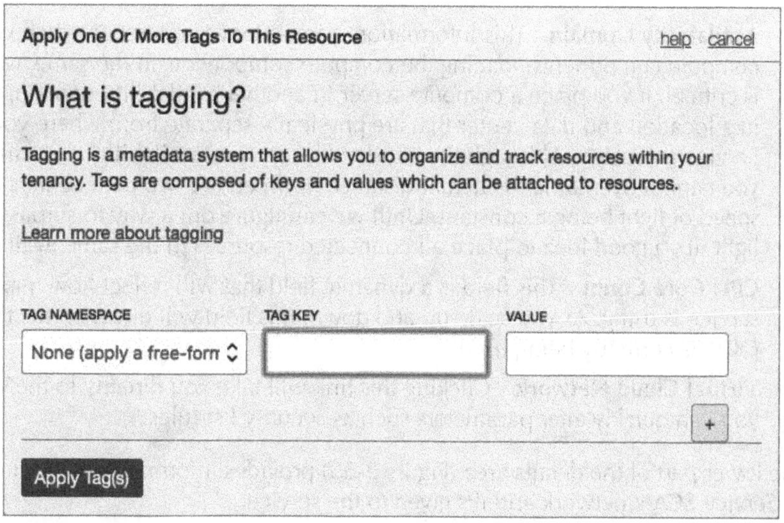

FIGURE 3-53. *Adding a tag to a resource*

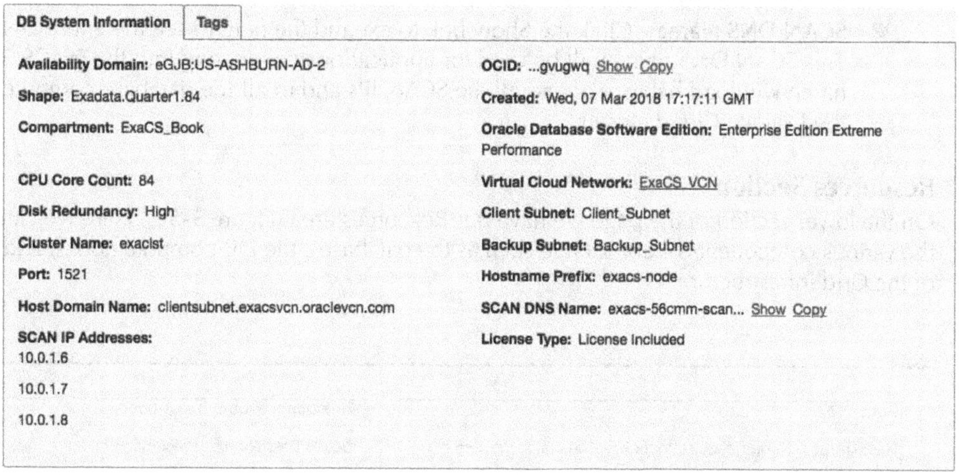

FIGURE 3-54. *DB System Information area*

Here's a rundown of some of the most important information details:

- **Availability Domain** This information is important to reference when you're using compute components. Placing the compute components in the same availability domain is critical. If you place a compute server in another availability domain, you are placing it in a location and data center that are physically separate from where your Exadata Cloud Service is located. Although the bandwidth between availability domains is excellent, you cannot overcome the actual distance between the two data centers because of the speed of light being a constant. Until we can figure out a way to surpass the speed of light, it's a good idea to place all connected resources in the same availability domain.

- **CPU Core Count** This field is a dynamic field that will reflect how many OCPUs your service is using. As you scale up and down, this field will always reflect the number of OCPUs currently being used.

- **Virtual Cloud Network** Clicking this link will take you directly to the VCN page so that you can quickly alter parameters such as security list rules.

The lower part of the details area (Figure 3-55) provides information regarding the Exadata Cloud Service SCAN network and IPs given to the service.

- **Port** This field shows the port number that the Exadata Cloud SCAN listener is on—usually 1521.

- **SCAN IP Addresses** Three SCAN listener IP addresses are listed. Depending on the subnet assigned to the client network, these IP addresses will reflect the range contained in that subnet. We assigned a 10.0.1.0/16 range to this particular ExaCS, so the SCANs are 10.0.1.6, 10.0.1.7, and 10.0.1.8.

- **SCAN DNS Name** Click the Show link to expand the field to see the entire DNS name. This SCAN DNS name will be used for applications connecting into the ExaCS. This DNS name will load balance across all the SCAN IPs and to all the database compute nodes in the Exadata Cloud cluster.

Resources Section

On the lower section of the page we have our Resources area (Figure 3-56). Here we can manage the various components of our service such as the databases, the DB compute nodes, and patching of the Grid Infrastructure.

Port: 1521	**Hostname Prefix:** exacs-node
Host Domain Name: clientsubnet.exacsvcn.oraclevcn.com	**SCAN DNS Name:** exacs-56cmm-scan... Show Copy
SCAN IP Addresses:	**License Type:** License Included
10.0.1.6	
10.0.1.7	
10.0.1.8	

FIGURE 3-55. *Exadata Cloud Service SCAN network details*

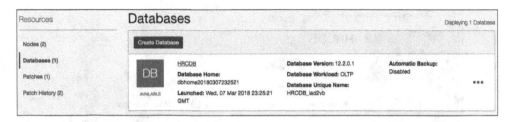

FIGURE 3-56. *The Resources section*

Database Details and Operations   Starting with the Database Resources section, we see details on the individual databases on the service. Using the menu on the right of the database section (Figure 3-57), we can perform actions upon this database right in this area; no need to go to a details page.

Using this menu, we can view the database details, create an on-demand backup, restore from an existing backup, enable Data Guard, apply tags, or terminate the database. We will go into these options on the database details page.

You can click a database service name to view the details. Once on the database details page (Figure 3-58), we can see that it is broken up into two sections: the details of the database on the top and the Resources and Actions on the lower section of the page.

The Details section on the upper part of the page is mainly informational, telling us when the database was created, are backups enabled, and what home it is in, as well as a subpanel with any tags applied to it. Of importance to note is the Restore button. Clicking this button will bring up the Restore Database modal (Figure 3-59). Here we can restore the database to the latest backup, to a point in time, or to a particular system change number (SCN).

The lower Resources section is where we can perform actions upon the database. Backups is the first section (Figure 3-60). The backup section lets us create on-demand backups, enable or disable automatic backups, or delete individual keep-forever backups, not incremental ones.

FIGURE 3-57. *Database Action menu on Service Details page*

Database » DB Systems » DB System Details » Database » Backups
HRCDB
Restore
Apply Tag(s)
Terminate
DB
AVAILABLE
Database Information
Tags
Database Home: dbhome20180307232521
Launched: Wed, 07 Mar 2018 23:25:21 GMT
Database Workload: OLTP
Character Set: AL32UTF8
National Character Set: AL16UTF16
OCID: ...ftzbha Show Copy
Database Version: 12.2.0.1.171017
Database Unique Name: HRCDB_iad2vb
Automatic Backup: Enabled
Resources
Backups (6)
Patches (3)
Patch History (1)
Data Guard Associations (0)
Backups
Displaying 6 Backups
Create Backup
Disable Automatic Backup
Automatic Backup
OCID: ...jl3ivq Show Copy
Type: Incremental
Started: Fri, 09 Mar 2018 04:15:08 GMT
Ended: Fri, 09 Mar 2018 04:18:03 GMT
Delete
ACTIVE

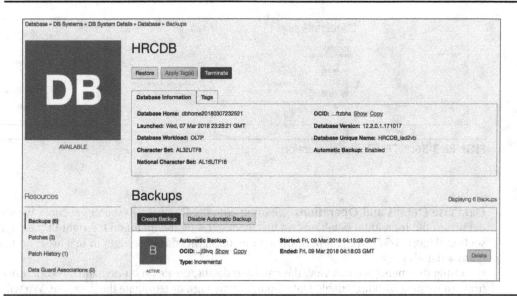

FIGURE 3-58. *The Database Details page*

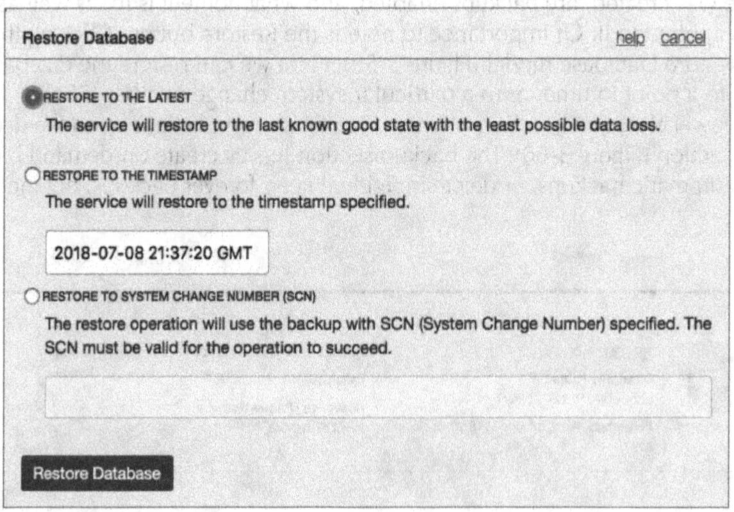

Restore Database
help cancel
RESTORE TO THE LATEST
The service will restore to the last known good state with the least possible data loss.
RESTORE TO THE TIMESTAMP
The service will restore to the timestamp specified.
2018-07-08 21:37:20 GMT
RESTORE TO SYSTEM CHANGE NUMBER (SCN)
The restore operation will use the backup with SCN (System Change Number) specified. The SCN must be valid for the operation to succeed.
Restore Database

FIGURE 3-59. *Restore Database modal*

FIGURE 3-60. *Database Backups*

The next action or resource is Patches. Here we can pre-check or apply a patch to this database. We can choose the patch via the UI and then select Pre-Check or Apply (Figure 3-61).

Once the pre-check is complete with no errors, we can apply the patch to our database here in the UI. You can look in the next Resources section, Patch History (Figure 3-62), to see any patches that have been applied to this service.

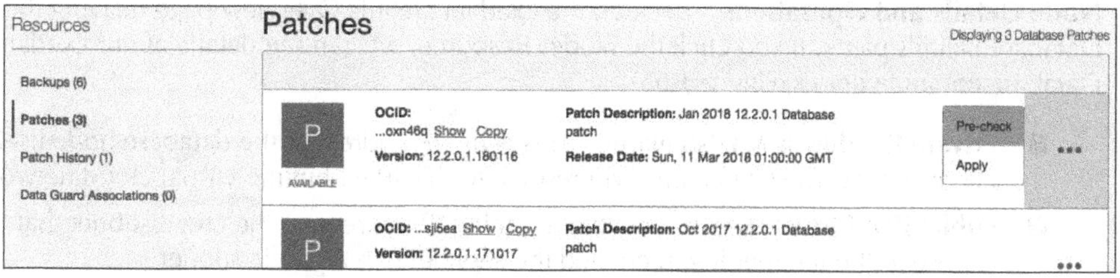

FIGURE 3-61. *Database patching options*

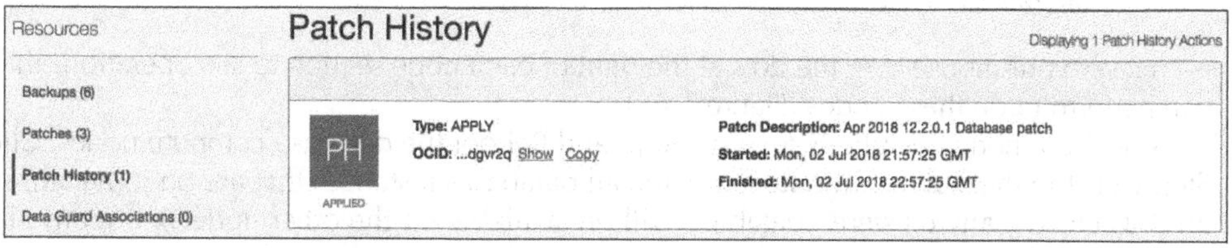

FIGURE 3-62. *History of applied patches to the database*

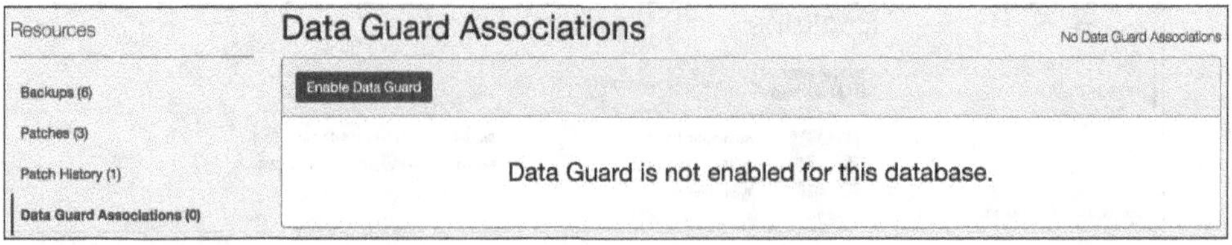

FIGURE 3-63. *Data Guard Associations modal*

The last Resource section is Data Guard Associations (Figure 3-63). Here we can click the Enable Data Guard button to create a Data Guard instance on another Exadata Cloud Service. Upon clicking the Enable Data Guard button, the Enable Data Guard Modal pops up (Figure 3-64). Here we first select the database system we want to use. The only other item we need to fill in is the Database Admin Password for the source database. Once done, click the Enable button and the service will automatically create a Data Guard Instance for you. Before you enable Data Guard between two instances, ensure that you have opened up two-way communications on port 1521 between both Exadata Cloud Services in the security lists for the client subnet.

Node Details and Operations   Back on the Exadata Details Overview page (leaving the Database Details page), if you click the Nodes Resource, we can see details of our Exadata Database compute nodes (Figure 3-65).

- **Private IP Address & DNS Name**   This is the IP address of the database node itself on the client subnet. The DNS name will resolve to this IP within the virtual cloud network.
- **Public IP Address**   This is an external-facing IP address on the client subnet that you may expose to the Internet if you created the service with a public subnet.
- **Backup Private IP Address & DNS Name**   These IPs, especially the private IPs, will be available only in the VCN. The public IP, again if you used a public subnet, will be available in both the VCN and on the public Internet.
- **Floating IP Address**   This is the SCAN VIP that is used by the database listener. The listener will pass connections from the SCAN IPs to the VIPs for connection to the database.

Hover your mouse over the dots at the right of each node section to see operations that you can perform upon these nodes (Figure 3-65).

Use these node operations to Start, Stop, and Reboot the database compute nodes. Clicking Stop will stop the actual compute node and all databases instances that are on it. Because this is an RAC cluster, any clustered database will be available on the other node(s), but any single instance databases will become unreachable.

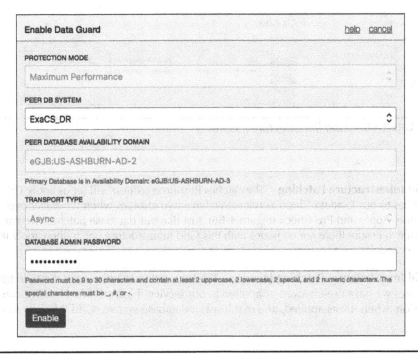

FIGURE 3-64. *Enable Data Guard modal*

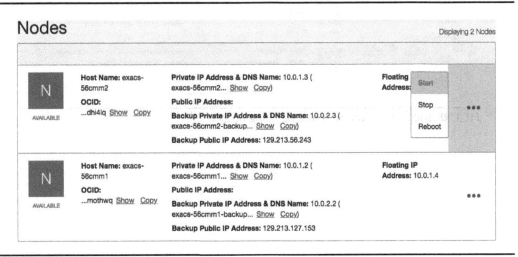

FIGURE 3-65. *Node operations*

Resources
Patches
Displaying 1 Database Patches
Nodes (2)
Databases (1)
Patches (1)
Patch History (2)
P
AVAILABLE
OCID: ...dlfknq Show Copy
Version: 12.2.0.1.180417
Patch Description: Apr 2018 12.2.0.1 Db System patch
Release Date: Wed, 25 Apr 2018 01:00:00 GMT
Pre-check
Apply

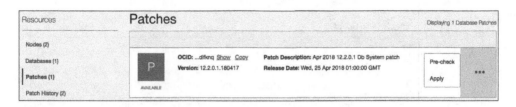

FIGURE 3-66. *Grid Infrastructure patches*

Grid Infrastructure Patching The Patches Resource section will let us apply Grid Infrastructure patches to our Exadata Cloud Service. We have two choices when we hover over the right menu section: Apply and Pre-Check (Figure 3-66). Just like our database patches, we can pre-check the service to ensure there are no issues with this Grid Infrastructure patch, then apply it if the pre-check is successful.

Grid Infrastructure Patching History The last section is a history of the Grid Infrastructure patches we have pre-checked or applied to our service (Figure 3-67). Here we can see what version, when it was applied, and that it was a database system (Grid Infrastructure) patch.

Resources
Patch History
Displaying 2 Patch History Actions
Nodes (2)
Databases (1)
Patches (1)
Patch History (2)
PH
AVAILABLE
Type: PRECHECK
OCID: ...aq2kqa Show Copy
Patch Description: Jan 2018 12.2.0.1 Db System patch
Started: Fri, 23 Mar 2018 15:55:49 GMT
Finished: Fri, 23 Mar 2018 16:01:16 GMT
PH
CHECKING...
Type: PRECHECK
OCID: ...4y4dma Show Copy
Patch Description: Apr 2018 12.2.0.1 Db System patch
Started: Tue, 01 May 2018 22:33:14 GMT
Finished: -

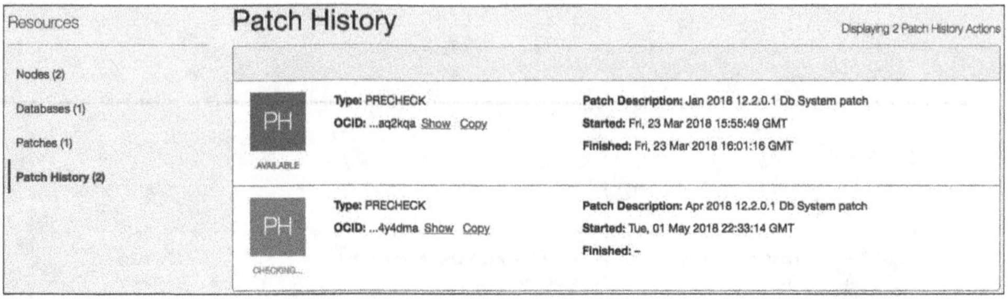

FIGURE 3-67. *Grid Infrastructure patching history*

Summary

With a single button click, you can perform many tasks in the Exadata Cloud Service that once required you to engage multiple teams and resources. Patching can be done on your own time, at your convenience, and creating backups is no longer a job for a DBA when he or she can find the time. The UI allows for scaling of OCPU resources when you need them on demand to handle holiday rush, tax time, or a weekend close of books. The goal of the Exadata Cloud Service is to put many of the tools and tasks into the hands of people who would normally not be able to perform these tasks without the help of others—it makes running an Exadata easy and simple.

CHAPTER 4

Exadata Cloud Services Tooling and CLIs

The Exadata Cloud Service includes Representational State Transfer (REST) APIs and tooling that can be used in many ways. For example, if a current in-house process is used to provision hardware, systems, and databases, you can use these REST services in the existing provisioning flow to provide users with seamless access to databases on the ExaCS. In the current provisioning system, they simply ask for a database and it is provisioned without the need to access additional elements on the UI. REST services also help users access the OS or command line interface (CLI) to create databases, configure backups, or change settings.

Setting Up Your Local Environment

In this book, when we call REST services in either Oracle Cloud Infrastructure (OCI) or Oracle Cloud Infrastructure Classic (OCI-C), we can use the Client for URLs (cURL), an open-source command line tool. The cURL tool enables you to pass over HTTP header information, JavaScript Object Notation (JSON) payloads, and authentication credentials to the REST server in a single line of code. This tool is packaged with most UNIX and Linux operating systems (including macOS). If you're using Windows, you may need to download the open-source libraries or use a browser plug-in.

NOTE
For more information about cURL, go to https://curl.haxx.se/. To download and install cURL, visit http://curl.haxx.se/download.html. You must download and install a version of cURL that supports the Secure Sockets Layer (SSL).

For secure communication between cURL and our REST servers, you'll need to have a local bundle of trusted certificates. This not only ensures that the connection to the REST service is secure and encrypted, but that the certificates match up in your local certificate authority (CA) certificate store.

NOTE
When you run cURL commands to call the REST services in this chapter, be sure to set the environment variable CURL_CA_BUNDLE to the location of your local CA certificate bundle. You can also specify the location of your local CA certificate bundle in the REST call by using the --cacert option. If you need a CA bundle, you can download one from http://curl.haxx.se/docs/caextract.html or work with your local network security organization to get an approved bundle that adheres to the internal policies of your company.

The Exadata Cloud Service REST Services

The Oracle Exadata Cloud Services have tooling and APIs at two levels: REST APIs and CLI APIs. This section covers the REST services for both OCI-C and OCI.

The REST, or RESTful, web service provides a method of talking between two systems on a network. That network may be an intranet, internal to a company or the Internet. A RESTful web service makes a request to a particular URI, with the response being in HTML, XML, or JSON. The requests are made over HTTP (or HTTPS for secure services) and use operations predefined by the HTTP methods—usually GET, POST, PUT, and DELETE. The key to these REST services is that they are extremely fast and efficient. You can look at these HTTP methods as verbs. GET is a read operation, POST is a create operation, PUT can be a create or an update operation, and DELETE is a delete operation.

The ExaCS uses the following group of REST APIs to manage various aspects of the operation. To manage backup and recovery:

- Start a backup operation
- Start a recovery operation
- View all backup operations
- View all recovery operations

To manage SSH access:

- Add an SSH public key
- View details for selected SSH keys
- View summaries for selected SSH keys
- View the details for an SSH key
- View the status of an SSH add key job
- View the summary for an SSH key

To control Exadata I/O Resource Manager (IORM):

- Set IORM shares
- View IORM shares

To manage database deployments:

- Create a database deployment
- Delete a database deployment
- Replace a database using a cloud backup

To manage patching:

- Apply a patch
- Perform a patching pre-check
- Roll back a patch
- View a patch operation
- View all patching pre-check operations
- View applied patches
- View available patches
- View the status of a patching pre-check operation

To manage snapshots:

- Create a snapshot master
- Delete a snapshot master
- View a snapshot master
- View all snapshot masters

To manage compute node operations:

- Stop, start, or restart a compute node
- Scale Oracle Compute Units (OCPUs)

To view service details:

- View a database deployment
- View all database deployments
- View compute nodes
- View the status of an operation

REST Services in OCI-C

The REST services use the format https://*rest-server/endpoint-path*, with the *rest-server* being the regional server name. Two servers are available with IDM-based accounts:

- **https://dbaas.oraclecloud.com** If your ExaCS is deployed in Ashburn, Virginia; or Chicago, Illinois
- **https://dbcs.emea.oraclecloud.com** If your service is in Slough or London, UK; or Amsterdam, the Netherlands

The *endpoint-path* is the service you want to use.
With IDCS-based accounts, we can use the following servers:

- https://psm.us.oraclecloud.com
- https://psm.europe.oraclecloud.com
- https://psm.usgov.oraclecloud.com

Using the REST Services in OCI-C

Let's go over the structure of the REST service call, starting with building the endpoint URI. Following is an example from start to the call itself.

First we indicate our location. As mentioned, we have two choices of REST server names based on our location, and we need to determine which choice is best. For this example, we'll use the ExaCS in the Chicago data center—the https://dbaas.oraclecloud.com REST server URL if we have an IDM-based account and https://psm.us.oraclecloud.com if we have an IDCS-based account.

Next, we choose a REST endpoint or operation to use. For this example, we can start a recovery operation on a database. Here's the endpoint path for that service:

/paas/service/dbcs/api/v1.1/instances/*identityDomainId/serviceId*/backups/recovery

There are two variables in this endpoint: *identityDomainId* and *serviceId*. The *identityDomainId* is the same ID we used to log into the service if using an older IDM-based account. If using a newer IDCS-based account, the *identityDomainId* will be in the format idcs-letters-and-numbers (idcs-e48d50317djdjhd8923d). You can find this ID in the Identity Service Id field on the Exadata Cloud Service Overview page, Additional Information section.

The *serviceId* is the service name we gave to our database deployment. For this example, we can use a fictional identity domain ID, jetdogresearch, and a service ID of HRCDB. We input these values and the correct regional REST server URI for an IDM-based account:

```
https://dbaas.oraclecloud.com/paas/service/dbcs/api/v1.1/instances/
jetdogresearch/HRCDB/backups/recovery
```

For an IDCS-based account, the URL will use the IDCS-based value and the appropriate regional server:

```
https://psm.us.oraclecloud.com/paas/service/dbcs/api/v1.1/instances/
idcs-e48d50317djdjhd8923d/HRCDB/backups/recovery
```

The next part is to create the call itself. This example call we are building will use cURL. Each endpoint has specific requirements, but the following will outline each part of the cURL call:

```
curl -i -X GET --cacert ~/cacert.pem --user username:password
-H "X-ID-TENANT-NAME:identity_domain_id" -d '{ }'
https://dbaas.oraclecloud.com/paas/service/dbcs/api/v1.1/instances/identity_domain_id
```

Let's take a look at the variables used in this example:

- **-i** Fetch only the headers of the response.
- **-X** Used in conjunction with the HTTP request type (GET, POST, DELETE, PUT).
- **--cacert** Indicates the location of our trusted CA bundle.
- **--user or -u** A credential variable, with a username and password of the user able to use the cloud service with the correct roles in Identity Management/Identity Cloud Service (IDM/IDCS).
- **-H** The HTTP header information. In this example, it's X-ID-TENANT-NAME, but we can also indicate the content type of the request document with -H "Content-Type:XXX", with *XXX* being a value such as application/JSON. Again, the value will depend on if this is an IDM- or IDCS-based account.
- **-d** The request document (in JSON format), which can be a location on the local computer or a JSON object, entered between curly brackets ({ }).
- **https://dbaas.oraclecloud.com/paas/service/dbcs/api/v1.1/instances/identity_domain_id** The endpoint URI we want to use. This is also based on region and identity account type (IDM or IDCS).

Now let's put the two parts together: the structure of the cURL call and the endpoint we want to use. Let's use the endpoint we created previously. For IDM-based accounts:

```
https://dbaas.oraclecloud.com/paas/service/dbcs/api/v1.1/instances/
jetdogresearch/HRCDB/backups/recovery
```

And for IDCS-based accounts:

```
https://psm.us.oraclecloud.com/paas/service/dbcs/api/v1.1/instances/
idcs-e48d50317djdjhd8923d/HRCDB/backups/recovery
```

We'll use this to create the cURL call. We start with the following (assuming we are going to use a local CA bundle located at /Users/btspendo):

```
curl -i -X GET --cacert /Users/btspendo/cacert.pem
```

Next, we add the user credentials. For this example, we'll use my username and password (replace these with your username and password):

```
-u brian.spendolini@oracle.com:Awes0mePassw0rd
```

Headers are next. Again, we'll use my identity domain ID, jetdogresearch or idcs-e48d50317djdjhd8923d (you will supply your own ID based on the IDM or IDCS value). IDM based:

```
-H "X-ID-TENANT-NAME:jetdogresearch"
```

IDCS based:

```
-H "X-ID-TENANT-NAME:idcs-e48d50317djdjhd8923d"
```

Seeing all new accounts are IDCS based, we will be using that format going forward.

This particular endpoint requires a JSON document. The document needed is quite simple but has four options we can choose between: `latest`, `scn`, `tag`, and `timestamp`. Each of these options for recovery has a particular value:

- **"latest"** `"yes"`
- **scn** System change number
- **tag** Database backup tag
- **"timestamp"** Must be in the format *dd-MM-yyyy hh:mm:ss*

To restore to a particular timestamp, we would enter the following JSON document:

```
{"timestamp":"31-OCT-2017 13:13:13"}
```

To use the latest backup, we'd enter the following:

```
{"latest":"yes"}
```

Let's use the latest backup—so the next part would be this:

```
-d {"latest":"yes"}
```

Remember that we need to tell the service in the headers that there is a JSON document coming, so add the following before the `-d` section:

```
-H "Content-Type:application/json"
```

Finally, we add the URI for the recovery operation. First, for IDM accounts:

```
https://dbaas.oraclecloud.com/paas/service/dbcs/api/v1.1/instances/
jetdogresearch/HRCDB/backups/recovery
```

And for IDCS accounts:

```
https://psm.us.oraclecloud.com/paas/service/dbcs/api/v1.1/instances/
idcs-e48d50317djdjhd8923d/HRCDB/backups/recovery
```

Putting it all together, we create the following REST call that will recover our database to the latest backup. For IDM:

```
curl -i -X GET --cacert /Users/btspendo/cacert.pem
-u brian.spendolini@oracle.com:Awes0mePassw0rd
-H "X-ID-TENANT-NAME:jetdogresearch" -H "Content-Type:application/json"
-d {"latest":"yes"}
https://dbaas.oraclecloud.com/paas/service/dbcs/api/v1.1/instances/jetdogresearch/
HRCDB/backups/recovery
```

And for IDCS:

```
curl -i -X GET --cacert /Users/btspendo/cacert.pem
-u brian.spendolini@oracle.com:Awes0mePassw0rd
-H "X-ID-TENANT-NAME:idcs-e48d50317djdjhd8923d"
-H "Content-Type:application/json"
-d {"latest":"yes"}
https://psm.us.oraclecloud.com/paas/service/dbcs/api/v1.1/instances/
idcs-e48d50317djdjhd8923d/HRCDB/backups/recovery
```

Once you issue this call, you should see a response similar to the following:

```
HTTP/2.0 202
server: Oracle-Application-Server-11g
strict-transport-security: max-age=31536000;includeSubDomains
location: https://psm.us.oraclecloud.com/paas/service/dbcs/api/v1.1/instances/
idcs-e48d50317djdjhd8923d/status/recovery/job/4182006
content-language: en
access-control-allow-origin: *
access-control-allow-headers: Content-Type, api_key, Authorization, X-ID-TENANT-
NAME, X-USER-IDENTITY-DOMAIN-NAME
retry-after: 60
access-control-allow-methods: GET, POST, DELETE, PUT, OPTIONS, HEAD
x-oracle-dms-ecid: izxsbKR3FYGWWyToFU6nTPcTr6fuCwBxA2
x-oracle-dms-ecid: izxsbKR3FYGWWyToFU6nTPcTr6fuCwBxA2
service-uri: https://psm.us.oraclecloud.com/paas/service/dbcs/api/v1.1/instances/
idcs-e48d50317djdjhd8923d/HRCDB
x-frame-options: DENY
content-type: application/json
vary: user-agent
date: Mon, 29 May 2017 23:31:23 GMT
```

This is the format used for calling REST services in OCI-C. Let's structure some more REST calls for another few endpoints, such as create database, list available patches, and control IORM.

The service for creating a database uses a JSON document for the parameters. The URI is similar to the service we just used:

```
curl -i -X GET --cacert /Users/btspendo/cacert.pem
-u brian.spendolini@oracle.com:Awes0mePassw0rd
-H "X-ID-TENANT-NAME: idcs-e48d50317djdjhd8923d"
-H "Content-Type:application/json" -d @createDatabase.json
https://psm.us.oraclecloud.com/paas/service/dbcs/api/v1.1/instances/
idcs-e48d50317djdjhd8923d
```

One of the differences we see is with the JSON payload. In the previous example, we put the JSON into the request. Here we reference the document, @createDatabase.json. The createDatabase .json document is located on a local desktop in this example.

This following JSON document is created with common create database parameters we can use for the REST call:

```
{
  "serviceName": "DB122",
  "description": "My Exadata Cloud Service 12.2 Database via a REST Service",
  "edition": "EE_EP",
  "exadataSystemName": "myexadatasys",
  "level": "PAAS_EXADATA",
  "subscriptionType": "MONTHLY",
  "version": "12.2.0.1",
  "vmPublicKeyText": " ssh-rsa AAAAB3NzaC1yc2EAAAADAQABAAABA... ",
  "parameters": [
    {
      "adminPassword": "AwesomePassword123",
      "oracleHomeName":"DatabaseHome12",
      "backupDestination": "OSS",
      "cloudStorageContainer": "Storage-myIdentityDomain/backupContainer",
      "cloudStorageUser": "myUserName",
      "cloudStoragePwd": "AwesomePassword",
      "isRac": "yes",
      "pdbName": "PDB122",
      "sid": "CDB122",
      "type": "db"
    }
  ]
}
```

Let's look at a few important parameters: The `oracleHomeName` parameter will indicate the Oracle home where this database will be placed. You can use a new name to create a new Oracle home or use an existing Oracle home location to share homes with other database instances.

The `backupDestination` parameter indicates how you want to back up the database. Just as we saw in the UI, you have three options: NONE, OSS, and BOTH. If you specify OSS or BOTH, you will need to include the `cloudStorageContainer`, `cloudStorageUser`, and `cloudStoragePwd` to indicate where the object storage backups are going and the user/password needed.

A parameter not used in the earlier sample but that is available in the UI and via the REST service is `ibkup`. Using the `ibkup` parameter, you can indicate whether you want to create this database using a backup that exists in the object store. If using the `ibkup` parameter, you will also need to specify the values for the following parameters:

- `ibkupCloudStorageContainer`
- `ibkupCloudStoragePassword`
- `ibkupCloudStorageUser`
- `ibkupDatabaseID`
- `ibkupDecryptionKey`
- `ibkupOnPremise`
- `ibkupServiceID`
- `ibkupWalletFileContent`

Next up is the List Patches REST API, which will return all the patches you can apply to a particular database deployment on your ExaCS. This service is run against each individual home or database deployment. Here is the URL for mine:

```
curl -i -X GET --cacert ~/cacert.pem
-u brian.spendolini@oracle.com:Awes0mePassw0rd
-H "X-ID-TENANT-NAME:idcs-e48d50317djdjhd8923d"
https://psm.us.oraclecloud.com/paas/api/v1.1/instancemgmt/idcs-e48d50317djdjhd8923d/
services/dbaas/instances/HRCDB/patches/available
```

Once you issue this request, the response will look similar to the following if a patch is available:

```
[{
        "availablePatchGuiMetadata": {
            "supportsPreCheck": false
        },
        "patchId": "24968615",
        "patchNumber": "Patch_12.1.0.2.170117",
        "patchCategory": "DB",
        "patchSeverity": "Normal",
        "includesConfigUpgrade": false,
        "patchDescription": "DB 12.1.0.2.170117 QUARTERLY DATABASE PATCH FOR
EXADATA - JAN2017",
        "patchReleaseUrl":
"https://support.oracle.com/epmos/faces/PatchDetail?patchId\u003d24968615",
        "serviceType": "DBaaS",
        "serviceVersion": "12.1.0.2",
        "releaseDate": "2017-01-17T01:40:00.000+0000",
        "entryDate": "2017-05-13T06:07:22.073+0000",
        "entryUserId": "smctl",
        "componentPatches": {
            "EXADATA": {
                "id": 2651,
                "version": "12.1.0.2.170117",
                "releaseVersion": "12.1.0.2.170117",
                "zipBundles": {
                    "EXADATA": {
                        "id": 4721,
```

```
                                    "md5sum": "48a500c7f4b50e703011",
                                    "storageKey": "PATCH/DB/12c/database.zip",
                                    "zipVersion": "12.1.0.2.170117"
                        }
                },
                    "preserveFiles": []
            }
        },
        "patchType": "PSU",
        "requiresRestart": true,
        "serviceTypeVersions": "ANY",
        "isDeleted": false,
        "isCustomerVisible": false,
        "isAutoApply": false,
        "induceDownTime": false,
        "displayName": "12.1.0.2.170117",
        "supportedStrategy": "Rolling",
        "releaseVersion": "12.1.0.2.170117",
        "serviceEditions": "EE_EP",
        "patchCustomActions": []
    }
]
```

The last service we will take a look at is setting IORM. The REST URI is as follows:

```
curl -i -X GET --cacert /Users/btspendo/cacert.pem
-u brian.spendolini@oracle.com:Awes0mePassw0rd
-H "X-ID-TENANT-NAME:idcs-e48d50317djdjhd8923d"
-H "Content-Type:application/json"
-d '{"DBPlan":[{"dbname":"DB122","share":"12"},
{"dbname":"HRCDB","share":"7"},
{"dbname":"default","share":"1"}]}'
https://dbaas.oraclecloud.com/paas/service/dbcs/api/v1.1/instances/
idcs-e48d50317djdjhd8923d/DB122/iorm
```

In this call, we have included the JSON in the request. Look closely to see the string.

```
{"DBPlan":[{"dbname":"DB122","share":"12"},
{"dbname":"HRCDB","share":"7"},
{"dbname":"default","share":"1"}]}
```

Here we are setting the shares for the DB122 database to 12, the shares for our HRCDB database to 7, and the default shares to 1. This plan would give priority to the DB122 database, with secondary priority to the HRCDB database, and all other databases getting a default priority of 1.

REST Services in OCI

OCI includes a CLI we can download and use for all REST service calls. After being configured, this CLI will pass over all the authentication you need to use the features of the OCI console but at a CLI level.

To start, we need to install the CLI. In this example, we'll be using an Oracle Linux VM for the install. (You can also use PowerShell in Windows if you are more comfortable with that environment.) The install on Linux starts with getting and installing the packages. We can do this with one simple command:

```
[opc@Linux ~]$ bash -c "$(curl -L https://raw.githubusercontent.com/oracle/
oci-cli/master/scripts/install/install.sh)"
```

After issuing this command, we need to answer a couple of questions on where the executable will go:

```
===> In what directory would you like to place the install? (leave blank to use
'/home/opc/lib/oracle-cli'):
-- Creating directory '/home/opc/lib/oracle-cli'.
-- We will install at '/home/opc/lib/oracle-cli'.
===> In what directory would you like to place the 'oci' executable? (leave blank
 to use '/home/opc/bin'):
-- Creating directory '/home/opc/bin'.
-- The executable will be in '/home/opc/bin'.
===> Modify profile to update your $PATH and enable shell/tab completion now? (Y/n):
```

The CLI is downloaded and installed. Next, we'll configure it for our environment.

Configure the OCI CLI

Configuring the OCI CLI is easy. You can do this in two ways: you can manually create the config file, or you can let the CLI walk you through it. Let's have the CLI do the work. Start by issuing the following command from the Linux prompt:

```
[opc@Linux ~]$ oci setup config
```

Next set a location for the config file. I'll use the default by not entering a value and just pressing ENTER:

```
Enter a location for your config [/home/opc/.oci/config]:
```

User OCID is the next parameter needed:

```
Enter a user OCID:
```

You can find this in the web console if you look at the details of a user. In the outlined box shown in Figure 4-1, you can see the User OCID in the User Information section of the User Details page. Click the Copy link to copy the OCID into your clipboard, or click Show to see it and copy and paste it yourself.

Next, enter the Tenancy OCID of our account.

```
Enter a tenancy OCID:
```

This OCID is located at the bottom of the OCI web console, as shown in Figure 4-2.

The following question asks us to choose a region:

```
Enter a region
```

Enter the region where the service you wish to use is located in. My Exadata Cloud Service is in Ashburn, so I'll choose us-ashburn-1.

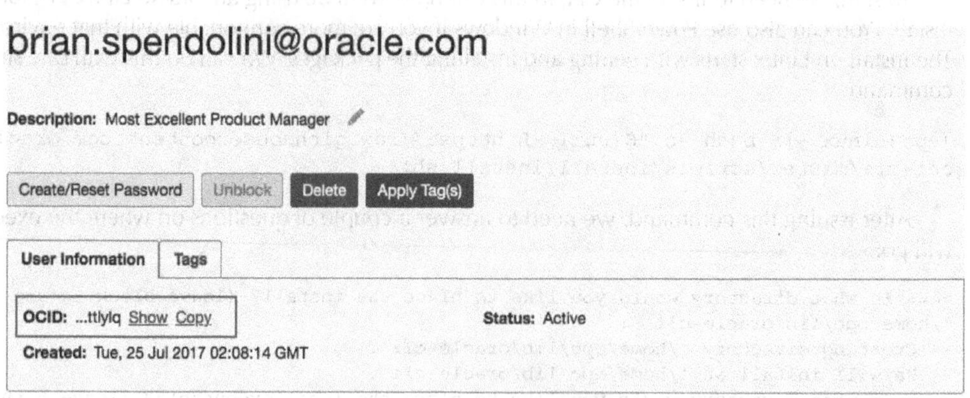
brian.spendolini@oracle.com
Description: Most Excellent Product Manager
Create/Reset Password
Unblock
Delete
Apply Tag(s)
User Information
Tags
OCID: ...ttlylq Show Copy
Status: Active
Created: Tue, 25 Jul 2017 02:08:14 GMT

FIGURE 4-1. *The User OCID in the OCI web console, User Details page*

The next question requires some thought. The CLI can generate a public/private key pair for you or you can use an existing one. For this example, I'll go through the CLI to create one and the steps required to add the keys to a user. So, for the question,

```
Do you want to generate a new RSA key pair? (If you decline you will be asked
to supply the path to an existing key.) [Y/n]:
```

choose Y.

Next, choose a directory where we want to store this key. I'll keep the default by again leaving the prompt blank and pressing ENTER:

```
Enter a directory for your keys to be created [/home/opc/.oci]:
```

Now choose a name for the key or use the default—I'll use the default by pressing ENTER with a blank prompt:

```
Enter a name for your key [oci_api_key]:
```

Do you want a passphrase for this key? If you do, now is the time to enter it; otherwise, just press ENTER and continue with no passphrase:

```
Enter a passphrase for your private key (empty for no passphrase):
```

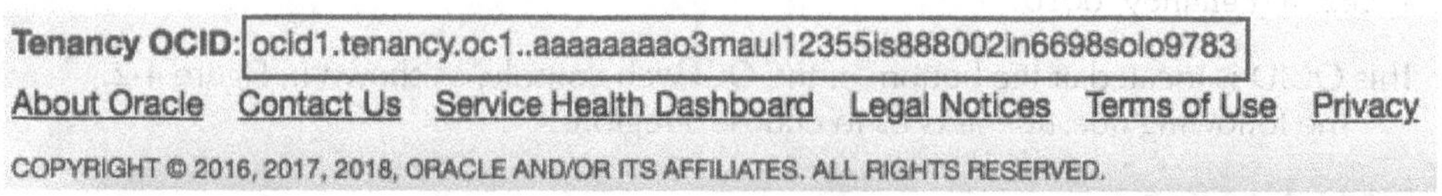
Tenancy OCID: ocid1.tenancy.oc1..aaaaaaaao3maul12355ls888002ln6698solo9783
About Oracle
Contact Us
Service Health Dashboard
Legal Notices
Terms of Use
Privacy
COPYRIGHT © 2016, 2017, 2018, ORACLE AND/OR ITS AFFILIATES. ALL RIGHTS RESERVED.

FIGURE 4-2. *The Tenancy OCID in the OCI web console*

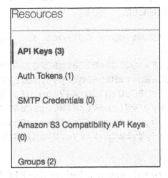

FIGURE 4-3. *Choosing API Keys in the User Details page*

That's it! We've configured the CLI, but before we can use it, we must add the key to our user in the OCI web console.

Go back to the User Details page (Figure 4-1). Under Resources on the left side of the page, click API Keys (Figure 4-3).

Click the Add Public Key button. In the Add Public Key modal (Figure 4-4), paste the key.

Where do you get this key? You actually created it when we configured the CLI. Back at the Linux prompt where you configured the CLI, you need to get the contents of the public key. You

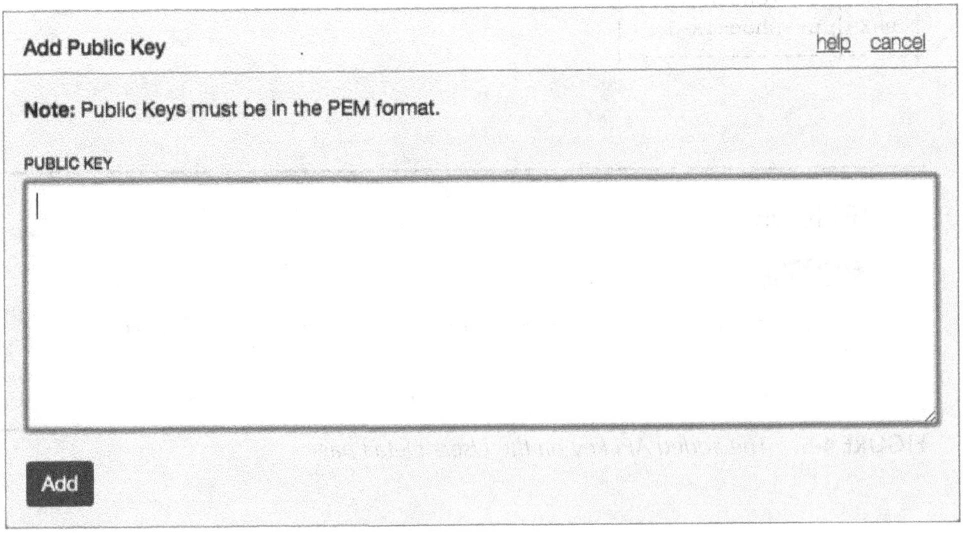

Add Public Key   help   cancel

Note: Public Keys must be in the PEM format.

PUBLIC KEY

Add

FIGURE 4-4. *The Add Public Key modal*

can do that with the following command (this assumed that you took the default values for key location when configuring the CLI):

```
[opc@Linux .oci]$ cat /home/opc/.oci/oci_api_key_public.pem
-----BEGIN PUBLIC KEY-----
MIIBIjANBgkqhkiG9w0BAQEFAAOCAQ8AMIIBCgKCAQEA6b8CdlRed6iKtFbbL3AC
olboMcBMYyKnXgKaMIDxK3k+Eq+ywMk96PqhPpvl/iu2NRHNxwioc0iY9+El3Ncz
o5GkPYISPTMWv6TRRbWF421pUPGuU4q78QjXSV4gn1gf9/DiJD7TDi9xid/1j/0O
7PORvGfMcvYPD6HxH/sQMnWyD/wNtcLevttXTWCwg9Ca63Tg0z6j+9MFE6z1Q4pi
HGdDPE8AzOTcX/XSSAvc7ZB0jdYt41bXPRQsxIGIeaoQ5THRQDEsvZ1HGCt3O9LD
f4CZiYMsraGwl+qUAYisbL/9yYvEzCz+f/ryerBVDKllNchxphtL9o6sCqt7Dtlo
-----END PUBLIC KEY-----
```

Now copy the contents of this key (including the BEGIN and END text) and paste it into the Add Public Key modal window from Figure 4-4 then click the blue Add button. The result, seen in Figure 4-5, will be an added key and a resulting fingerprint.

This fingerprint should also match the fingerprint the CLI setup had displayed in the final section:

```
Private key written to: /home/opc/.oci/oci_api_key.pem
Fingerprint: 4f:35:f4:26:1b:22:fb:0c:b7:22:55:11:tt:bb:b8:c6
Config written to /home/opc/.oci/config
```

Now try the CLI:

```
[opc@Linux ~]$ oci iam region list --output table
+-----+----------------+
| key | name           |
+-----+----------------+
| FRA | eu-frankfurt-1 |
| IAD | us-ashburn-1   |
| LHR | uk-london-1    |
| PHX | us-phoenix-1   |
+-----+----------------+
```

FIGURE 4-5. *The added API key on the Users Detail page*

The `--output table` Parameter

Notice that in this call we added the `--output table` parameter at the end. This formats the results into a table, as you can see in the preceding output. If we did not specify this, the results would have been returned in a JSON format:

```
[opc@Linux ~]$ oci iam region list
{
  "data": [
    {
      "key": "FRA",
      "name": "eu-frankfurt-1"
    },
    {
      "key": "IAD",
      "name": "us-ashburn-1"
    },
    {
      "key": "LHR",
      "name": "uk-london-1"
    },
    {
      "key": "PHX",
      "name": "us-phoenix-1"
    }
  ]
}
```

By default, all output is JSON, but it can be put into a table format for readability using the `--output table` parameter in the CLI calls.

Using the OCI CLI

Using the CLI, you can perform any of the OCI web console operations that you have privileges to access, modify, delete, and create. For example, you can list all the virtual cloud networks (VCNs) in a particular compartment. Here's the syntax:

```
oci network vcn list --compartment-id
```

You can also use `-c` for `--compartment-id` if you so choose. You can get the compartment IDs or OCIDs from the OCI web console or with another CLI command:

```
oci iam compartment list
```

Using either method, you can create a compartment OCID you can use to run the command that lists all the VCNs in that compartment:

```
[opc@Linux ~]$ oci network vcn list -c ocid1.compartment.oc1..
aaaaaaaa2pwvgqxnqqmd2olkt5jivtyt4ffiyga7wfsdfsdfsdf
{
  "data": [
    {
      "cidr-block": "10.0.0.0/16",
      "compartment-id":
"ocid1.compartment.oc1..aaaaaaaa2pwvgqxnqqmd2olkt5jivtyt4ffiyga",
      "default-dhcp-options-id":
"ocid1.dhcpoptions.oc1.iad.aaaaaaaaim3zoez6ae4kopjnzugqvft7zxoz",
      "default-route-table-id":
"ocid1.routetable.oc1.iad.aaaaaaaaztxlp2zexhkwrhmhqqupoxqekfcpp",
      "default-security-list-id":
"ocid1.securitylist.oc1.iad.aaaaaaaa6fgomp4aiyr5cfec3irs72pysej",
      "defined-tags": {},
      "display-name": "ExaCS_VCN",
      "dns-label": "exacsvcn",
      "freeform-tags": {},
      "id":
"ocid1.vcn.oc1.iad.
aaaaaaaaaooh2iqkebzvz7raceje26evlggv3sdfsdfsdfsdfsdfsdfsdfsdfsdf",
      "lifecycle-state": "AVAILABLE",
      "time-created": "2018-03-07T16:05:04.183000+00:00",
      "vcn-domain-name": "exacsvcn.oraclevcn.com"
    }
  ]
}
```

This CLI command lists all the VCNs in that compartment, but it also returns the OCID of the VCN. You can use that to list all the subnets in the VCN:

```
[opc@Linux ~]$ oci network subnet list -c
  ocid1.compartment.oc1..aaaaaaaa2pwvgqxnqqmd2olkt5jivtyt4ffi
--vcn-id ocid1.vcn.oc1.iad.aaaaaaaaaooh2iqkebzvz7raceje26evlggv3
```

The CLI offers much more than listings. Again, you can use the CLI to create, delete, modify, and list.

Moving on from here, let's work with our databases via the OCI CLI. Starting simple, you can list all the databases on your ExaCS. You need the compartment OCID the Exadata Cloud Service is in, as well as the ExaCS OCID. The ExaCS OCID can be found via the CLI or on the OCI web console:

```
[opc@Linux ~]$ oci db database list
--compartment-id ocid1.compartment.oc1..aaaaaaaa2pwvgqxnqqmd2olkt5jivtyt4ffi
--db-system-id ocid1.dbsystem.oc1.iad.abuwcljtzkm7zagahrapsptz7sgbs2cowh7
{
  "data": [
    {
```

```
      "character-set": "AL32UTF8",
      "compartment-id":
"ocid1.compartment.oc1..aaaaaaaa2pwvgqxnqqmd2olkt5jivtyt4ffiyga7wvkzaitn7z2ovcdbn2
6q",
      "db-backup-config": {
        "auto-backup-enabled": false
      },
      "db-home-id":
"ocid1.dbhome.oc1.iad.abuwcljtvu2y72jvd5nr6iwedswtfawerz3mmc5smq73gphrfdhlnityqcfq
",
      "db-name": "HRCDB",
      "db-unique-name": "HRCDB_iad2mn",
      "db-workload": "OLTP",
      "defined-tags": {},
      "freeform-tags": {},
      "id": "ocid1.database.oc1.iad.
abuwcljtlzv6w5vrjq5kmaxurouckw2zon4pvjqyj3eipjexlasrmn2rek
ia",
      "lifecycle-details": null,
      "lifecycle-state": "AVAILABLE",
      "ncharacter-set": "AL16UTF16",
      "pdb-name": "HRPDB",
      "time-created": "2018-03-07T17:17:11.086000+00:00"
    }
  ]
}
```

Next, let's create a database with the CLI. We use the `oci db database create` command, along with a few mandatory options:

- `--db-system-id`
- `--admin-password`
- `--db-name`
- `--db-version`

We have the DB system ID or OCID from the previous command. Combine that with the `create` command (and adding `pdb-name`):

```
[opc@Linux ~]$ oci db database create
--db-system-id ocid1.dbsystem.oc1.iad.abuwcljtzkm7zagahrapsptz7sgbs2cowh7
--admin-password PASSWORD --db-name CLIDB --pdb-name CLIPDB --db-version 18.0.0.0
{
  "data": {
    "character-set": "AL32UTF8",
    "compartment-id":
"ocid1.compartment.oc1..aaaaaaaa2pwvgqxnqqmd2olkt5jivtyt4ffi",
    "db-backup-config": null,
    "db-home-id": "ocid1.dbhome.oc1.iad.
abuwcljsqlbayl6qrpw2u2ljle7niyd5kydohan5rwtgqzvqiwqflzyikgjq",
    "db-name": "CLIDB",
    "db-unique-name": "CLIDB_iad26m",
    "db-workload": "OLTP",
```

```
    "defined-tags": {},
    "freeform-tags": {},
    "id": "ocid1.database.ocl.iad.
abuwcljszmtq2bbkqngpoon3rpea3sz32ht56z2p37fuqsjpxzyl6g4iie
ea",
    "lifecycle-details": null,
    "lifecycle-state": "PROVISIONING",
    "ncharacter-set": "AL16UTF16",
    "pdb-name": "CLIPDB",
    "time-created": "2018-07-01T18:06:06.602000+00:00"
    }
}
```

In the OCI web console, you can see this newly created database (Figure 4-6).

NOTE
We provided only the bare minimums in the CLI call to create the databases, but we could have added other parameters as well, such as character set.

And just as you can create a database, you can also delete it:

```
[opc@Linux ~]$ oci db database delete --database-id
ocid1.database.ocl.iad.
abuwcljszmtq2bbkqngpoon3rpea3sz32ht56z2p37fuqsjpxzyl6g4iie
```

A database's lifecycle can be completely controlled by the OCI CLI. You can patch, back up, create Data Guard instances, and control IORM. Any feature you can do on the OCI web console can be performed by the OCI CLI.

Databases

Displaying 2 Databases

Create Database

DB PROVISIONING...	CLIDB Database Home: dbhome20180701180606 Launched: Sun, 01 Jul 2018 18:06:06 GMT	Database Version: 12.2.0.1 Database Workload: OLTP Database Unique Name: CLIDB_iad26m	Automatic Backup: Disabled •••
DB AVAILABLE	HRCDB Database Home: dbhome20180307232521 Launched: Wed, 07 Mar 2018 23:25:21 GMT	Database Version: 12.2.0.1.171017 Database Workload: OLTP Database Unique Name: HRCDB_iad2vb	Automatic Backup: Disabled •••

FIGURE 4-6. *New database from the CLI created in the UI*

For a final OCI CLI example, let's look at patching. First we need to see the available patches for a particular database. We have a choice here as well: we can see the patches for an individual database or patches for the Exadata Cloud Service System (Grid Infrastructure patches). We can control this by either passing in a database system ID:

```
[opc@Linux ~]$ oci db patch list by-db-system --db-system-id
ocid1.dbsystem.oc1.iad.abuwcljsa3hvv3sfaw33abzeocfd7fplueupoes5rsdfrexdfertdfer
{
  "data": [
    {
      "available-actions": [],
      "description": "Apr 2018 12.2.0.1 Db System patch",
......
```

or a database ID:

```
[opc@Linux ~]$ oci db patch list by-database --database-id
ocid1.database.oc1.iad.abuwcljszmtq2bbkqngpoon3rpea3sz32ht56z2p3sadferfzsdfvfa
{
  "data": [
    {
      "available-actions": [
        "APPLY",
        "PRECHECK"
      ],
      "description": "Apr 2018 12.2.0.1 Database patch",
      "id": "ocid1.dbpatch.oc1.iad.
abuwcljs5r4stsxkroismxjkiuoux33u24uldeewiy3qmrdg3qkrd47usg3
a",
...
```

Let's apply a database patch. To apply the patch, use this format:

```
oci db database patch --database-id database_id --patch-action APPLY or PRECHECK
--patch-id patch_id
```

Here it is in practice:

```
[opc@Linux ~]$ oci db database patch --database-id
ocid1.database.oc1.iad.abuwcljsorq6gxdgnnjcxax6rv5qzvpw35ewng6hdbpvvamh2mk7rmftzbh
 -patch-action APPLY -patch-id
ocid1.dbpatch.oc1.iad.abuwcljs5r4stsxkroismxjkiuoux33u24uldeewiy3qmrdg3qkrd47usg3a
{
  "data": {
    "character-set": "AL32UTF8",
    "compartment-id": "ocid1.compartment.oc1..
aaaaaaaa2pwvgqxnqqmd2olkt5jivtyt4ffiyga7wvkzaitn7z2ovcdbn2
6q",
    "db-backup-config": {
      "auto-backup-enabled": false
    },
    "db-home-id": "ocid1.dbhome.oc1.iad.
abuwcljsk3win44geeewbww37opkkxewz5is3ndqgqqblmfvyn2zqwld2g2a",
    "db-name": "HRCDB",
    "db-unique-name": "HRCDB_iad2vb",
    "db-workload": "OLTP",
```

```
    "defined-tags": {},
    "freeform-tags": {},
    "id": "ocid1.database.ocl.iad.
abuwcljsorq6gxdgnnjcxax6rv5qzvpw35ewng6hdbpvvamh2mk7rmftzb
ha",
    "lifecycle-details": null,
    "lifecycle-state": "UPDATING",
    "ncharacter-set": "AL16UTF16",
    "pdb-name": "HRPDB",
    "time-created": "2018-03-07T23:25:21.757000+00:00"
  }
}
```

But wait! There is one more important command for scaling OCPUs. We can scale a service to the OCPU count we want to use. The command is in the following format:

```
[opc@Linux ~]$ oci db system update --cpu-core-count core_count
--db-system-id dbsystemOCID
```

Here's an example of setting the core count of a quarter rack to 44 OCPUs:

```
[opc@Linux ~]$ oci db system update --cpu-core-count 44 --db-system-id
ocid1.dbsystem.ocl.iad.abuwcljtzkm7zagahrapsptz7sgbs2cowh7shfeida32sdfsdfefsdczhee
wrss
```

You can view the service information to see the change as well:

```
[opc@Linux ~]$ oci db system get --db-system-id
ocid1.dbsystem.ocl.iad.abuwcljtzkm7zagahrapsptz7sgbs2cowh7shfeida32sdfsdfefsdczhee
wrss
{
  "data": {
    "availability-domain": "eGJB:US-ASHBURN-AD-2",
    "backup-subnet-id": "ocid1.dbsystem.ocl.iad.
abuwcljtzkm7zagahrapsptz7sgbs2cowh7shfeida32sdfsdfefsdczhe
ewrss",
    "cluster-name": "exaclst",
    "compartment-id": "ocid1.compartment.ocl..
aaaaaaaa2pwvgqxnqqmd2olkt5jivtyt4ffiyga7wvkzaitn7z2ovcdbn2
6q",
    "cpu-core-count": 44,
    "data-storage-percentage": 40,
    "data-storage-size-in-gbs": null,
    "database-edition":"ENTERPRISE_EDITION_EXTREME_PERFORMANCE",
    "defined-tags": {},
    "disk-redundancy": "HIGH",
    "display-name": "ExaCS",
...
```

Oracle Cloud Infrastructure SDKs

Using the OCI CLI to work with OCI components is not the only method available. You can use multiple programing languages to access these APIs via different methods. The OCI CLI is a Python-based CLI, and, depending on the config file you created, you call the REST APIs with the proper authentication. OCI also provides methods for Java, Ruby, and Go.

The Exadata Cloud Service CLIs

The ExaCS also has many tools in the CLIs that you can use to perform many of the functions of the REST services. The biggest difference is that you need to be on the actual service to use these command line tools. The following CLIs work on both OCI and OCI-C.

Connecting to Your Exadata Cloud Service

Let's start by logging into the service from the OS level. To do this, we must have port 22 open. Previous chapters showed you how you can alter the firewall rules in OCI and OCI-C to enable this access at the OS level. To connect into this service, we need to know the IP address of the first database compute node, which can be found on the details page of a database in OCI-C (Figure 4-7) or on the Exadata Cloud Service details page in OCI (Figure 4-8).

NOTE
The samples we'll use are from a UNIX, Linux, macOS-based system. If you're using Windows, the open-source program PuTTY will work as well.

Once we have this address, we can SSH into this database compute node.

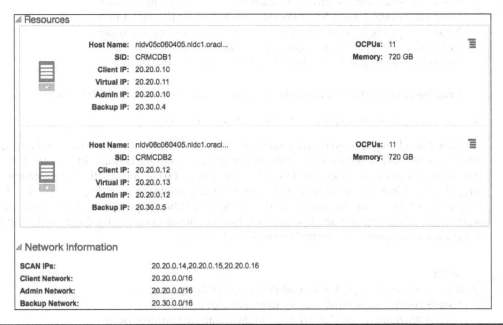

FIGURE 4-7. *The database compute node IP addresses in OCI-C*

Nodes

Displaying 2 Nodes

N AVAILABLE	**Host Name:** exacs-56cmm2 **OCID:** ...dhi4lq <u>Show</u> <u>Copy</u>	**Private IP Address & DNS Name:** 10.0.1.3 (exacs-56cmm2... <u>Show</u> <u>Copy</u>) **Public IP Address:** **Backup Private IP Address & DNS Name:** 10.0.2.3 (exacs-56cmm2-backup... <u>Show</u> <u>Copy</u>) **Backup Public IP Address:** 129.213.56.243	**Floating IP Address:** 10.0.1.5 •••
N AVAILABLE	**Host Name:** exacs-56cmm1 **OCID:** ...mothwq <u>Show</u> <u>Copy</u>	**Private IP Address & DNS Name:** 10.0.1.2 (exacs-56cmm1... <u>Show</u> <u>Copy</u>) **Public IP Address:** **Backup Private IP Address & DNS Name:** 10.0.2.2 (exacs-56cmm1-backup... <u>Show</u> <u>Copy</u>) **Backup Public IP Address:** 129.213.127.153	**Floating IP Address:** 10.0.1.4 •••

FIGURE 4-8. *The database compute node IP addresses in OCI*

NOTE
The IP addresses may be private IP addresses, so we need to connect either via a bastion/jump box, through FastConnect, or through a VPN. If you have public IPs on your compute nodes, this would just require a change in the firewall rules. You can also connect over the backup network if it has a public IP where the client network is private.

From the command line on a UNIX- or Linux-based machine, run the following:

```
ssh -i your_private_key.ppk -l opc 111.111.111.111
```

Now a quick explanation of this command. Starting with the –i, we need to use the matching private key we have when we created the public key upon service creation in Chapter 2. If using Windows, you will need to load and export this key using PuTTYgen, another open-source program. The -l indicates what user to use when logging into the system (login, -l, get it?). When logging in to manage the databases, use the oracle user. When logging in to do administration and using the APIs, log in as the opc user. The last part of our command is the IP address of the first database compute node in the Exadata Cloud Service.

NOTE
If this command hangs, the firewall port may not be open. If so, double-check your firewall settings to ensure that a path is open from your local computer (and IP address) to the database compute node.

Once on the system, you can use the CLIs. Once you're in, as the opc user, issue the following command:

```
[root@exacs-node1 opc]# sudo -s
```

You will now be the root user on the system.

 CAUTION
As root, you can do anything. And when I say anything, I mean anything. You can delete everything on this service with a single command, so tread lightly and double-check all commands you issue.

Updating the Exadata dbaasapi Tooling in OCI and OCI-C

Before using dbaasapi tooling, we first should check for updates. This is a simple procedure that needs to be run on every node of your service. Start by issuing the following command as the root user:

```
[root@exacs-node1 ~]# rpm -qa|grep -i dbaastools_exa
```

The output of this will give you a version. Here's an example:

```
[root@exacs-node1 ~]# rpm -qa|grep -i dbaastools_exa
dbaastools_exa-1.0-1+18.1.2.1.180423.x86_64
```

This shows that my tooling version is 18.1.2.1.180423. You can then issue a command to determine whether there are any newer available versions out there—aka upgrades. Run the following command:

```
[root@exacs-node1 ~]# /var/opt/oracle/exapatch/exadbcpatch -list_tools
```

The output of this command will be similar to the following:

```
[root@exacs-node1 ~]# /var/opt/oracle/exapatch/exadbcpatch -list_tools
INFO: Starting init module
Starting EXADBCPATCH
Logfile is /var/opt/oracle/log/exadbcpatch/exadbcpatch_2018-07-01_23:59:36.log
Config file is /var/opt/oracle/exapatch/exadbcpatch.cfg
INFO: Completed init module
Location of inventory.xml is set to /u01/app/oraInventory/ContentsXML/inventory.xml
INFO: getting rdbname from creg
INFO: oss_container_url is not given, using the default
INFO: Completed validate_params
INFO: tools images available for patching
$VAR1 = {
          'last_async_precheck_txn_id' => ' ',
          'last_async_apply_txn_id' => ' ',
          'errmsg' => '',
          'err' => '',
          'current_version' => '18.1.2.1.180423',
          'last_async_precheck_patch_id' => ' ',
          'current_patch' => '180423',
          'last_async_apply_patch_id' => ' ',
          'patches' => [
```

```
                                         {
                                           'patchid' => '18.1.4.1.0_180620.0000',
                                           'last_precheck_txnid' => '',
                                           'description' => 'DBAAS Tools for Oracle Public Cloud'
                                         },
                                         {
                                           'patchid' => '18.1.4.1.0_180627.0000',
                                           'last_precheck_txnid' => '',
                                           'description' => 'DBAAS Tools for Oracle Public Cloud'
                                         }
                };
...
```

This shows that there is a tooling update. Upgrading my ExaCS tooling from 18.1.2.1.180423 to 18.1.4.1.0_180627.0000 is very simple, by issuing the following command:

```
[root@exacs-node1 ~]# /var/opt/oracle/exapatch/exadbcpatch -toolsinst
-rpmversion=patchid
```

with the new tooling version indicated where `patchid` is

```
[root@exacs-node1 ~]# /var/opt/oracle/exapatch/exadbcpatch -toolsinst
-rpmversion=18.1.4.1.0_180627.0000
```

If you're using OCI, you can update in async mode by removing the old tooling and installing the new version in the background:

```
[root@exacs-node1 ~]# /var/opt/oracle/exapatch/exadbcpatchsm
-toolsinst_async pachid
```

Here's the example using our 18.1.4.1.0_180627.0000 tooling:

```
[root@exacs-node1 ~]# /var/opt/oracle/exapatch/exadbcpatchsm
-toolsinst_async 18.1.4.1.0_180627.0000
INFO: async case
INFO: patch number given is : 18.1.4.1.0_180627.0000
INFO: check for this action toolsinst_async
<start txn>292<end txn>
INFO: command to be run is: /var/opt/oracle/exapatch/exadbcpatch -toolsinst_async
-rpmversion=18.1.4.1.0_180627.0000
INFO: system cmd is: "nohup /var/opt/oracle/exapatch/exadbcpatch -toolsinst_async
-rpmversion=18.1.4.1.0_180627.0000 "
```

You can also manually download the tooling.

Manually Updating the Tooling   Issue the following command if you're in the United States and in an OCI-C data center:

```
wget https://storage.us2.oraclecloud.com/v1/
dbcsswlibp-usoracle29538/dbaas_patch/shome/dbaastools_exa.rpm
```

Use the following if you're in Europe, the Middle East, or Africa:

```
wget https://a88717.storage.oraclecloud.com/v1/
Storage-a88717/dbaas_patch/shome/dbaastools_exa.rpm
```

Issue the following commands if you're in the United States or Europe and in an OCI data center.

For Phoenix (PHX) region:

```
wget https://swiftobjectstorage.us-phoenix-1.oraclecloud.com/
v1/exadata/patches/dbaas_patch/shome/dbaastools_exa.rpm
```

For Ashburn (IAD) region:

```
wget https://swiftobjectstorage.us-ashburn-1.oraclecloud.com/
v1/exadata/patches/dbaas_patch/shome/dbaastools_exa.rpm
```

For Frankfurt (FRA) region:

```
wget https://swiftobjectstorage.eu-frankfurt-1.oraclecloud.com/
v1/exadata/patches/dbaas_patch/shome/dbaastools_exa.rpm
```

For London (LHR) region:

```
wget https://swiftobjectstorage.uk-london-1.oraclecloud.com/
v1/exadata/patches/dbaas_patch/shome/dbaastools_exa.rpm
```

Next, check the version of the downloaded .rpm package:

```
rpm -qpi ./dbaastools_exa.rpm
```

The output would be similar to this:

```
[root@exacs-node1 ~]# rpm -qpi ./dbaastools_exa.rpm
Name         : dbaastools_exa              Relocations: (not relocatable)
Version      : 1.0                              Vendor: Oracle
Release      : 1+18.1.4.1.0_180627.0000     Build Date: Wed 27 Jun 2018 09:32:47
AM UTC
Install Date: (not installed)               Build Host: den00jnj.us.oracle.com
Group        : Applications/Administrative  Source RPM: dbaastools_exa-1.0-
1+18.1.4.1.0_180627.0000.src.rpm
Size         : 349251016                       License: Copyright (c) 2013, Oracle
and/or its affiliates. All rights reserved.
Signature    : (none)
Packager     : mmoteka
URL          : http://dbdev.us.oracle.com/
Summary      : DBAAS Tools for exadata
Description  :
DBAAS Tools for Oracle Public Cloud - Exadata
```

Now that we have a newer version of the tooling, we need to remove the old version. Remove it with the command:

```
rpm -ev CURRENT_INSTALLED_VERSION
```

with the current installed version being what we got from running `rpm -qa|grep -i dbaastools_exa`.

Here it is, put together:

```
[root@exacs-node1 ~]# rpm -qa|grep -i dbaastools_exa
dbaastools_exa-1.0-1+18.1.2.1.0_180423.0203.x86_64
[root@exacs-node1 ~]# rpm -ev dbaastools_exa-1.0-1+18.1.2.1.0_180423.0203.x86_64
```

To finish the manual install, run the following:

```
[root@exacs-node1 ~]# rpm -ivh ./dbaastools_exa.rpm
```

Here's the output:

```
[root@exacs-node1 ~]# rpm -ivh ./dbaastools_exa.rpm
Preparing...                 ######################################### [100%]
   1:dbaastools_exa           ######################################### [100%]
```

Remember that this needs to be done on all database compute nodes in your service.
If the tooling update check hangs or times out, look at the "Accessing a Storage Container in OCI for Database Backups Prerequisites" sidebar later in this chapter to see how you can open a route to the storage container where the updates are located.

Using dbaasapi Tooling

After you've updated tooling, you can start using it. The dbaasapi tool can be used to manage the lifecycle of the databases on your ExaCS system.

Database Creation Using dbaasapi Tooling

To create a database, first create a local JSON file with the parameters for this new database. This file is very similar to the JSON file we used for creating a database with the REST service.
Here is a sample database JSON file we will use for our new OCI database:

```
{
  "object": "db",
  "action": "start",
  "operation": "createdb",
  "params": {
    "nodelist":            "",
    "dbname":              "MY122DB",
    "edition":             "EE_EP",
    "version":             "12.2.0.1",
    "adminPassword":       "Awes0mePassw0rd",
    "sid":                 "CDB122",
    "pdbName":             "PDB122",
    "charset":             "AL32UTF8",
    "ncharset":            "AL16UTF16",
    "backupDestination":   "OSS",
    "cloudStorageContainer":
"https://swiftobjectstorage.<region>.oraclecloud.com/v1/mycompany/myDBBackup",
    "cloudStorageUser":    "brian.spendolini@oracle.com",
    "cloudStoragePwd":     "Awes0mePassw0rd"
  },
  "outputfile": "/home/oracle/createdb.out",
  "FLAGS": ""
}
```

You can create this file on your local OS with your favorite Linux text editor (vi for me). Let's name this file createDB.json using our text editor. Here it is using vi:

```
[root@exacs-node1 ~]# vi createDB.json
```

Copy and paste this code into the file, change the parameters to meet your needs, and save it.
After the file is created, issue the following dbaasapi command:

```
[root@exacs-node1 ~]# /var/opt/oracle/dbaasapi/dbaasapi -i createDB.json
```

In the JSON file, you'll see "outputfile" : "/home/oracle/createdb.out". You can cat this file to view the output using this command:

```
[root@exacs-node1 ~]# cat /home/oracle/createdb.out
```

The result will be similar to this JSON file:

```
{
    "msg" : "",
    "object" : "db",
    "status" : "Starting",
    "errmsg" : "",
    "outputfile" : "/home/oracle/createdb.out",
    "action" : "start",
    "id" : "21",
    "operation" : "createdb",
    "logfile" : "/var/opt/oracle/log/gsa1/dbaasapi/db/createdb/1.log"
}
```

To monitor the status of this service, you can create a status.json file and run the dbaasapi on that JSON file to keep tabs on the service. Again, using your favorite Linux text editor, create a status.json file and place the following text into it:

```
{
  "object": "db",
  "action": "status",
  "operation": "createdb",
  "id": 21,
  "params": {
    "dbname": " MY122DB "
  },
  "outputfile": "/home/oracle/dbstatus.out",
  "FLAGS": ""
}
```

Notice that the id and dbname parameters reflect the ID in the output file and the dbname we used in the createDB.json file. If these do not match, the result of the next call will be incorrect. Once this status.json file is created, run the following command:

```
[root@exacs-node1 ~]# /var/opt/oracle/dbaasapi/dbaasapi -i status.json
```

This will result in an output file dbstatus.out, as used for the outputfile parameter in the status.json file. You can see the status of the create process using the following command:

```
[root@exacs-node1 ~]# cat /home/oracle/dbstatus.out
```

The result of the command shows the status of the database creation:

```
"status" : "Success",
   "errmsg" : "",
   "outputfile" : "/home/oracle/createdb_exadb.out",
   "action" : "start",
   "id" : "21",
   "operation" : "createdb",
   "logfile" : "/var/opt/oracle/log/exadb/dbaasapi/db/createdb/21.log"
```

Database Deletion Using dbaasapi Tooling

Deleting a database is similar to creating it, starting with a JSON file. Using a text editor, create a deleteMyDB.json file and add the following text:

```
{
  "object":    "db",
  "action":    "start",
  "operation": "deletedb",
  "params": {
    "dbname": "MY122DB"
  },
  "outputfile":   "/home/oracle/delete_myDatabase.out",
  "FLAGS": ""
}
```

You need to customize the parameter dbname, using the same name as when you created it. Once this file is created, issue the following command:

```
[root@exacs-node1 ~]# /var/opt/oracle/dbaasapi/dbaasapi -i deleteMyDB.json
```

Like the create process, you can cat the output file to see the results of the command:

```
cat /home/oracle/delete_myDatabase.out
```

You'll see results similar to the following:

```
{
  "msg" : "",
  "object" : "db",
  "status" : "Starting",
  "errmsg" : "",
  "outputfile" : "/home/oracle/deletedb.out",
  "action" : "start",
  "id" : "12",
  "operation" : "deletedb",
  "logfile" : "/var/opt/oracle/log/exadb/dbaasapi/db/deletedb/12.log"
}
```

As with the create process, you can create a status JSON file to keep tabs on the job. Let's call this file deleteDBstatus.json and add the following text:

```
{
  "object": "db",
  "action": "status",
  "operation": "deletedb",
```

```
"id": 12,
"params": {
  "dbname": "MY122DB"
},
"outputfile": "/home/oracle/deletedb.out",
"FLAGS": ""
}
```

Be sure to enter the ID you saw in the delete_myDatabase.out file, as well as the dbname you used in the initial deleteMyDB.json file. Run the following command:

```
[root@exacs-node1 ~]# /var/opt/oracle/dbaasapi/dbaasapi -i deleteDBstatus.json
```

Then view the output:

```
[root@exacs-node1 ~]# cat /home/oracle/deletedb.out
```

Keep an eye on the following section of the deletedb.out file for status updates:

```
"status" : "InProgress",
  "errmsg" : "",
  "outputfile" : "/home/oracle/deletedb.out",
  "action" : "start",
  "id" : "12",
  "operation" : "deletedb",
  "logfile" : "/var/opt/oracle/log/exadb/dbaasapi/db/deletedb/12.log"
```

Using dbaascli Tooling

Another ExaCS CLI tool, dbaascli, mainly deals with database lifecycle management and functionality at the core database level. The actions that can be performed on the following components of your databases on the ExaCS are

- **Database**   bounce, changepassword, move, start, status, stop, elastic
- **dbhome**   info, purge
- **listener**   bounce, status, start, stop
- **orec (Oracle recovery)**   latest, list, pitr, scn
- **Transparent Data Encryption (TDE)**   addcronjob, backup, rotate masterkey, status
- **regdb**   begin, prereqs

NOTE
dbaascli can be run by the oracle user or by root, depending on the command and subcommand used. Database, Listener, and TDE are used by oracle with dbhome, regdb, and orec used by root. An exception is TDE addcronjob; normally run by oracle, this subcommand is run by root because it needs to update the crontab file.

Let's look at these commands in depth.

Database Commands

Seven database commands are available.

bounce   Stop and start the database:

```
[oracle@exacs-node1 ~]$ dbaascli database bounce -dbname HRCDB
```

changepassword   Change the specified database user's password:

```
[oracle@exacs-node1 ~]$ dbaascli database changepassword -dbname HRPDB
DBAAS CLI version 18.1.4.1.0
Executing command database changepassword
Enter username whose password change is required: REX
Enter new  password:
Re-enter new password:
```

move   Move the database from one Oracle home into another existing Oracle home (as root):

```
[root@exacs-node1 ~]$  dbaascli database move --dbname CRMCDB
--ohome /u02/app/oracle/product/12.2.0/dbhome_2
```

status   The status command gives us information about the databases and the nodes they are running on:

```
[oracle@exacs-node1 ~]$ dbaascli database status --dbname HRCDB
DBAAS CLI version 18.1.4.1.0
Executing command database status
Database Status:
Instance HRCDB1 is running on node exacs-node1. Instance status: Open.
Instance HRCDB2 is running on node exacs-node2. Instance status: Open.
Database name: HRCDB
Oracle Database 12c EE Extreme Perf Release 12.2.0.1.0 - 64bit Production
PL/SQL Release 12.2.0.1.0 - Production
CORE      12.2.0.1.0     Production
TNS for Linux: Version 12.2.0.1.0 - Production
NLSRTL Version 12.2.0.1.0 - Production
```

start and stop   Using the CLI, we can start a database:

```
[oracle@exacs-node1 ~]$ dbaascli database start --dbname HRCDB
DBAAS CLI version 18.1.4.1.0
Executing command database start
Database started!
```

As well as stop it:

```
[oracle@exacs-node1 ~]$ dbaascli database stop --dbname HRCDB
DBAAS CLI version 18.1.4.1.0
Executing command database stop
Database stopped!
```

elastic   Change the CPU_CPOUNT value and SGA_TARGET of the specified database. Use the --precheck parameter to see recommended values before making the actual change. If the memory parameter is not passed, the tooling will recommend or change the values based on best practices:

```
Using --precheck:
[oracle@exacs-node1 ~]$ dbaascli database update --dbname HRCDB --cpu 4
--memory 9g --precheck
DBAAS CLI version 18.1.4.1.0
Executing command database update  --cpu 4 --memory 9g --precheck
INFO: Update log - /var/opt/oracle/log/HRCDB/update/update_2018-06-13_12:16:36.log
INFO : Running Pre-Checks
Database Name : HRCDB
Current values
$EXISTING = '{
    "PGA_AGGREGATE_TARGET" : "2.00 GB",
    "SESSIONS" : "1568",
    "SGA_TARGET" : "3.00 GB",
    "CPU_COUNT" : "16"
}';
Recommended values
$NEW = '{
    "PGA_AGGREGATE_TARGET" : "3.00 GB",
    "SESSIONS" : 2000,
    "SGA_TARGET" : "5.00 GB",
    "CPU_COUNT" : "4"
}';
INFO : Precheck completed
```

Now remove the `--precheck` parameter and change the `CPU_COUNT` and `SGA_TARGET`:

```
[oracle@exacs-node1 ~]$ dbaascli database update --dbname HRCDB --cpu 4
--memory 5g
DBAAS CLI version 18.1.4.1.0
Executing command database update  --cpu 4
INFO: Update log - /var/opt/oracle/log/HRCDB/update/update_2018-06-13_12:17:33.log
INFO : Running Pre-Checks
Database Name : HRCDB
Current values
$EXISTING = '{
    "PGA_AGGREGATE_TARGET" : "2.00 GB",
    "SESSIONS" : "1568",
    "SGA_TARGET" : "3.00 GB",
    "CPU_COUNT" : "16"
}';
Recommended values
$NEW = '{
    "PGA_AGGREGATE_TARGET" : "3.00 GB",
    "SESSIONS" : 2000,
    "SGA_TARGET" : "5.00 GB",
    "CPU_COUNT" : "4"
}';
INFO: Restarting the DB Instance in rolling method to take an effect of changes
        INFO: Stopping the DB Instance on exacs-node1
        INFO: Starting the DB Instance on exacs-node1
        INFO: Stopping the DB Instance on exacs-node2
        INFO: Starting the DB Instance on exacs-node2
INFO: Updated successfully
```

dbhome Commands
There are the two `dbhome` commands.

info   Display information about all the Oracle homes on the service:

```
[root@exacs-node1 ~]# dbaascli dbhome info
DBAAS CLI version 18.1.4.1.0
Executing command dbhome info
Location of inventory.xml is set to /u01/app/oraInventory/ContentsXML/inventory.xml
Enter a homename or just press enter if you want details of all homes
1.HOME_NAME=OraHome1
  HOME_LOC=/u02/app/oracle/product/12.2.0/dbhome_2
  PATCH_LEVEL=122010_0
  DBs installed= HRCDB
2.HOME_NAME=OraHome104_12201_dbbp180417_0
  HOME_LOC=/u02/app/oracle/product/12.2.0/dbhome_5
  PATCH_LEVEL=122010_0
  DBs installed= CRMCDB
```

purge   Delete unused/empty Oracle homes (the directories and files). You can choose the home either by location or home name:

```
[root@exacs-node1 ~]# dbaascli dbhome purge
DBAAS CLI version 18.1.4.1.0
Executing command dbhome purge
Location of inventory.xml is set to /u01/app/oraInventory/ContentsXML/inventory.xml
Enter
1 - If you wish to enter homename to be purged
2 - If you wish to enter home path to be purged
1
Enter the homename
OraHome101_122010_0_0
```

Listener Commands
These commands are similar to using `lsnrctl`.

bounce   Stop and start the listener. Dbname is required, but on ExaCS, there is only one listener:

```
[oracle@exacs-node1 ~]$ dbaascli listener bounce --dbname HRCDB
DBAAS CLI version 18.1.4.1.0
Executing command listener bounce
Bouncing listener
Executing command listener stop
Stopping listener
Listener stopped!
Executing command listener start
Starting listener
Listener started!
```

stop or start   Stop the listener:

```
[oracle@exacs-node1 ~]$ dbaascli listener stop --dbname HRCDB
DBAAS CLI version 18.1.4.1.0
Executing command listener stop
Stoping listener
Listener stopped!
```

Start the listener:

```
[oracle@exacs-node1 ~]$ dbaascli listener start --dbname HRCDB
DBAAS CLI version 18.1.4.1.0
Executing command listener start
Starting listener
Listener started!
```

status   Display the status of the listener, with the same output as lsnrctl status:

```
[oracle@exacs-node1 ~]$ dbaascli listener status --dbname HRCDB
```

orec Commands
These commands deal with database recovery.

latest   Recover the database from the most recent backup:

```
[root@exacs-node1 ~]# dbaascli orec --args -latest --dbname HRCDB
```

list   List the current backups you can use to recover the database:

```
[root@exacs-node1 ~]# dbaascli orec --args -list --dbname HRCDB
```

pitr   Restore the database from a specific backup. Pass in the tag of the backup you want to restore from:

```
[root@exacs-node1 ~]# dbaascli orec --args -pitr TAG20180625T000036 --dbname HRCDB
```

SCN   Restore the database to a specific system change number (SCN):

```
[root@exacs-node1 ~]# dbaascli orec --args -scn 145321 --dbname HRCDB
```

TDE Commands
There are four TDE commands.

addcronjob   The add CRON job (addcronjob) command will add an entry into the OS's crontab file in /etc. This entry will back up the TDE wallet automatically by running the dbaascli tde backup command with the -alldb parameter indicating all databases on the service:

```
[root@exacs-node1 ~]# dbaascli tde addcronjob
DBAAS CLI version 18.1.4.1.0
Executing command tde addcronjob
INFO: addcronjob: TDE wallet backup entry is added to crontab successfully.
```

backup   The backup command takes a database name as a parameter so that you can back up the wallet for a specific database or all databases using the -alldb parameter. Backups are placed in /u02/app/oracle/admin/DB_NAME/tde_wallet:

```
[oracle@exacs-node1 ~]$ dbaascli tde backup --dbname HRCDB
DBAAS CLI version 18.1.4.1.0
Executing command tde backup
INFO: backup: TDE wallet backup completed successfully
```

rotate masterkey   Rotate the master key of the specified database. You will need the current wallet password to use this command:

```
[oracle@exacs-node1 ~]$ dbaascli tde rotate masterkey --dbname HRCDB
DBAAS CLI version 18.1.4.1.0
Executing command tde rotate masterkey
Enter keystore password:
```

status   Display the current status of the software keystore for the specified database:

```
[oracle@exacs-node1 ~]$ dbaascli tde status --dbname HRCDB
DBAAS CLI version 18.1.4.1.0
Executing command tde status
TDE is configured on this instance with:
 keystore login: auto
 keystore status: open
 keystore type: autologin
```

regdb Commands

The two register database (regdb) commands are used to register a database you imported from on-premises to the cloud. Start by creating a database via the UI or CLI with the same name as the on-premises database. Once that database is created, you can replace it with an on-premises database of the same name. After re-creating the database, we can use regdb to ensure that the cloud tooling works with the imported database (assuming it passes the prereqs check; same name, same patch level).

begin   Use the begin command to start the database registration process:

```
[root@exacs-node1 ~]# dbaascli regdb begin --dbname HRCDB
DBAAS CLI version 18.1.4.1.0
Executing command regdb begin
Logfile Location: /var/opt/oracle/log/HRCDB/regdb/regdb_2018-09
13_02:30:10.log
Running prereqs
DBAAS CLI version 18.1.4.1.0
Executing command regdb prereqs
INFO: Logfile Location: /var/opt/oracle/log/HRCDB/regdb/regdb_2018-09
13_02:30:12.log
INFO: Prereqs completed successfully
Prereqs completed
Running OCDE .. will take time ..
OCDE Completed successfully.
Database HRCDB registered as Cloud database
```

prereqs   Run the prereqs command using the dbname of the home where you imported your on-premises database:

```
[root@exacs-node1 ~]$ dbaascli regdb prereqs --dbname HRCDB
DBAAS CLI version 18.1.4.1.0
Executing command regdb prereqs
INFO: Logfile Location: /var/opt/oracle/log/HRCDB/regdb/regdb_2018-09
13_02:27:42.log
INFO: Prereqs completed successfully
```

Patching a Database Using exadbcpatchmulti

You can patch OCI and OCI-C databases from the command line using the exadbcpatchmulti API.

NOTE
All of the following commands can be used for Oracle database homes as well as the Grid Infrastructure. Though this section does use an Oracle database home, we could have just as easily swapped out the Oracle path with a Grid Infrastructure path (/u01/app/12.1.0.2/ grid, /u01/app/12.2.0.1/grid or /u01/app/18.1.0.0/grid).

To start, you again need to be root on the service. To see all patches available for an Oracle home, use the following command:

```
[root@exacs-node1 ~]# /var/opt/oracle/exapatch/exadbcpatchmulti -list_patches
-sshkey=sshkey_file -oh=hostname:oracle_home
```

The parameter `sshkey` points to where a private key is for the opc user so that the user can log into all the nodes in the ExaCS. The `-oh` parameter needs the compute node hostname and oracle_home directory you want to check. For example, if my hostname was exacs-node1 and I wanted to list the patches for my Oracle home at /u02/app/oracle/product/12.2.0/dbhome_2, I'd use this command:

```
[root@exacs-node1 ~]# /var/opt/oracle/exapatch/exadbcpatchmulti -list_patches
-sshkey=/home/opc/.ssh/id_rsa
-oh=exacs-node1:/u02/app/oracle/product/12.2.0/dbhome_2
```

The output would look similar to the following:

```
INFO: Completed init module
Location of inventory.xml is set to /u01/app/oraInventory/ContentsXML/inventory.xml
INFO: Finding db_active_nodes and local sid for HRCDB: 0
INFO: db_active_nodes for HRCDB: 1
INFO: getting rdbname from creg
INFO: dbversion detected : 12201
INFO: patching type : psu
INFO: oss_container_url is not given, using the default
INFO: Completed validate_params
INFO: images available for patching
INFO: patch_all_dbs is set to
INFO: going to read spool file
12.2.0.1.0, ee
$VAR1 = {
        'last_async_precheck_txn_id' => '245',
        'last_async_apply_txn_id' => '289',
        'errmsg' => '',
        'err' => '',
        'current_version' => '12.2.0.1.0',
        'last_async_precheck_patch_id' => '27486326',
        'current_patch' => '',
        'last_async_apply_patch_id' => '27010930',
        'patches' => [
                    {
                        'patchid' => '26610291',
                        'last_precheck_txnid' => '',
```

```
                              'description' => 'DB 12.2.0.1.170814 DATABASE RELEASE
UPDATE (Aug 2017)'
                    },
                    {
                      'patchid' => '26737266',
                      'last_precheck_txnid' => '',
                      'description' => 'DB 12.2.0.1.171017 DATABASE RELEASE
UPDATE (Oct 2017)'
                    },
                    {
                      'patchid' => '27100009',
                      'last_precheck_txnid' => '',
                      'description' => 'DB 12.2.0.1.180116 DATABASE RELEASE
UPDATE (Jan 2018)'
                    },
                    {
                      'patchid' => '27468969',
                      'last_precheck_txnid' => 217,
                      'description' => 'DB 12.2.0.1.180417 DATABASE RELEASE
UPDATE (Apr 2018)'
                    }
                 ]
        };
...
```

You can use this information to patch the database home.

TIP
Remember that it's best to pre-check a patch to ensure that it will apply with no issues.

Using the information received in the list patches call, you can structure your `precheck` command. Using the hostname and patch version, you can structure a `precheck` command into the following:

```
[root@exacs-node1 ~]# /var/opt/oracle/exapatch/exadbcpatchmulti
-precheck_async 27468969 -sshkey=/home/opc/.ssh/id_rsa
-instance1=exacs-node1:/u02/app/oracle/product/12.2.0/dbhome_2
-instance2=exacs-node2:/u02/app/oracle/product/12.2.0/dbhome_2
```

We have also listed both hostnames and oracle homes on both compute nodes, assuming we have a quarter rack. This will pre-check on both nodes.

Applying a patch uses a command very similar to `precheck`. You can use the same structure to create the patching command (`precheck_async` changes to `apply_async`):

```
[root@exacs-node1 ~]# /var/opt/oracle/exapatch/exadbcpatchmulti
-apply_async 27468969 -sshkey=/home/opc/.ssh/id_rsa
-instance1=exacs-node1:/u02/app/oracle/product/12.2.0/dbhome_2
-instance2=exacs-node2:/u02/app/oracle/product/12.2.0/dbhome_2
-run_datasql=1
```

The other change is the `-run_datasql`. This addition instructs the `exadbcpatchmulti` command to execute patch-related SQL commands after the patch has been applied.

Lastly, you can roll back a patch by replacing `apply_async` with `rollback_async`:

```
[root@exacs-node1 ~]# /var/opt/oracle/exapatch/exadbcpatchmulti
-rollback_async 27468969 -sshkey=/home/opc/.ssh/id_rsa
-instance1=exacs-node1:/u02/app/oracle/product/12.2.0/dbhome_2
-instance2=exacs-node2:/u02/app/oracle/product/12.2.0/dbhome_2
 -run_datasql=1
```

You can list applied patches to an Oracle home or a Grid Infrastructure, in this case using OPatch. As the oracle user, set the ORACLE_HOME environment variable on the Linux OS (.DB_NAME in the /home/oracle directory). Then run OPatch:

```
[root@exacs-node1 ~]# $ORACLE_HOME/OPatch/opatch lspatches
```

This will list all applied patches to that home. If you want to run this on the Grid Infrastructure, log in as opc and issue the following commands:

```
[root@exacs-node1 ~]# sudo -s
[root@exacs-node1 ~]# su - grid
```

You are now the grid user. Same as the oracle user, run the following command:

```
[root@exacs-node1 ~]# $ORACLE_HOME/OPatch/opatch lspatches
```

The Database Backup CLI

As you saw in Chapter 2, we can set up backups and recover our database from the UI. We can also set up backups using the bkup CLI—but if we do this after the database is created, we will not see these changes in the UI. To alter or add backups to a particular database, you can use this CLI. To start, log in as opc to the first database compute node of your ExaCS via SSH:

```
ssh -i your_private_key.ppk -l opc 111.111.111.111
```

Then change to the root user from opc:

```
[root@exacs-node1 ~]# sudo -s
```

Now you can change your directory to the bkup CLI home by issuing the following command:

```
[root@exacs-node1 ~]# cd /var/opt/oracle/ocde/assistants/bkup/
```

You can now create a configuration file for backups. If you do an `ls` in the directory, you'll see a bkup.cfg file. Copy this file and create a new one. You can do that quickly with the cp command:

```
[root@exacs-node1 ~]# cp bkup.cfg bkup.cfg.original
```

This will create a copy you can work from. Edit this file with your favorite Linux text editor. Here we use vi:

```
[root@exacs-node1 ~]# vi bkup.cfg
```

Accessing a Storage Container in OCI for Database Backups Prerequisites
When creating a storage container in OCI, you need to allow your VCN to access it. Depending on how you have set up your VCN, you have a few choices.

First, you can add an Internet gateway or service gateway to your VCN to access the storage container. Remember, however, that an Internet gateway is used for accessing the Internet from your VCN, and traffic to the object store will not go outside the OCI data center networks.

Next, alter some static routes for your network. Run the following command as root to get the gateway IP:

```
[root@exacs-node1 ~]# grep GATEWAY /etc/sysconfig/network-scripts/ifcfg-bondeth1
|awk -F"=" '{print $2}'
10.0.2.1
```

It returns 10.0.2.1. Remember this IP address to use again. Now add this route and the IPs of the storage service to the /etc/sysconfig/network-scripts/route-bondeth1 file on all nodes of your service:

```
[root@exacs-node1 ~]# vi /etc/sysconfig/network-scripts/route-bondeth1
```

Then add to the file:

```
134.70.0.0/17 via <gateway_IP_from_previous_step> dev bondeth1
```

My final file that I will save will look like this:

```
10.0.2.0/26 dev bondeth1 table 211
default via 10.0.2.1 dev bondeth1 table 211
134.70.0.0/17 via 10.0.2.1 dev bondeth1
```

Once you add the line to the route-bondeth1 file, bounce the network adapter with the following command:

```
[root@exacs-node1 ~]# ifdown bondeth1; ifup bondeth1;
```

Once the network is restarted, make this change and bounce the network adapter on all nodes of your ExaCS.

After the routes have been updated, add an entry to your route tables in the OCI web console. To do this, find your VCN in the OCI web console and click Route Tables on the lower-left area of the Details page (Figure 4-9).

Next, select the route table you used when creating the backup network. Then click the blue Edit Route Rules button. In the Edit Route Rules modal (Figure 4-10), if you have no route rules, click the + Another Route Rule button. How you create the rule depends on whether you used an Internet gateway or a service gateway.

If you have an **Internet gateway**, do the following:

1. Set the Target Type as Internet Gateway.
2. For Destination CIDR Block, enter **134.70.0.0/17**.
3. Set the Compartment to the compartment where your Internet gateway is located.
4. Set the Target Internet Gateway to the name of your Internet gateway.

Figure 4-10 shows an example of setting up the route rule for an Internet gateway.

If you have a **service gateway**, do the following:

1. Set the Target Type to Service Gateway.
2. For Destination Service, select the object store that corresponds to the region you are in. I am in Ashburn, so I would select OCI IAD ObjectStorage.
3. For Compartment, use the compartment where your service gateway is located.
4. For Target Service Gateway, enter the name of your service gateway.

Figure 4-11 shows an example of setting up the route rule for a service gateway.
Next, you need to create an egress rule in the backup subnets security list. Find the security list you created for the backup traffic and click it to view the details.

1. On the details page, click the Edit All Rules button. On the Edit All Rules modal, you will add an egress rule in the Allow Rules For Egress section of the modal.
2. For Destination Type, choose CIDR.
3. For Destination CIDR, enter the IP range of the Storage service, **134.70.0.0/17**.
4. For IP Protocol, use TCP.
5. For Destination Port Range, enter **443**. Your rule should look similar to Figure 4-12.
6. After you have created the rule, save it by clicking the blue Save Security List Rules button at the lower left of the Edit Security List Rules page.

You are now done with the backup prerequisites.

You'll need to add the correct parameters to this file to enable your database to back up:

- **bkup_disk**   Set to yes or no. This will set backups to use the RECO disk group local to the ExaCS.
- **bkup_oss**   Set to yes or no. This parameter is used if you want to back up the database to the database backup service in the cloud. Required if `bkup_oss` is set to yes.
- **bkup_oss_url**   If backing up to the cloud, this is the container URL parameter. Required if `bkup_oss` is set to yes.
- **bkup_oss_user**   The username used to authenticate against the database backup service. Required if `bkup_oss` is set to yes.
- **bkup_oss_passwd**   Password used for the user authenticating against the backup service. Required if `bkup_oss` is set to yes.
- **bkup_oss_recovery_window**   The number of days that backups and archived redo logs are retained in the database backup service. Valid inputs are in days, from 1 to 30. Required if `bkup_oss` is set to yes.
- **bkup_disk_recovery_window**   The number of days that backups and archived redo logs are retained in RECO local to the service. Valid inputs are in days, from 1 to 30. Required if `bkup_oss` is set to yes.
- **bkup_daily_time**   Time the service will back up the database in the format *hh:mm*, using UTC.

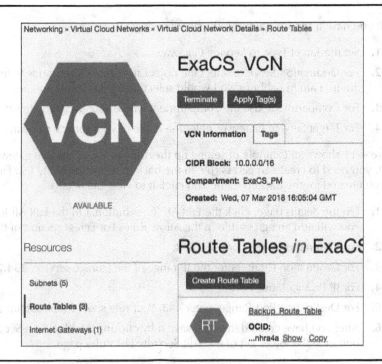

FIGURE 4-9. *Selecting Route Tables from the VCN Details page*

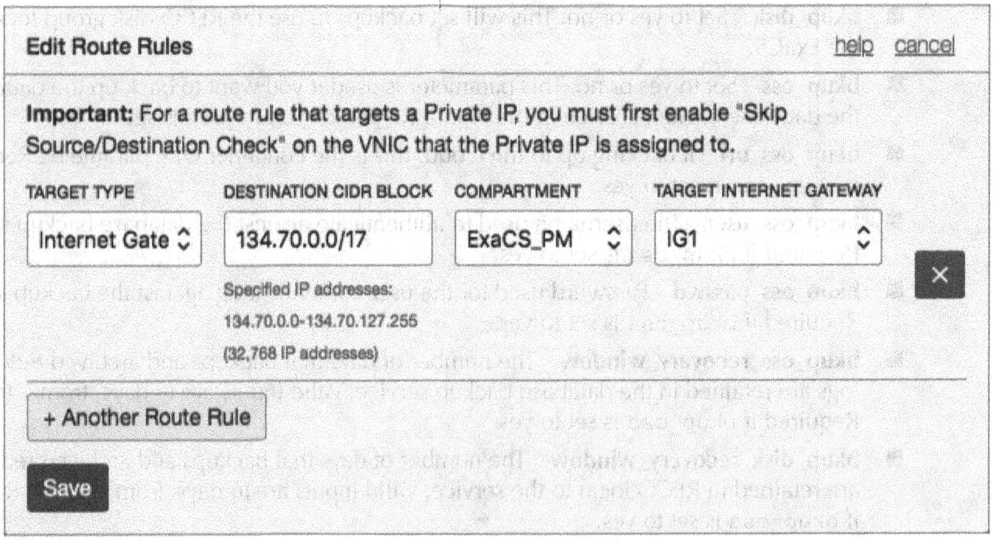

FIGURE 4-10. *Creating an Internet Gateway route rule*

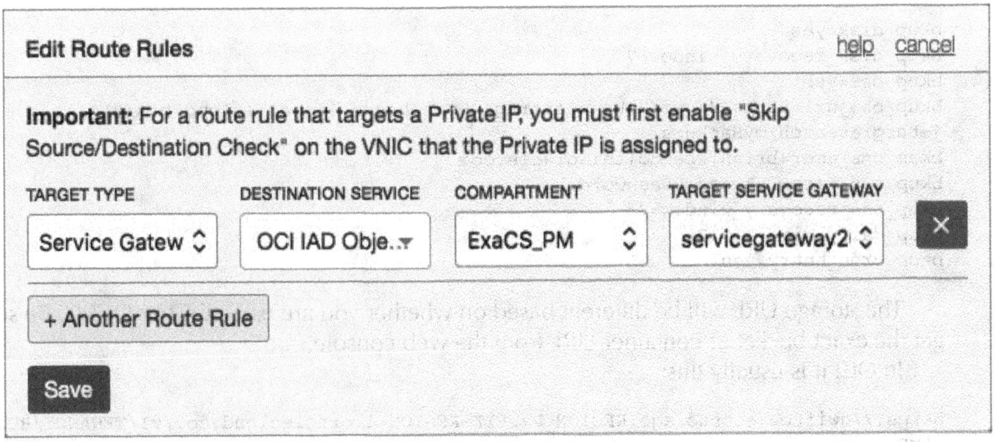

Edit Route Rules   help   cancel

Important: For a route rule that targets a Private IP, you must first enable "Skip Source/Destination Check" on the VNIC that the Private IP is assigned to.

TARGET TYPE	DESTINATION SERVICE	COMPARTMENT	TARGET SERVICE GATEWAY	
Service Gatew ⌄	OCI IAD Obje..▾	ExaCS_PM ⌄	servicegateway2 ⌄	✕

+ Another Route Rule

Save

FIGURE 4-11. *Creating a Service Gateway route rule*

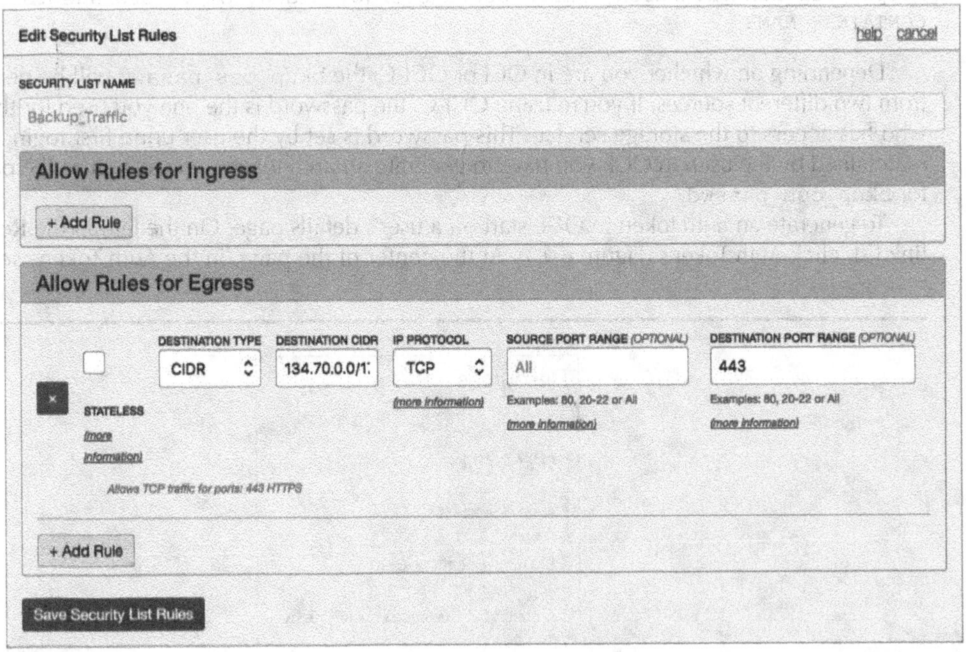

Edit Security List Rules   help   cancel

SECURITY LIST NAME

Backup_Traffic

Allow Rules for Ingress

+ Add Rule

Allow Rules for Egress

		DESTINATION TYPE	DESTINATION CIDR	IP PROTOCOL	SOURCE PORT RANGE *(OPTIONAL)*	DESTINATION PORT RANGE *(OPTIONAL)*
✕	☐	CIDR ⌄	134.70.0.0/1:	TCP ⌄	All	443
	STATELESS		*(more information)*		Examples: 80, 20-22 or All	Examples: 80, 20-22 or All
	more information				*(more information)*	*(more information)*
	Allows TCP traffic for ports: 443 HTTPS					

+ Add Rule

Save Security List Rules

FIGURE 4-12. *Adding an egress rule for accessing storage containers*

Taking these parameters into consideration, here is a sample you can use for a database:

```
bkup_disk=yes
bkup_disk_recovery_window=7
bkup_oss=yes
bkup_oss_url=https://swiftobjectstorage.us-ashburn-1.oraclecloud.com/v1/
jetdogresearch/myBackups
bkup_oss_user=brian.spendolini@oracle.com
bkup_oss_passwd=AwesomePassword
bkup_oss_recovery_window=7
bkup_daily_time=21:12
bkup_cron_entry=yes
```

The storage URL will be different based on whether you are using OCI or OCI-C. Be sure to get the exact bucket or container URL from the web console.

In OCI it is usually this:

```
https://swiftobjectstorage.REGION_PREFIX-REGION-1.oraclecloud.com/v1/TENANCY/BUCKET_
NAME
```

In OCI-C it can be two different formats. If using a legacy zone, it would be in this format:

```
https://storage.us.oraclecloud.com/v1/ID_DOMAIN/CONTAINER_NAME
```

If using an AD in OCI-C, it would be in this format:

```
https://ID_DOMAIN.REGION_PREFIX.storage.oraclecloud.com/v1/Storage-ID_DOMAIN/
CONTAINER_NAME
```

Depending on whether you are in OCI or OCI-C, the `bkup_oss_passwd` will be derived from two different sources. If you're using OCI-C, the password is the one you used for the user who has access to the storage service. This password is set by the user upon first login and maintained by the user. In OCI, you have to generate an auth token and use that as the password for `bkup_oss_passwd`.

To generate an auth token in OCI, start on a user's details page. On the left, in the Resources link list, click Auth Tokens (Figure 4-13). At the center of the page, in the Auth Tokens section

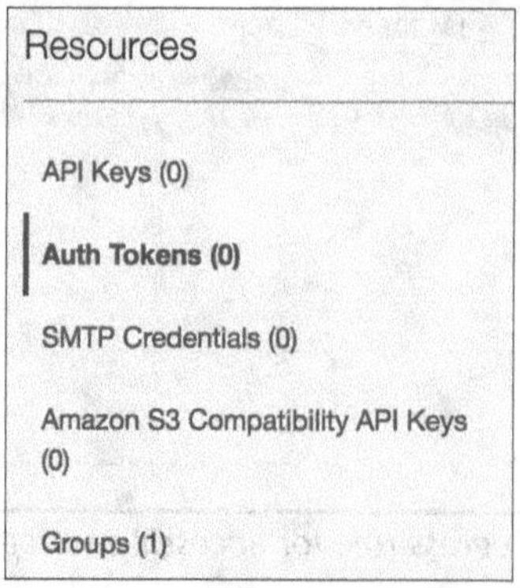

FIGURE 4-13. *Selecting Auth Tokens from the Resources link list*

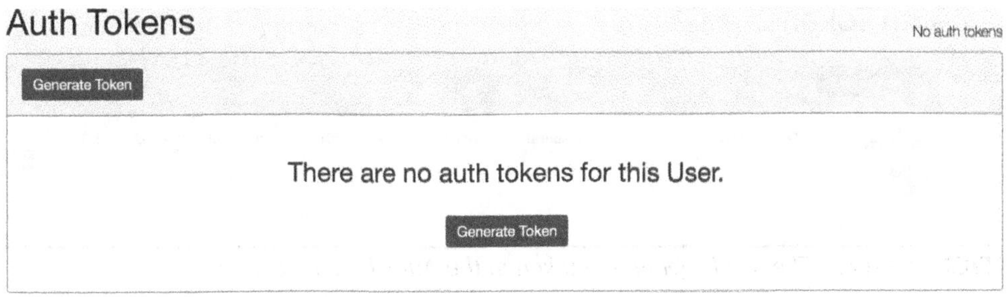

Auth Tokens

No auth tokens

Generate Token

There are no auth tokens for this User.

Generate Token

FIGURE 4-14. *Click the Generate Token button.*

(Figure 4-14), click the Generate Token button. In the Generate Token modal (Figure 4-15), enter a Description and click Generate Token.

The modal will display the generated token (Figure 4-16). Click the Copy button or highlight and copy the token. You will use this for the `bkup_oss_passwd` parameter in the bkup.cfg file.

Generate Token   help   cancel

DESCRIPTION

Generate Token

FIGURE 4-15. *Enter a description in the Generate Token modal.*

Generate Token   help   close

GENERATED TOKEN

#0HhII4f3fLG3{lbgXW9

Copy this token for your records. It will not be shown again.

Copy

Close

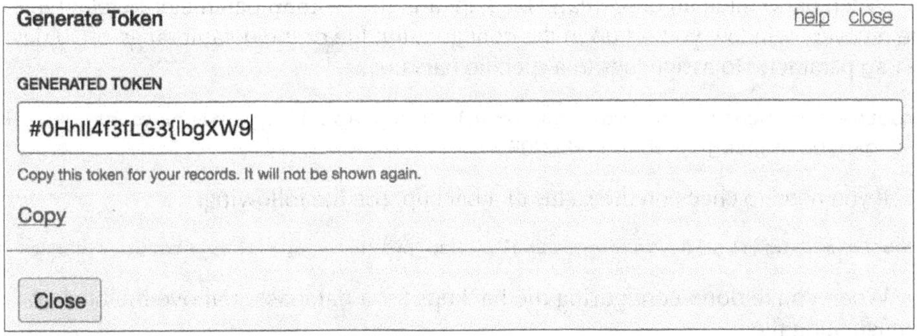

FIGURE 4-16. *The generated auth token*

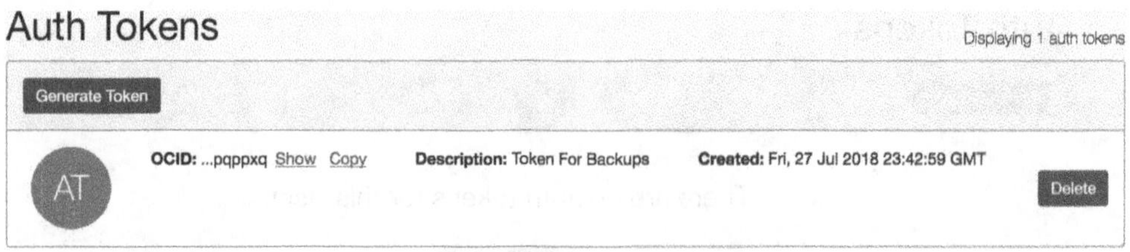

Auth Tokens

Displaying 1 auth tokens

Generate Token

AT   OCID: ...pqppxq _Show_ _Copy_   **Description:** Token For Backups   **Created:** Fri, 27 Jul 2018 23:42:59 GMT

Delete

FIGURE 4-17. *The newly generated token in the Auth Tokens section*

Close the modal, and you'll see in the Auth Tokens section (Figure 4-17) the token that you created and can reference in the future if needed. If you delete this token, the backups will no longer work because the token will be invalid.

Once you have created this file, change the permissions using the following:

```
[root@exacs-node1 ~]# chmod 600 bkup.cfg
```

Then let root own this file:

```
[root@exacs-node1 ~]# chown root bkup.cfg
```

Now configure the backups against a specific database with the following command:

```
[root@exacs-node1 ~]#./bkup -cfg bkup.cfg -dbname=<database_name>
```

The database name would be the service name. If you were using our HRCDB database, you would use this:

```
[root@exacs-node1 ~]#./bkup -cfg bkup.cfg -dbname=HRCDB
```

If you want to perform an on-demand backup outside of the scheduled backup window, you can use the following command, again as root and using HRCDB as the database name:

```
[root@exacs-node1 ~]# /var/opt/oracle/bkup_api/bkup_api bkup_start --dbname=HRCDB
```

When performing an on-demand backup, add the `--keep` parameter to retain this outside of the recovery window you set up in the configuration file or the default range of 30 days. Use the `--tag` parameter to assign tags to a specific backup:

```
[root@exacs-node1 ~]# /var/opt/oracle/bkup_api/bkup_api bkup_start --keep
--tag=mybackuptag --dbname=HRCDB
```

If you need to check on the status of a backup, use the following:

```
[root@exacs-node1 ~]# /var/opt/oracle/bkup_api/bkup_api bkup_status --dbname=HRCDB
```

When you're done configuring the backups for a database, remove the backup configuration file:

```
[root@exacs-node1 ~]# rm bkup.cfg
```

When you set up the backups using the API, the system was set up to back up your service automatically (the `bkup_daily_time` parameter). The following section will show you what happened behind the scenes. Again, this was done for you automatically.

The backup API uses the Linux job scheduler system. As root, go to the /etc directory:

```
[root@exacs-node1 ~]# cd /etc
```

You need to work with the crontab file. If you have set up backups to run at 9:21 P.M. every day, for example, you would add the following entry into the crontab file. Use your Linux text editor to add the following:

```
21 12 * * * root /var/opt/oracle/bkup_api/bkup_api bkup_start --dbname=HRCDB
```

The OS would now run this job every day at the specified time. If you need to change this time, you can just alter this file again. Again, the initial setup would have added this line, but you now know where it is and how to alter it if you need to.

Working with Backups Using the bkup CLI

Once your backups are set, you can use the same CLI to alter retention periods, backup cycles, and even to delete backups.

Let's start by changing the retention period. Using the following command, you can alter the retention period with the `--retention=days` parameter, a number between 1 and 30:

```
[root@exacs-node1 ~]# /var/opt/oracle/bkup_api/bkup_api bkup_chgcfg
--retention=30 --dbname=HRCDB
```

You can also change the cycle of the time frame for level 0 plus level 1 backups. The default is 7, which means a level 0 backup will be performed on, say, Sunday, and level 1 backups the rest of the week. Add the `--retention=30` parameter:

```
[root@exacs-node1 ~]# /var/opt/oracle/bkup_api/bkup_api bkup_chgcfg
--retention=30 --cycle=7 --dbname=HRCDB
```

NOTE
Make sure that the retention number of days is always greater than the cycle number of days.

Deleting a backup is easy using the bkup CLI. Start by listing all the backups you have for a database:

```
[root@exacs-node1 ~]# /var/opt/oracle/bkup_api/bkup_api list --dbname=HRCDB
```

Here's the output:

```
[root@exacs-node1 ~]# /var/opt/oracle/bkup_api/bkup_api list --dbname=HRCDB
DBaaS Backup API V1.5 @2016 Multi-Oracle home
DBaaS Backup API V1.5 @2015 Multi-Oracle home
-> Action : list
-> logfile: /var/opt/oracle/bkup_api/log/bkup_api.log
-> Listing all backups
```

Backup Tag	Completion Date (UTC)	Type	keep
TAG20171003T155207	10/03/2017 15:52:07	Full	True
TAG20171004T010403	10/04/2017 01:04:03	incremental	False
TAG20171005T010528	10/05/2017 01:05:28	incremental	False
TAG20171006T010744	10/06/2017 01:07:44	incremental	False

Using the backup tag and the database name, you can delete the Keep Forever backups. This will not work with incremental backups, however:

```
[root@exacs-node1 ~]# /var/opt/oracle/bkup_api/bkup_api bkup_delete
--bkup= TAG20171003T155207 --dbname=HRCDB
```

Database Recovery Using the bkup CLI

Not only can you back up using the bkup CLI, but you can recover a database just as you did in the UI. To restore from the latest backup, issue this command:

```
[root@exacs-node1 ~]# /var/opt/oracle/bkup_api/bkup_api recover_start --latest
--dbname=HRCDB
```

You can also recover from an SCN number, TAG, or a UTC timestamp, as you did in the UI. For SCN recovery (with SCN# being the SCN number), use this:

```
[root@exacs-node1 ~]# /var/opt/oracle/bkup_api/bkup_api recover_start --scn SCN#
--dbname=HRCDB
```

To recover from a specific TAG (incorporate with the previous list command), use this:

```
[root@exacs-node1 ~]# /var/opt/oracle/bkup_api/bkup_api recover_start
-b TAGXXXXXXXXX --dbname=HRCDB
```

To recover from a UTC timestamp, use this:

```
[root@exacs-node1 ~]# /var/opt/oracle/bkup_api/bkup_api recover_start
-t '31-JAN-2018 14:50:07' -dbname=HRCDB
```

To recover from a non-UTC timestamp (using the DB's time zone), use this:

```
[root@exacs-node1 ~]# /var/opt/oracle/bkup_api/bkup_api recover_start
-t '31-JAN-2018 14:50:07' --nonutc --dbname=HRCDB
```

As with the backup process, you can also check on the recovery status:

```
[root@exacs-node1 ~]# /var/opt/oracle/bkup_api/bkup_api recover_status
--dbname=HRCDB
```

Summary

By utilizing the REST services included with the ExaCS, you can integrate this functionality into existing systems to create a seamless user experience. By using the CLI tools, you can quickly and easily create databases, patch Grid Infrastructures, and back up or recover databases with a single-line command, making these tasks easy and efficient and reducing many of the manual steps required in the past.

CHAPTER 5

Smart Scans and Storage Indexes

The next few chapters discuss the Exadata in the Exadata Cloud Service—what makes an Exadata so different from anything else any company has produced and why we can get hyper-fast performance from an engineered system. This chapter starts with the basics of what an Exadata Database Machine is and how all the pieces work together to deliver the best Oracle Database performance possible. After you understand how the Exadata hardware works, you'll learn about one of its main features: query offloading.

The Exadata Database Machine Architecture

Exadata is what Oracle calls an "engineered system" (Figure 5-1), a system in which the hardware and software are created in unison to provide the best possible performance in an Oracle database.

FIGURE 5-1. *An Exadata Database machine*

Hardware Components

In its simplest form, an Exadata is made of up three major components: database compute nodes, storage cells, and the InfiniBand network that connects the two. Let's take a look at these components one at a time.

Exadata Database Compute Nodes

The database compute nodes are where the actual Oracle Database software is installed (the Oracle homes). Also stored on these nodes are the Grid Infrastructure, Automatic Storage Management (ASM), and the operating system (Oracle Linux) on which the Oracle software runs. With the latest generation of Exadata Database Machine, the X7, these compute nodes can have up to 48 CPU cores in the X7-2s (two socket) and 192 CPU cores in the X7-8 (eight socket). Memory on these database compute nodes can go up to 1.5TB for an X7-2 and up to 6TB for an X7-8. As for networking, the compute nodes in the X7 can have 25 Gigabit Ethernet, a change from all previous models that had 10 Gigabit Ethernet.

NOTE
The "-2" and "-8" in the model number designates the number of sockets they have (if you didn't already figure that out).

Exadata Storage Servers (Storage Cells)

The Exadata Storage Servers come in two types: Extreme Flash (EF) and High Capacity (HC). The EF Storage Servers have 20 CPUs and 192GB or more of DDR4 memory. They also contain eight 6.4TB state-of-the-art Flash Accelerator F640 NVMe PCI flash drives, giving each EF Storage Server 51.2TB of raw flash. The High Capacity Storage Servers offer the same amount of CPU and memory but are outfitted with twelve 10TB SAS disk drives offering 120TB total raw disk space. The HC Storage Servers also contain four 6.4TB Flash Accelerator F640 NVMe PCI flash drives, providing 25.6TB of flash memory (configured as Smart Flash Cache in the cloud). Both the EF and HC servers are connected to the database compute nodes via 40 Gbps InfiniBand.

The InfiniBand Network

The InfiniBand network is used to create a high-speed (40 Gbps) network between the storage servers (or storage cells) and the database compute nodes. It is also used as the interconnect for communications between the database compute nodes for the RAC cluster. There are two InfiniBand switches with the X7-2 and X7-8 Exadata Database Machines.

The diagram in Figure 5-2 shows a full rack layout for an Exadata X7-2. You can see the placement of the Exadata Database compute nodes (database server), the storage servers (storage cells), and the InfiniBand switches.

The Exadata Database Machine uses the Intelligent Database protocol (iDB) to communicate from the database compute nodes to the storage servers using InfiniBand. iDB is built on the Reliable Datagram Sockets (RDS v3) protocol and is also implemented directly in the Oracle Database kernel. iDB is used for sending SQL operations down to the Exadata Storage Servers for execution. Along with these messages are additional data about the query that the storage cells will use in prioritization and execution.

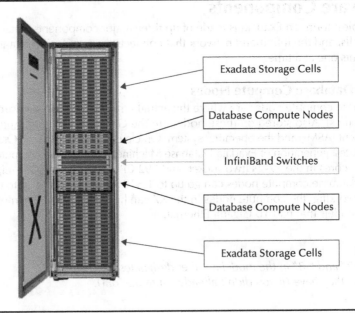

Exadata Storage Cells

Database Compute Nodes

InfiniBand Switches

Database Compute Nodes

Exadata Storage Cells

FIGURE 5-2. *The Exadata X7-2 full rack layout*

Software Components

As with the hardware, there are three major software components with the Exadata Database Machine: the Oracle Database software, the Oracle Grid Infrastructure, and the Exadata Storage Server software (Figure 5-3).

Oracle Database Server

Before we get to the database server software, keep in mind that the database compute nodes are running the Oracle Linux operating system. Upon this OS is the Oracle Database Server software. Here we create the Oracle Database instances, which can also use Real Application Clusters (RACs) to scale across nodes. All the database binaries are in these Oracle homes as well, such as SQL*Plus. All Oracle homes on the Exadata Cloud Service are kept at /u02/app/oracle/product/ *DATABASE_VERSION*, while the grid home is under /u01/app/*GI_VERSION*/grid.

Oracle Grid Infrastructure

The Grid Infrastructure combines ASM and Oracle Clusterware into a single Oracle home. The Clusterware enables the creation of database clusters for RAC databases, creating a network of servers that act as a single entity. This Clusterware provides the infrastructure for node failover, the SCAN Listener, and the pooling of resources.

The second part of the Grid Infrastructure is Automatic Storage Management (ASM). ASM is a volume manager that provides file storage for clustered databases using RAC. ASM will also take care of disk errors and failures. In an Exadata environment in the Oracle Cloud, ASM provides the high redundancy (triple mirroring of the data) on the storage servers (storage cells) for high availability for your data. The ASM disk groups also live on the storage servers and use the iDB protocol to communicate with the database compute nodes.

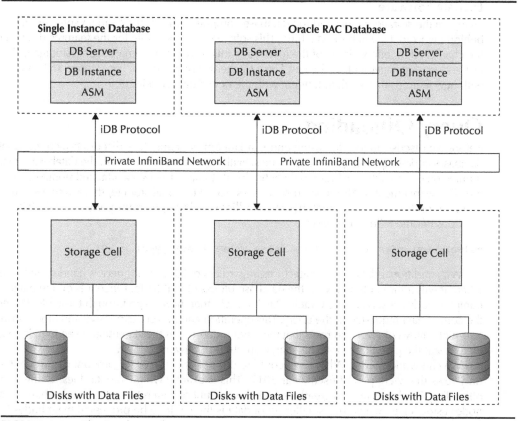

FIGURE 5-3. *The Exadata software components*

NOTE
If you were to issue **df -h** *on the database compute nodes, you would not see the ASM disks. Only the database and related tools via iDB can see the grid disk volumes. In the cloud, three main disk groups are created: RECO for the fast recovery area, DATA for your database data files, and SPARSE for any sparse clones you have created. There are also Automatic Storage Management Cluster File System (ACFS) disk mounts created to store Oracle images and to be used as a stage area for patching and your own data. The Grid Infrastructure home is maintained by the grid OS user. You cannot log in directly with this user but have to use the* **su** *(substitute user) command as root (or OPC). The Oracle home for the Grid Infrastructure is located at /u01/app/GI_VERSION/grid in the cloud, with GI_VERSION being the installed version upon Exadata Cloud Service creation.*

Exadata Software

Living on the storage servers and the database compute nodes is the Exadata software, the magic behind the Exadata Database Machine. This software is responsible for the features discussed in the chapters that follow. Some of the features of this software are Smart Scans, storage indexes, I/O resource management, and Smart Flash Cache. Every version of the Exadata software comes with new features that work in tandem with the new database release.

Query Offloading

Before we discuss query offloading and Exadata Smart Scans, let's discuss how traditional databases address querying from large tables. With non-Exadata hardware, the database is usually running on commodity hardware, with either local storage or network attached storage. And with today's advancement in NVMe solid-state disks (SSDs) for local storage, these systems can get hundreds of thousands, or sometimes even millions, of I/O operations per second (IOPS).

Consider the following query:

```
select sum(order_amount) from sales where fiscal_year = 2017;
```

With traditional database architectures, regardless of IOPS, that query is handed off to storage, where it will return potentially all the database blocks of that table. Once it is on the database compute nodes or servers, the Oracle Database will then have to go through these blocks and get the correct data requested in the query. This operation can be very expensive and time consuming, returning many columns and rows that were not requested in the statement. Even with indexes, there is still the potential of returning large amounts of unwanted data.

We can work smarter. What if we could return not only the order_amount column but also only rows that were part of fiscal year 2017? This is exactly what Exadata does. Using query offloading, Exadata is able to greatly reduce the amount of data returned to the database compute nodes using Smart Scans. This smaller set of data is then able to be processed magnitudes faster for reduced query times.

Let's return to the query:

```
select sum(order_amount) from sales where fiscal_year = 2017;
```

And let's follow its path on Exadata. Once the query is issued via a client or application, it is sent using the iDB protocol to the storage cells. Here on the storage cells, we can see what an engineered system can do.

The first feature that is part of Smart Scans is Column Projection. As with the traditional database architecture with local or network storage, if we issued this query and the sales table had 200 columns, all these columns would be returned to the System Global Area (SGA), where it would be processed. Column Projection returns only the columns requested in the select statement. In our query, we would be returning only two columns out of 200—this is a huge savings in time and data returned to the database compute nodes for processing.

The next optimization of Smart Scans is Predicate Filtering. Let's look at the query and how a traditional database would handle the where clause or the predicate. We want only rows that are in fiscal year 2017. A traditional database would apply this predicate to return a subset of rows once

Query Offloading and Query Predicates
Query offloading can improve the following comparisons in query predicates:

- IS NULL
- IS NOT NULL
- Greater than or equal to (>=)
- Less than or equal to (<=)
- Equality (=)
- Inequality (<, !=, or >)

Want a full list? Just run the following query on your system:

```
SELECT * FROM v$sqlfn_metadata WHERE offloadable = 'YES';
```

the data was returned from storage to the database compute nodes. Once there, Oracle would apply the predicate, throw out the rows not matching `fiscal_year = 2017`, and return the correct ones. With Exadata, this is done on the storage cells even before the data is returned via the iDB protocol to the database compute nodes, again further reducing the amount of data returned.

The third level of query optimization that Smart Scans offer are storage indexes. A storage index holds information about a region of the disk on the storage cells, with one region index for each 1MB of disk space. Storage indexes are automatically created and are transparent to the database. The indexes contain minimum, maximum, and null values for up to 27 columns on a table as of software version 18.1.4. These values are then used to eliminate regions or blocks of data that would result in unnecessary I/O; this is also called I/O filtering.

Let's take a conceptual look at how storage indexes work. Suppose we have a products table with a column called product_id. Now this table is rather large—a few terabytes in size. The storage servers (storage cells) automatically create storage indexes on this table for us and then store these indexes in the memory of the storage cells.

We issue a query against this table:

```
select product_id, product_name from products where product_id < 100;
```

When this query is passed down to the storage cells, we'll use the storage indexes to eliminate a large chunk of the product table. When the storage indexes are used, we instantly know what regions of the table contain product IDs that fit our predicate of `product_id < 100`. Any regions of this table that do not have a storage index that fits this where clause are instantly discarded, saving gigabytes of data being returned to the database compute nodes. This process is summarized in Figure 5-4.

Storage indexes can also help with table joins by, again, skipping unnecessary I/O operations and with range-sorted columns.

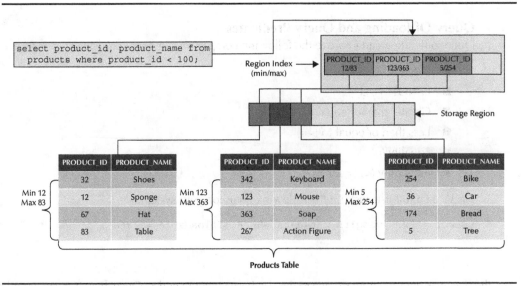

FIGURE 5-4. *Summary of storage indexes*

Using Smart Scans with an Exadata Cloud Service

Now let's see Smart Scans in action. In the next section, we'll set up our environment by creating a large table with random data. Then we'll issue queries against this table using various optimizer hints.

If these three conditions exist, a Smart Scan will be used:

- The object must be stored on the Exadata Storage Servers (cells).

- A full table scan occurs. This can also be a full scan of a partition, view, or materialized view. Offloading can also be used with fast full index scans.

- A direct path read must happen. A direct read bypasses the buffer cache and reads from disk.

Setting Up Your Environment

We'll use the pluggable database (PDB) that was created when we created the database service in Chapter 2. Log into your service via SSH as the oracle user, into the first database compute node and source the environment file that was created for you. The environment file is named after the container database (CDB) or system identifier (SID) you used when creating the database. For example, if my CDB was HRPROD, my environment file would be named HRPROD.env. To source it, or set up the environment of the OS to use the database, we issue the following command:

```
[oracle@exacs-node1 ~]$. HRPROD.env
```

NOTE
*All code used in the book is available for download, as explained in
the "Introduction" of this book.*

The environment will now be ready to use. We next need to use SQL*Plus as SYS to log into
the service. We can do that by using the command `sqlplus`. If your environment is set up
correctly with the environment file, you should see something similar to the following:

```
[oracle@exacs-node1 ~]$ sqlplus
SQL*Plus: Release 12.1.0.2.0 Production on Sat Nov 18 20:33:55 2017
Copyright (c) 1982, 2014, Oracle.  All rights reserved.
Enter user-name:
```

For username, we'll use the following:

```
/ as sysdba
```

We could have also combined these two steps into one and issued the following:

```
[oracle@exacs-node1 ~]$ sqlplus / as sysdba
```

At the SQL prompt, we can see the pluggable databases (PDBs) we have by issuing the
command `show pdbs`:

```
SQL> show pdbs

    CON_ID CON_NAME                       OPEN MODE  RESTRICTED
---------- ------------------------------ ---------- ----------
         2 PDB$SEED                       READ ONLY  NO
         3 HRPDB                          READ WRITE NO
```

We'll work in our PDB with a 12c or 18c database. To change to that container or
PDB, we issue the following command (you'll use the name of your PDB and not the one
referenced here):

```
SQL> alter session set container = HRPDB;
```

We are now in the PDB. We can double-check with the `show con_name` command:

```
SQL> SHOW CON_NAME
CON_NAME
------------------------------
HRPDB
```

Next, we need to create a user for the SQL examples and tables in the next chapters. Let's use
book as the username. We can create this user with the following SQL:

```
SQL> create user book identified by exadatabook;
```

Now we grant the rights (a bit liberal, but these are examples) so we can create tables and run
SQL statements:

```
SQL> grant connect, resource, dba to book;
```

And, finally, we switch from SYS to the book user (remember to use your PDB's name):

```
SQL> connect book/exadatabook@hrpdb;
```

We are now ready to create the tables.

Sample Data with an External Table

Let's use some data that is a bit more interesting. I have included a .csv file in the downloadable material for this book, called census_data.csv, that uses some of the 2010 U.S. Census data. Getting this data into the database is a bit more complex than using a SQL statement. The .csv file needs to be copied to both database compute nodes of the service. We use very similar syntax that we used to SSH into the node: the following command on a Linux or macOS system to use Secure Copy Protocol (SCP) to copy the file to the service:

```
scp -i your_private_key.ppk LOCATION_OF_CSV_FILE oracle@node_one_ip_address:/tmp
```

NOTE
You will need to substitute a few values here. Use your private key, the location of the file, and the IP address of the first compute node of the service.

Once you have those values, the command will look similar to the following:

```
scp -i myExaKey.ppk /Users/brian/census_data.csv oracle@111.111.111.111:/tmp
census_data.csv                          100% 3754KB   1.2MB/s   00:03
```

NOTE
This is a RAC environment, so we need to place the file on all nodes. Just rerun the previous scp command on all additional nodes:

```
scp -i myExaKey.ppk /Users/brian/census_data.csv oracle@222.222.222.222:/tmp
census_data.csv                          100% 3754KB   1.2MB/s   00:03
scp -i myExaKey.ppk /Users/brian/census_data.csv oracle@333.333.333.333:/tmp
census_data.csv                          100% 3754KB   1.2MB/s   00:03
```

We now have the file on our Exadata Cloud Service. Next, we need to load the data into the database using the external table feature. We log back into the PDB. We can do this quickly with the following SQL:

```
[oracle@exacs-node1 ~]$ sqlplus book/exadatabook@hrpdb
SQL*Plus: Release 12.2.0.1.0 Production on Sun Nov 26 18:50:30 2017
Copyright (c) 1982, 2016, Oracle.  All rights reserved.
Last Successful login time: Sun Nov 26 2017 18:43:48 +00:00
Connected to:
Oracle Database 12c EE Extreme Perf Release 12.2.0.1.0 - 64bit Production
SQL>
```

CAUTION
If you are sharing a system with other people, they can look at the command line history and see your password. Best to enter it in at the password prompt in SQL*Plus. If this is a personal system, then have at it.

To use an external table, a directory needs to be created in the database pointing to the location of the file. Use the following command to create the directory where we used SCP to put the file in /home/oracle:

```
SQL> create or replace directory EXTERNAL_TABLES as '/tmp';
```

Next, as the book user, we can load the data into a table from the .csv file with the following SQL:

```
CREATE TABLE census_ext (
PERSON_ID               NUMBER,
AGE                     NUMBER,
WORKCLASS               VARCHAR2(100),
EDUCATION               VARCHAR2(100),
      EDUCATION_ID      NUMBER,
      MARITAL_STATUS    VARCHAR2(100),
OCCUPATION              VARCHAR2(100),
HOUSE_SERV              VARCHAR2(100),
RACE                    VARCHAR2(100),
GENDER                  VARCHAR2(100),
WORK_HOURS_WEEK         NUMBER,
NATIVE_COUNTRY          VARCHAR2(100),
SALARY                  VARCHAR2(100)
)
organization external
(
  type oracle_loader
  default directory EXTERNAL_TABLES
  access parameters
  (
    records delimited by newline
    fields terminated by ','
)
  location ('census_data.csv')
);
```

Now create a table in the book schema from the external file:

```
SQL> create table big_census as select * from census_ext;
```

Just to be secure, we should delete this table:

```
SQL> drop table census_ext;
```

And also delete the external directory:

```
SQL> drop directory EXTERNAL_TABLES;
```

A date column needs to be added and filled in with random dates for later use. This is pretty simple to do. We start by adding the column:

```
SQL> alter table big_census add (person_date date);
```

Then we need to update this column with random dates. Use the following SQL for that:

```
SQL> update big_census set person_date = to_date(trunc(dbms_random.value
(2433283, 2458484)),'J')  where person_date is null;
```

And commit the data:

```
SQL> commit;
```

This SQL will fill the column with a random date between January 1, 1945, and December 31, 2018.

We now have a table created from the census data in the .csv file we used SCP to place on the Exadata Database compute node. Though this table is large (30,000 rows), we need to make it much bigger. To do this, we'll use some SQL to insert into this table from the rows that are current in the table. First, though, we need to turn off logging:

```
SQL> alter table big_census nologging;
```

This SQL includes the /*+ append */ optimizer hint. This hint tells the database to do a direct-path insert, which will improve performance with a large insert. It does this by bypassing the buffer cache and bypassing triggers, and it appends the data to the table rather than looking for free space within the existing table blocks. Now we'll do the inserts:

```
SQL> insert /*+ append */ into big_census select * from big_census;
32561 rows created.
```

And then commit the changes:

```
SQL> commit;
```

TIP
If you want to speed things up, you can flex more Exadata muscle by running the command

```
SQL> alter session force parallel dml;
```

We want to perform this same SQL multiple times so we can get a large table. We can see how big the table is now by running the following size SQL:

```
SQL> select segment_name, bytes/1024/1024/1024 as gigs from user_segments;

SEGMENT_NAME           GIGS
-------------------    -----
BIG_CENSUS             .0087
```

TIP
*To grow a table to multiple gigabytes, if you have the space available,
you can run the same insert /*+ append */ SQL again. Use the
size SQL to check how many gigabytes the table is.*

After running the `insert` command multiple times (about eight), we have a table of
16,671,232 rows that is just over 2GB in size:

```
SQL> select segment_name, bytes/1024/1024/1024 as gigs from user_segments;

SEGMENT_NAME          GIGS
-------------------   -----
BIG_CENSUS            2.0625
```

Last, we need to run stats for the table:

```
SQL> exec dbms_stats.gather_table_stats('book','big_census');
```

Using Smart Scans

Now our data is ready, it's time to see Smart Scans in action. We'll use a system parameter to
prevent the database from using Smart Scans: `cell_offload_processing`. Setting this to
`false` will prevent Smart Scans. Ready? Here we go.
    Start by flushing the buffer cache and shared pool of the database:

```
SQL> alter system flush shared_pool;
System altered.
SQL> alter system flush buffer_cache;
System altered.
```

Next, as stated earlier, we need to set the system parameter to prevent Smart Scans:

```
SQL> alter session set cell_offload_processing=false;
Session altered.
```

Now we turn on the timings so we can see how long each query takes:

```
SQL> set timing on
```

The first query we will run on the census table will be a simple count with a predicate. We
are adding a SQL comment between the /* */. We will use this next to find the explain plan:

```
SQL> select /* NO_OFFLOADING */ count(*) from big_census where gender = 'Female';

COUNT(*)
----------
5514752

Elapsed: 00:00:03.72
```

We run the following SQL to find and see the explain plan:

```
SQL> set linesize 90
SQL> select sql_id from v$sql where sql_text like '%NO_OFFLOADING%' and sql_text
not like '%v$sql%';
SQL_ID
-------------
aqm7zkkrrmgk8

SQL> select plan_table_output from table
(dbms_xplan.display_cursor('aqm7zkkrrmgk8'));

PLAN_TABLE_OUTPUT
-------------------------------------------------------------------------------
SQL_ID         aqm7zkkrrmgk8, child number 0
-------------------------------------
select /* NO_OFFLOADING */ count(*) from big_census where gender =
'Female'

Plan hash value: 1271265830


-------------------------------------------------------------------------------
| Id| Operation                   | Name        | Rows  | Bytes | Cost(%CPU)| Time     |
-------------------------------------------------------------------------------
|  0| SELECT STATEMENT            |             |       |       | 67895(100)|          |
PLAN_TABLE_OUTPUT
-------------------------------------------------------------------------------
|  1| SORT AGGREGATE             |             |     1 |     6 |           |          |
|* 2|   TABLE ACCESS STORAGE FULL| BIG_CENSUS  | 5514K |   31M | 67895 (1) |00:00:03|
-------------------------------------------------------------------------------

Predicate Information (identified by operation id):
-------------------------------------------------

   2 - filter("GENDER"='Female')


20 rows selected.
```

As you can see from the explain plan (TABLE ACCESS STORAGE FULL), the query did a full table scan as expected but did not use Smart Scans. How can we tell? Let's turn Smart Scans on and see the differences.

Start by flushing the buffer cache of the database:

```
SQL> alter system flush buffer_cache;
System altered.
```

Now set the system parameter to enable Smart Scans:

```
SQL> alter session set cell_offload_processing=true;
Session altered.
```

Now we can run the same query as before:

```
SQL> select /* WITH_OFFLOADING */ count(*) from big_census where gender = 'Female';

COUNT(*)
----------
5514752

Elapsed: 00:00:00.27
```

So immediately we see a difference in the timings alone. We went from 3.72 seconds down to 0.27, for a better than 70 percent improvement. The explain plan will be telling as well:

```
SQL> select sql_id from v$sql where sql_text like '%WITH_OFFLOADING%' and sql_text
not like '%v$sql%';

SQL_ID
-------------
gkbw1j9523a6c

Elapsed: 00:00:00.07
SQL> select plan_table_output from table
(dbms_xplan.display_cursor('gkbw1j9523a6c'));

PLAN_TABLE_OUTPUT
--------------------------------------------------------------------------------
SQL_ID    gkbw1j9523a6c, child number 0
------------------------------------
select /* WITH_OFFLOADING */ count(*) from big_census where gender =
'Female'

Plan hash value: 1271265830

--------------------------------------------------------------------------------
| Id| Operation              | Name        | Rows | Bytes | Cost(%CPU)| Time     |
--------------------------------------------------------------------------------
|  0| SELECT STATEMENT       |             |      |       | 67895(100)|          |

PLAN_TABLE_OUTPUT
--------------------------------------------------------------------------------
|  1| SORT AGGREGATE         |             |    1 |     6 |           |          |
|* 2| TABLE ACCESS STORAGE FULL| BIG_CENSUS | 5514K|   31M | 67895 (1) |00:00:03|
--------------------------------------------------------------------------------

Predicate Information (identified by operation id):
---------------------------------------------------

   2 - storage("GENDER"='Female')
       filter("GENDER"='Female')


21 rows selected.
```

Notice the new line at the bottom of the explain plan:

```
 2 - storage("GENDER"='Female').
```

This indicates that the Smart Scans did filter on the query predicate, which accounts for the improved query times we saw. Now this indicates that a Smart Scan may have been used, but it does not guarantee it was. We need to dig into the system and session stats to be sure.

Looking at the data in v$mystat table, we can see how much data is being transferred to the compute nodes. Now we can run the following queries, which will return cumulative results, with all the data and savings that happened over the past queries. In this book, we start with empty stats so that you can easily see the results.

NOTE
The values in this book are not the values you will see in your system.
Your values will differ, but the concepts remain the same.

Running the following query will return many statistics, a few of which we are going to pay very close attention to:

```
SQL> select name, value/1024/1024 as gb from v$statname
natural join v$mystat where name in
(
'physical read total bytes',
'physical write total bytes',
'cell IO uncompressed bytes')
or
name like 'cell physical%'
;


NAME                                                               GB
----------------------------------------------------------------- ---
physical read total bytes                                          0
physical write total bytes                                         0
cell physical IO interconnect bytes                                0
cell physical IO bytes saved during optimized file creation        0
cell physical IO bytes saved during optimized RMAN file restore    0
cell physical IO bytes eligible for predicate offload              0
cell physical IO bytes eligible for smart IOs                      0
cell physical IO bytes saved by columnar cache                     0
cell physical IO bytes saved by storage index                      0
cell physical IO bytes sent directly to DB node to balance CPU     0
cell physical IO interconnect bytes returned by smart scan         0
cell physical write bytes saved by smart file initialization       0
cell IO uncompressed bytes                                         0
cell physical write IO bytes eligible for offload                  0
cell physical write IO host network bytes written during offload   0

15 rows selected.
```

Just as expected, we have very few statistics. We are going to run the queries with offloading on and off and refer to this query after each run. Let's start with offloading off.

We start by flushing the buffer cache of the database:

```
SQL> alter system flush buffer_cache;
System altered.
```

We then turn offloading off:

```
SQL> alter session set cell_offload_processing=false;
Session altered.
```

Now we turn the timings on so we can see how long each query takes:

```
SQL> set timing on
```

Now we run the query:

```
SQL> select /* NO_OFFLOADING */ count(*) from big_census where gender = 'Female';

COUNT(*)
----------
5514752


Elapsed: 00:00:03.84
```

Now we run the statistics query:

```
SQL> select name, value/1024/1024 as gb from v$statname
natural join v$mystat where name in
(
'physical read total bytes',
'physical write total bytes',
'cell IO uncompressed bytes')
or
name like 'cell physical%'
;
```

NAME	GB
physical read total bytes	1.9028244
physical write total bytes	0
cell physical IO interconnect bytes	1.9028244
cell physical IO bytes saved during optimized file creation	0
cell physical IO bytes saved during optimized RMAN file restore	0
cell physical IO bytes eligible for predicate offload	0
cell physical IO bytes eligible for smart IOs	0
cell physical IO bytes saved by columnar cache	0
cell physical IO bytes saved by storage index	0
cell physical IO bytes sent directly to DB node to balance CPU	0
cell physical IO interconnect bytes returned by smart scan	0
cell physical write bytes saved by smart file initialization	0
cell IO uncompressed bytes	0
cell physical write IO bytes eligible for offload	0
cell physical write IO host network bytes written during offload	0

```
15 rows selected.
```

As expected, the entire table was read and returned to the database compute nodes for processing:

```
physical read total bytes              1.9028244
cell physical IO interconnect bytes    1.9028244
```

We'll turn offloading back on and look at the statistics again.

We flush the buffer cache of the database:

```
SQL> alter system flush buffer_cache;
System altered.
```

Turn offloading on:

```
SQL> alter session set cell_offload_processing=true;
Session altered.
```

Now we run the same query as before:

```
SQL> select /* WITH_OFFLOADING */ count(*) from big_census where gender = 'Female';
COUNT(*)
----------
5514752

Elapsed: 00:00:00.28
```

Time to look at the statistics:

```
SQL> select name, value/1024/1024 as gb from v$statname
natural join v$mystat where name in
(
'physical read total bytes',
'physical write total bytes',
'cell IO uncompressed bytes')
or
name like 'cell physical%'
;
```

```
NAME                                                              GB
--------------------------------------------------------------   ----------
physical read total bytes                                        3.81765747
physical write total bytes                                       0
cell physical IO interconnect bytes                              2.01969211
cell physical IO bytes saved during optimized file creation      0
cell physical IO bytes saved during optimized RMAN file restore  0
cell physical IO bytes eligible for predicate offload            1.90031433
cell physical IO bytes eligible for smart IOs                    1.90031433
cell physical IO bytes saved by columnar cache                   0
cell physical IO bytes saved by storage index                    0
cell physical IO bytes sent directly to DB node to balance CPU   0
cell physical IO interconnect bytes returned by smart scan       .102348968
cell physical write bytes saved by smart file initialization     0
```

```
cell IO uncompressed bytes                                    1.90097809
cell physical write IO bytes eligible for offload                      0
cell physical write IO host network bytes written during offload 0
```

```
15 rows selected.
```

If you look at the following statistics, you see that the query was offloaded:

```
cell physical IO bytes eligible for predicate offload    1.90031433
cell physical IO bytes eligible for smart IOs            1.90031433
```

And, more importantly, look at how much data was returned to the database compute nodes:

```
cell physical IO interconnect bytes returned by smart scan    .102348968
```

Where without offloading it returned just shy of 2GB, with offloading it returned only 100MB, a huge savings of 95 percent!

Storage Indexes

Storage indexes can help improve query times as well. Before we run the SQL, we need to create a table that will highlight storage indexes. We run the following SQL to create this table:

```
SQL> create table big_census_si as select * from big_census where rownum = 0;
```

Next, we fill the table with values, but we are going to sort the person_date column with the next SQL statements.
Logging off:

```
SQL> alter table big_census_si nologging;
```

Sorted insert:

```
SQL> insert /*+ append */ into big_census_si select * from big_census order by
person_date;
```

Commit the insert:

```
SQL> commit;
```

Lastly, run stats on the table:

```
SQL> exec dbms_stats.gather_table_stats('book','big_census_si');
```

As with Smart Scans, we can start with a query.
Flush the system:

```
SQL> alter system flush buffer_cache;
System altered.
```

Turn offloading off:

```
SQL> alter session set cell_offload_processing=false;
Session altered.
```

Timings on:

```
SQL> set timing on
```

And run the query:

```
SQL> select /* NO_OFFLOADING */ count(*) from big_census_si where person_date =
to_date('12-NOV-55','DD-MON-RR');

  COUNT(*)
----------
       512

Elapsed: 00:00:03.73
```

Same as before, we run the statistics SQL (I bounced the database so we can get back to clean stats):

```
SQL> select name, value/1024/1024 as gb from v$statname
natural join v$mystat where name in
(
'physical read total bytes',
'physical write total bytes',
'cell IO uncompressed bytes')
or
name like 'cell physical%'
;

NAME                                                              GB
----------------------------------------------------------------- ----------
physical read total bytes                                         2.04419708
physical write total bytes                                        0
cell physical IO interconnect bytes                               2.04419708
cell physical IO bytes saved during optimized file creation       0
cell physical IO bytes saved during optimized RMAN file restore   0
cell physical IO bytes eligible for predicate offload             0
cell physical IO bytes eligible for smart IOs                     0
cell physical IO bytes saved by columnar cache                    0
cell physical IO bytes saved by storage index                    0
cell physical IO bytes sent directly to DB node to balance CPU    0
cell physical IO interconnect bytes returned by smart scan        0
cell physical write bytes saved by smart file initialization      0
cell IO uncompressed bytes                                        0
cell physical write IO bytes eligible for offload                 0
cell physical write IO host network bytes written during offload  0

15 rows selected.
```

As before, we turn offloading back on.
Flush the buffer cache of the database:

```
SQL> alter system flush buffer_cache;
System altered.
```

Offloading on:

```
SQL> alter session set cell_offload_processing=true;
Session altered.
```

And now the query:

```
SQL> select /* WITH_OFFLOADING */ count(*) from big_census_si where person_date =
to_date('12-NOV-55','DD-MON-RR');

  COUNT(*)
----------
       512
```

```
Elapsed: 00:00:00.05
```

That's a massive improvement on time. Running the statistics SQL, we should see some interesting values:

```
SQL> select name, value/1024/1024 as gb from v$statname
natural join v$mystat where name in
(
'physical read total bytes',
'physical write total bytes',
'cell IO uncompressed bytes')
or
name like 'cell physical%'
;
```

```
NAME                                                              GB
----------------------------------------------------------------- ----------
physical read total bytes                                         4.08879852
physical write total bytes                                        0
cell physical IO interconnect bytes                               2.04567031
cell physical IO bytes saved during optimized file creation       0
cell physical IO bytes saved during optimized RMAN file restore   0
cell physical IO bytes eligible for predicate offload             2.04314423
cell physical IO bytes eligible for smart IOs                     2.04314423
cell physical IO bytes saved by columnar cache                    0
cell physical IO bytes saved by storage index                     2.0412674
cell physical IO bytes sent directly to DB node to balance CPU    0
cell physical IO interconnect bytes returned by smart scan        .000016011
cell physical write bytes saved by smart file initialization      0
cell IO uncompressed bytes                                        .001876831
cell physical write IO bytes eligible for offload                 0
cell physical write IO host network bytes written during offload 0
```

```
15 rows selected.
```

To start, we see the following:

```
cell physical IO bytes saved by storage index        2.0412674
```

Using the storage index, we were able to prevent not only sending 2GB over to the database compute nodes to be processed, but it returned the following:

```
cell physical IO interconnect bytes returned by smart scan      .000016011
```

Running some quick math, that's 16KB returned. That's a savings of 99.992 percent. Imagine looking for a particular date in a set of orders across decades? It's the exact same principle we just saw here.

We can also use the storage indexes on date ranges. Let's run a few more queries. This next query will take a look at the average age over a range of dates.

Flush:

```
SQL> alter system flush buffer_cache;
System altered.
```

Turn offloading off:

```
SQL> alter session set cell_offload_processing=false;
Session altered.
```

Timings on:

```
SQL> set timing on
```

And run the query:

```
SQL> select /* NO_OFFLOADING */ avg(age) from big_census_si where person_date
between to_date('10-JAN-75','DD-MON-RR') and to_date('10-JAN-00','DD-MON-RR');
AVG(AGE)
----------
38.6035183
Elapsed: 00:00:04.27
```

And looking at the statistics:

```
SQL> select name, value/1024/1024 as gb from v$statname
natural join v$mystat where name in
(
'physical read total bytes',
'physical write total bytes',
'cell IO uncompressed bytes')
or
name like 'cell physical%'
;
```

NAME	GB
physical read total bytes	6.13440704
physical write total bytes	0
cell physical IO interconnect bytes	4.09127883
cell physical IO bytes saved during optimized file creation	0
cell physical IO bytes saved during optimized RMAN file restore	0
cell physical IO bytes eligible for predicate offload	2.04314423

```
cell physical IO bytes eligible for smart IOs             2.04314423
cell physical IO bytes saved by columnar cache            0
cell physical IO bytes saved by storage index            2.0412674
cell physical IO bytes sent directly to DB node to balance CPU  0
cell physical IO interconnect bytes returned by smart scan   0
cell physical write bytes saved by smart file initialization  0
cell IO uncompressed bytes                               0
cell physical write IO bytes eligible for offload         0
cell physical write IO host network bytes written during offload 0

15 rows selected.
```

The entire table went over to the database compute nodes. We can also see there is no change in the amount of data returned by the Smart Scans. Now turn offloading back on so we can see the savings that storage indexes will give us.

Flush the buffer cache of the database:

```
SQL> alter system flush buffer_cache;
System altered.
```

Offloading on:

```
SQL> alter session set cell_offload_processing=true;
Session altered.
```

And now the query:

```
SQL> select /* NO_OFFLOADING */ avg(age) from big_census_si where person_date
between to_date('10-JAN-75','DD-MON-RR') and to_date('10-JAN-00','DD-MON-RR');
AVG(AGE)
----------
38.6035183
Elapsed: 00:00:00.43
```

The timings tell us we already saved over four seconds; let's see what the statistics say:

```
SQL> select name, value/1024/1024 as gb from v$statname
natural join v$mystat where name in
(
'physical read total bytes',
'physical write total bytes',
'cell IO uncompressed bytes')
or
name like 'cell physical%'
;


NAME                                                             GB
---------------------------------------------------------------- ----------
physical read total bytes                                        8.17884827
physical write total bytes                                       0
cell physical IO interconnect bytes                              4.14134008
cell physical IO bytes saved during optimized file creation      0
cell physical IO bytes saved during optimized RMAN file restore  0
```

```
cell physical IO bytes eligible for predicate offload      4.08628845
cell physical IO bytes eligible for smart IOs              4.08628845
cell physical IO bytes saved by columnar cache             0
cell physical IO bytes saved by storage index             3.34081268
cell physical IO bytes sent directly to DB node to balance CPU  0
cell physical IO interconnect bytes returned by smart scan  .048780262
cell physical write bytes saved by smart file initialization  0
cell IO uncompressed bytes                                 .745727539
cell physical write IO bytes eligible for offload          0
cell physical write IO host network bytes written during offload 0

15 rows selected.
```

Again, we look at the data returned by the Smart Scan:

```
cell physical IO interconnect bytes returned by smart scan   .048780262
```

We see about 48MB out of a 2GB table was returned. Another significant savings.

Summary

With Exadata, it's all about working smarter. Why return the entire table to the database to be processed when we can return only the rows and columns that are of interest to us? That is exactly what we did in this chapter. Using predicate filtering, column projection, and storage indexes, we were able to run our queries faster than with regular storage or dumb networking attached storage. Regardless of the speed of the network for a NAS or how fast local NVMe storage is, returning 16K out of 2GB of table to the database is always going to be faster. You also may have noticed that we never added an index to any of these tables. The Exadata software does it all for us. The storage servers (cells) see the type of data in the columns and create the storage indexes for us; no intervention is needed from the DBA or a developer.

CHAPTER 6

Compression Techniques

U sers of the Exadata Cloud Service (ExaCS)—well, Exadata in general—have enjoyed the ability to use multiple compression techniques for many, many years. Utilizing the CPUs in the storage cells, a lot of the compress/decompress work is done in the back end. In this chapter, we will start with the basics: how Oracle stores data. This is important information, because many of the concepts that you'll learn about compression refer to the basic storage concepts of the Oracle Database. After the overview, we will work with five compression techniques you can use on the ExaCS for various types of data.

Data Blocks, Extents, and Segments

Back in 2000, when I interviewed at Oracle, my brother sent me an Oracle 7 book. He said, "You don't have to read the entire book, but be sure to study the chapters on how Oracle stores data. You need to know cold *data blocks*, *extents*, and *segments*."

As many new people come to use the Oracle Database, especially in the cloud, we never question the basic fundamentals on how the database actually works and how Oracle stores all that data on the disks. This section will go over data blocks, extents, and segments (Figure 6-1), so that when we get to compression techniques, you'll find the concepts much easier to understand.

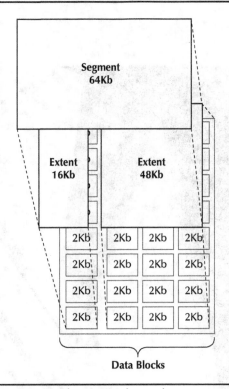

FIGURE 6-1. *Data blocks, extents, and segments hierarchy*

Data Blocks

It all starts with *data blocks*, the smallest logical unit of storage in an Oracle Database. A data block corresponds to a specific number of bytes of physical database space on disk, which is reflected in the database initialization parameter, DB_BLOCK_SIZE. The Exadata Cloud Service uses 8KB as the default block size based on Oracle best practices, and that 8KB performs the best in testing. Changing the default block size is very difficult after the database is created. As a workaround, you can create tablespaces with different block sizes if needed. Remember, on disk, these are physically stored as bytes, and the operating system block size does not have to be the same as the database block size.

So what's in a data block? Figure 6-2 shows the parts of the data block in a physical layout. A data block is made up of the following parts, or components:

- Common and variable header
- Table directory
- Row directory
- Free space
- Row data

Common and Variable Header Sometimes just referred to as the block header, this component does not store user data, but general information about the block, such as address and type. The header may also contain transaction information about current and past transactions performed on the block.

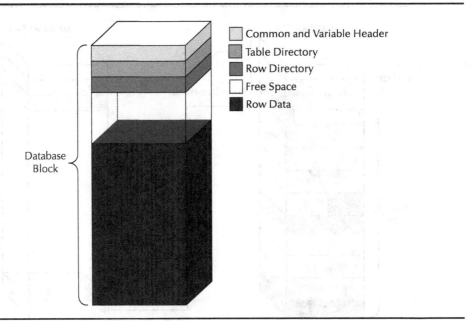

FIGURE 6-2. *Data block layout*

Table Directory   The table directory stores metadata about the tables that store data in this data block. In a common data block situation, multiple tables share a single data block.

Row Directory   This component contains data on the rows that are in the row data component of the data block. The row directory describes the location of the rows—in other words, it has the address of the row in the row data. The Oracle Database reuses space allocated in the row directory once row data is deleted; space is never reclaimed. In some cases, a block is empty of row data but still has space allocated in the row directory. That space will then be reused when new rows are inserted into that block.

Free Space   This is a complex component of a data block. Free space is reserved space in a block where future inserts and updates can be stored. Based on what the table/data is going to be doing, this space can either grow or shrink. The amount of free space in a data block can be managed by the database automatically (via automatic segment-space management) or by specifying a parameter on table creation (PCTFREE).

Incorrect free space management can result in either row chaining or row migration. Row chaining (Figure 6-3), which results when a new row is too large to fit into a single data block, causes the database to store the row in a chain of data blocks.

Row migration (Figure 6-4) occurs when a row that initially fit into a data block no longer fits because of an update and lack of free space. When this happens, the database moves the entire row into a new data block but keeps a pointer in the original data block.

The result of row chaining and row migration is a degradation of performance; the Oracle database must scan not only the initial data block, but other data blocks as well. This adds I/O to the query.

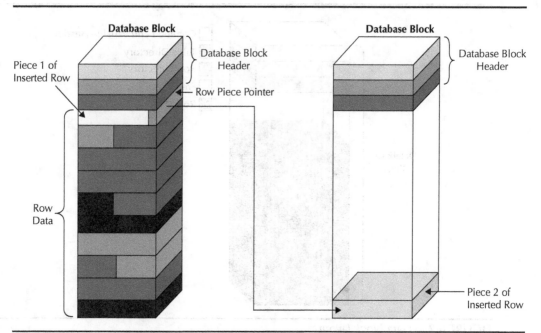

FIGURE 6-3.   *Row chaining*

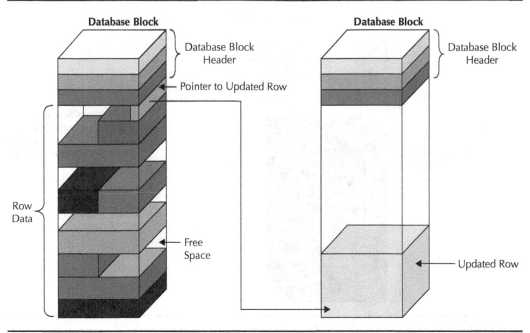

FIGURE 6-4. *Row migration*

As for `PCTFREE`, this table parameter dictates how much free space a data block contains. In Figure 6-5, this data block has been created with a `PCTFREE` of 20 percent.

This leaves 80 percent of the block for data and 20 percent free for updates. New data can be added until the block is 80 percent full, where a new block will be allocated for the table. Adding the `PCTFREE` parameter to a table create statement looks like this:

```
CREATE TABLE MY_COOL_TABLE
(
  COOL_ID    NUMBER,
  COOL_NAME  VARCHAR2(100)
)
PCTFREE    10;
```

Row Data   This section of a data block contains the table data or index data. Each row kept in the row data component has a row format (Figure 6-6).

Just like a data block, the row format is made up of different components—two to be precise: the row header and the column data. The row header contains information about the columns that are in the table in this particular row data piece. If the row spans across blocks, this row header information will reflect this. The column data component actually stores the row data itself. The data is stored in the order the create table statement specified, unless a LONG column is used; those are stored last. Lastly in the row data is a ROWID, a logical structure made up of four components: data object number, relative file number, block number, and row number. From this ROWID, the database can find the row even if it spans across multiple blocks.

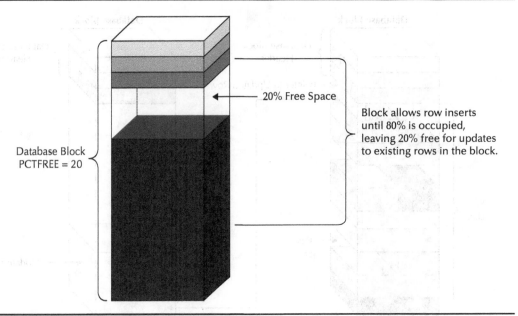

Database Block
PCTFREE = 20

20% Free Space

Block allows row inserts
until 80% is occupied,
leaving 20% free for updates
to existing rows in the block.

FIGURE 6-5. *Free space in a data block*

Extents

Leveling up from data blocks are extents, which are made up of logically contiguous data blocks. When you issue a CREATE TABLE command, an initial extent is created in preparation for data storage (Figure 6-7). Default extent allocations and sizes can be specified in table creation, or, if not specified, the default values of the database will be used.

As extents become full, the database will automatically create another extent to be used. Oracle recommends that you use locally managed tablespaces so that the database can determine the optimal size and placement of additional extents in free space within the tablespace. You can also manually add extents:

```
ALTER TABLE MY_COOL_TABLE ALLOCATE EXTENT;
```

Extents can also be deallocated and returned to a tablespace—for example, when you drop a table, truncate a table, or manually request it via SQL*Plus.

Segments

You know that extents are a logical collection of data blocks; segments are a collection of extents for a logical storage structure, such as a table. Data segments can hold a nonpartitioned table, a partition of a table, or a cluster of tables. An index segment is a segment that contains an index for a table. Segments can also contain large objects (LOBs), including character LOB (CLOB) and binary LOB (BLOB) partitions.

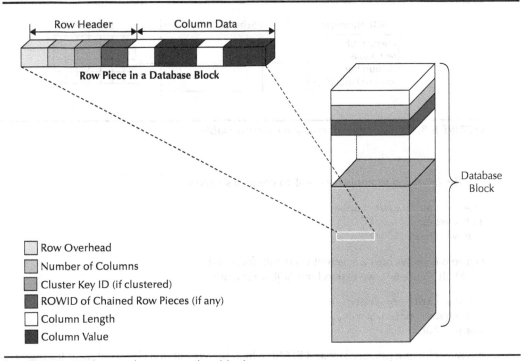

FIGURE 6-6. *The row format in a data block*

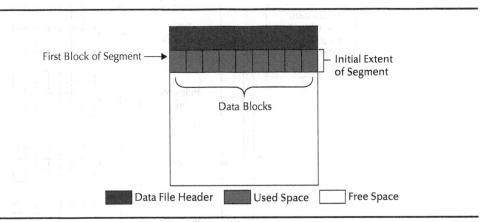

FIGURE 6-7. *Initial extent creation on a create table*

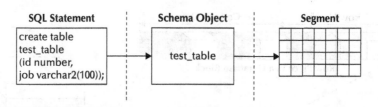

FIGURE 6-8. *Initial segment creation on create table*

The following example uses SQL to create a segment:

```
create table test_table
(id number,
job varchar2(100));
```

Figure 6-8 shows how a segment is created for a table.
With Figure 6-9, we expand our SQL statement:

```
create table my_table
(id number primary key,
image blob);
```

It now includes a primary key and BLOB, which both result in indexes—thus index segments.

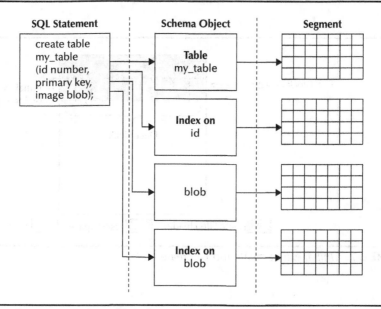

FIGURE 6-9. *Segment creation with indexes*

Finally, Oracle stores undo data in undo segments, which contain data records of transactions so that we can rollback, recover, and have read consistency across our database. Some Flashback database features use undo data as well. Temporary segments are yet another type that are created as temporary workspaces when parsing SQL statements.

Oracle Advanced Row Compression

Advanced Row Compression is an option of Oracle Advanced Compression. This option is included with ExaCS and can be used freely with the service. Advanced Row Compression works by eliminating duplicate values within database blocks, which works even across multiple columns. This compression type is best used for online transaction processing (OLTP) table types; tables with a lot of inserts, updates, and deletes. When compression occurs and duplicate values are removed, the database maintains a symbol table where this metadata is stored. As the duplicate values are removed, they are replaced with a short reference value that points back to the symbol table.

What are the benefits of Advanced Row Compression? To start, it reduces your storage space consumption by a factor of two to four times. So if you start with a 10GB table, use Advanced Row Compression; you may now have a 5GB, or smaller, table. Using Advanced Row Compression also results in a decrease in I/O times because there is less to read.

As they say, there is no such thing as free beer, so where is the hit? Although Advanced Row Compression can help in read operations, it can result in a performance hit on write operations. As you write to the database, the data blocks with uncompressed data are not instantly compressed, but compression happens once the blocks are filled. Uncompressed data queried within these blocks will not benefit from Advanced Row Compression until they are compressed.

Using Advanced Row Compression

Now let's use Advanced Row Compression in our database. For new tables, we can add the compression clause, as follows:

```
create table inventory (
inv_id number,
item_name varchar2(500),
item_description varchar2(2000),
item_number number
)
 row store compress advanced;
```

This SQL creates the inventory table with advanced row compression. Now all data going into this table will be compressed.

NOTE
When working with previous versions of Oracle, the clause used for Advanced Compression was different. This example used the 12c compression clause. In 11gR2, it was:

```
compress for OLTP;
```

Both methods are shown here because you can create 11.2 through 18c databases on the Exadata Cloud Service.

The table is compressed with the following SQL:

```
SQL> select table_name, compression, compress_for from user_tables;
```

And when we run this in our PDB, we see the following:

```
SQL> SELECT table_name, compression, compress_for FROM user_tables where
table_name = 'INVENTORY';
TABLE_NAME              COMPRESS       COMPRESS_FOR
--------------------    --------       ------------
INVENTORY               ENABLED        ADVANCED
```

The Inventory table is enabled for Advanced Row Compression. This is great for new tables, but what about using it on existing tables? With existing tables, we can enable Advanced Compression with the following SQL:

```
SQL> alter table my_table row store compress advanced;
```

This SQL will compress all new data manipulation language (DML) but not compress the existing data. To do that, we can use the following SQL:

```
SQL> alter table my_table move row store compress advanced;
```

Let's see what the savings is with our census table. We need to create a copy first, so we run the following SQL:

```
SQL> create table big_census_arc as select * from big_census;
```

Now, let's check the sizes:

```
SQL> select segment_name, bytes/1024/1024/1024 as gigs from user_segments;
SEGMENT_NAME             GIGS
-----------------------  ----------
BIG_CENSUS               2.0625
BIG_CENSUS_ARC           2.0625
BIG_CENSUS_SI            2.05957031
```

Next, we alter the table and compress it with Advanced Row Compression:

```
SQL> alter table big_census_arc move row store compress advanced;
```

(This SQL may take a few moments to process.)

Quick check: Is it enabled on the table after we just ran that SQL?

```
SQL> select table_name, compression, compress_for from user_tables where
table_name like 'BIG_CENSUS%';;
TABLE_NAME              COMPRESS COMPRESS_FOR
--------------------    -------- -------------------------------
BIG_CENSUS              DISABLED
BIG_CENSUS_SI           DISABLED
BIG_CENSUS_ARC          ENABLED  ADVANCED
```

And we run the size SQL again:

```
SQL> select segment_name, bytes/1024/1024/1024 as gigs from user_segments where
segment_name like 'BIG_CENSUS%';
SEGMENT_NAME             GIGS
------------------------ ----------
BIG_CENSUS               2.0625
BIG_CENSUS_ARC           .59375
BIG_CENSUS_SI            2.05957031
```

Our table went from just over 2GB to about 600MB. That's about a 2.5-times savings of space.

Despite this good news, there are some drawbacks to compressing existing tables. The move statement prevents DML statements against the table while it is running, but we can get around this with online redefinition. Also, all indexes will be invalid after the move, so we will have to rebuild them. With versions 12.2 and later, we remove some of these limitations by using the ONLINE predicate.

Change the previous SQL to the following by adding online:

```
SQL> alter table big_census_arc move row store compress advanced online;
```

This will enable DML to continue on this table, and indexes do not have to be rebuilt.

Advanced Row Compression and Partitioned Tables

Not only can we use Advanced Row Compression on full tables, but we can define compression on individual table partitions. Say we created our census table to be partitioned by half century (our data starts at 1950, so 1950–1974, 1975–1999, 2000–2049):

```
SQL> create table big_census_part
(person_id          number,
age                 number,
workclass           varchar2(100),
education           varchar2(100),
education_id        number,
marital_status      varchar2(100),
occupation          varchar2(100),
house_serv          varchar2(100),
race                varchar2(100),
gender              varchar2(100),
work_hours_week     number,
native_country      varchar2(100),
salary              varchar2(100),
person_date         date)
partition by range (person_date)
(partition person_date_1 values less than (to_date('01/01/1975', 'dd/mm/yyyy'))
tablespace users,
partition person_date_2 values less than (to_date('01/01/2000', 'dd/mm/yyyy'))
tablespace users,
partition person_date_3 values less than (to_date('01/01/2050', 'dd/mm/yyyy'))
tablespace users
);
```

For speed:

```
SQL> alter table big_census_part nologging;
And load the data into the table:
SQL> insert /*+ append */ into big_census_part select * from big_census;
```

Now that we have the table loaded and partitioned, we can see the sizing of the partitions:

```
SQL> column partition_name format a20
SQL> column segment_name format a20
SQL> select segment_name, partition_name, bytes/1024/1024/1024 as gigs from
user_segments where segment_name like 'BIG_CENSUS%';
```

SEGMENT_NAME	PARTITION_NAME	GIGS
BIG_CENSUS_PART	PERSON_DATE_1	.75
BIG_CENSUS_PART	PERSON_DATE_2	.75
BIG_CENSUS_PART	PERSON_DATE_3	.5703125

Using the following SQL, we can change a partition's compression without changing the entire table. We can also use the ONLINE predicate, as we used on the table:

```
SQL> alter table big_census_part move partition person_date_1 row store compress
advanced online;
```

We again see a difference in space:

```
SQL> select segment_name, partition_name, bytes/1024/1024/1024 as gigs from
user_segments where segment_name like 'BIG_CENSUS%';
```

SEGMENT_NAME	PARTITION_NAME	GIGS
BIG_CENSUS_PART	**PERSON_DATE_1**	**.21875**
BIG_CENSUS_PART	PERSON_DATE_2	.75
BIG_CENSUS_PART	PERSON_DATE_3	.5703125

And we can see that the partition is compressed:

```
SQL> select table_name, partition_name, compression, compress_for from
user_tab_partitions where table_name like 'BIG_CENSUS%';
```

TABLE_NAME	PARTITION_NAME	COMPRESS	COMPRESS_FOR
BIG_CENSUS_PART	PERSON_DATE_1	ENABLED	ADVANCED
BIG_CENSUS_PART	PERSON_DATE_2	DISABLED	
BIG_CENSUS_PART	PERSON_DATE_3	DISABLED	

Hybrid Columnar Compression Overview

Hybrid Columnar Compression (HCC) changes the fundamental way the database stores data. Think back to the storage review at the beginning of this chapter—in particular, Figure 6-6. In a traditional database block (no compression) we store the row data one after another in a contiguous pattern.

With Advanced Row Compression, we store the data in the same way, but we replace frequently used values with symbols that we keep in a symbol or lookup table. With HCC, we store the data in columnar format.

What's columnar format? In some databases, data is stored in columns rather than rows. Let's use the EMP table as an example. Just about everyone who has used an Oracle database has done this:

```
SQL> select * from emp;
```

And most of us are familiar with the results.

EMPNO	ENAME	JOB	MGR	HIREDATE	SAL	COMM	DEPTNO
7839	KING	PRESIDENT	-	17-NOV-81	5000	-	10
7698	BLAKE	MANAGER	7839	01-MAY-81	2850	-	30
7782	CLARK	MANAGER	7839	09-JUN-81	2450	-	10
7566	JONES	MANAGER	7839	02-APR-81	2975	-	20
7788	SCOTT	ANALYST	7566	19-APR-87	3000	-	20
7499	ALLEN	SALESMAN	7698	20-FEB-81	1600	300	30
7521	WARD	SALESMAN	7698	22-FEB-81	1250	500	30
7654	MARTIN	SALESMAN	7698	28-SEP-81	1250	1400	30

Break this down to a CSV, and we have this:

```
7839,KING,PRESIDENT, - ,17-NOV-81,5000, - ,10
7499,ALLEN,SALESMAN,7698,20-FEB-81,1600,300,30
7521,WARD,SALESMAN,7698,22-FEB-81,1250,500,30
7654,MARTIN,SALESMAN,7698,28-SEP-81,1250,1400,30
```

But if we store this table in columnar format, it would look like this:

```
7839:001,7499:002,7521:003,7654:004;
KING:001,ALLEN:002,WARD:003,MARTIN:004;
PRESIDENT:001,SALESMAN:002,SALESMAN:003,SALESMAN:004;
```

Many NoSQL databases store information using this method. You can see with this sample that SALESMAN repeats at the column level rather than the row level. That's a key point we will come back to.

With HCC, Oracle combines the best of the columnar format with a traditional Oracle data block, with the result being a *compression unit*. Figure 6-10 illustrates a logical compression unit.

As data is loaded into an HCC-enabled table, Oracle groups column values for rows and compresses them. After compression, they are stored into a compression unit with a single table potentially spanning multiple data blocks, as shown in Figure 6-10. The compression unit header holds information about where the columns are located, similar to the row header when storing a row in an uncompressed table.

Think of it this way: When we load data into the HCC table, Oracle stores it similarly to what's shown in Figure 6-6, but instead of it being just a single column in the column data area, each column area could potentially be thousands of compressed columns. For a table with ten columns, we will still have ten column areas, but data for a single row is *not* stored in each area; instead, data for the entire table (Figure 6-10) is stored in each area. And as in Advanced Row Compression, we can replace like values in the columns with symbols (as with the SALESMAN

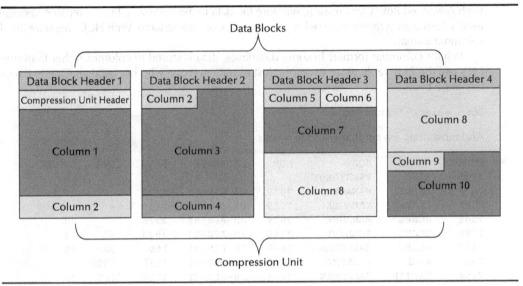

Data Blocks

Compression Unit

FIGURE 6-10. *A compression unit*

value). HCC combines the storage method of columnar format with the traditional Oracle data block row storage—thus it is a hybrid of the two methods.

Using Hybrid Columnar Compression

Before we look at HCC in action, let's talk about the various flavors. HCC comes in two versions, or methods: Warehouse Compression and Archive Compression. Depending on what you need to compress and the state of the data to be compressed, you can choose one over the other.

Warehouse Compression

One of the most popular use cases we see when customers use ExaCS are data warehouses. They use the service to consolidate multiple date stores from on-premises or other clouds into a single database using a variety of methods (such as Data Guard, GoldenGate, and so on). Some customers run into a space issue; with such large amounts of data, they need to be able to fit as much as possible onto their service. This is where Warehouse Compression can help.

Using Warehouse Compression, up to ten times more space can be saved than without using it. So, for example, if your database is 10TB, with Warehouse Compression, it can be compressed to 1TB. As an added benefit, Exadata Smart Scans also enjoy this decrease in space by having to perform fewer I/Os.

When setting a table up for Warehouse Compression, you can choose from two levels of compression, high or low. Where high will save you about ten times the space, it will also demand more of the cell CPU resources on data load. Using low will offer around six times the space savings but will use fewer CPU resources on data load.

Archive Compression

We all have that folder or directory on our computers or laptops that we can't get rid of, because someday we will need to put a file in it. It keeps growing and taking up valuable space that we could otherwise be using for photos of our cat. This is the situation that Archive Compression addresses—it makes room for cat photos.

Archive Compression is best used on historical data that we need to keep around but cannot get rid of yet. Sometimes, based on company or organizational policy, we need to keep historical data for decades (information lifecycle management). As this data piles up, it takes up more and more space that we need to budget and pay for. Archive Compression can reduce the amount of space our data takes up, but at the cost of speed to access. If you have data that is accessed infrequently or only when you need a particular piece of data, such as once a year for historical reasons, this is the compression method for you. As mentioned, query performance will be much slower when going against data that has been archive compressed, but it will be better than going back into the archives or your off-site storage vendor and asking for a particular backup. The other benefit is that if data model changes have occurred, you don't have to worry about restore issues with older archives or tapes.

Just like Warehouse Compression, Archive Compression can be used with two levels: low and high. A tenfold savings can be seen with low and typically 15 times with high, with high also needing more CPU for the load processes.

Examples of HCC Use

Let's create some HCC tables based on our census data and see what level of compression we can achieve.

Warehouse Compression Example

We'll start with Warehouse Compression. The following SQL will create a table for Warehouse Compression, query low:

```
SQL> create table big_census_wh_low as select * from big_census;
```

We check the table size before compression:

```
SQL> select segment_name, bytes/1024/1024/1024 as gigs from user_segments where
segment_name = upper('big_census_wh_low');

SEGMENT_NAME          GIGS
-------------------- ----------
BIG_CENSUS_WH_LOW    2.05175781
```

Next, we alter or move the table and compress it with Warehouse Compression, query low:

```
SQL> alter table big_census_wh_low move column store compress for query low;
```

NOTE
Remember that if you're performing this with a table with existing indexes, all indexes will be invalid after the move, so you will have to rebuild them. With 18c, we can now do this ONLINE with HCC, like we previously did with Advanced Row Compression.

```
SQL> alter table big_census_wh_low move column store compress for query low
online;
```

We run the SQL to check the size again:

```
SQL> select segment_name, bytes/1024/1024/1024 as gigs from user_segments where
segment_name = upper('big_census_wh_low');

SEGMENT_NAME          GIGS
--------------------  ----------
BIG_CENSUS_WH_LOW     .3828125
```

This shows that we have a space savings of about five times, very close to the advertised amount.

Next, we can see what query high gets us. Again, we create a new table:

```
SQL> create table big_census_wh_high as select * from big_census;
```

And check the table size before compression:

```
SQL> select segment_name, bytes/1024/1024/1024 as gigs from user_segments where
segment_name = upper('big_census_wh_high');

SEGMENT_NAME          GIGS
--------------------  ----------
BIG_CENSUS_WH_HIGH    2.0625
```

As with query low, we can move the table and set the compression level to Warehouse Compression, query high:

```
SQL> alter table big_census_wh_high move column store compress for query high
online;
```

And we see the size of the table:

```
SQL> select segment_name, bytes/1024/1024/1024 as gigs from user_segments where
segment_name = upper('big_census_wh_high');

SEGMENT_NAME          GIGS
--------------------  ----------
BIG_CENSUS_WH_HIGH    .1953125
```

This gave us a compression ratio of ten times, exactly the advertised amount (it's actually a bit more than ten times). Not bad at all.

Archive Compression Example

Let's create the two tables using Archive Compression high and low compression algorithms just as we did with Warehouse Compression. To start, we create a new table:

```
SQL> create table big_census_ar_low as select * from big_census;
```

We check the before compression size:

```
SQL> select segment_name, bytes/1024/1024/1024 as gigs from user_segments where
segment_name = upper('big_census_ar_low');

SEGMENT_NAME          GIGS
--------------------  ----------
BIG_CENSUS_AR_LOW     2.0625
```

We alter the table now to use the Archive Compression, archive low:

```
SQL> alter table big_census_ar_low move column store compress for archive low
online;
```

And we see the size of the table:

```
SQL> select segment_name, bytes/1024/1024/1024 as gigs from user_segments where
segment_name = upper('big_census_ar_low');
```

```
SEGMENT_NAME          GIGS
-------------------- ----------
BIG_CENSUS_AR_LOW     .1796875
```

We got a compression ratio of just over ten times. It's now time for archive high. How much can we shrink 2GB down to?

First, we create the table:

```
SQL> create table big_census_ar_high as select * from big_census;
```

Check the table size before compression:

```
SQL> select segment_name, bytes/1024/1024/1024 as gigs from user_segments where
segment_name = upper('big_census_ar_high');
```

```
SEGMENT_NAME          GIGS
-------------------- ----------
BIG_CENSUS_AR_HIGH    2.0625
```

We alter the table now to use the Archive Compression, archive high:

```
SQL> alter table big_census_ar_high move column store compress for archive high
online;
```

And here we go. How small were we able to get this table down to using archive high?

```
SQL> select segment_name, bytes/1024/1024/1024 as gigs from user_segments
where segment_name = upper('big_census_ar_high');
```

```
SEGMENT_NAME          GIGS
-------------------- ----------
BIG_CENSUS_AR_HIGH    .1171875
```

There it is—a compression ratio of more than 18 times. That's pretty amazing if you think about it; the original table was 2GB and it is now a bit over 100MB.

So the next question we can ask is how many compression units are being used per table? Using the PL/SQL package in MOS document 1374169.1, at https://support.oracle.com, we can compute just that. Use the package:

```
WITH blocks AS (
    SELECT COUNT(*) usedblocks, AVG(rowcount) avgrowsperusedblock
    FROM (
        SELECT
            DBMS_ROWID.ROWID_RELATIVE_FNO(ROWID),
            DBMS_ROWID.ROWID_BLOCK_NUMBER(ROWID),
            COUNT(*) rowcount
```

```
        FROM &tablename
        GROUP BY
            DBMS_ROWID.ROWID_RELATIVE_FNO(ROWID),
            DBMS_ROWID.ROWID_BLOCK_NUMBER(ROWID)
        )
)
SELECT extents, blocks allocatedblocks, usedblocks, avgrowsperusedblock
FROM blocks, user_segments
WHERE segment_name = upper('&tablename')
/
```

We can see how many compression units each table is using. Following are the results for all four tables. Pay close attention to USEDBLOCKS, which indicates how many compression units we are using:

```
BIG_CENSUS_WH_LOW
EXTENTS   ALLOCATEDBLOCKS USEDBLOCKS AVGROWSPERUSEDBLOCK
--------  --------------- ---------- -------------------
120       50176           12421      1342.18114
BIG_CENSUS_WH_HIGH
EXTENTS   ALLOCATEDBLOCKS USEDBLOCKS AVGROWSPERUSEDBLOCK
--------  --------------- ---------- -------------------
96        25600           6234       2674.24318
BIG_CENSUS_AR_LOW
EXTENTS   ALLOCATEDBLOCKS USEDBLOCKS AVGROWSPERUSEDBLOCK
--------  --------------- ---------- -------------------
94        23552           2297       7257.82847
BIG_CENSUS_AR_HIGH
EXTENTS   ALLOCATEDBLOCKS USEDBLOCKS AVGROWSPERUSEDBLOCK
--------  --------------- ---------- -------------------
86        15360           597        27925.0117
```

You can see from these values that the greater the compression, the more the average rows per block increases.

HCC and Partitioned Tables

As with Advanced Row Compression, we can use HCC on table partitions. This can be very powerful, because instead of rolling off partitions to tape and storing them offsite, we can use Archive Compression and keep the partitions in the database and online.

Let's use the same table, the BIG_CENSUS_PART table, and archive-compress a different partition. Referring back to the current state:

```
SQL> select table_name, partition_name, compression, compress_for from
user_tab_partitions where table_name = 'BIG_CENSUS_PART';

TABLE_NAME        PARTITION_NAME      COMPRESS COMPRESS_FOR
----------------- ------------------- -------- ---------------
BIG_CENSUS_PART   PERSON_DATE_1       ENABLED  ADVANCED
BIG_CENSUS_PART   PERSON_DATE_2       DISABLED
BIG_CENSUS_PART   PERSON_DATE_3       DISABLED
```

We see that partition 1 is compressed using Advanced Row Compression. Using Archive Compression high, let's compress partition 3—but first, a quick refresher on the sizes of the current partitions:

```
SQL> select segment_name, partition_name, bytes/1024/1024/1024 as gigs from
user_segments where segment_name = 'BIG_CENSUS_PART';
```

SEGMENT_NAME	PARTITION_NAME	GIGS
BIG_CENSUS_PART	PERSON_DATE_1	.21875
BIG_CENSUS_PART	PERSON_DATE_2	.75
BIG_CENSUS_PART	**PERSON_DATE_3**	**.5703125**

And now we compress partition 3, Archive Compression high:

```
SQL> alter table big_census_part move partition person_date_3 column store
compress for archive high online;
```

How much did we save?

```
SQL> select segment_name, partition_name, bytes/1024/1024/1024 as gigs from
user_segments where segment_name = 'BIG_CENSUS_PART';
```

SEGMENT_NAME	PARTITION_NAME	GIGS
BIG_CENSUS_PART	PERSON_DATE_2	.75
BIG_CENSUS_PART	**PERSON_DATE_3**	**.0234375**
BIG_CENSUS_PART	PERSON_DATE_1	.21875

We got a savings of about 28 times.

Lastly, let's take a final look at the partitions and their compression types:

```
SQL> select table_name, partition_name, compression, compress_for from
user_tab_partitions where table_name = 'BIG_CENSUS_PART';
```

TABLE_NAME	PARTITION_NAME	COMPRESS	COMPRESS_FOR
BIG_CENSUS_PART	PERSON_DATE_3	ENABLED	ARCHIVE HIGH
BIG_CENSUS_PART	PERSON_DATE_2	DISABLED	
BIG_CENSUS_PART	PERSON_DATE_1	ENABLED	ADVANCED

HCC Performance

Now that we have created the tables, we can see how fast we can load the data into each type of HCC. We know that we have to load the data with the /*+ append */ hint to ensure a direct path load. Otherwise, the data would not be compressed correctly.

To start, we can truncate the tables we are going to use:

```
SQL> truncate table big_census_wh_low;
Table truncated.
SQL> truncate table big_census_wh_high;
Table truncated.
SQL> truncate table big_census_ar_low;
```

```
Table truncated.
SQL> truncate table big_census_ar_high;
Table truncated.
```

And now let's load each one from the big_census table. We'll turn timings on here as well so we can see how long each load takes. First, turn logging off for all four tables:

```
SQL> alter table big_census_wh_low nologging;
Table altered.
SQL> alter table big_census_wh_high nologging;
Table altered.
SQL> alter table big_census_ar_low nologging;
Table altered.
SQL> alter table big_census_ar_high nologging;
Table altered.
```

And check to see all the tables and how they are compressed:

```
SQL> select table_name, compression, compress_for from user_tables;
TABLE_NAME            COMPRESS COMPRESS_FOR
-------------------- -------- -------------
BIG_CENSUS            DISABLED
BIG_CENSUS_BASELINE   DISABLED
BIG_CENSUS_ARC        ENABLED  ADVANCED
BIG_CENSUS_WH_LOW     ENABLED  QUERY LOW
BIG_CENSUS_WH_HIGH    ENABLED  QUERY HIGH
BIG_CENSUS_AR_LOW     ENABLED  ARCHIVE LOW
BIG_CENSUS_AR_HIGH    ENABLED  ARCHIVE HIGH
```

Now we can start the insert process—but first a baseline. How long does it take in a noncompressed table?

```
SQL> create table big_census_baseline as select * from big_census
where 1 = 2;
SQL> set timing on
SQL> insert /*+ append */ into big_census_baseline select * from
big_census;
16671232 rows created.
Elapsed: 00:00:38.74
SQL> commit;
```

And now into Warehouse Compression low:

```
SQL> set timing on
SQL> insert /*+ append */ into big_census_wh_low select * from big_census;
16671232 rows created.
Elapsed: 00:00:35.58
SQL> commit;
```

And Warehouse Compression high:

```
SQL> insert /*+ append */ into big_census_wh_high select * from big_census;
16671232 rows created.
Elapsed: 00:01:10.07
SQL> commit;
```

Archive Compression low:

```
SQL> insert /*+ append */ into big_census_ar_low select * from big_census;
16671232 rows created.
Elapsed: 00:01:14.34
SQL> commit;
```

Archive Compression high:

```
SQL> insert /*+ append */ into big_census_ar_high select * from big_census;
16671232 rows created.
Elapsed: 00:04:41.42
SQL> commit;
```

Table 6-1 sums it all up.

What about query performance? We can run the same query across all five tables to see the timings of each. Again, we start with the baseline using a query from Chapter 5. We will flush the buffer cache to start:

```
alter system flush buffer_cache;
```

And now the query:

```
SQL> select count(*) from big_census_baseline where gender = 'Female';

COUNT(*)
----------
5514752

Elapsed: 00:00:00.33
```

Warehouse Compression low:

```
SQL> select count(*) from big_census_wh_low where gender = 'Female';

COUNT(*)
----------
5514752

Elapsed: 00:00:00.14
```

Compression Type	Elapsed Time (in Minutes)
None	0:38.74
Warehouse Compression low	0:35.58
Warehouse Compression high	1:10.07
Archive Compression low	1:14.34
Archive Compression high	4:41.42

TABLE 6-1. *Loading Data into Different Compressed Tables*

Warehouse Compression high:

```
SQL> select count(*) from big_census_wh_high where gender = 'Female';

COUNT(*)
----------
5514752

Elapsed: 00:00:00.12
```

Archive Compression low:

```
SQL> select count(*) from big_census_ar_low where gender = 'Female';

COUNT(*)
----------
5514752

Elapsed: 00:00:00.13
```

Archive Compression high:

```
SQL> select count(*) from big_census_ar_high where gender = 'Female';

COUNT(*)
----------
5514752

Elapsed: 00:00:00.20
```

Table 6-2 provides a summary.

These loads and queries give you a better view into the performance differences between all four types of HCC. HCC not only compresses data to save space, but the hit on query times is not as drastic as you might think. Although these are only 2GB tables, these examples do give you a window into the performance you will get on larger tables.

Table 6-3 provides an overview of the compression types used in this chapter.

Compression Type	Elapsed Time (in Seconds)
None	0.33
Warehouse Compression low	0.14
Warehouse Compression high	0.12
archive Compression low	0.13
Archive Compression high	0.20

TABLE 6-2. *Querying Data from Different Compressed Tables*

Table Compression Method	CREATE/ALTER TABLE Syntax	CPU Overhead	(Query/Insert) Usage Notes
Advanced Row Compression	`ROW STORE COMPRESS ADVANCED`	Minimal	Rows inserted with or without using direct-path or array insert. Updated rows are compressed using Advanced Row Compression.
Warehouse Compression low	`COLUMN STORE COMPRESS FOR QUERY LOW`	High	DML performed on this table without using direct-path loads will not be compressed.
Warehouse Compression high	`COLUMN STORE COMPRESS FOR QUERY HIGH`	Highest	DML performed on this table without using direct-path loads will not be compressed.
Archive Compression low	`COLUMN STORE COMPRESS FOR ARCHIVE LOW`	High	DML performed on this table without using direct-path loads will not be compressed.
Archive Compression high	`COLUMN STORE COMPRESS FOR ARCHIVE HIGH`	Highest	DML performed on this table without using direct-path loads will not be compressed.

TABLE 6-3.   *Overview of the Compression Types*

DBMS_COMPRESSION

Oracle 11.2 and later versions include a built-in compression advisor in the form of DBMS_COMPRESSION. Using this package, the database will tell you the best method of compression for a particular table. The Oracle Support Document 1589879.1 contains a nice procedure we can use for our testing. The procedure is as follows (with some modifications):

```
set serveroutput on

declare
    v_blkcnt_cmp pls_integer;
    v_blkcnt_uncmp pls_integer;
    v_row_cmp pls_integer;
    v_row_uncmp pls_integer;
    v_cmp_ratio number;
    v_comptype_str varchar2(60);
begin
    dbms_compression.get_compression_ratio(
        scratchtbsname => upper('&ScratchTBS'),
        ownname => upper('&ownername'),
        objname => upper('&TableName'),
        subobjname => NULL,
        comptype => &compression_type_number,
        subset_numrows=> &num_rows,
        blkcnt_cmp => v_blkcnt_cmp,
        blkcnt_uncmp => v_blkcnt_uncmp,
        row_cmp => v_row_cmp,
        row_uncmp => v_row_uncmp,
```

```
               cmp_ratio => v_cmp_ratio,
               comptype_str => v_comptype_str );

dbms_output.put_line('.');
dbms_output.put_line('OUTPUT: ');
dbms_output.put_line('Estimated Compression Ratio: '||to_char(v_cmp_ratio));
dbms_output.put_line('Blocks used by compressed sample: '||to_char(v_blkcnt_cmp));
dbms_output.put_line('Blocks used by uncompressed sample: '||to_char(v_blkcnt_uncmp));
dbms_output.put_line('Rows in a block in compressed sample: '||to_char(v_row_cmp));
dbms_output.put_line('Rows in a block in uncompressed sample: '||to_char(v_row_uncmp));
end;
/
```

We can create a script with this procedure or just run it from SQL*Plus. I quickly created a script so that the next few code sections would be easier to read.

The procedure takes in five values:

```
        scratchtbsname => upper('&ScratchTBS'),
        ownname => upper('&ownername'),
        objname => upper('&TableName'),
        comptype => &compression_type_number,
        subset_numrows=> &num_rows,
```

The first one is tablespace—more on this one in a minute. The next variable is the owner name or the table owner, and the third is the object name. In our case, this will be the name of the table, big_census.

The compression type, or `&compression_type_number`, takes in a number that corresponds to a compression type. We will use the following values for this:

Compression Type	Compression Type Number	Description
COMP_ADVANCED	2	Advanced Compression level
COMP_QUERY_HIGH	4	Warehouse Compression high
COMP_QUERY_LOW	8	Warehouse Compression low
COMP_ARCHIVE_HIGH	16	Archive Compression high
COMP_ARCHIVE_LOW	32	Archive Compression low

The fifth variable is number of rows. To perform this procedure for HCC, we need at the minimum one million rows—thus we need to use 1000000 for this value.

With tablespace, the procedure itself will use as much space as the table you are looking to compress, so you need to ensure that you have enough space in the tablespace you want to use. You can also use a staging temporary tablespace if you have the ability/roles to create a new one. This is not a traditional temp tablespace, but just a temporary workspace. If you want to create one, you can use the following SQL:

```
create tablespace workspace_temp_compress_tbs
   datafile '+datac3/hrcdb/hrpdb/datafile/mytablespace5.dbf'
      size 10m
      reuse
      autoextend on next 10m maxsize 200m;
```

To get the data file location, we can use the following SQL:

```
SQL> select tablespace_name,file_name from sys.dba_data_files;
```

TABLESPACE_NAME	FILE_NAME
SYSTEM	+DATAC1/HRPROD/HRPDB/DATAFILE/system.268.960794695
SYSAUX	+DATAC1/HRPROD/HRPDB/DATAFILE/sysaux.269.960794695
UNDOTBS1	+DATAC1/HRPROD/HRPDB/DATAFILE/undotbs1.270.960794695
UNDO_2	+DATAC1/HRPROD/HRPDB/DATAFILE/undo_2.272.960794723
USERS	+DATAC1/HRPROD/HRPDB/DATAFILE/users.273.960794737

This will return the FILE_NAME location we can use in the create tablespace SQL.

Now that we have the tablespace created, we can run the procedure. Again, I put it into SQL script so the following code will reflect that. The variables will be workspace_temp_compress_tbs for the table space, book for the owner, and big_census for the table or object name. The fourth variable will be 4 for Warehouse Compression high and number of rows is 1000000 (one million).

```
SQL> @compress.sql
Enter value for scratchtbs: temp_compress_tbs
old   10:           scratchtbsname => upper('&ScratchTBS'),
new   10:           scratchtbsname => upper('temp_compress_tbs'),
Enter value for ownername: book
old   11:           ownname => upper('&ownername'),
new   11:           ownname => upper('book'),
Enter value for tablename: big_census
old   12:           objname => upper('&TableName'),
new   12:           objname => upper('big_census'),
Enter value for compression_type_number: 4
old   14:           comptype => &compression_type_number,
new   14:           comptype => 4,
Enter value for num_rows: 1000000
old   15:           subset_numrows=> &num_rows,
new   15:           subset_numrows=> 1000000,
Compression Advisor self-check validation successful. select count(*) on both
Uncompressed and EHCC Compressed format = 1000001 rows
.
OUTPUT:
Estimated Compression Ratio: 10.9
Blocks used by compressed sample: 1472
Blocks used by uncompressed sample: 16063
Rows in a block in compressed sample: 679
Rows in a block in uncompressed sample: 62
```

Using only 1 million rows from a 16-million-row table, the ratio is actually quite close to what we saw when we compressed the table previously in the chapter. Let's see if it can estimate the ratio we saw with Archive Compression high (18 times):

```
SQL> @compress.sql
Enter value for scratchtbs: temp_compress_tbs
old   10:           scratchtbsname => upper('&ScratchTBS'),
```

```
new  10:                 scratchtbsname => upper('temp_compress_tbs'),
Enter value for ownername: book
old  11:                 ownname => upper('&ownername'),
new  11:                 ownname => upper('book'),
Enter value for tablename: big_census
old  12:                 objname => upper('&TableName'),
new  12:                 objname => upper('big_census'),
Enter value for compression_type_number: 16
old  14:                 comptype => &compression_type_number,
new  14:                 comptype => 16,
Enter value for num_rows: 1000000
old  15:                 subset_numrows=> &num_rows,
new  15:                 subset_numrows=> 1000000,
Compression Advisor self-check validation successful. select count(*) on both
Uncompressed and EHCC Compressed format = 1000001 rows
.
OUTPUT:
Estimated Compression Ratio: 18
Blocks used by compressed sample: 889
Blocks used by uncompressed sample: 16062
Rows in a block in compressed sample: 1125
Rows in a block in uncompressed sample: 62
```

Uncanny.

Compression Tips

You need to be aware of a few issues when using HCC on your data:

- HCC is not supported for long data types. Not many people still use this data type, but if you use the Oracle E-Business Suite, you have long data types.

- HCC is used for relational data and not unstructured data. CLOBs and BLOBs are best stored in Oracle SecureFiles and compressed using Advanced Compression.

- Not that this is an issue for this book, but HCC is available only on Exadata Storage and ZFS Storage Appliances. With an Exadata Cloud Service, obviously, you get HCC and the benefits of the smart Exadata software and the extra CPU horsepower on the cells to help with compression and decompression. With a ZFS Storage Appliance, you get only HCC.

- HCC is best used on data that is being queried and not being intensively updated and deleted. Advanced Row Compression is better suited for volatile data experiencing many DML operations.

Summary

Today, so much data is being collected that space has become a concern. As we use the Exadata Cloud Service for a data warehouse, data lake, or a consolidation platform, we need to be able to fit as much data on to our disks as possible. Advanced Row Compression can help with volatile data, or data that is constantly changing. As for data that is mainly static, at rest, or archived, we can use the four flavors of HCC to reach compression ratios of better than 28 times.

CHAPTER 7

Exadata Resource Management

One of the key features of the Exadata Cloud Service (ExaCS) is the ability to create multiple databases of different versions all on the same service or platform. Having mixed workloads on a single service does incorporate some challenges, however—in particular, deciding what database or workload gets what resources. Fortunately, the Exadata Cloud Service includes features that help with resource management, and using the included tools, you can decide which workloads get which resources across the entire service.

This chapter covers three features of ExaCS that deal with resource management: I/O Resource Manager (IORM), Database Resource Manager, and Instance Caging. These three utilities will help you include mixed workloads on the service while dictating what database gets what resources.

To help you better understand how and where these utilities work with ExaCS, examine Figure 7-1.

Database Resource Manager and Instance Caging are set in the database instances themselves. We can set these limits and priorities via PL/SQL or from Enterprise Manager. IORM is set at the Exadata Storage Server level and can be set via the Cloud Service UI, ExaCLI, or a Representational State Transfer (REST) service. With an Exadata Database Machine on-premises, IORM is set at the storage server level using the CellCLI utility in the Exadata Cloud Service, which we will go over later in Chapter 9 when discussing ExaCLI.

I/O Resource Manager

We briefly touched on IORM in Chapter 3, but here we will see how it works in the Exadata Cloud Service and how to set it up for mixed workloads. To start, let's look at what IORM is and how it works.

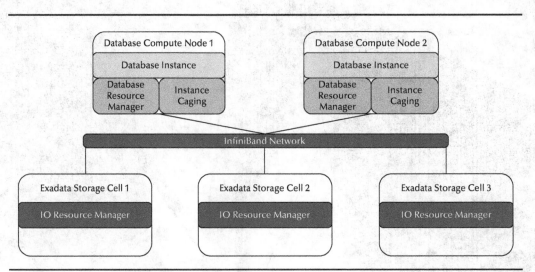

FIGURE 7-1. *Resource management in the Exadata Cloud Service*

Consider the following scenario: Two databases are running on an Exadata Cloud Service. One is a financial database and the other is an HR database for the same company/organization. When the storage servers are underutilized, I/O requests from both databases are serviced immediately; there's no need for resource management because neither database is affecting the performance of the other. Now let's assume it's the close of a quarter or month, and the financial database needs to be the star of the service, getting priority over the HR database. Here, the HR database could potentially affect the I/O resources from the financial database, so we need to have IORM prioritize requests. This is called an *interdatabase resource plan* because it is shared across multiple databases.

As the storage servers become inundated with requests from the financial database, the HR database's query requests get queued until there are resources available to complete those requests. IORM ensures that the financial database's performance is never hindered by the HR database.

Configuring IORM in ExaCS

ExaCS enables you to set shares of database I/O resources to individual databases using the UI, a REST service, or ExaCLI. The share system for IORM was introduced in Exadata Cell Software Version 11.2.3.1. This feature enables you to assign a certain number of shares to a particular database to give it priority over others. The shares range from 1 to 32, with 32 being the greatest priority. If you do not alter IORM in ExaCS, all databases get a share of 1 by default.

Let's return to our financial and HR database scenario. To expand a bit on this, we can add a third database, a test or development database. We know the financial database is the most important one, with the HR coming in second, and the test database in third. We need to distribute shares to each of these databases accordingly. The financial database gets a 10 with HR getting a 5. So, not only is the financial database the number one priority, but it also gets the majority of the I/O resources. The test database gets a 2, putting it slightly above the default of 1. If we use the equation $(d / (a + b + c)) \times 100$, we can see the total percentages for our shares. In this equation, d represents the database shares we want to find the percentage of, with a, b, and c being the shares themselves. So, in our example, a will be the financial database. It has 10 shares and the other databases have 5 and 2. Our equation would now look like the following:

$$(10 / (10 + 5 + 2)) \times 100 = 58.8\%$$

This gives the financial database almost 60 percent of the I/O resources. Once we do the math, we may want to increase the shares to make it more of a priority. If we set the shares to 20, our equation yields the following:

$$(20 / (20 + 5 + 2)) \times 100 = 74\%$$

This grants the financial database 74 percent of the I/O resources.

With setting these shares for the databases, not only do we prioritize I/O resources, but the amount of flash storage accessible on the storage cells is also prioritized with this implementation in ExaCS. The more shares given, the more flash storage the database can use.

Setting IORM in Oracle Cloud Infrastructure Classic

In Oracle Cloud Infrastructure Classic (OCI-C), we can set IORM in the UI. On the database console page (shown in Figure 7-2), to the right of each database name is a pop-up menu defined by four horizontal lines (Figure 7-3).

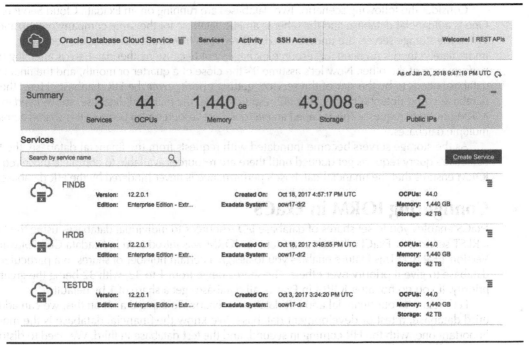

FIGURE 7-2. *The database console page*

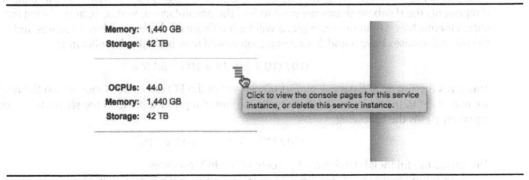

FIGURE 7-3. *Selecting the pop-up menu*

We click the pop-up menu to reveal the Update Exadata IORM option (Figure 7-4).

We click that option to bring up the Exadata IORM modal window. Here we can set the shares of the databases, as discussed in the previous section. The Financial database, or FINDB, will get 20; HRDB will get 5; and the TESTDB will get 2. Once we set the shares (Figure 7-5) we click Save.

We can also set the database shares using the IORM REST service. There are two REST services you can use with IORM: Set IORM Shares and View IORM Shares.

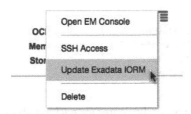

FIGURE 7-4. *Selecting the Update Exadata IORM pop-up menu option*

NOTE
In Chapter 4, we went over using the REST APIs with OCI-C, so if you need a quick refresher, please reference that chapter.

The first REST service we will look at with IORM is Set IORM Shares. Using the same credentials and format we used in Chapter 4, the Set IORM Shares REST call would look like the following:

```
curl -i -X PUT --cacert /Users/btspendo/cacert.pem
-u brian.spendolini@oracle.com:Awes0mePassw0rd -H
"X-ID-TENANT-NAME:jetdogresearch" -H "Content-Type:application/json" -d
'{"DBPlan":[
{"dbname":"FINDB","share":"20"},
{"dbname":"HRDB","share":"5"},
{"dbname":"TESTDB","share":"2"},
{"dbname":"default","share":"1"}
]}' https://dbaas.oraclecloud.com/paas/service/dbcs/api/v1.1/instances/jetdogresearch
/findb/iorm
```

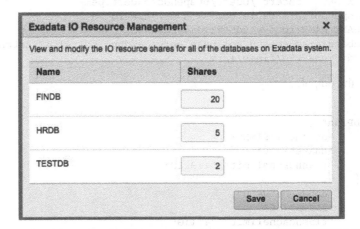

FIGURE 7-5. *Setting shares in the Exadata IORM modal window*

Taking a closer look at this API, we can see a JSON string with values for DBPlan:

```
'{"DBPlan":[
    {"dbname":"FINDB","share":"20"},
    {"dbname":"HRDB","share":"5"},
    {"dbname":"TESTDB","share":"2"},
    {"dbname":"default","share":"1"}
]}'
```

Just as we did in the UI, we set the shares for each database in our service in the JSON string. We can also set the default shares as well in the REST API. Also, in the REST API we can see the endpoint contains one of our database service names. This URL uses IDM-based authentication:

```
https://dbaas.oraclecloud.com/paas/service/dbcs/api/v1.1/instances/jetdogresearch
/findb/iorm
```

This next URL uses IDCS-based authentication:

```
https://psm.us.oraclecloud.com/paas/service/dbcs/api/v1.1/instances/idcs-
e48d50317djdjhd8923d/findb/iorm
```

In this example, we use the findb database. Remember that you must use a database service name when using this REST API—here jetdogresearch is the identity domain.

Using the View IORM Shares REST API is similar to the Set IORM Shares API. Again, using the same structure for ID domain and user credentials as the previous example, the View IORM Shares REST call would look like the following for an IDM based account:

```
curl -i -X GET --cacert /Users/btspendo/cacert.pem
-u brian.spendolini@oracle.com:AwesOmePasswOrd -H
"X-ID-TENANT-NAME:jetdogresearch"
https://dbaas.oraclecloud.com/paas/service/dbcs/api/v1.1/instances/jetdogresearch
/findb/iorm
```

This REST call uses IDCS-based authentication:

```
curl -i -X GET --cacert /Users/btspendo/cacert.pem
-u brian.spendolini@oracle.com:AwesOmePasswOrd -H
"X-ID-TENANT-NAME:idcs-e48d50317djdjhd8923d"
https://dbaas.oraclecloud.com/paas/service/dbcs/api/v1.1/instances/idcs-
e48d50317djdjhd8923d/findb/iorm
```

And here's the output:

```
{
    "DbPlan":[{
        "dbname":"FINDB",
        "share":"20",
        "flashcachelimit":"11922G"
    },{
        "dbname":"HRDB",
        "share":"5",
        "flashcachelimit":"4111G"
```

```
     }, {
           "dbname":"TESTDB",
           "share":"2",
           "flashcachelimit":"1644G"
     }, {
           "dbname":"default",
           "share":"1",
           "flashcachelimit":"851G"
     }]
}
```

Again, the REST API brings back a bit more information—mainly the `flashcachelimit` parameter. This is very useful information that lets us see exactly how much flash cache a database can use.

Setting IORM in the Oracle Cloud Infrastructure

At the time of writing this book, the ability to set IORM shares was not available in the Exadata Cloud Service in OCI. This functionality is planned in the near future and should function similar to how it does in OCI-C. For now, we can use ExaCLI to set IORM. There's more on using ExaCLI in Chapter 9.

Storage Cells and IORM

So, what is happening in the back end on the storage servers when we set the shares for the database? Here is what it's actually doing: It's using the command line interface (CLI) tool CellCLI to set the IORM profiles for each database with the following command (more on ExaCLI/CellCLI in Chapter 9):

```
CellCLI> ALTER IORMPLAN
         dbPlan=(
                   (name=findb, share=20, flashcachelimit=11922G),
                   (name=hrdb, share=5, flashcachelimit=4111G),
                   (name=testdb, share=2, flashcachelimit=1644G),
                   (name=default, share=1, flashcachelimit=851G))
```

Database Resource Manager

Database Resource Manager (DBRM) was introduced in Oracle Database Enterprise Edition Version 8i. It's a method for controlling resources from within your databases—resources such as CPU, Program Global Area (PGA) resources, Exadata I/O, parallel queries, and active sessions. This type of resource management from within the database is also referred to as intradatabase resource management.

First, let's quickly go over what DBRM is and how it's structured. We'll just scratch the surface of DBRM here, so if you would like a more in-depth look, refer to the latest Database Administrator's Guide, Resource Management section.

DBRM is made up of three major parts: resource consumer groups, resource plan directives, and resource plans.

Resource Consumer Groups

Resource consumer groups, or simply consumer groups, are a collection of user sessions that are grouped together based on their processing requirements. The database will automatically map a user session to a consumer group based on user-defined rules. A user with the correct role or an application can dynamically move a session from one consumer group to another; this is very useful for controlling sessions and resources.

With every Oracle Database, two consumer groups are always present:

- **SYS_GROUP** Included for all sessions created by the SYS or SYSTEM user account
- **OTHER_GROUPS** Contains all sessions that have not been assigned a consumer group

With ExaCS, or any Exadata service, are three other groups that come out of the box:

- **ETL_GROUP** Used for ETL (extract, transform, and load) jobs
- **DSS_GROUP** Used for noncritical DSS (decision support system) queries
- **DSS_CRITICAL_GROUP** Used for critical/important DSS queries

Resource Plan Directives

Resource plan directives dictate what resources a consumer group can utilize for the currently active resource plan. A single resource plan directive can reference one resource consumer group. A directive can control or limit resources allocated to a consumer group, resources such as CPU or number of active sessions, as noted previously in this chapter. Note that you cannot have multiple directives referencing the same resource consumer group in a current active plan.

Resource Plans

Resource plans specify how resources are allocated to resource consumer groups. Think of a resource plan as a container or box where we can add consumer groups and dictate how they utilize resources (resource plan directives), creating a parent-child relationship between a resource plan and its resource plan directives. We can create as many resource plans as we want, but only one can be active at a time. When creating custom resource plans, we must ensure that we include the OTHER_GROUPS resource consumer group.

With Exadata, we have two pre-created resource plans:

- **DSS_PLAN** Prioritizes DSS-related queries
- **ETL_CRITICAL_PLAN** Prioritizes ETL workloads

Putting It All Together

Now that we have discussed the parts of Resource Manager, let's put them together into a simple example before we focus on Exadata and multitenancy. For this example, we'll use the same resources we used for the IORM example—three databases: the financial, the HR, and the test. We'll work with the financial database here, because DBRM is intradatabase, a defining resource within a single database.

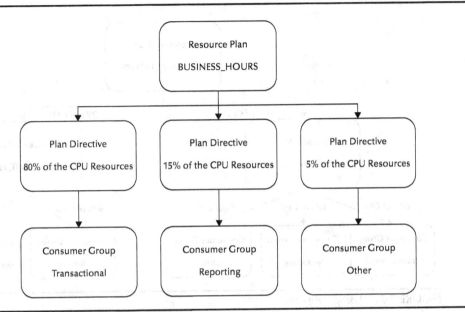

FIGURE 7-6. *Database Resource Manager component relationships*

With our financial database, let's assume we have three groups of users or sessions: transactional, reporting, and other. Being a financial database, the transactional sessions need to be of the highest priority, with reporting as secondary, and other as the least important. The resource plan for this grouping will be called BUSINESS_HOURS, a name that will become more apparent as we go through this example. Within this resource plan, we can set up the plan directives that allocate CPU resources for each group. Transactions get 80 percent of the CPU, reporting gets 15 percent, and other gets 5 percent. Figure 7-6 shows that our resource consumer groups are transactional, reporting, and other. Our directives are 80 percent of the CPU, 15 percent, and 5 percent. Lastly, this is all under the BUSINESS_HOURS resource plan.

We can also have an AFTER_HOURS resource plan that kicks in at, say, 9 P.M. every night. This plan can shift resources to the reporting group so that we can run reports to be delivered in the morning while there are few OLTP transactions going on. We then shift to the BUSINESS_HOURS plan at 6 A.M. the next morning. Lastly, we can have a WEEKEND_HOURS resource plan that shifts the resources to yet another group for weekend activities. Plans can also nest within each other. These subplans pull from the resource plan above it. So back to our example, if this BUSINESS_HOURS plan were just one of many, it could roll up to the COMPANY_HOURS plan. The COMPANY_HOURS plan gives 80 percent of the resources to BUSINESS_HOURS, while the other 20 percent is given to the DEVELOPMENT_HOURS plan used for the development organization. This use of subplans would look like Figure 7-7.

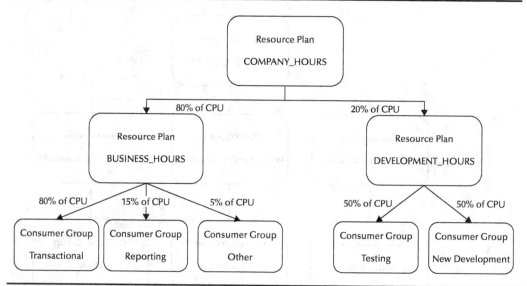

FIGURE 7-7. *Using subplans*

Database Resource Manager and Multitenancy

With Oracle Database versions 12.1 and later, multitenancy offers the ability to have multiple pluggable databases (PDBs) under a single container database (CDB). DBRM can also be used with multitenancy. As you would expect, DBRM can manage resources at both the CDB and PDB level. At the CDB level, DBRM will manage the resources allocated to each of the PDBs in a single CDB. At the PDB level, DBRM will manage the resources within that particular PDB. You can quickly see the parent-child relationship with DBRM and the CDB/PDB architecture. Just as we saw with DBRM plans at the database level, with multitenancy, some PDBs will be more important than others, so the ability to prioritize resources is a key feature. DBRM can control the following at the CDB level:

- Prioritization of multiple PDBs in a single CDB
- CPU usage of a single PDB
- Number of parallel execution servers that a single PDB can use
- Maximum amount of memory a single PDB can use
- Set performance profiles for different sets of PDBs

A performance profile can specify shares of system resources, the CPU, and the number of parallel execution servers for a single or set of PDBs in a CDB. PDB performance profiles are useful because we can group multiple PDBs into a single profile rather than having to place individual Resource Manager plans on each one. Because Exadata is a consolidation platform, imagine a service with 100 PDBs; being able to group many PDBs into a single performance profile saves time and effort, and it makes management easier. The PDB performance profiles let you do the following:

- Limit the resource usage of sessions connected to a single PDB
- Limit the I/O
- Ease the monitoring of resource usage in one or multiple PDBs

Just as we saw earlier with database resource plans, we have CDB resource plans. And as a resource plan allocated resources to a particular database based on resource plan directives, a CDB resource plan does the same, but upon PDBs with resource plan directives. The plans can be put on a single PDB or multiple PDBs using a PDB performance profile.

Configuring DBRM in the Exadata Cloud Service

Now that you understand how DBRM is structured, let's configure it in the Exadata Cloud Service. We will continue to use our HRCDB and PDB created in Chapter 3. Oracle's strategic plan is to move to a CDB/PDB architecture for all databases—in fact, in version 12.2, the ability to create non-CDB databases, while present, is deprecated. With that said, the following section will be using DBRM with CDBs and PDBs.

We next need to generate some load so we can see how the PDB acts before we put a Resource Manager profile upon it. A quick and simple method for load generation is to use Dominic Giles's SwingBench. This tool will not only load your database with sample data but will generate a load with graphs and charts telling you exactly what is going on. For this part of the book, SwingBench will be installed on an Infrastructure as a Service (IaaS) virtual machine (VM) image in the same virtual cloud network (VCN) as our Exadata Cloud Service. This makes contacting the service easy, and we can VNC into the Linux box to see the GUI of SwingBench. We will also use the sample Order Entry data that SwingBench provides.

NOTE
You'll find more information on SwingBench and how to use it at
http://dominicgiles.com/swingbench.html.

Prerequisites for Using Resource Manager with a CDB

Before we can create our CDB resource plans, we have to be sure we can use the Resource Manager packages and procedures. To start, we need to have the system privilege ADMINISTER_RESOURCE_MANAGER to, well, administer the Resource Manager. Once we have this system privilege, we can then execute all of the procedures in the DBMS_RESOURCE_MANAGER PL/SQL package. By default, this privilege (with the ADMIN option) is granted to database administrators through the DBA role. If we want to grant it to other users, we can use DBMS_RESOURCE_MANAGER_PRIVS.GRANT_SYSTEM_PRIVILEGE. Here's an example:

```
BEGIN
DBMS_RESOURCE_MANAGER_PRIVS.GRANT_SYSTEM_PRIVILEGE (
  grantee_name => 'book',
  privilege_name => 'ADMINISTER_RESOURCE_MANAGER',
  admin_option => FALSE);
END;
/
```

The `admin_option` enables users to grant this privilege to other users.

In the previous example, the user book is granted the privilege to use the DBMS_RESOURCE_MANAGER PL/SQL packages but not to grant this privilege to others. We can revoke this privilege using the REVOKE_SYSTEM_PRVILEGE procedure as follows:

```
BEGIN
    DBMS_RESOURCE_MANAGER_PRIVS.REVOKE_SYSTEM_PRIVILEGE ('book');
END;
/
```

Creating a CDB Resource Plan

As discussed previously, a CDB resource plan dictates what resources a PDB will get using a set of resource plan directives. The CDB resource plan forms a parent-child relationship with its directives. These directives can control CPU and parallel execution servers in a single or a set of PDBs. We can allocate shares to PDBs using directives much like we did with IORM. The shares are allocated using the CREATE_CDB_PLAN_DIRECTIVE procedure in the DBMS_RESOURCE_MANAGER package. In this procedure, we assign the directive a share value. This value is used when the CDB is allocating resources across all PDBs. Our CDB has three PDBs: the HRPDB, the TESTPDB, and the SALESPDB.

We can assign shares to each of them based on priority: 3 for the HRPDB, 2 for the TESTPDB, and 5 for the SALESPDB, giving us a total of 10. The SALESPDB is guaranteed 50 percent, or 5/10 ((5/10) × 100 = 50%) of the resources. The HRPDB is going to get 3/10 ((3/10) × 100 = 30%) and the TESTPDB 2/10 ((2/10) × 100 = 20%). With this said, if the SALES and HR PDBs are not active, the TESTPDB can consume more resources than allocated. If the SALES or HR PDB demand resources, they will be taken away from the TESTPDB. We also have the option of setting the utilization_limit and parallel_server_limit via the CDB resource plan. These limits will constrain the overall resources a PDB can use at any time, with utilization_limit controlling system resources and parallel_server_limit controlling parallel execution servers. Both settings can have a maximum value of 100, allowing all resources to be used, and a minimum of 1. The numbers correspond to the percentage of our CDB's available CPU resources that will be available to the PDBs.

Now that we know the values we want to set, we can start creating the plan. The entire process consists of the following steps:

1. Create the pending area. Think of the pending area as a worksheet where we will create the plans without affecting the existing active plans.

2. Create the CDB resource plan procedure.

3. Create directives for the PDBs.

4. Validate and submit the pending area.

To create our worksheet or pending area, we run the following SQL:

```
SQL> exec DBMS_RESOURCE_MANAGER.CREATE_PENDING_AREA();
```

Next, we create a CDB resource plan named my_cdb_plan using the CREATE_CDB_PLAN procedure:

```
BEGIN
  DBMS_RESOURCE_MANAGER.CREATE_CDB_PLAN(
    plan    => 'my_cdb_plan',
    comment => 'My CDB resource plan');
END;
/
```

Now, we create the directives for the CDB resource plan. From this example, we have three PDBs: SALESPDB, HRPDB, and TESTPDB. The shares we are assigning are 5, 3, and 2, respectively. Also, to ensure our SALESPDB gets the most resources when needed, we will set the `utilization_limit` and `parallel_server_limit` to 100, 70 for HRPDB, and 50 for the TESTPDB. We use the following SQL for creating the directives:

```
BEGIN
  DBMS_RESOURCE_MANAGER.CREATE_CDB_PLAN_DIRECTIVE(
    plan                  => 'my_cdb_plan',
    pluggable_database    => 'SALESPDB',
    shares                => 5,
    utilization_limit     => 100,
    parallel_server_limit => 100);
END;
/


BEGIN
  DBMS_RESOURCE_MANAGER.CREATE_CDB_PLAN_DIRECTIVE(
    plan                  => 'my_cdb_plan',
    pluggable_database    => 'HRPDB',
    shares                => 3,
    utilization_limit     => 70,
    parallel_server_limit => 70);
END;
/


BEGIN
  DBMS_RESOURCE_MANAGER.CREATE_CDB_PLAN_DIRECTIVE(
    plan                  => 'my_cdb_plan',
    pluggable_database    => 'TESTPDB',
    shares                => 2,
    utilization_limit     => 50,
    parallel_server_limit => 50);
END;
/
```

Any other PDBs we create at a later time will use the default directive. We can set those parameters with this SQL:

```
BEGIN
  DBMS_RESOURCE_MANAGER.UPDATE_CDB_DEFAULT_DIRECTIVE(
    plan                      => 'my_cdb_plan',
    new_shares                => 1,
    new_utilization_limit     => 30,
    new_parallel_server_limit => 30);
END;
/
```

This default plan ensures that any new PDBs will get resources, but not enough to affect the SALESPDB. If a new PDB warrants more resources, we can always give it a new directive. We have one more "default" directive: the AUTOTASK directive. This directive applies to automatic maintenance tasks or operations. These tasks are run in a maintenance window that we can define with the Oracle Scheduler. Tasks performed in these maintenance windows are Automatic

Optimizer Statistics Collection, Automatic Segment Advisor, Automatic SQL Tuning Advisor, and the SQL Plan Management (SPM) Evolve Advisor. We can set that directive with the following PL/SQL:

```
BEGIN
  DBMS_RESOURCE_MANAGER.UPDATE_CDB_AUTOTASK_DIRECTIVE(
    plan                       => 'my_cdb_plan',
    new_shares                 => 1,
    new_utilization_limit      => 70,
    new_parallel_server_limit  => 70);
END;
/
```

Lastly, we validate our pending area:

```
SQL> exec DBMS_RESOURCE_MANAGER.VALIDATE_PENDING_AREA();
```

If the plan validates successfully, we finally submit it:

```
SQL> exec DBMS_RESOURCE_MANAGER.SUBMIT_PENDING_AREA();
```

Now that the plan is in the data dictionary, we can use or enable it to our CDB. Again, we must be in the root container (CDB) to enable a CDB plan; we cannot be in a PDB. Once we are sure we are in the CDB, we run the following:

```
SQL> alter system set resource_manager_plan=my_cdb_plan scope=both sid='*';
```

That's it; we have enabled the plan and resources will now be allocated to the PDBs accordingly.

Making Plan Changes

Don't like how the plans are running? Want to remove them? No problem. Just run the following SQL to remove the CDB resource plan:

```
SQL> alter system set resource_manager_plan='';
```

Need to update a plan? Suppose we need to give more resources to the TESTPDB. Easy enough: we can do that with the following SQL and change the shares from 2 to 3, and the limits from 50 to 55:

```
SQL> exec DBMS_RESOURCE_MANAGER.CREATE_PENDING_AREA();
BEGIN
  DBMS_RESOURCE_MANAGER.UPDATE_CDB_PLAN_DIRECTIVE(
    plan                       => 'my_cdb_plan',
    pluggable_database         => 'TESTPDB',
    new_shares                 => 3,
    new_utilization_limit      => 55,
    new_parallel_server_limit  => 55);
END;
/
SQL> exec DBMS_RESOURCE_MANAGER.VALIDATE_PENDING_AREA();
SQL> exec DBMS_RESOURCE_MANAGER.SUBMIT_PENDING_AREA();
```

Deleting a plan is also simple. Say we need to delete the TESTPDB plan and have it use the default plan. We can use this SQL:

```
SQL> exec DBMS_RESOURCE_MANAGER.CREATE_PENDING_AREA();
BEGIN
  DBMS_RESOURCE_MANAGER.DELETE_CDB_PLAN_DIRECTIVE(
```

```
    plan                     => 'my_cdb_plan',
    pluggable_database       => 'TESTPDB');
END;
/
SQL> exec DBMS_RESOURCE_MANAGER.VALIDATE_PENDING_AREA();
SQL> exec DBMS_RESOURCE_MANAGER.SUBMIT_PENDING_AREA();
```

Creating a CDB Resource Plan that Uses PDB Performance Profiles

What we just did would be fine for a small number of PDBs. But what if we are managing hundreds in a single CDB? That's where we can use PDB performance profiles. We discussed them previously, and now it's time to see how we create them. We'll create a set of PDB performance profiles. Then we'll enable them in a PDB. Once a PDB has a profile, it inherits the directives that were assigned when creating the profile. Similar to before, here are the steps:

1. Create the pending area.
2. Create the CDB resource plan procedure.
3. Create PDB performance profiles.
4. Validate and submit the pending area.
5. Assign a profile to a PDB.

Let's begin. Just as before, we start with the pending area in the CDB:

```
SQL> exec DBMS_RESOURCE_MANAGER.CREATE_PENDING_AREA();
```

And, again, we create the CDB resource plan:

```
BEGIN
  DBMS_RESOURCE_MANAGER.CREATE_CDB_PLAN(
    plan    => 'my_cdb_plan_profile',
    comment => 'My CDB resource plan with Profiles');
END;
/
```

Next, we create the profiles. We can create a tiered profile system, pulling from the Maximum Availability Architecture plan names of Platinum, Gold, Silver, and Bronze.

```
BEGIN
  DBMS_RESOURCE_MANAGER.CREATE_CDB_PROFILE_DIRECTIVE(
    plan                  => 'my_cdb_plan_profile',
    profile               => 'platinum',
    shares                => 8,
    utilization_limit     => 100,
    parallel_server_limit => 100);
END;
/

BEGIN
  DBMS_RESOURCE_MANAGER.CREATE_CDB_PROFILE_DIRECTIVE(
    plan                  => 'my_cdb_plan_profile',
    profile               => 'gold',
```

```
   shares                  => 5,
   utilization_limit       => 90,
   parallel_server_limit   => 90);
END;
/


BEGIN
  DBMS_RESOURCE_MANAGER.CREATE_CDB_PROFILE_DIRECTIVE(
     plan                    => 'my_cdb_plan_profile',
     profile                 => 'silver',
     shares                  => 2,
     utilization_limit       => 40,
     parallel_server_limit   => 40);
END;
/


BEGIN
  DBMS_RESOURCE_MANAGER.CREATE_CDB_PROFILE_DIRECTIVE(
     plan                    => 'my_cdb_plan_profile',
     profile                 => 'bronze',
     shares                  => 1,
     utilization_limit       => 20,
     parallel_server_limit   => 20);
END;
/
```

We also need to set the default and AUTOTASK directives. We can reuse the values from our previous plan; we just need to change the plan name. First the default:

```
BEGIN
  DBMS_RESOURCE_MANAGER.UPDATE_CDB_DEFAULT_DIRECTIVE(
     plan                       => 'my_cdb_plan_profile',
     new_shares                 => 1,
     new_utilization_limit      => 30,
     new_parallel_server_limit  => 30);
END;
/
```

And then the AUTOTASK:

```
BEGIN
  DBMS_RESOURCE_MANAGER.UPDATE_CDB_AUTOTASK_DIRECTIVE(
     plan                       => 'my_cdb_plan_profile',
     new_shares                 => 1,
     new_utilization_limit      => 70,
     new_parallel_server_limit  => 70);
END;
/
```

Lastly, we validate:

```
SQL> exec DBMS_RESOURCE_MANAGER.VALIDATE_PENDING_AREA();
```

If the validation was successful, we submit the following:

```
SQL> exec DBMS_RESOURCE_MANAGER.SUBMIT_PENDING_AREA();
```

After the plan and profiles are created, we can apply or enable the CDB resource plan in the CDB. Remember that we need to be in the CDB to run this SQL:

```
SQL> alter system set resource_manager_plan=my_cdb_plan_profile scope=both
sid='*';
```

And now we can apply a profile to a PDB. Alter the session to be in the PDB of choice. Here we'll go into the HRPDB:

```
SQL> alter session set container = HRPDB;
```

Then set the profile:

```
SQL> alter system set DB_PERFORMANCE_PROFILE=gold scope=spfile sid='*'
instances=all;
```

Now close the PDB:

```
SQL> alter pluggable database close immediate instances=all;
```

And open the PDB for the profile to become active:

```
SQL> alter pluggable database open instances=all;
```

Updating a PDB performance profile is easy. Just create the pending area, update the profile, validate, and submit. Here we update the Bronze plan from 1 share to 2, as well as increase the limits from 20 to 25. Remember that we need to be in the CDB to perform the following SQL:

```
SQL> exec DBMS_RESOURCE_MANAGER.CREATE_PENDING_AREA();
BEGIN
  DBMS_RESOURCE_MANAGER.UPDATE_CDB_PROFILE_DIRECTIVE(
    plan                      => 'my_cdb_plan_profile',
    profile                   => 'bronze',
    new_shares                => 2,
    new_utilization_limit     => 25,
    new_parallel_server_limit => 25);
END;
/
SQL> exec DBMS_RESOURCE_MANAGER.VALIDATE_PENDING_AREA();
SQL> exec DBMS_RESOURCE_MANAGER.SUBMIT_PENDING_AREA();
```

And just as with the CDB plans, we can delete PDB performance profiles, performing the following SQL in the CDB:

```
SQL> exec DBMS_RESOURCE_MANAGER.CREATE_PENDING_AREA();
BEGIN
  DBMS_RESOURCE_MANAGER.DELETE_CDB_PROFILE_DIRECTIVE (
plan                      => 'my_cdb_plan_profile',
    profile               => 'bronze');
END;
```

```
/
SQL> exec DBMS_RESOURCE_MANAGER.VALIDATE_PENDING_AREA();
SQL> exec DBMS_RESOURCE_MANAGER.SUBMIT_PENDING_AREA();
```

Seeing DBRM in Action

We have our limits set; now let's see how the databases behave when we place loads upon them. We are going to use the stress test in SwingBench—the exact same test on both the HRPDB and the SALESPDB, with 300 users logging on. To exaggerate this test, we'll reduce the shares on the HRPDB to 2 and both the `utilization_limit` and `parallel_server_limit` to 5. This is a bit extreme but will help get the point across.

Enterprise Manager Express will assist us in visualizing this test, or demo.

TIP
The issue with EM Express is that it's Flash-based, and it's very difficult to justify installing Adobe Flash on your laptop/desktop these days. I suggest downloading a pre-created VM from Oracle or using another VM you may have. Take a snapshot and install Flash; that way, you can always revert to the snapshot after using EM Express.

To use EM Express with the CDB, we need to set the port. We log into the database with SQL*Plus as sysdba:

```
[oracle@exacs-node1 ~]$ sqlplus
SQL*Plus: Release 12.2.0.1.0 Production on Sat Jan 27 19:04:53 2018
Copyright (c) 1982, 2016, Oracle.  All rights reserved.

Enter user-name: / as sysdba
```

Now we need to check whether EM Express is running on an existing port using the following SQL in the CDB:

```
SQL> select dbms_xdb_config.getHttpsPort() from dual;

DBMS_XDB_CONFIG.GETHTTPSPORT()
------------------------------
5502
```

If the result is 0 (zero), we can set the port with the following SQL:

```
SQL> exec dbms_xdb_config.sethttpsport(desired port number);
```

So, if we want port 5502, we would use this SQL:

```
SQL> exec dbms_xdb_config.sethttpsport(5502);
```

Once the port is set, we open the firewall port (Chapter 2) and connect with the following URL: https://*your_ExaCS_client_IP_address:port_set*/em. (The port is the one we just set with this SQL, so I used the URL https://172.168.80.2:5502/em, because I set my port to 5502 for the CDB.)

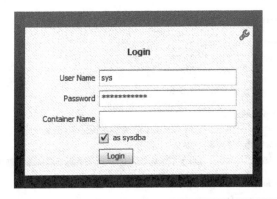

FIGURE 7-8.   *Logging into EM Express*

NOTE
If you are running EM Express on a version 12.1 database, you will need to set the port not only in the CDB but also on each of the PDBs you want to use EM Express with, and on different ports. If you are using version 12.2 or later, you just have to set the port in the CDB.

Once on the login page, we log in as sys, enter sys's password, and check the box As Sysdba (Figure 7-8). Leave the Container Name field blank.

TIP
You can also set the EM Express port on a PDB by running
SQL> exec dbms_xdb_config.sethttpsport(5503);
in the PDB and assigning it a port other than the one you use for the CDB.

In EM, we'll go to the Resource Management page under the Configuration drop-down menu on the top of the page (Figure 7-9).

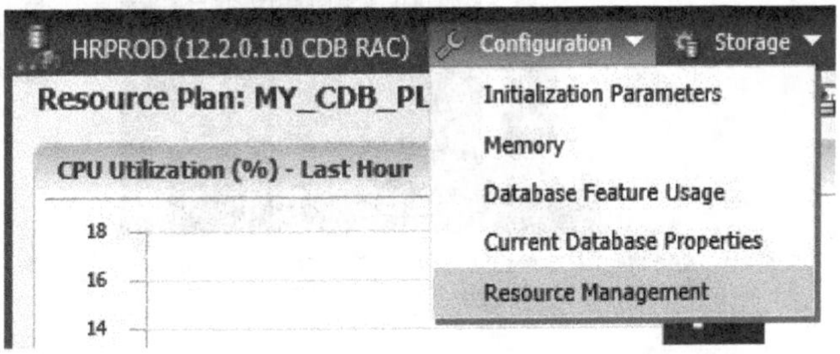

FIGURE 7-9.   *Getting to the Resource Management page in EM Express*

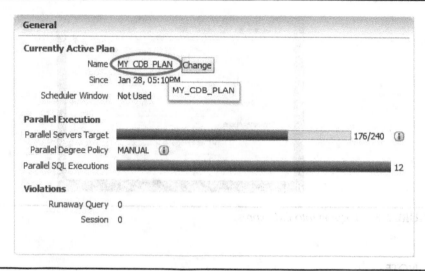

FIGURE 7-10. *Clicking the current active plan*

At the upper-left corner of the page, in the General panel, we click the name of the resource plan: in this case, MY_CDB_PLAN (Figure 7-10).

As the database load is running on both PDBs in SwingBench, we can see in the upper CPU Utilization graph that the majority of the resources are going to the SALESPDB (Figure 7-11).

In the lower/middle section (Figure 7-12), we can see a breakdown of the PDBs and how the plans are applied to them.

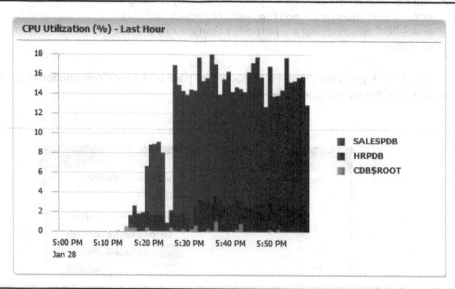

FIGURE 7-11. *CPU utilization for the PDBs using the plan MY_CDB_PLAN*

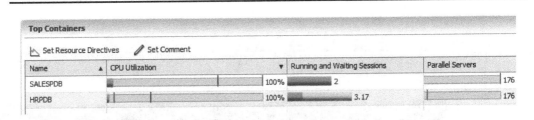

FIGURE 7-12. *Breakdown of the PDBs and resources being used*

In the CPU Utilization cells of the report, we can see that the SALESPDB is using more CPU, but we also see gray and red lines. These lines correspond to the limits we set when creating the directives (Figure 7-13).

In the Running and Waiting Sessions cells, we see that again that the SALESPDB has no waiting sessions, but the HRPDB has many (Figure 7-14).

If we take a look at SwingBench to see how the stress test is going, we can see that, again, the SALESPDB is doing an average of around 340,000 transactions per minute (top chart), while the HRPDB is doing only around 51,000 transactions per minute (bottom chart). Again, same test, same number of users (Figure 7-15).

These charts truly show that we can limit resources using DBRM at the CDB and PDB levels, isolating resources per PDB.

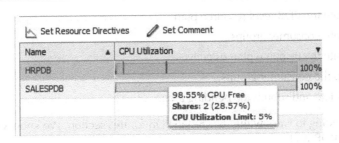

FIGURE 7-13. *The CPU utilization and directives*

FIGURE 7-14. *Running and Waiting Sessions cells*

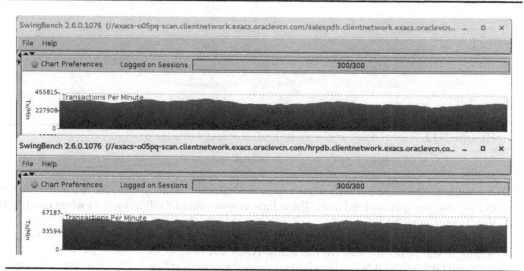

FIGURE 7-15. *SwingBench transactions per minute*

Intra-Database Resource Manager

Now that we have set the limits on the PDBs themselves, we can set limits on users and groups within the actual PDB. Here are the steps involved:

1. Create the pending area.
2. Create the PDB level resource plan.
3. Create consumer groups.
4. Create the resource plan directives.
5. Map the consumer groups.
6. Validate and submit the pending area.

We are going to work within our SALESPDB for this section. We know what resources we granted the PDB itself:

```
BEGIN
DBMS_RESOURCE_MANAGER.CREATE_CDB_PLAN_DIRECTIVE(
    plan                 => 'my_cdb_plan',
    pluggable_database   => 'SALESPDB',
    shares               => 5,
    utilization_limit    => 100,
    parallel_server_limit => 100);
END;
/
```

Now we can use Resource Manager to allocate resources to individual users and groups. Just as we did in the previous plans, we need to create our worksheet or pending area:

```
SQL> exec DBMS_RESOURCE_MANAGER.CREATE_PENDING_AREA();
```

Now let's create our plan, which will be used only in the SALESPDB and not in any other PDBs. In the previous section, we were working at the CDB level, so all PDBs were affected.

We create a plan for our PDB with the following SQL:

```
BEGIN
  DBMS_RESOURCE_MANAGER.CREATE_PLAN(
       PLAN      => 'MY_PDB_PLAN',
MGMT_MTH => =>'RATIO');
END;
/
```

We have set the resource allocation method (MGMT_MTH), or management method, to RATIO. With RATIO, we can use a share, similar to the system we used for the CDP plans. Our other option is to use the value EMPHASIS. The EMPHASIS option uses percentages to specify how the CPU is allocated among our consumer groups. One advantage of RATIO over EMPHASIS is that if you add another group in the future, the ratio of shares will balance without having to revisit every group.

Speaking of consumer groups, let's create them now. We'll create three groups: OLTP, REPORTING, and TESTDEV. These three groups will be allocated resources based on priority. To create the groups, we use this PL/SQL:

```
BEGIN
  DBMS_RESOURCE_MANAGER.CREATE_CONSUMER_GROUP (
    CONSUMER_GROUP => 'OLTP');
END;
/
BEGIN
  DBMS_RESOURCE_MANAGER.CREATE_CONSUMER_GROUP (
    CONSUMER_GROUP => 'REPORTING');
END;
/
BEGIN
  DBMS_RESOURCE_MANAGER.CREATE_CONSUMER_GROUP (
    CONSUMER_GROUP => 'TESTDEV');
END;
/
```

That's it; we have created our groups. Next, we need to define the resource plan directives. We know we want the OLTP group to have the most resources, so we use the following to create a resource plan directive for exactly that:

```
BEGIN
  DBMS_RESOURCE_MANAGER.CREATE_PLAN_DIRECTIVE (
       PLAN              => 'MY_PDB_PLAN',
       GROUP_OR_SUBPLAN => 'OLTP',
MGMT_P1          => 25);
END;
/
```

The MGMT_P1 parameter is where we'll place the shares of resources amount. The REPORTING group needs even fewer resources, at least during the day or business hours:

```
BEGIN
  DBMS_RESOURCE_MANAGER.CREATE_PLAN_DIRECTIVE (
      PLAN              => 'MY_PDB_PLAN',
      GROUP_OR_SUBPLAN  => 'REPORTING',
MGMT_P1               => 15);
END;
/
```

Now the TESTDEV group:

```
BEGIN
  DBMS_RESOURCE_MANAGER.CREATE_PLAN_DIRECTIVE (
      PLAN              => 'MY_PDB_PLAN',
      GROUP_OR_SUBPLAN  => 'TESTDEV',
MGMT_P1               => 5);
END;
/
```

We need to add an OTHER_GROUPS directive as a fallback for anything not mapped to one of our groups:

```
BEGIN
  DBMS_RESOURCE_MANAGER.CREATE_PLAN_DIRECTIVE (
      PLAN              => 'MY_PDB_PLAN',
      GROUP_OR_SUBPLAN  => 'OTHER_GROUPS',
MGMT_P1               => 1);
END;
/
```

We have a total amount of 46 shares. If we do the math to the CDB plans, we can see that the OLTP group gets $((25/46) \times 100) = 54$ percent of the resources, where the REPORTING group gets $((15/46) \times 100) = 33$ percent, with TESTDEV getting $((5/46) \times 100) = 11$ percent, and OTHER_ GROUPS getting $((1/46) \times 100) = 2$ percent.

Now let's map our consumer groups. Before we map, an explanation will help. With Resource Manager, we can map to ten consumer groups:

- **ORACLE_USER**   Oracle Database username
- **SERVICE_NAME**   Database service name used by the client with establishing connections
- **CLIENT_OS_USER**   OS username of the client logging in; think SQL*Plus on the OS
- **CLIENT_PROGRAM**   Name of the client program used to log in to the database; maybe an OS batch job
- **CLIENT_MACHINE**   Hostname of the client that is making the connection to the database
- **CLIENT_ID**   Client ID for the session

- **MODULE_NAME** Module name of an app connected to the database; set with DBMS_APPLICATION_INFO.SET_MODULE

- **MODULE_NAME_ACTION** Combination of the current module (module name) and the action being done that is set with one of the PL/SQL packages DBMS_APPLICATION_INFO.SET_MODULE or DBMS_APPLICATION_INFO.SET_ACTION

- **SERVICE_MODULE** Name when combining the service and module names in the format *service_name.module_name*

- **SERVICE_MODULE_ACTION** Like the SERVICE_MODULE, but with an action name in the format: *service_name.module_name.action_name*

We can use each of these groups when mapping with Resource Manager, but more importantly, we can prioritize them with the following package:

```
DBMS_RESOURCE_MANAGER.SET_CONSUMER_GROUP_MAPPING_PRI (
    EXPLICIT                IN  NUMBER,
    ORACLE_USER             IN  NUMBER,
    SERVICE_NAME            IN  NUMBER,
    CLIENT_ID               IN  NUMBER,
    CLIENT_OS_USER          IN  NUMBER,
    CLIENT_PROGRAM          IN  NUMBER,
    CLIENT_MACHINE          IN  NUMBER,
    MODULE_NAME             IN  NUMBER,
    MODULE_NAME_ACTION      IN  NUMBER,
    SERVICE_MODULE          IN  NUMBER,
    SERVICE_MODULE_ACTION   IN  NUMBER);
```

The following is an example that can be used:

```
BEGIN
  DBMS_RESOURCE_MANAGER.SET_CONSUMER_GROUP_MAPPING_PRI (
    EXPLICIT              => 1,
    ORACLE_USER           => 2,
    SERVICE_NAME          => 3,
    CLIENT_ID             => 4,
    CLIENT_OS_USER        => 5,
    CLIENT_PROGRAM        => 6,
    CLIENT_MACHINE        => 7,
    MODULE_NAME           => 8,
    SERVICE_MODULE        => 9,
    MODULE_NAME_ACTION    => 10,
    SERVICE_MODULE_ACTION => 11);
    END;
/
```

You may have noticed the EXPLICIT group. The pseudo-attribute EXPLICIT not only must be set to 1 at all times, but it indicates that consumer group switches using DBMS_SESSION.SWITCH_CURRENT_CONSUMER_GROUP, DBMS_RESOURCE_MANAGER.SWITCH_CONSUMER_GROUP_FOR_SESS, or DBMS_RESOURCE_MANAGER.SWITCH_CONSUMER_GROUP_FOR_USER have the highest priority. (More on consumer group switching in the next section.)

Now that we have set the group priorities, we can map our groups. First, we can map an OLTP user named OE to the OLTP group:

```
BEGIN
  DBMS_RESOURCE_MANAGER.SET_CONSUMER_GROUP_MAPPING(
    ATTRIBUTE       => DBMS_RESOURCE_MANAGER.ORACLE_USER,
    VALUE           => 'OE',
    CONSUMER_GROUP => 'OLTP');
END;
/
```

Next, we can map a REPORTING user, named BIUSER, to the REPORTING group:

```
BEGIN
  DBMS_RESOURCE_MANAGER.SET_CONSUMER_GROUP_MAPPING(
    ATTRIBUTE       => DBMS_RESOURCE_MANAGER.ORACLE_USER,
    VALUE           => 'BIUSER',
    CONSUMER_GROUP => 'REPORTING');
END;
/
```

And, finally, we can map a module that is in testing to the TESTDEV group:

```
BEGIN
  DBMS_RESOURCE_MANAGER.SET_CONSUMER_GROUP_MAPPING(
    ATTRIBUTE       => DBMS_RESOURCE_MANAGER.MODULE_NAME,
    VALUE           => 'TEST_SALES_APPLICATION',
    CONSUMER_GROUP => 'TESTDEV');
END;
/
```

Now we validate and submit the pending area:

```
SQL> exec DBMS_RESOURCE_MANAGER.VALIDATE_PENDING_AREA();
SQL> exec DBMS_RESOURCE_MANAGER.SUBMIT_PENDING_AREA();
```

Switching Groups

As noted previously, we need to revisit the switch commands with Resource Manager. We may want a user or application to switch to a different consumer group. We first need to grant that entity permission to switch groups. That is done with the GRANT_SWITCH_CONSUMER_GROUP procedure. In this example, the BIUSER in the REPORTING group can now switch to the OLTP group:

```
BEGIN
  DBMS_RESOURCE_MANAGER_PRIVS.GRANT_SWITCH_CONSUMER_GROUP (
    GRANTEE_NAME    => 'BIUSER',
    CONSUMER_GROUP => 'OLTP',
    GRANT_OPTION    => TRUE);
END;
/
```

The GRANT_OPTION says that BIUSER can now grant this ability to switch consumer groups to other users. You may or may not want this ability; set to FALSE if you want to restrict this behavior. Want to revoke this privilege? Just use the procedure:

```
BEGIN
  DBMS_RESOURCE_MANAGER_PRIVS.REVOKE_SWITCH_CONSUMER_GROUP (
    REVOKEE_NAME    => 'BIUSER',
    CONSUMER_GROUP => 'OLTP');
END;
/
```

Now with the ability to switch, we can use three different procedures to do the actual switch:

- **SWITCH_CONSUMER_GROUP_FOR_SESS** This procedure switches the group for a particular session. It is used in the following format

```
DBMS_RESOURCE_MANAGER.SWITCH_CONSUMER_GROUP_FOR_SESS (
    session_id     IN NUMBER,
    session_serial IN NUMBER,
    consumer_group IN VARCHAR2);
```

  with the session_id being SID column from the V$SESSION view, the session_serial being the SERIAL# in the V$SESSION view, and the consumer_group being the group you want to switch to.

- **SWITCH_CONSUMER_GROUP_FOR_USER** This procedure changes the consumer group for all sessions being used by a particular database user. Here's the format:

```
DBMS_RESOURCE_MANAGER.SWITCH_CONSUMER_GROUP_FOR_USER (
    user            IN VARCHAR2,
    consumer_group  IN VARCHAR2);
```

  The user is the database username, and consumer_group is the group you want to switch to.

- **SWITCH_CURRENT_CONSUMER_GROUP** This procedure is a bit different because it uses the DBMS_SESSION package. Using the procedure lets the user change the consumer group within a session, such as a SQL session. Here's the format:

```
DBMS_SESSION.switch_current_consumer_group (
    new_consumer_group      IN  VARCHAR2,
    old_consumer_group      OUT VARCHAR2,
    initial_group_on_error  IN  BOOLEAN);
```

  The new_consumer_group is the group you want to switch to. The old_consumer_group is an OUT variable and returns the old group you just switched from. If the initial_group_on_error is set to TRUE, being a Boolean, it will return you to the original group if this produces errors for any reason.

Here the BIUSER is switching from the REPORTING group to the OLTP group:

```
BEGIN
DBMS_RESOURCE_MANAGER.SWITCH_CONSUMER_GROUP_FOR_USER (
    user            => 'BIUSER',
    consumer_group  => 'OLTP');
END;
/
```

Changing Plans Using DBMS_SCHEDULER

Early in this chapter we talked about having a plan for business hours, a plan for night, and a weekend plan. The best way to move from plan to plan is to use the Oracle Scheduler.

Here is an example of creating windows for the plans to be active. The three plans we are going to reference are BUSINESS_HOURS, AFTER_HOURS, and WEEKEND_HOURS. Here is the code to do just that:

```
BEGIN
 DBMS_SCHEDULER.CREATE_WINDOW(
   window_name      => 'BUSINESS_HOURS',
   resource_plan    => 'BUSINESS_HOURS',
   start_date       => systimestamp,
   duration         => INTERVAL '14' HOUR,
   repeat_interval  => 'FREQ=WEEKLY;BYDAY=MON,TUE,WED,THU,FRI;BYHOUR=6;BYMINUTE=0;BYSECO
ND=0',
   end_date         => null);
 DBMS_SCHEDULER.ENABLE('"SYS"."BUSINESS_HOURS"');
END;
/
BEGIN
 DBMS_SCHEDULER.CREATE_WINDOW(
   window_name      => 'AFTER_HOURS',
   resource_plan    => 'AFTER_HOURS',
   start_date       => systimestamp,
   duration         => INTERVAL '10' HOUR,
   repeat_interval  => 'FREQ=WEEKLY;BYDAY=MON,TUE,WED,THU,FRI;BYHOUR=20;BYMINUTE=0;BYSEC
OND=0',
   end_date         => null);
 DBMS_SCHEDULER.ENABLE('"SYS"."AFTER_HOURS"');
END;
/
BEGIN
 DBMS_SCHEDULER.CREATE_WINDOW(
   window_name      => 'WEEKEND_HOURS',
   resource_plan    => 'WEEKEND_HOURS',
   start_date       => systimestamp,
   duration         => INTERVAL '24' HOUR,
   repeat_interval  => 'FREQ=WEEKLY;BYDAY=SAT,SUN;BYHOUR=0;BYMINUTE=0;BYSECOND=0',
   end_date         => null);
 DBMS_SCHEDULER.ENABLE('"SYS"."WEEKEND_HOURS"');
END;
/
```

Instance Caging

To isolate resources further, we can use Instance Caging to determine an exact number of processors that an instance or CDB can utilize.

NOTE
When we use the term "instance" in this section, think of a single instance database, a non-CDB architecture like what we find in version 11gR2.

To start, run the following SQL in the CDB to see how many processers we have to work with:

```
SQL> select value from v$osstat where stat_name = 'NUM_CPUS';

    VALUE
----------
       22
```

Here in our quarter rack, we have 11 processors per node, or 22 total. We see 22 because of hyperthreading (11 cores that can use two threads each). Now there are two schools of thought on Instance Caging: We can only give out the total number of CPUs to all the instances or CDBs so that the total count equals the total number of processors. Or we oversubscribe the number of CPUs to all the instances or CDBs so that the total number we use for Instance Caging is more than the total number of CPUs. This assumes that not all the instances will need all the CPUs at the same time. When you're configuring and planning Instance Caging, keep these two options in mind.

To set up Instance Caging on an instance or CDB, we can run the following SQL:

```
SQL> alter system set cpu_count = 4 scope=both sid='*';
```

In this case, we are limiting the service to four CPUs. For this to work correctly, we also need to have a resource plan in place. If there is no resource plan, then Instance Caging will not work. You don't need a particular plan, because even the default plan will do, but you need an active resource plan.

To check to see if Instance Caging is enabled, run the following SQL:

```
SQL> select instance_caging from v$rsrc_plan where is_top_plan = 'TRUE';

INS
---
ON
```

If Instance Caging is enabled, the result will be ON. We can also check the database parameter CPU_COUNT:

```
SQL> show parameter cpu_count;
NAME                            TYPE        VALUE
------------------------------- ----------- ----------------------
cpu_count                       integer     4
```

That's it; Instance Caging is enabled.

TIP
Be sure you don't set the value to 1, because that will cause the database to become unstable and it may crash.

You can also limit CPU for a PDB in versions 12.2 and 18c by setting the CPU_COUNT parameter as we did for a CDB or single instance. But note that if both utilization_limit in a CDB plan directive and CPU_COUNT are set, then the more restrictive (lower) value is enforced. With that said, using the utilization_limit along with Instance Caging may be more flexible because we can set the CPU_COUNT at the CDB level, and the limit will dynamically change.

We can also alter the shares in a directive, yet again dynamically increasing or decreasing the CPU utilization limits, as well as alter CPU_COUNT.

Summary

Exadata is a true consolidation platform. Through IORM, Instance Caging, and Database Resource Manager, we can have mixed workloads on a single platform, all living in harmony. Resource Manager also lets us decide when we want a particular type of workload to have priority with a simple scheduler window. IORM can control who gets what on the storage cells, and we can further delineate resources with Instance Caging. The Exadata Cloud Service is a very flexible platform, and these three tools prove that claim.

CHAPTER 8

Exadata Smart Flash Cache

With Exadata X2, Oracle introduced Flash Cache on the storage cells, not only to help with reads by caching frequently accessed data but to help with log writing as well (Flash Logging, available with 11.2.2.4 Storage Software). The X2 had a total of 5.3TB of flash cache in a full rack. As flash prices have decreased and capacities have increased, the X7, the newest version as of the beginning of 2018, has a maximum of 307.2TB (full rack) in the Exadata Cloud Service and Cloud at Customer models. With an on-premises Extreme Flash X7 version, you can have up to 716.8TB of flash—a better than 5500 percent increase in just seven years!

The Rise of Flash

Flash storage is everywhere now—from our phones to our laptops—and its small size has enabled personal technology to hold gigabytes of data in a medium smaller than a postage stamp. Consider digital cameras, for example. I bought my first digital camera for a trip to Hawaii in 2005. At the time, there were many formats of flash memory available. We had compact flash cards, SD cards, and some outliers such as SmartMedia flash cards, which was used in the camera I purchased. I had two SmartMedia cards, both with about 16MB in capacity, which was fine for a 4-megapixel camera. Flash forward (get it?) to today, and we have cameras that are 45 megapixels, where one picture is about 100MB. SD cards are by far the most popular, with some challengers such as XQD cards that are used for professional photography.

In the mid-2000s we also saw a move to flash drives in laptops. The first flash drives in laptops had problems, in that that they were connecting to a legacy interface—Serial AT Attachment, or SATA. SATA versions 2 and 3 provided a much greater throughput, but the SATA interface itself was designed for spinning disks, not flash storage. Regardless, there was an immediate noticeable difference when replacing a spinning drive in a computer or laptop with a flash drive, even with the SATA connection. With enterprise storage arrays, SCSI/SAS (Small Computer System Interface/Serial Attached SCS) is the interface of choice, with 10,000-RPM spinning drives. Regardless of your storage and interface choices, you were bottlenecked by the hard drive controllers.

In around 2012 came the first laptops with NVM Express (NVMe) flash, which was attached directly to the PCI bus. The Peripheral Component Interconnect Express was not a new technology; it was being used in home computers for the graphics cards. This high-bandwidth connector was the key to having high-definition graphics for gaming computers, and the PCI Express (PCIe) slots enabled multiple graphics cards to work in parallel to provide that 60 frames per second needed for *Call of Battlefield 4*.

PCI provided multiple lanes of high bandwidth, much more than SATA could provide. By attaching flash storage directly via PCIe, read and write speeds increased dramatically. Where a laptop with a SATA flash drive solid-state drive (SSD) saw reads of around 500 MBps, these NVMe drives were seeing more than five times that amount. With writes, SATA flash was in at around 450 MBps, with NVMe coming in sometimes at four times that amount. Today, NVMe flash is the standard in laptops, tablets, and phones.

There were other advantages to switching from a spinning to a flash drive. One was power consumption. SSDs and flash drives had no moving parts. The laptop no longer had to use some of its precious battery power for moving the mechanical hard drive. Just switching out the drive on a laptop with one of these drives could increase the battery life by about 30 to 60 minutes. That was huge when early laptops lasted only about 4 hours. For data centers with many, many spinning drives, the power bill was lowered as well, moving from about 7 watts per spinning drive to less than 3 watts for a flash drive.

Other advantages of flash include reductions in noise and heat. No moving parts and less power draw mean an instant savings on heat, so the enclosures needed less cooling. Lastly, failure rates improved. Everyone at some point has heard the dreaded "clicking noise of death" in a spinning drive—the noise you hear just before the drive with your entire digital life on it is about to die. Failure rates on flash drives are vastly decreased, saving costs of replacements and extending life of equipment.

The drawback of flash, however, is that capacities have not caught up to spinning drives. Where spinning drives now have reached 15TB per drive, flash is just cresting at a few terabytes. And as you increase capacity of these flash drives, their cost increases. As of writing this, I can buy a commodity 12TB drive for about $350, but a flash drive of similar size is $10,000. A commodity flash drive of 4TB is around $1500.

Exadata and Flash

As mentioned, the X2 was the first Exadata version to use flash in the storage servers, creating the Exadata Smart Flash Cache. These storage cards were the Sun Flash Accelerator F20. There were four cards per storage server, with 96GB of single-level cell (SLC) flash on each card. In a full rack with 14 storage cells, that offered around 5.3TB of flash. With the Exadata X5, Oracle moved from SLC flash to NVMe and all the advantages that came with it. An X5 had four 1.6TB Oracle Flash Accelerator F160 PCIe cards in each storage server, giving an X5 quarter rack in the Exadata Cloud Service 19.2TB of flash. For on-premises Exadata Database Machines, an Extreme Flash option replaces all spinning disks in the storage servers, doubling the amount of flash offered in a high-capacity storage server. This Extreme Flash option is still available today with the X7 and 716.8TB of raw flash.

Exadata Smart Flash Cache

With the X2 we saw the marriage of flash and spinning disks that continues today, providing speed and large capacities. The question now is, how does this flash work with an Exadata and what are the advantages? What's so smart about the Exadata Smart Flash Cache?

One of the main jobs of the Exadata Smart Flash Cache is to store frequently accessed and/or read data so that queries can take advantage of the flash speeds. The "Smart" comes in to play here because this happens transparently to the users. The Exadata Storage Servers decide what data to cache in the flash cache based on how regularly that data is being requested. The flash cache also knows the types of requests coming in, so only those that are querying data will be considered for placing in the cache. Plus, you can pin tables into flash cache, as we discuss later in this chapter in the section "The CELL_FLASH_CACHE Storage Clause."

When the Flash Cache Is Used

Let's walk through a typical query to see when the flash cache will be accessed. Consider a simple query:

```
SQL> select product_name from products where product_id > 10;
```

The first stop to look for this data is Database In-Memory. Has this table been placed in memory using the Oracle Database In-Memory option? If the data is not there, we can check the local buffer cache or use Cache Fusion to check in the other nodes of the Exadata Cloud Service's global cache. If we cannot find it locally or in the global cache, we then send the request down to the storage servers.

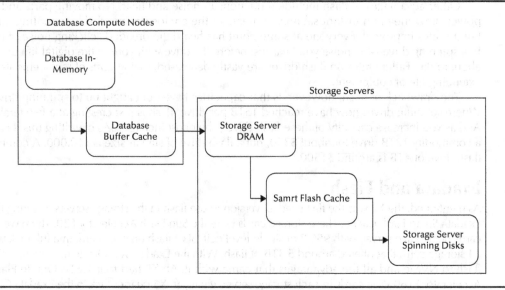

FIGURE 8-1. *The query path on an Exadata Database Machine*

There is where things get interesting, especially with version 18.1. In Exadata Storage Servers X6 and X7, on 18.1, we can store data that ages out of the buffer cache on the database compute nodes into the DRAM of the storage cells. This cache sits in front of the flash cache on the storage cells. If the data is found in this storage server DRAM cache, it is removed and sent back to the database compute nodes buffer cache.

If you are using a version earlier than 18.1 or version X5 or earlier storage servers, the next stop will be the flash cache. When the request comes in, the storage servers look for that data in the flash cache and, if needed, on the spinning disks as well. If the data is found in the Smart Flash Cache, it is returned to the database compute nodes. If it is not found in the Smart Flash Cache, the request is sent to the spinning disks, where it is retrieved. Because the database and the storage servers were created to work together, the database can inform the storage servers that this data will be accessed frequently. The data is then put into the Smart Flash Cache. A complete flow is shown in Figure 8-1.

WriteThrough and WriteBack

The Smart Flash Cache can also be used for database writes. The storage servers have two options, or methods, for database writes: WriteThrough and WriteBack. With WriteThrough, the Exadata will write directly to the disk. If the storage servers determine this data is frequently used, it will be put into the flash cache, but not until the database transaction is completed and the disk signals so. This flow is shown in Figure 8-2.

With Exadata Storage Software release 11.2.3.2, Oracle introduced WriteBack (see Figure 8-3). This enables the Exadata Storage Server to keep changed or active blocks in the flash cache to be later written to disk. This speeds up OLTP operations because we no longer have to wait for the slower spinning drives to signal complete. Once this change is committed to the disk, the Smart

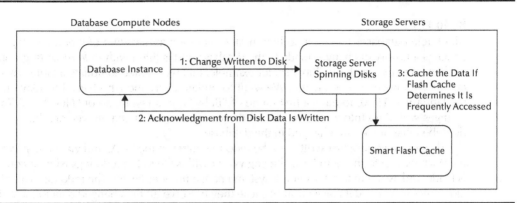

FIGURE 8-2.   *WriteThrough method of writing data*

Flash Cache will also determine whether this data is frequently accessed, and as a result, whether it should be kept in the flash cache for faster reads.

WriteBack mode is the default for the Exadata Cloud Service and Cloud at Customer and cannot be changed. As an Exadata system admin once told me, "Friends don't let friends use WriteThrough." Also, seeing the storage is set to HIGH redundancy in the cloud (triple mirrored), there are three copies of the changes in the flash cache, ensuring that data is never lost. Just as we saw with other features of Exadata, this is all done transparently to the users and no setup/ configure tasks need to be performed to enable this.

Exadata Smart Flash Logging

With version 11.2.2.4 of the Exadata Storage software, Oracle enabled the Exadata Smart Flash Log. This feature was created to deal with the latency of log writes.

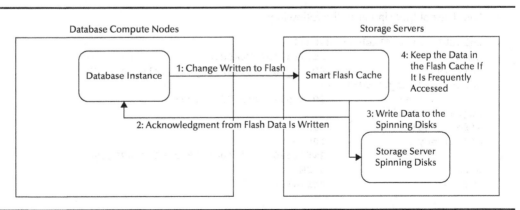

FIGURE 8-3.   *WriteBack method of writing data*

Redo Logs

All Oracle databases have a redo log; in fact, there are at least two of them. This log contains a history of changes made to the database and is filled with *redo records*, groups of changes to the database. Suppose, for example, that we wanted to update a table, say the census data we have been using. We want to update everyone who has a birthday on the January 1, 1980, to have a first name of "Baby" and a last name of "New Year." These changes would go into a redo log as a redo record as a set of change vectors that describe what blocks are changed in the database.

These changes are first written to the redo log buffer in the SGA, and via the Log Writer (LGWR), written to the redo logs. The Log Writer will write to the redo logs when a commit is made and assign that transaction a system change number (SCN). The redo logs can also aid in recovery in a database crash because they preserve all the changed data to the point of the crash.

The Exadata Smart Flash Cache will write to the redo log on both the flash cache and the spinning disks of the Exadata Storage Server in parallel. Whichever one of these writes completes first will inform the database that it has completed. This improves response times and throughput, because if the disk or flash is experiencing slow response times, the other medium will pick up the slack and complete the write. The flash cache will not permanently store the redo information in flash, but hold it until it is safely written to disk.

For OLTP workloads, Smart Flash Logging will help with the many log writes that occur, removing the latency in writes that sometimes happens with slow disk performance. As with many of the Exadata features, Smart Flash Logging is transparent to the database and set up automatically for you.

In the Exadata Cloud Service, Smart Flash Logging is enabled by default. It uses only 512MB per storage server, so there is little effect on the total amount of flash available. If you have access to a storage server (or use ExaCLI; see Chapter 9), you can issue the following command:

```
CellCLI> list flashlog detail
```

You'll see output similar to the following:

```
CellCLI> list flashlog detail
name:                   rdrlrx1402_FLASHLOG
cellDisk:               FD_03_rdrlrx1402,FD_00_rdrlrx1402,FD_01_
rdrlrx1402,FD_02_rdrlrx1402
creationTime:           2016-03-31T15:55:45+00:00
degradedCelldisks:
effectiveSize:          512M
efficiency:             100.0
id:                     2wf0re40-a444-40d1-8800-92b86678e900
size:                   512M
status:                 normal
```

Creating the Flash Cache and Flash Grid Disks

In the Exadata Cloud Service, the flash cache is created for you upon service creation. With that said, let's go over the commands in the process of manually creating the flash cache to help you better understand the process. You can also look into the setWBFC.sh script in Oracle Support Note 1500257.1. If you were to perform the following manual steps, you would need to do this on each storage cell.

First, you have to flush the flash cache to ensure that any data stored there is synchronized with the spinning disks (if this was an existing system):

```
CELLCLI> alter flashcache all flush
```

Then drop the flash cache, flash log, and cell disks:

```
CELLCLI> drop flashcache
CELLCLI> drop flashlog
CELLCLI> drop celldisk all flashdisk
```

Next, create the cell disks, flash cache, and the flash log; for this, you won't specify a size but will use all available flash.

First, the disks:

```
CELLCLI> create celldisk all flashdisk
```

Now the flash log (the flash log must be created before the flash cache):

```
CELLCLI> create flashlog all
```

And, finally, the flash cache:

```
CELLCLI> create flashcache all
```

You can also run commands in the following format:

```
CellCLI -e create flashlog all
CellCLI -e create flashcache all
```

NOTE
You may notice the -e flag in some of the commands we are going to use. The -e will cause CellCLI to exit after running the command. If you have multiple commands you need to run via CellCLI, you can just skip using the -e flag. For most of this chapter, we will be at the CellCLI prompt.

Once the flash cache is created, you can see the details using the `list` command:

```
CellCLI> list flashcache detail
```

Or, if you need a specific attribute listed, you can use the following:

```
CellCLI> list flashcache attributes size
```

Here you will just see the size attribute. The following attributes can be passed into this command, or you can use multiple attributes separated by a comma (size,name,and_so_on):

- `name`
- `cellDisk`
- `creationTime`
- `degradedCelldisks`
- `effectiveCacheSize`
- `id`
- `size`
- `status`

From CellCLI, you can list this attributes with the following command:

```
CellCLI> describe flashcache
```

Another option with the flash disks is to create usable volumes for grid disk groups. This is an option that is not yet included in the Exadata Cloud Service but something that you should know exists. Why would you do this? Using flash disks for storage can greatly accelerate I/O for tables that can fit in a smaller amount of space. Again, the Extreme Flash version of the Exadata Storage Servers are 100 percent flash, but at the cost of less storage.

As before, you need to flush the flash cache:

```
CELLCLI> alter flashcache all flush
```

Next, drop the flash cache:

```
CELLCLI> drop flashcache
CELLCLI> drop flashlog
```

Create the flash cache, but of a smaller size using the `size` attribute. This example uses an X7, which has four 6.4TB flash cards. The flash cache will be 6TB on each card, leaving 400GB for the grid disk volume.

```
CELLCLI> create flashlog all
CellCLI> create flashcache all size=6000G
```

Now create the flash volumes:

```
CellCLI> create griddisk all flashdisk prefix=flashdisk01
```

As with any disks at the CellCLI level, you can list the attributes. Here you can use the following to see the attributes of the new flash-based grid disk:

```
CellCLI> list griddisk attributes where disktype='flashdisk'
```

Just as with the flash cache attributes, the grid disk has attributes you can see as well:

- `name`
- `asmDeactivationOutcome`
- `asmDiskgroupName`
- `asmDiskName`
- `asmDiskRepairTime`
- `asmDiskSize`
- `asmFailGroupName`
- `asmModeStatus`
- `availableTo`
- `cachedBy`
- `cachingPolicy`
- `cellDisk`
- `comment`
- `creationTime`
- `diskType`
- `errorCount`
- `id`
- `size`
- `sparse`
- `status`
- `virtualSize`

And you can also list them with the following command:

```
CellCLI> describe griddisk
```

Now add to this command to list only the attributes you want to see:

```
CellCLI> list griddisk attributes name,status,size where disktype='flashdisk'
```

Now, as sysadm, connect to the ASM instance where you can create the new flash volume:

```
SQL> create diskgroup FLASH01
high redundancy
disk 'o/*/flashdisk01*'
attribute 'compatible.rdbms' = '12.2',
'compatible.asm' = '12.2',
'cell.smart_scan_capable' = 'TRUE',
'au_size' = '4M';
```

The disk group is created, and that's it. You can now create objects using this flash volume on the flash cache of the storage cells.

Columnar Flash Caching and Storage Server In-Memory Cache

New in Oracle Exadata Storage Server release 12.1.2.1.0 is Columnar Flash Caching. This feature takes hybrid columnar compressed data and places it into the flash cache in pure columnar format for very fast analytics processing. Not only does this accelerate reads to the data, but Smart Scans can also take advantage of this format by reading only the selected columns already in columnar format. With Storage Server release 18.1.0, Columnar Flash Caching is extended to regular tables as well as tables compressed with Advanced Row Compression. Columnar Flash Caching is enabled by default in the Exadata Cloud Service for Hybrid Columnar Compression (HCC) compressed tables, but the `INMEMORY_SIZE` database initialization parameter must be set to use Columnar Flash Caching on regular and advanced row-compressed tables.

Also new with Storage Server release 18.1.0 is the ability to use the DRAM of the storage servers as an in-memory cache. The RAM cache, or DRAM, is a cache in front of the Smart Flash Cache on storage servers and is an extension of the database cache. This RAM cache is much faster than the Smart Flash Cache but also much smaller. Where the flash cache is terabytes in size, the RAM cache is only a few hundred gigabytes by default in the Cloud Service. The RAM cache accepts aged out buffers from the database buffer cache. If the data block from that aged-out buffer cache is needed, it is evicted from the RAM cache and placed back into the database buffer cache. That data block can exist only in the buffer cache of the database *or* the RAM cache in the storage servers; it cannot exist in both places at the same time. This RAM cache adds a layer when querying data in front of the flash cache. This feature needs to have the 18.1.0 Storage Server software as well as the Storage Servers being an X6 or X7 variant.

The CELL_FLASH_CACHE Storage Clause

Where the Smart Flash Cache will automatically cache frequently used data, we can force a table into the cache via SQL. We can use the `CELL_FLASH_CACHE` clause in an `alter table` command to pin the table into the flash cache. The `CELL_FLASH_CACHE` has three values: `KEEP`, `NONE`, and `DEFAULT`. `KEEP` will pin it in the flash cache as long as the flash cache is large enough, `DEFAULT` will let the Smart Flash Cache decide, and `NONE` will prevent it from going into the flash cache.

NOTE
KEEP doesn't mean it will stay in the flash cache forever. It will eventually expire (24 hours) if not accessed and will be placed back once accessed again.

If we want to move our census table into the flash cache, we would issue the following SQL:

```
SQL> alter table big_census storage (cell_flash_cache keep);
```

The table is now in the flash cache. To move it out permanently, we would issue this:

```
SQL> alter table big_census storage (cell_flash_cache none);
```

And, finally, to set it so that the Smart Flash Cache decides, we use this:

```
SQL> alter table big_census storage (cell_flash_cache default);
```

We can view whether the table is set to be in the flash cache by KEEP, NONE, or DEFAULT with the following SQL:

```
SQL> select table_name, num_rows, compression, cell_flash_cache from all_tables
  where table_name in upper('big_census');
TABLE_NAME               NUM_ROWS COMPRESS CELL_FL
-------------------- -------- -------- -------
BIG_CENSUS               16671232 DISABLED DEFAULT
```

This storage clause can also be used on a table partition level:

```
SQL> alter table big_census_part modify partition person_date_1 storage
  (cell_flash_cache keep);
```

Overall, it's best to let the Smart Flash Cache decide what gets cached and what does not.

Summary

As flash prices decrease, the Exadata Database Machine will continue to use more and more of it. We have seen a dramatic increase of the amount of flash available in Exadata in just five short years. Exadata Storage Software has taken advantage of flash with features such as Smart Flash Cache, Smart Flash Logging, and Columnar Flash Caching. These features, along with a new RAM cache on the storage servers, continue to accelerate query speed and analytics; a SQL statement that took minutes to run on commodity hardware can now be done in less than a second.

CHAPTER 9

Managing and Monitoring the Exadata Cloud Service

S everal Oracle products help us manage and monitor the Exadata Cloud Service (ExaCS) on various levels. This chapter covers some of the tools and software we can use to manage the service. Although Oracle provides methods for fast provisioning and setup, it is an unmanaged service and we need to ensure that it stays healthy. The tools we are covering in this chapter mainly deal with managing the databases on the service. The "ExaCLI" section will cover Exadata-specific management and monitoring.

11g Database Control and Enterprise Manager Express

We briefly covered Enterprise Manager Express (EM Express) in Chapter 7, but here we discuss the product more in depth. We'll also go over Enterprise Manager 11g Database Control, the console included with version 11.2.0.4. In 12c and 18c databases we have EM Express, a light, or stripped down, version of Enterprise Manager used for managing a single database and doing some day-to-day tasks. It offers a good deal of functionality and should not be dismissed.

Database Control

Database Control is enabled out of the box after you create an 11g database on your Exadata Cloud Service. To see what port the Database Control is running on, SSH into your service. Once on the service, source the 11g environment and view the emd.properties file at $ORACLE_HOME/*nodehostname_sid*/sysman/config/emd.properties. (Change *nodehostname_sid* to your hostname and database SID.)

Let's look at an example. Say our 11g database is named JANE (to match the following example). First, we log into node 1, and then we can change the directory to the Oracle home (/home/oracle), so we source the database environment file:

```
[oracle@exacs-node1 ~]$ . JANE.env
```

We change the directory to the Oracle home:

```
[oracle@exacs-node1 ~]$ cd $ORACLE_HOME
```

In this directory, we can see the *nodehostname_sid* directory. In this example, it's exacs-node1_JANE and exacs-node2_JANE. Two nodes are in a quarter rack, so two directories. We can now view the file:

```
[oracle@exacs-node1 dbhome_2]$ more exacs-node1_JANE/sysman/config/emd.properties
| grep REPOSITORY_URL
```

This will return something similar to the following:

```
REPOSITORY_URL=https://exacs-node1.us2.oraclecloud.com:1159/em/upload/
```

We now know the console is running on port 1159.

NOTE
If you are using Oracle Cloud Infrastructure Classic (OCI-C), you will have to enable the port in either a security list if you're using an IP network or the firewall rules in the Exadata Details Overview page, as discussed in Chapter 3.

Once the rule is applied, we can access the console by going to the following URL: https://ExaCS-ip-address-for-node-N:1159/em

In this example, if my IP address was 10.0.0.10 for node 1 of my database compute node and 10.0.0.12 for the other database compute node (assume a quarter rack, two nodes), then the URL for node 1 would be https://10.0.0.10:1159/em.

NOTE
Be aware that if your ExaCS has a private IP address, you will have to be using a FastConnect network service, a virtual private network (VPN) service into the IP networks (OCI-C), or a VPN/FastConnect Network into an OCI Dynamic Routing Gateway to resolve the IP addresses. You can also SSH into a bastion server and tunnel the connection and forward the port to the console.

Tunneling over SSH

For accessing an ExaCS that has a private IP address, you can use a bastion server or jump box to access the service. Bring up an IaaS instance (Solaris for Intel or Linux) and assign a public IP to that instance. Then SSH into that instance and jump over to the ExaCS that's in the private cloud network. This jump box acts as a gateway into your ExaCS.

Sometimes you'll need to tunnel EM Express access over an SSH connection rather than have port 5501 open to the Internet. You can do this in two ways. On a Linux, macOS, or Unix system, run the following command at the command prompt:

```
ssh -i private-key -L 3333:10.0.0.1:5501 opc@10.0.0.1
```

For this example, my ExaCS database compute node has an IP address of 10.0.0.1 and my local port will be 3333. (Always use a port greater than 1024 and less than 49152 so that you don't have conflicts with services running on the system. Most services use ports less than 1024.) This enables you to access EM Express/Database Console via a browser on this ExaCS over the SSH tunnel.

If you're using Windows, you have to use a third-party program such as PuTTY to accomplish the same task. Once your connection to the ExaCS is created, you need to expand the SSH node and then the Tunnels node via the left-hand navigation bar in the PuTTY interface (Figure 9-1).

Next, set the Source Port Text field to a port that is available on your system. For this example, let's use 3333 again. In the Destination text field, specify the ExaCS database compute node, as we did earlier, and the EM Express port number. Here I would use 10.0.0.1:5201.

(Continued)

Ensure that the Local and Auto radio buttons are selected. Then click the Add button. You can see that the entry is added into the Forwarded Ports section (Figure 9-2). Save your PuTTY session after this is complete.

Connect using PuTTY, and you should be able to access EM Express using a browser over the SSH connection.

If you're using OCI-C, you can also use the menu to the right of the service in the database console to open a new window with the correct URL filled in. From the menu, select Open EM Console, as shown in Figure 9-3.

NOTE
Unless you open up the firewall to these ports, you will not be able to access the web consoles. Be sure to open the port for the specific console you are going to use in the firewall; use the security lists in OCI and OCI-C IP networks or the Software Firewall page in OCI-C without IP networks. Refer to Chapters 2 and 3.

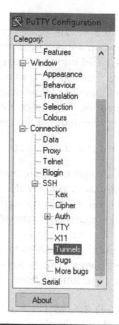

FIGURE 9-1. *Accessing the Tunnels option in PuTTY*

```
┌─────────────────────────────────────────────────┐
│        Options controlling SSH port forwarding    │
│  ┌───────────────────────────────────────────┐   │
│  Port forwarding                                  │
│  ☐ Local ports accept connections from other hosts│
│  ☐ Remote ports do the same (SSH-2 only)          │
│  Forwarded ports:                    ┌─────────┐  │
│                                      │ Remove  │  │
│  ┌─────────────────────────────┐     └─────────┘  │
│  │ L3333    10.0.0.1:5201       │                  │
│  │                             │                  │
│  └─────────────────────────────┘                  │
│  Add new forwarded port:                          │
│  Source port    ┌──────┐         ┌─────────┐      │
│                 │ 3333 │         │   Add   │      │
│                 └──────┘         └─────────┘      │
│  Destination   ┌────────────────────┐            │
│                │ 10.0.0.1:5201      │            │
│                └────────────────────┘            │
│  ◉ Local       ○ Remote      ○ Dynamic           │
│  ◉ Auto        ○ IPv4        ○ IPv6              │
└─────────────────────────────────────────────────┘
```

FIGURE 9-2. *Forwarding a port in PuTTY*

Because the service uses self-signed certificates, your browser will warn you about an insecure connection. Depending on the browser you are using, you can either click to get past this message or add a temporary exception to the session.

Once you are able to reach this URL, you will see a login page, with a login box on the left side (Figure 9-4).

Enter the credentials shown in Figure 9-5. Enter the password you used to create the service. Then click Login.

Upon logging in, you'll see the details of your database you just created (Figure 9-6).

Enterprise Manager Express

Chapter 7 discussed how to enable EM Express for 12c databases; here, we will revisit this. EM Express can be used with 12c and 18c databases, and configuring it is the same in both versions. To start, we need to find out what port it's running on, very much like we just did with 11g Database Control. The difference between the two is that Database Control uses a small app server, where in 12c and 18c, it is served out of the database on the XML DB port. Remember that we need to ensure that the firewall is opened to these ports, just as we did previously.

With OCI-C, we can access the console just as we did for 11g Database Control. We find the database we want to use on the database console page and use the menu to the right to select Open EM Console, as shown in Figure 9-3. Just remember, if this ExaCS is using private IPs, the URL will need to be accessed via a VPN, FastConnect, bastion server, or SSH tunnel.

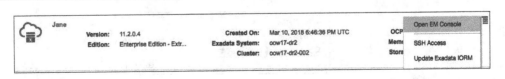

FIGURE 9-3. *Open the EM console in the OCI-C database console UI*

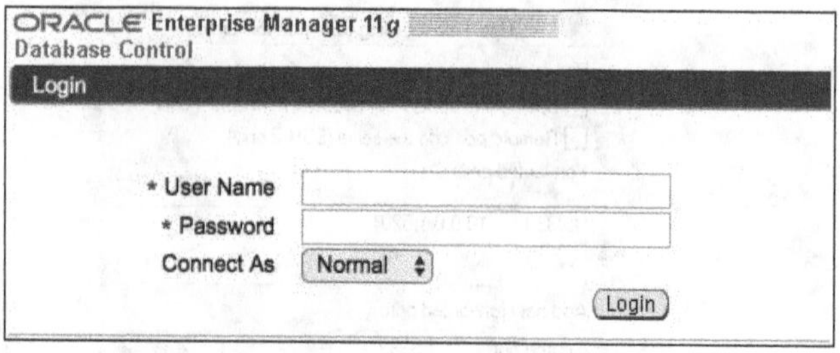

FIGURE 9-4. *11g Database Control login*

If using OCI, we need to get/set the port. We SSH into our service, node 1, and source the 12c or 18c database we want to work with. In this example, we will use the HRCDB database again:

```
[oracle@exacs-node1 ~]$ . HRCDB.env
```

Next, we log into the database with SQL*Plus, as sysdba:

```
[oracle@exacs-o05pq1 ~]$ sqlplus
SQL*Plus: Release 12.2.0.1.0 Production on Sat Jan 27 19:04:53 2018
Copyright (c) 1982, 2016, Oracle.  All rights reserved.

Enter user-name: / as sysdba
```

EM Express could be running on a port already, so we need to check, using the following SQL in the CDB:

```
SQL> select dbms_xdb_config.getHttpsPort() from dual;

DBMS_XDB_CONFIG.GETHTTPSPORT()
------------------------------
                          5502
```

If the result is a number other than 0 (usually 5500 through 5510), we do not need to set the port. If 0 is returned, we can use the following SQL to set the port:

```
SQL> exec dbms_xdb_config.sethttpsport(desired port number);
```

So if we want port 5502, we would use

```
SQL> exec dbms_xdb_config.sethttpsport(5502);
```

FIGURE 9-5. *Credentials for logging into 11g Database Control*

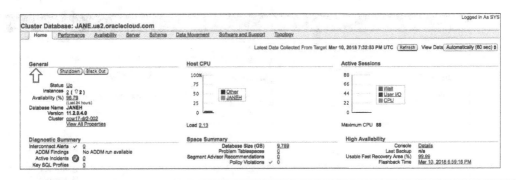

FIGURE 9-6. *Database Control database details*

Once the port is set, we open the port (see Chapter 3) and connect with the following URL: https://your_ExaCS_IP_address:port_set/em. The port is the one we just set with the previous SQL. We use https://10.0.0.10:5502/em because we set our port to 5502 for the CDB and are connecting to the first node.

NOTE
If you are running EM Express on a version 12.1 database, you will need to set the port not only in the CDB, but on each of the PDBs you want to use EM Express with, and on different ports. If you are using 12.2 or later, you just have to set the port in the CDB.

When you're performing this operation, you may face the self-signed certificate issue. As before, add the exception or click through.

Once on the login page, we find the Login box on the right, as shown in Figure 9-7, and enter the credentials shown in the figure. We use the password we used when we created the database instance, leave the Container field blank, and check the As Sysdba box.

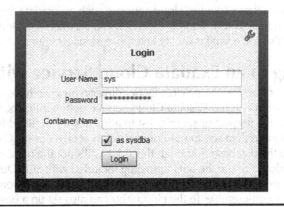

FIGURE 9-7. *EM Express Login box*

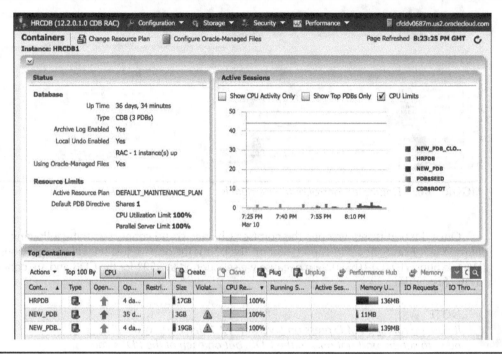

FIGURE 9-8.   *Managing PDBs in EM Express 12.2*

Once we're logged into EM Express, we can manage and monitor our CDBs and PDBs (Figure 9-8).

SQL Developer

SQL Developer is Oracle's all-encompassing tool for working with databases. It has evolved over the years to include many cloud-specific functions such as SSH tunneling and a native ability to connect into some of the database-specific cloud services such as Exadata Express, Autonomous Data Warehouse, Autonomous OLTP, and the older Schema Service. SQL Developer also has the ability to manage your database in a similar way to Enterprise Manager with a breadth of DBA-specific tools.

Connecting to an Exadata Cloud Service with SQL Developer

First, we need to connect to the service. Depending on how we have set up our service, we have a few options. If we set up our Exadata Cloud Service with public IPs, we have an easy job ahead of us. We can use the firewall or security list to allow a specific IP address in over 1521, the SQL*Net port. We can then set up our connection to access our ExaCS right over that port and direct connect to the database. Although this is easy, it's not the most secure way.

A better solution is to use the SSH tunneling included with SQL Developer to connect via SSH and tunnel 1521 over that connection. This ensures that the connection is secure and encrypted as we move data from on-premises to the cloud. You can also set up a bastion server to forward traffic on 1521 to an ExaCS if the service is using private IPs after SSHing into that bastion.

After we have the public IP, we need one more item for our secured connection: the private key. When you created a Database-as-a-Service (DBaaS) instance, you created a public and private key. The public key was used on instance creation. The private key will be used to connect to the instance at the OS level. We need this key for our SQL Developer connection.

After we open SQL Developer, we choose View | SSH (Figure 9-9).

At the bottom left of SQL Developer, a new SSH panel should appear. We right-click SSH Hosts and select New SSH Host (Figure 9-10).

In the New SSH Host modal, for the Name field, we enter **ExaCS**. For Host, we enter the IP address of one of the ExaCS database nodes. For Username, we enter **opc**.

We select the checkbox next to Use Key File and use the .ppk key file we used to log into the Exadata database compute nodes. Also, we click the checkbox next to Add A Local Port Forward. For Name, we enter **VIP**. For the Host field, we use the VIP of the node we selected in the Host field (called *floating IP address* in OCI). Lastly, we leave the port as 1521. The modal now looks like Figure 9-11. We click OK to save the information.

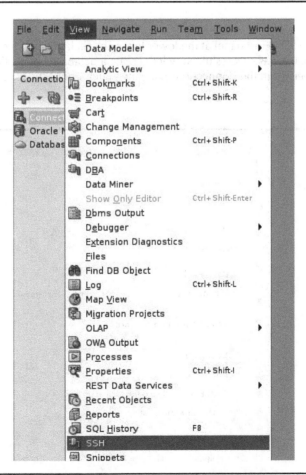

FIGURE 9-9. *Accessing the SSH panel*

FIGURE 9-10. *Creating a new SSH host*

Back in the SSH Host panel at the lower left, right-click the ExaCS connection and select Test. It should come back as successful. Now let's create a database connection.

At the upper left in the Connections panel, we click Connections and select New Connection (Figure 9-12).

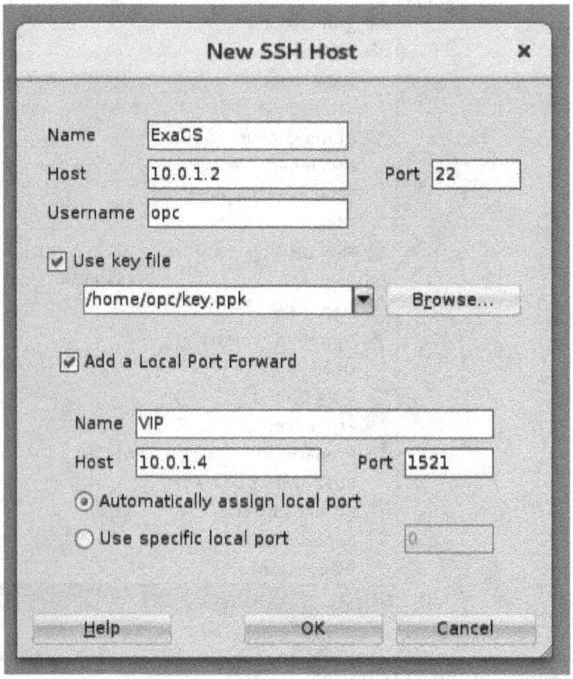

New SSH Host ✕

Name	ExaCS
Host	10.0.1.2	Port 22
Username	opc

☑ Use key file

/home/opc/key.ppk ▼ Browse...

☑ Add a Local Port Forward

Name VIP

Host 10.0.1.4 Port 1521

◉ Automatically assign local port

○ Use specific local port 0

Help OK Cancel

FIGURE 9-11. *The completed New SSH Host modal*

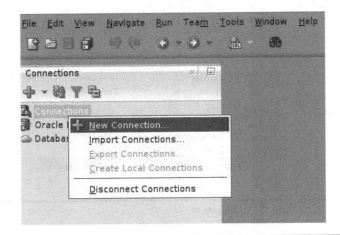

FIGURE 9-12.   *Creating a new database connection*

In the New/Select Database Connection modal, in the Connection Name field, we enter **ExaCS Database**. For Username and Password, we enter **sys** and the password for sys (what was entered on database creation). Then click the Save Password checkbox.

In the Oracle section, for Connection Type we choose SSH. Then change the Role to SYSDBA. We select the Service Name radio button and enter the service name of the CDB of the database we want to connect to. The Service Name is the URL-like name; in the example it is HRCDB .clientsubnet.exacsvcn.oraclevcn.com. Figure 9-13 shows how the modal should look. We click the Test button to see if our connection works. It we have a successful connection, we click the Connect button.

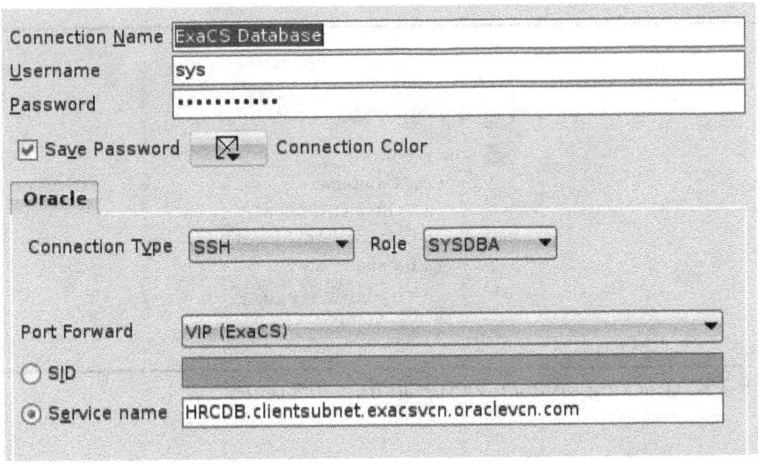

Connection Name ExaCS Database

Username sys

Password ....

☑ Save Password   ⬛   Connection Color

Oracle

Connection Type SSH ▼   Role SYSDBA ▼

Port Forward VIP (ExaCS) ▼

○ SID

◉ Service name HRCDB.clientsubnet.exacsvcn.oraclevcn.com

FIGURE 9-13.   *Creating a database connection in SQL Developer*

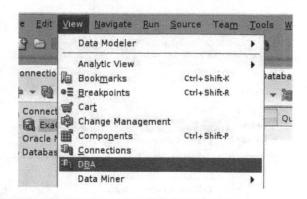

FIGURE 9-14. *Selecting the DBA panel*

Managing the Database with the DBA Panel

Once we're connected, back in SQL Developer, we select View | DBA (Figure 9-14).

The DBA panel is presented at the lower left of the window, just as the SSH panel was. Right-click the Connections node and in the Select Connection modal, we select our ExaCS Database connection. Now, on the left, we expand the ExaCS Database connection node, expand the Database Status node, and click Instance Viewer (Figure 9-15).

The main panel will refresh, and we can see the status of our database with auto-refreshing charts and graphs (Figure 9-16).

Through the Instance Viewer and the DBA panel, we can monitor and manage the database. If we need to work at a PDB level, we can copy the SQL Developer connection we created and point the service name to a PDB rather than the CDB.

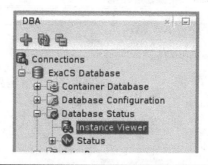

FIGURE 9-15. *Clicking Instance Viewer in the DBA panel*

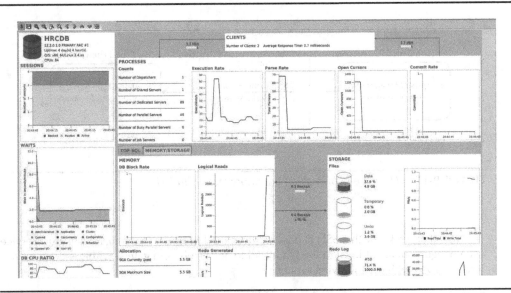

FIGURE 9-16. *Viewing the status of our database in the Instance Viewer*

Enterprise Manager Cloud Control 13cR2

This next section is going to make a big assumption: I assume you have installed Enterprise Manager Cloud Control 13cR2 (or greater) so that it can access the Exadata Cloud Service. For this section, I've installed EM on an IaaS instance within an OCI VCN where my ExaCS is located. We will pick up from where we configured the EM instance to accept hybrid agents and then deploy one to the ExaCS.

Configure the Hybrid Gateway

The first step in setting up Enterprise Manager to be used with the ExaCS is to enable the hybrid gateway. The hybrid gateway is used to manage cloud instances. A regular EM agent communicates bidirectionally on a few ports. If you were to deploy a regular agent on your cloud instance with an EM instance on-premises, you would need to open up incoming ports from the open Internet back into your intranet. This is usually frowned upon by corporate IT departments. To get over this issue, we can deploy hybrid agents, which communicate over SSH and never initiate communication. It is always started from EM to the agent, as shown in Figure 9-17.

To enable the hybrid gateway, you need to log into the on-premises server/IaaS VM where EM is installed. In the following example, we use an IaaS VM hosted in OCI in the same VCN as an ExaCS. The IaaS VM has a public IP address where we can access EM, but the ExaCS has all private IP addresses.

Once on the server, we ensure that we can SSH into the Exadata Cloud Service:

```
[opc@em1 ~]$ ssh -i key.ppk -l opc 10.0.2.2
Last login: Sun Mar 25 01:32:47 2018 from em1.apexsub.exacsvcn.oraclevcn.com
[opc@exacs-node1 ~]$
```

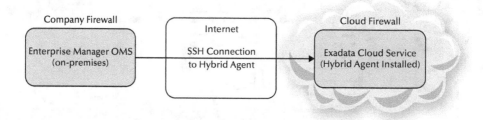

FIGURE 9-17. *How the hybrid agent communicates with EM*

Now that we know that SSH is possible from the EM server to the Exadata Cloud Service, we can configure an agent local to the EM install to act as a hybrid gateway. This is done on the EM instance's VM with the following syntax:

```
$<emcli_install_location>/bin/emcli login -username=sysman
```

We first log into EM via `emcli`. We then register the gateway with the local agent:

```
$<emcli_install_location>/bin/emcli register_hybridgateway_agent
-hybridgateway_agent_list="<On-premises target name for the Agent>"
-ignore_network_check -ignore_central_agent_check
```

Here's a quick explanation of the two flags used:

- **–ignore_network_check** Using `ignore_network_check` will not attempt to communicate with a cloud service. We already know we have a connection, so we can skip this.
- **–ignore_central_agent_check** This is used so that we can use the OMS agent running on the main instance of EM as the hybrid gateway. Best practice is to have the hybrid agent on another server, but for this example, we will use the central OMS agent.

The trick is getting the on-premises or local target name for the agent we want to use as the gateway. We can do this by logging into EM from a web UI. Once logged in, we can view all targets by selecting the All Targets option from the Targets drop-down menu in the upper right (Figure 9-18).

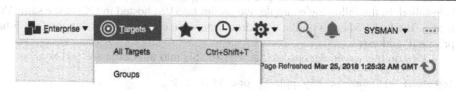

FIGURE 9-18. *Selecting All Targets from the Targets drop-down menu*

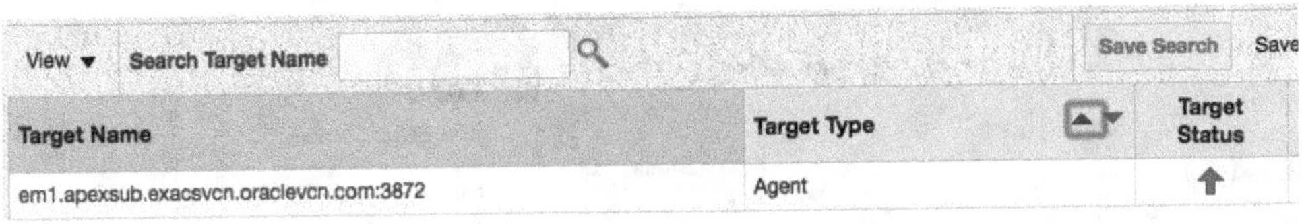

View ▼ Search Target Name	[_____] 🔍	Save Search	Save
Target Name	**Target Type**	◢▸	**Target Status**
em1.apexsub.exacsvcn.oraclevcn.com:3872	Agent		⬆

FIGURE 9-19. *Using the ascend/descend sort arrows to sort by ascending*

On the following page, the targets report, use the ascend/descend sort arrows to sort by ascending (Figure 9-19).

One of the first items, if not the first item, in the list should be the agent. Copy the target name for the agent. In our example, we would use em1.apexsub.exacsvcn.oraclevcn.com:3872 as the agent name. We can now use this agent to enable the hybrid gateway. For our example, the code would look like the following:

```
$<emcli_install_location>/bin/emcli login -username=sysman
$<emcli_install_location>/bin/emcli register_hybridgateway_agent
-hybridgateway_agent_list="em1.apexsub.exacsvcn.oraclevcn.com:3872"
-ignore_network_check -ignore_central_agent_check
```

And here's what it looks like in practice:

```
[opc@em1 bin]$ ./emcli login -username=sysman
Enter password :

Login successful
[opc@em1 bin]$ ./emcli register_hybridgateway_agent
-hybridgateway_agent_list="em1.apexsub.exacsvcn.oraclevcn.com:3872"
-ignore_network_check -ignore_central_agent_check
Successfully registered list of agents as hybridgateways.
[opc@em1 bin]$
```

Next we will deploy the agent onto our ExaCS. We do this in a few steps. First, we register the SSH keys with EM. Back in the EM web console, from the Setup drop-down menu, select Security, then Named Credentials (Figure 9-20).

On the Named Credentials page, we click Create. On the Create Credential page, General Properties section, for Credential Name, we enter **ExaCS_Login**. Authenticating Target Type is set as Host, but we change Credential Type to SSH Key Credentials. Finally, in this section, we select the Global radio button for Scope. The General Properties section should look like Figure 9-21.

Now, in the Credential Properties section, for UserName, we enter **oracle**. For the SSH Private Key, we enter the private key text for the key we used to log in to the Exadata Cloud Service as oracle. Or we can use the buttons next to Upload Private Key to select the key on our local computer and upload it. Once the Credential Properties section looks like Figure 9-22, we click

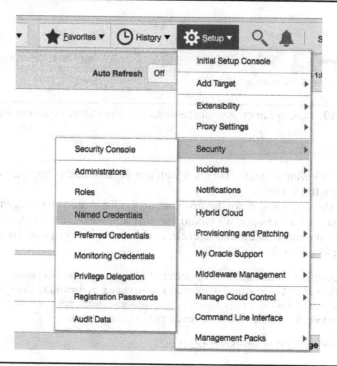

FIGURE 9-20. *Selecting Named Credentials*

the Save button in the upper-right corner of the page. (Click the Save button, not the Test And Save button.) When we get the warning message, "Credential may not be valid as you have not chosen 'Test and Save'. Do you wish to continue to save?", we click Save.

Now that we have created the Named Credentials, we can start to deploy the agent onto the ExaCS database nodes. Back in the Setup drop-down menu, we select Add Target, then Add Targets Manually (Figure 9-23).

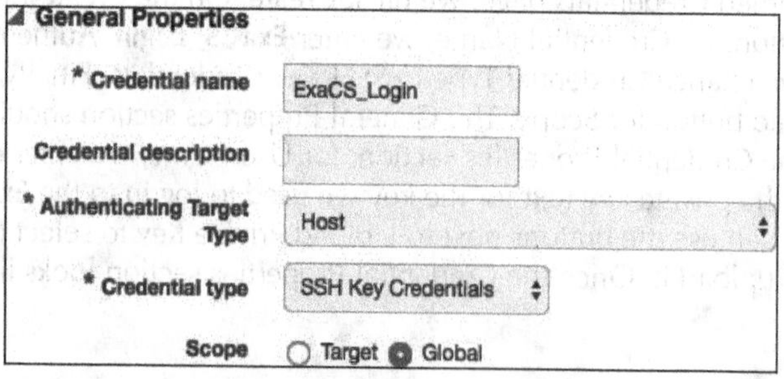

FIGURE 9-21. *The General Properties section*

Credential Properties

* **UserName**	oracle

* **SSH Private Key**

```
gv4qvgur/incuzzuuuuzun/ntruripuuvucuuiv
+QbNkebc6bKV/sHYvfilvoagaeW5Pu
xauQw526+J/+Zdll1BTt0UB4XXxRqwrYqUR
oOs8ynUr9kCc0v8J9awkJ4yCJ+IvY
-----END RSA PRIVATE KEY-----
```

Upload Private Key [Choose File] No file chosen

SSH Public Key

Upload Public Key [Choose File] No file chosen

Run Privilege | None ⬍

FIGURE 9-22. *The Credential Properties section*

On the following page, we click Install Agent On Host from the Add Host Targets panel (Figure 9-24).

On the Add Host Targets: Host And Platform page, click the Add button in the middle left of the page. A new row appears in the report section. For Host, we enter the IP address of the first database compute node in our Exadata Cloud Service. For Platform, we select Linux x86-64 (Figure 9-25).

We click Next in the upper-right part of the page, and the following warning message is displayed: "The host names specified include IP addresses or short names. It is advised to provide Fully Qualified Host Names, such as foo.mydomain.com, that are persistent over the life of the targets. It is recommended for ease of maintenance and overall security. However, you can choose to ignore this warning and proceed by clicking Next." We click Next again after clicking OK to clear the warning.

On the next page, the Add Host Targets: Installation Details page, at the bottom section of the page is Linux x86-64: Agent Installation Details. For Installation Base Directory, we use

```
/u02/app/oracle/agent
```

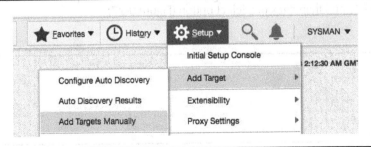

FIGURE 9-23. *Selecting Add Targets Manually*

FIGURE 9-24. *The Add Host Targets panel*

Usually the Instance Directory will auto-complete. If not, enter the following:

```
/u02/app/oracle/agent/agent_inst
```

We select the checkbox next to Configure Hybrid Cloud Agent, and a Hybrid Cloud Gateway Agent field is displayed (Figure 9-26).

Now, click the magnifying glass icon to the left of the new Hybrid Cloud Gateway Agent field. In the Select Hybrid Cloud Gateway Agent modal, click on the agent we configured in the table in the middle and then click the Select button (Figure 9-27).

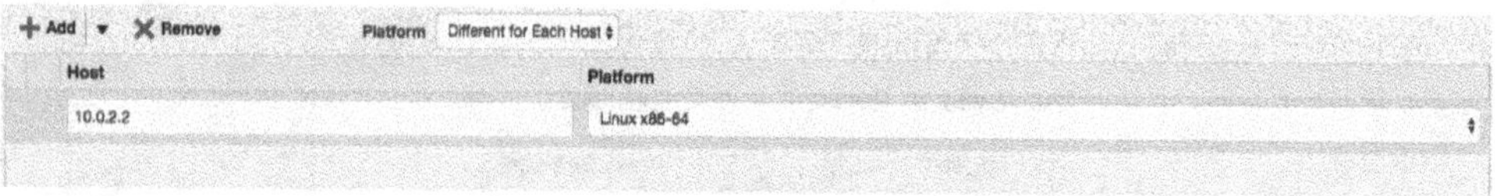

+ Add ▾ ✕ Remove	Platform Different for Each Host ⬧	
Host	**Platform**	
10.0.2.2	Linux x86-64	⬧

FIGURE 9-25. *Adding a host and platform for the first agent*

FIGURE 9-26. *Hybrid Cloud Gateway Agent field*

Leave the Hybrid Cloud Gateway Proxy Port set to the default value. For Named Credential, we select the one we previously created: EXACS_LOGIN. Once the Linux x86-64: Agent Installation Details section looks like Figure 9-28, we click Next in the upper-right corner of the page.

On the last page of the Add Target flow, we click Deploy Agent in the upper-right corner of the page.

As the install page is displayed, we can run into a few issues. First, if we are running this on an ExaCS in OCI, the installer will not see .oraclecloud.internal when it runs a `hostname -d` command on the database compute node. We can get around this by changing the network file in /etc/sysconfig, the hosts file in /etc, and running the `hostname` command to change the hostname temporarily to return oraclecloud.internal when issuing the `hostname -d` command.

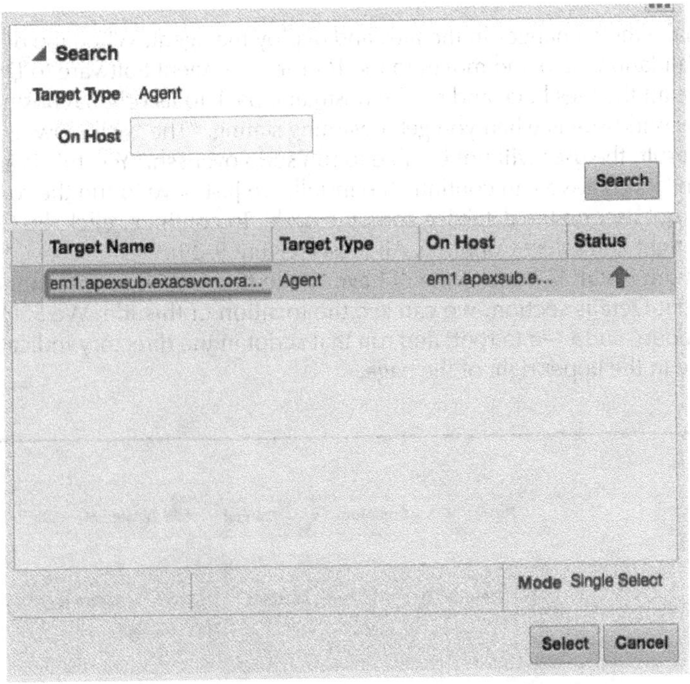

FIGURE 9-27. *Select the Hybrid Cloud Gateway Agent in the modal*

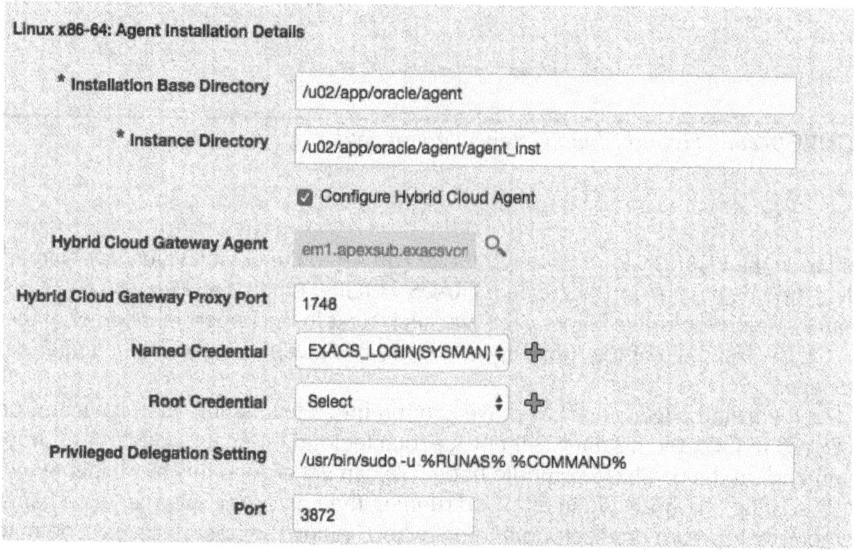

Linux x86-64: Agent Installation Details

* Installation Base Directory	/u02/app/oracle/agent
* Instance Directory	/u02/app/oracle/agent/agent_inst
	☑ Configure Hybrid Cloud Agent
Hybrid Cloud Gateway Agent	em1.apexsub.exacsvcn 🔍
Hybrid Cloud Gateway Proxy Port	1748
Named Credential	EXACS_LOGIN(SYSMAN) ▲▼ ➕
Root Credential	Select ▲▼ ➕
Privileged Delegation Setting	/usr/bin/sudo -u %RUNAS% %COMMAND%
Port	3872

FIGURE 9-28. *The Linux x86-64: Agent Installation Details section*

We make these changes in the files and deploy the agent. When the deployment gets past the Remote Validations step and moves to the Transferring Agent Software to Destination Host step, we change all the files back and set the hostname back to its original hostname.

The second issue is when you get a warning stating, "The 'visiblepw' is not set the sudoers file and as a result, the user will not be able to run sudo over ssh." Yes, this is a strange error and it is missing an "in," but we can continue the install; we just have to run the root.sh script manually using the root user on the database compute node. To continue, click the Continue drop-down in the upper right and select Continue, All Hosts (Figure 9-29).

When the install is done, we will have to run the root.sh script manually. In the Agent Deployment Details section, we can see the location of this file. We SSH into the database compute node, sudo -s to root, and run that script in the directory indicated. After it is run, we click Done in the upper right of the page.

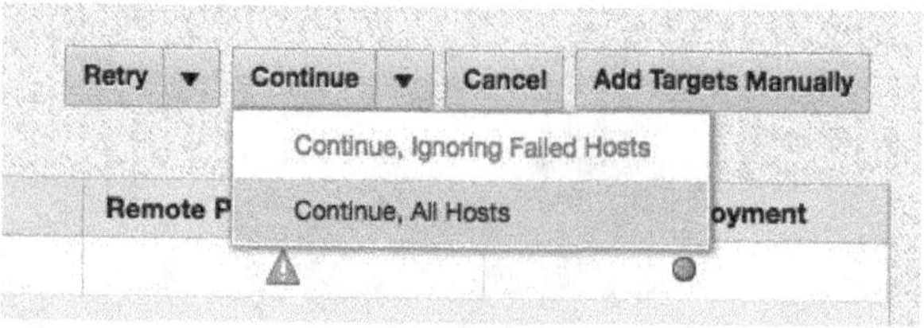

Retry ▼	Continue ▼	Cancel	Add Targets Manually
	Continue, Ignoring Failed Hosts		
Remote P	Continue, All Hosts		oyment
	⚠		◉

FIGURE 9-29. *Continuing the install after the warning*

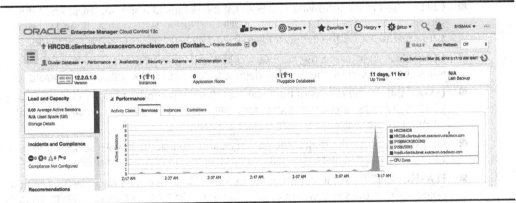

FIGURE 9-30.   *ExaCS in EM*

To deploy the agent on the other nodes of our service, we follow the previous directions for each node. Shortly after the agent is deployed, the services on that node will be registered with EM. We can hurry things along on the Auto Discovery Results page in EM. Once EM registers the components on the ExaCS, we can manage and monitor them via the EM console pages (Figure 9-30). We can even see how the database's compute nodes are running, including CPU and memory utilization. The only difference here between this hybrid agent and an on-premises Exadata Agent is that we can see only to the cluster level. Cell health and hardware metrics are not available.

ExaCLI

If you have an on-premises Exadata, you know that you can use CellCLI or DBMCLI on your hosts to get information and statistics back from your storage cells. With the Exadata Cloud Service, you have access to ExaCLI, which brings with it a subset of the available commands for working with the storage cells. Where DBMCLI runs on the database compute nodes and CellCLI runs on the storage servers, ExaCLI runs on the DB compute nodes and can use commands from both CellCLI and DBMCLI.

With the Exadata Cloud Service, you can use the LIST command with ExaCLI for gathering information about the storage servers. Now much of this information can be seen in an Automatic Workload Repository (AWR) report, but if you need up-to-date, real-time information, ExaCLI is the tool to use. Using the LIST command, you can see information for the following objects/ services:

- **ACTIVEREQUEST**   Lists all active requests that are currently being served by the storage servers.
- **ALERTDEFINITION**   Used with the LIST command, displays all the alerts and their sources for the storage servers.
- **ALERTHISTORY**   Lists all the alerts that have happened on the storage servers.

- **CELL**   Used in the following syntax to list the details of a specific attribute of the storage servers or storage cells, `LIST CELL ATTRIBUTES A,B,C`, with A, B, and C being attributes. To see all the cell attributes, use `ATTRIBUTES ALL` in the command.

- **CELLDISK**   Lets us see the attributes of the cell disks in the storage servers. Use the following syntax to list the cell disk details: `LIST CELLDISK CELL_DISK_NAME DETAIL`.

- **DATABASE**   View details of the databases. Syntax is similar to other LIST commands: `LIST DATABASE` and `LIST DATABASE DETAIL`. And it can look at an individual attribute: `LIST DATABASE ATTRIBUTES NAME`.

- **DIAGPACK**   Lists the diagnostic packages and their status in your service. The syntax is `LIST DIAGPACK [DETAIL]`, with `DETAIL` being an optional attribute.

- **FLASHCACHE**   See the details of the Exadata Cloud Service's flash cache. Using this object follows the same syntax as other commands: `LIST FLASHCACHE DETAIL` or `ExaCLI LIST FLASHCACHE ATTRIBUTES [ATTRIBUTE(S)]`.

- **FLASHCACHECONTENT**   View all the details of the objects in the flash cache or by a specific object ID. To list all the contents, issue the following command: `LIST FLASHCACHECONTENT DETAIL`. To see the details for a specific object, first find the object ID. For example, use the user_objects to get the object_id of, say, a partition or table:

```
select object_name, data_object_id from user_objects where object_name =
'BIG_CENSUS';
OBJECT_NAME              DATA_OBJECT_ID
--------------------     --------------
BIG_CENSUS               29152
```

  Using the data_object_id, you can then see the details of this using the FLASHCACHECONTENT object: `LIST FLASHCACHECONTENT WHERE objectNumber=29152 DETAIL`.

- **FLASHLOG**   Using `LIST FLASHLOG` displays the attributes for the Oracle Exadata Smart Flash Log.

- **GRIDDISK**   Similar to the CELLDISK object syntax, you can see details of a particular grid disk. You can see all the attributes: `LIST GRIDDISK GRIDDISK_NAME DETAIL`. Or see just an attribute of the grid disk: `LIST GRIDDISK GRIDDISK_NAME ATTRIBUTES size, name`.

- **IBPORT**   Shows details about the InfiniBand ports. Syntax is `LIST IBPORT DETAIL`.

- **IORMPLAN**   Offers a bit more freedom than just `LIST`. You can create custom IORM plans and apply them to the storage servers as well as view information about these plans. To start, as with the other `LIST` commands, you can see the details of all the IORM plans with the following command: `ExaCLI LIST IORMPLAN DETAIL`. You can also alter and create plans. Here is an example of creating a plan:

```
ALTER IORMPLAN dbplan= ((name=db1, limit=50),
(name=db2, limit=50),
(name=other, level=1, allocation=25))
```

  IORMPLAN is discussed later in this chapter in the section "ExaCLI Examples."

- **IORMPROFILE**   Used with the `LIST` command, lets you view any profiles you have set on the storage servers. You can also refer back to the profile attribute on the DATABASE object if a database has an IORM profile upon it. Syntax is `LIST IORMPROFILE`.

- **LUN** Logical Unit Number object returns the number and the detail of the physical disks in the storage servers. You can see the LUNs of the disks with `LIST LUN` and the details of each LUN with `LIST LUN LUN_NUMBER DETAIL`.

- **METRICCURRRENT** The metric current object lists the current metrics for a particular object type. Syntax is `LIST METRICCURRENT WHERE objectType = 'CELLDISK'`. This object also allows for sorting and results limits as seen in the following command:

  ```
  LIST METRICCURRENT attributes name, metricObjectName ORDER BY metricObjectName
  asc, name desc LIMIT 5
  ```

- **METRICDEFINITION** Lists metric definitions for the object that you can then get details for. With the command `LIST metricDefinition WHERE objectType=cell`, you can get all the metrics for that object type. You can then use the metric definition object again and get details for one of those specific metrics just listed: `LIST metricDefinition WHERE name= IORM_MODE DETAIL`.

- **METRICHISTORY** Lets you see a list of metrics over a specified period of time. In the example `LIST METRICHISTORY WHERE ageInMinutes < 30`, you can see all the metrics collected over the past 30 minutes. You can also use the predicate `collectionTime` to set a range from a specific time. You would use that in the following way: `LIST METRICHISTORY WHERE collectionTime > '2018-04-01T21:12:00-10:00'`. The metric history object can also be used to see a specific metric using the object's name (`LIST METRICHISTORY CT_FD_IO_RQ_SM`) or a where clause to get objects with similar attributes like name (`LIST METRICHISTORY WHERE name like 'CT_.*'`).

- **OFFLOADGROUP** Using `LIST OFFLOADGROUP` shows the attributes for the offload group that are running on your storage servers. You can see all the details for all groups with `LIST OFFLOADGROUP DETAIL`, the attributes for a specific group with `LIST OFFLOADGROUP offloadgroup4`, or as with other `LIST` commands, specific attributes with `LIST OFFLOADGROUP ATTRIBUTES name`.

- **PHYSICALDISK** Works in a similar way to the `LUN` object. You can first list all the physical disks with `LIST PHYSICALDISK`. You can then see the details of a particular physical disk, with `LIST PHYSICALDISK 20:10 DETAIL`, and flash disks, with `LIST PHYSICALDISK FLASH_1_0 DETAIL`.

- **PLUGGABLEDATABASE** Lists all PDBs with `LIST PLUGGABLEDATABASE` or see the details of a specific PDB with `LIST PLUGGABLEDATABASE PDB_NAME`.

- **QUARANTINE** Lists all SQL statements that you prevented from using Smart Scans. The syntax is `LIST QUARANTINE DETAIL`, or using a where clause on any of the available attributes.

Using ExaCLI

To use ExaCLI, we construct our commands in the following syntax using the opc user:

```
exacli -c [username@]remotehost [-l username] [--xml] [--cookie-jar [filename]]
[-e command]
```

The username is cloud_user. The password for the cloud_user is the same password we used for the sys/system accounts on the first database we created on the service. The remote host is going to be one of the storage servers. Use `--xml` to display the output from the commands in XML. This is an optional flag. The `--cookie-jar` flag will store the authentication cookie returned by the storage server locally in a file. If we do not specify a file name, the cookie is stored at the default location of HOME/.exacli/cookiejar, with HOME being the user's home directory. For the opc user, for example, the home is /home/opc. Finally, the `-e` flag is used to list the command we want to issue.

We need to find the cells' IP addresses or hostnames. We can use the cellip.ora to find the IP addresses. Taking a look at my cellip.ora file, I see the following IP addresses (this is a quarter rack shape so three storage cells, two connections each, six total connections).

Here are my cell IPs and hostnames in the hosts file on an ExaCS in OCI:

```
[root@exacs-node1 ~]# cat /etc/oracle/cell/
network-config/cellip.ora
cell="192.168.136.5;192.168.136.6"
cell="192.168.136.7;192.168.136.8"
cell="192.168.136.9;192.168.136.10"
```

Here are my cell IPs and hostnames in the hosts file on an ExaCS in OCI-C:

```
[root@exacs-node1 ~]# cat /etc/oracle/cell/
network-config/cellip.ora
cell="10.196.112.5;10.196.112.6"
cell="10.196.112.7;10.196.112.8"
cell="10.196.112.9;10.196.112.10"
```

When using ExaCLI, I need to connect to one of these storage cells. An example of connecting into a storage cell with ExaCLI would be

```
[opc@exacs-node1 ~]$ exacli -l cloud_user -c 192.168.136.7
```

Putting this all together, here is an example of using the ExaCLI command to list the griddisk's details.

```
[opc@exacs-node1 ~]$ exacli -l cloud_user -c 192.168.136.7
--cookie-jar -e list griddisk detail
No cookies found for cloud_user@192.168.136.7.
Password: *********
name:                  ACFSC1_DG1_CD02_cell3
asmDiskGroupName:      ACFSC1_DG1
asmDiskName:           ACFSC1_DG1_CD02_CELL3
asmFailGroupName:      IAD300127EXDCL12
availableTo:
cachedBy:              FD_01_iad300127exdcl12
cachingPolicy:         default
cellDisk:              CD_02_iad300127exdcl12
comment:
creationTime:          2018-03-08T10:26:40+00:00
diskType:              HardDisk
errorCount:            0
id:                    0f2af869-f4ab-4c31-8f82-181101c434c9
size:                  24G
status:                active
......
```

ExaCLI will list the grid disk details and exit out of the tool. Also, seeing that I used the `--cookie-jar` command, I no longer need to supply the password when logging into ExaCLI on this particular node (192.168.136.7).

If this is the first time I was accessing the storage cells via ExaCLI, I might be prompted to accept a certificate. I would then accept this self-signed certificate and continue using the tool:

```
[opc@exacs-node1 ~]$ exacli --login-name cloud_user
--cookie-jar -c 192.168.136.7
No cookies found for cloud_user@192.168.136.7.
Password: *********
EXA-30016: This connection is not secure. You have asked ExaCLI to connect to cell
 192.168.136.7 securely. The identity of 192.168.136.7 cannot be verified.
Got certificate from server:
C=US,ST=California,L=Redwood City,O=Oracle Corporation,OU=Oracle
 Exadata,CN=ed1c103clu01-priv2.usdc2.oraclecloud.com
Do you want to accept and store this certificate? (Press y/n)
```

ExaCLI Examples

Let's run some actual commands on our ExaCS and see what ExaCLI returns. We can start by logging into ExaCLI and listing all the databases on the service (no need to use a password because of the `--cookie-jar`):

```
[opc@exacs-node1 ~]$ exacli -l cloud_user -c 192.168.136.7
```

Now that we are in ExaCLI, we can list all the databases:

```
exacli cloud_user@192.168.136.7> LIST DATABASE
        ASM
        HRCDB
```

Remember that each object type has multiple attributes. Taking a look at the DATABASE object type using the `DESCRIBE` command yields the following:

```
exacli cloud_user@192.168.136.7> DESCRIBE DATABASE
        name
        databaseID
        flashCacheLimit
        flashCacheMin
        flashCacheSize
        iormShare
        lastRequestTime
        profile
```

And we can list one or many attributes now using `LIST` and `ATTRIBUTES`:

```
exacli cloud_user@192.168.136.7> LIST DATABASE ATTRIBUTES name,databaseID,iormshare
        ASM     0               0
        CRMCDB  3000709034      1
        HRCDB   550225509       20
```

We can also zero in on a single database's details by adding its name into the `LIST DETAIL` command:

```
exacli cloud_user@192.168.136.7> LIST DATABASE HRCDB DETAIL
        name:                      HRCDB
        databaseID:                550225509
        iormShare:                 1
        lastRequestTime:           2018-05-26T19:13:15+00:00
        profile:
        flashCacheMin:             0
        flashCacheLimit:           11.642578125T
        flashCacheSize:            0
```

Next, we can view all pluggable databases:

```
exacli cloud_user@192.168.136.7> LIST PLUGGABLEDATABASE
        CDB$ROOT
        PDB$SEED
        HRPDB
```

And see a specific pluggable database's details:

```
exacli cloud_user@192.168.136.7> LIST PLUGGABLEDATABASE HRPDB DETAIL
        name:                      HRPDB
        pdbID:                     1312617605
        containerName:             HRCDB
        flashCacheMin:             0
        flashCacheLimit:           3.816436767578125T
        flashCacheSize:            0
```

We can view the IORM plan and shares on our databases (which we created via the UI, API, or ExaCLI):

```
exacli cloud_user@192.168.136.7> LIST IORMPLAN DETAIL
        name:                      cfclcx2649_IORMPLAN
        catPlan:
        dbPlan:                    name=CLONECDB,share=2,flashcachelimit=1703G
                                   name=HRCDB,share=20,flashcachelimit=11922G
                                   name=HRSNCDB,share=5,flashcachelimit=4258G
                                   name=default,share=1,flashcachelimit=851G
        objective:                 auto
        status:                    activeexacli
```

Using ExaCLI, we can also create custom IORM plans.

NOTE
If you do alter the IORM plan, you need to alter it on all of the storage cells in your Exadata Cloud Service shape:

```
exacli cloud_user@192.168.136.7> ALTER IORMPLAN
        dbPlan=(
                (name=findb, share=20, flashcachelimit=11922G),
                (name=hrdb, share=5, flashcachelimit=4111G),
                (name=testdb, share=2, flashcachelimit=1644G),
                (name=default, share=1, flashcachelimit=851G))
```

As the uncle of a comic book hero once said, "With great power comes great responsibility." Having the ability to change IORM plans is a very powerful feature, and you need to take great care when altering them. If you change the plan at the ExaCLI level, all the settings you made in the UI will be erased and this new plan will be used. If you do choose to use ALTER IORMPLAN, be sure to take a good long look at the documentation set. Setting IORM plans will change the way your Exadata Cloud Service handles requests—and not in a good way if it's done incorrectly.

In Chapter 8, we discussed the Exadata Smart Flash Log. We can view the Flash Log details with the LIST FLASHLOG DETAIL command:

```
exacli cloud_user@192.168.136.7> LIST FLASHLOG DETAIL
        name:                  iad300127exdcl12_FLASHLOG
        cellDisk:              FD_00_iad300127exdcl12,FD_01_
iad300127exdcl12,FD_03_iad300127exdcl12,FD_02_iad3001
27exdcl12
        creationTime:          2018-03-08T09:37:54+00:00
        degradedCelldisks:
        effectiveSize:         512M
        efficiency:            100.0
        id:                    f8604435-5490-42d7-8b5a-76aed9d5cd1b
        size:                  512M
        status:                normal
```

ExaCLI can also be used to see details about the cell disks:

```
exacli cloud_user@192.168.136.7> LIST CELLDISK
        CD_00_cfclcx2647    normal
        CD_01_cfclcx2647    normal
        CD_02_cfclcx2647    normal
...
```

And we can see the details of a particular cell disk:

```
exacli cloud_user@192.168.136.7> LIST CELLDISK CD_00_cfclcx2647 DETAIL
        name:                  CD_00_cfclcx2647
        comment:
        creationTime:          2017-09-25T22:13:34+00:00
        deviceName:            /dev/sda
        devicePartition:       /dev/sda3
        diskType:              HardDisk
        errorCount:            0
        freeSpace:             435.0625G
        id:                    56d8a54c-5d76-4dab-9c97-00917dee1fb8
        physicalDisk:          PW9E0V
        size:                  7.11924743652343 75T
        status:                normal
```

Metrics and Diagnostics

Knowing how the service is running is always important. ExaCLI offers some deeper insight into how the storage cells are health-wise, as well as how they are performing. We can even see what objects are cached in the flash cache.

Using ExaCLI, we can see if a particular object is for sure cached in the flash cache. To start, we need to get the DATA_OBJECT_ID from the database using SQL*Plus. In this example, we are in the HRPDB as sys:

```
SQL> select object_name, subobject_name, data_object_id from user_objects where
 object_name = 'BIG_CENSUS';

OBJ_NAME              SUBOBJECT_NAME        DATA_OBJECT_ID
-------------------   -------------------   ---------------
BIG_CENSUS                                  29152
```

Now that we have the DATA_OBJECT_ID, we can look in the flash cache using ExaCLI back as the opc user:

```
[opc@exacs-node1 ~]$ exacli -l cloud_user -c 192.168.136.7
```

After we have logged into ExaCLI, we can issue the following command:

```
exacli cloud_user@192.168.136.7> LIST FLASHCACHECONTENT WHERE objectNumber=29152
DETAIL
        cachedKeepSize:         0
        cachedSize:             826007552
        cachedWriteSize:        49152
        columnarCacheSize:      91750400
        columnarKeepSize:       0
        dbID:                   999933986
        dbUniqueName:           HRCDB.HRPDB
        hitCount:               311966
        missCount:              1407
        objectNumber:           29152
        tableSpaceNumber:       0
```

For diagnostics information, we can start by looking at all the current metrics on the cell with LIST METRICCURRENT:

```
exacli cloud_user@192.168.136.7> LIST METRICCURRENT
        CD_BY_FC_DIRTY        CD_00_cfclcx2647        0.000 MB
        CD_BY_FC_DIRTY        CD_01_cfclcx2647        0.000 MB
        CD_BY_FC_DIRTY        CD_02_cfclcx2647        0.000 MB
        CD_BY_FC_DIRTY        CD_03_cfclcx2647        0.000 MB
        CD_BY_FC_DIRTY        CD_04_cfclcx2647        0.000 MB
        CD_BY_FC_DIRTY        CD_05_cfclcx2647        0.000 MB
        CD_BY_FC_DIRTY        CD_06_cfclcx2647        0.000 MB
...
```

Using DESCRIBE on METRICCURRENT shows what attributes we can use:

```
exacli cloud_user@192.168.136.7> DESCRIBE METRICCURRENT
        name
        alertState
        collectionTime
        metricObjectName
        metricType
        metricValue
        objectType
```

ExaCLI also enables us to use SQL-like clauses to choose what attributes we want to see, how to order them, and to limit the number of results:

```
exacli cloud_user@192.168.136.7> LIST METRICCURRENT attributes name,
 metricobjectname, alertstate, metricvalue order by metricvalue desc,
 metricobjectname asc, name desc limit 3
         CD_IO_TM_R_LG     CD_01_cfclcx2647    normal      88,638,551,241 us
         CD_IO_TM_R_LG     CD_00_cfclcx2647    normal      87,962,500,742 us
         CD_IO_TM_R_LG     CD_10_cfclcx2647    normal      87,699,982,103 us
```

We can also use the where clause in our ExaCLI commands:

```
exacli cloud_user@192.168.136.7> LIST METRICCURRENT WHERE
objectType = 'CELLDISK'
```

If we have issues on our storage cells, we can see what alerts were raised. Start by listing all the alerts on the cells:

```
exacli cloud_user@192.168.136.7> LIST ALERTDEFINITION
         ADRAlert
         HardwareAlert
         MetricAlert
         SoftwareAlert
```

As with preceding commands, we can see the details of the listed alerts:

```
exacli cloud_user@192.168.136.7> LIST ALERTDEFINITION ADRAlert DETAIL
         name:                 ADRAlert
         alertShortName:       ADR
         alertSource:          "Automatic Diagnostic Repository"
         description:          "Incident Alert"
exacli cloud_user@192.168.136.7> LIST ALERTDEFINITION HardwareAlert DETAIL
         name:                 HardwareAlert
         alertShortName:       Hardware
         alertSource:          Hardware
         description:          "Hardware Alert"
```

Finally, we can list all the alerts with ALERTHISTORY:

```
exacli cloud_user@192.168.136.7> LIST ALERTHISTORY
```

With objects like ALERTHISTORY, we can use a time-based where clause as shown next:

```
exacli cloud_user@192.168.136.7> LIST ALERTHISTORY WHERE ageInMinutes < 30
```

and

```
exacli cloud_user@192.168.136.7> LIST ALERTHISTORY
WHERE begintime > 'Jun 1, 2009 11:37:00 AM PDT'
```

The last command we will look at is for creating diagnostics for our storage cells. We will do this with the CREATE DIAGPACK command, which will gather logs and trace files into a single compressed file for us to download. Here is how it's done.

The `CREATE DIAGPACK` command takes in a `packStartTime` as an attribute. The format for this attribute is *yyyy_MM_ddTHH_mm_ss*:

```
exacli cloud_user@192.168.136.7> CREATE DIAGPACK
packStartTime=2018_06_01T00_00_00
```

We can also use now:

```
exacli cloud_user@192.168.136.7> CREATE DIAGPACK packStartTime=now
```

Once we run this command, the service will start to create this file for us:

```
Processing cfclcx2647_diag_2018_06_03T00_44_24_1
```

To check on the status, we can use the `LIST DIAGPACK DETAIL` command:

```
exacli cloud_user@192.168.136.7> LIST DIAGPACK  DETAIL
    name: cfclcx2760_diag_2018_06_17T00_00_00_1
    alertDescription: Processing...
```

When finished processing, the file is ready to download:

```
exacli cloud_user@192.168.136.7> LIST DIAGPACK
        cfclcx2647_diag_2018_06_03T00_44_24_1.tar.bz2
```

Next, we can download the file to our local file system. We use this format:

```
DOWNLOAD DIAGPACK PACK_NAME LOCAL_DIRECTORY
```

So for this example, it would be

```
DOWNLOAD DIAGPACK cfclcx2647_diag_2018_06_03T00_44_24_1 /tmp
```

This would download the diagpack to the /tmp directory:

```
exacli cloud_user@ 192.168.136.7> DOWNLOAD DIAGPACK
 cfclcx2647_diag_2018_06_03T00_44_24_1 /tmp

Downloading cfclcx2647_diag_2018_06_03T00_44_24_1.
Diagpack downloaded: /tmp/cfclcx2647_diag_2018_06_03T00_44_24_1.
```

We can now decompress this file or provide it to support for evaluation.

Summary
The Exadata Cloud Service has multiple built-in tools you can use for managing your databases as well as your service. Use Enterprise Manager Express or the DB console to manage and monitor your individual databases. If you want a fleet-based view, Enterprise Manager will give you just that. Deploy the agents and discover all the databases on your service and manage them from a single console. You can also monitor the health of your storage cells with ExaCLI. Create diagnostic packs, see alerts, and dictate which databases get the most I/O resources. ExaCLI is a very powerful tool, and you will see more functionality unlocked as the service matures.

CHAPTER 10

Migrating to the Exadata Cloud Service

I n this chapter, you'll see explanations for and examples of some common migration methods for moving your databases to the Exadata Cloud Service. Depending on what you are moving, some methods may be more appropriate than others, so be sure to evaluate the tools and their strengths when planning your migration. Some methods covered here are good for entire database migration, while others work not only for full databases but for schemas and tablespaces as well.

TDE Location

In some of the following examples, we'll use Transparent Data Encryption (TDE) because it's used on the ExaCS by default. Where the TDE wallet is located depends on when your database and service were created. In later versions of the ExaCS, the wallet is stored on shared storage. Check the database's sqlnet.ora file at $ORACLE_HOME/network/admin/DB_NAME for the location. In the file, look for the DIRECTORY location.

In this example, the wallet is located in shared storage:

```
ENCRYPTION_WALLET_LOCATION =
 (SOURCE=
  (METHOD=FILE)
   (METHOD_DATA=
    (DIRECTORY=/var/opt/oracle/dbaas_acfs/HRCDB/tde_wallet)))
```

Here, it is stored locally:

```
ENCRYPTION_WALLET_LOCATION =
 (SOURCE=
  (METHOD=FILE)
   (METHOD_DATA=
    (DIRECTORY=/u02/app/oracle/admin/HRCDB/tde_wallet)))
```

NOTE
When using local storage, you need to use the scp *command or move files across to all nodes. When using shared storage, you do not have to do this extra step.*

Data Pump

Introduced in version 10g, Data Pump remains one of the fastest ways to move data from database to database. Even better, it can also move data across platforms (big or little endian) as well as upgrade from one version to another. Data Pump can move data at various levels, from metadata only all the way to a full database. Previous to version 10g, a regular import/export process was used, but Data Pump is a much faster and feature-rich utility.

Schema Export and Import

In the following examples, we will move data; in the process, we'll accomplish some tasks you would face with migrating to the Exadata Cloud Service. The first task is quite elementary but something everyone will face when moving data: moving a schema or table from one database to another.

On this example system, we have a new version 12.2 database just created on our ExaCS. On premises, we have another version 12.2 database. Let's use Data Pump to move either a schema or table from that on-premises database to the cloud.

Let's start with the on-premises database. We have a pluggable database (PDB) named SRCPDB and a schema called move_it, with a password of move_it (awesome security). In this schema, we have a table (my_table) and some objects. We start by connecting to the PDB via SQL*Plus and then set our session to the SRCPDB:

```
[oracle@on-prem-server ~]$ sqlplus
SQL*Plus: Release 12.2.0.1.0 Production on Sun Apr 8 23:09:41 2018
Copyright (c) 1982, 2016, Oracle.  All rights reserved.
Enter user-name: / as sysdba
Connected to:
Oracle Database 12c EE Extreme Perf Release 12.2.0.1.0 - 64bit Production
SQL> alter session set container = SRCPDB;
Session altered.
```

Once in the PDB, we need to create a directory in the database that maps to a physical directory on the file system. If you remember back in Chapter 3, we did the same for our census_ data table load:

```
SQL> create or replace directory dp_export_dir as '/home/oracle/';
Directory created.
```

Next, we can export the schema using Data Pump Export (dpexp). Start by exiting or quitting out of the SQL session and running the following command:

```
[oracle@on-prem-server ~]$ expdp move_it/move_it@SRCPDB schemas=move_it
 directory=dp_export_dir dumpfile=move_it.dmp logfile=expdp.log
Export: Release 12.2.0.1.0 - Production on Sun Apr 8 23:15:17 2018
Copyright (c) 1982, 2017, Oracle and/or its affiliates.  All rights reserved.
Connected to: Oracle Database 12c EE Extreme Perf Release 12.2.0.1.0 - 64bit
 Production
Starting "MOVE_IT"."SYS_EXPORT_SCHEMA_01":  move_it/********@SRCPDB
schemas=move_it directory=dp_export_dir dumpfile=move_it.dmp logfile=expdp.log
Processing object type SCHEMA_EXPORT/TABLE/TABLE_DATA
Processing object type SCHEMA_EXPORT/TABLE/INDEX/STATISTICS/INDEX_STATISTICS
Processing object type SCHEMA_EXPORT/TABLE/STATISTICS/TABLE_STATISTICS
Processing object type SCHEMA_EXPORT/USER
Processing object type SCHEMA_EXPORT/SYSTEM_GRANT
Processing object type SCHEMA_EXPORT/ROLE_GRANT
Processing object type SCHEMA_EXPORT/DEFAULT_ROLE
Processing object type SCHEMA_EXPORT/PRE_SCHEMA/PROCACT_SCHEMA
Processing object type SCHEMA_EXPORT/SEQUENCE/SEQUENCE
Processing object type SCHEMA_EXPORT/TABLE/TABLE
Processing object type SCHEMA_EXPORT/TABLE/COMMENT
Processing object type SCHEMA_EXPORT/TABLE/INDEX/INDEX
Processing object type SCHEMA_EXPORT/TABLE/CONSTRAINT/CONSTRAINT
. . exported "MOVE_IT"."MY_TABLE"                          10 KB       100 rows
Master table "MOVE_IT"."SYS_EXPORT_SCHEMA_01" successfully loaded/unloaded
******************************************************************************
Dump file set for MOVE_IT.SYS_EXPORT_SCHEMA_01 is:
  /home/oracle/move_it.dmp
Job "MOVE_IT"."SYS_EXPORT_SCHEMA_01" successfully completed at Sun Apr 8 23:16:19
2018 elapsed 0 00:00:53
```

This is quite a small export, but if this were a large export, we could add the `parallel` parameter, break it up into multiple dump files, and set the size of the dump files (`filesize`). Here's an example:

```
[oracle@on-prem-server ~]$ expdp move_it/move_it@SRCPDB parallel=4 schemas=move_it
directory=dp_export_dir dumpfile=move_it_%U.dmp logfile=expdp.log filesize=1g
```

Next, we need to import the file into our HRPDB. Again, we need to create a directory in the HRPDB PDB on the ExaCS using SQL*Plus, similar to what we did in the SRCPDB, but we will name it a bit differently:

```
SQL> create or replace directory dp_import_dir as '/home/oracle/';
Directory created.
```

We called it `dp_import_dir`, rather than `db_export_dir`. Notice in the export shown earlier is this line:

```
Processing object type SCHEMA_EXPORT/USER
```

When exporting, and if the user has the CREATE USER privilege, you can export the user and re-create it on import. If you do not have this privilege and do not see this line, the user must exist before you import the .dmp file:

```
[oracle@exacs-node1 ~]$ impdp system/Password@HRPDB schemas=move_it
directory=dp_import_dir dumpfile=move_it.dmp logfile=impdp.log
Import: Release 12.2.0.1.0 - Production on Sun Apr 8 23:35:53 2018
Copyright (c) 1982, 2017, Oracle and/or its affiliates.  All rights reserved.
Connected to: Oracle Database 12c EE Extreme Perf Release 12.2.0.1.0 - 64bit
Production
Master table "SYSTEM"."SYS_IMPORT_SCHEMA_01" successfully loaded/unloaded
Starting "SYSTEM"."SYS_IMPORT_SCHEMA_01":  system/********@HRPDB schemas=move_it
directory=dp_import_dir dumpfile=move_it.dmp logfile=impdp.log
Processing object type SCHEMA_EXPORT/USER
Processing object type SCHEMA_EXPORT/SYSTEM_GRANT
Processing object type SCHEMA_EXPORT/ROLE_GRANT
Processing object type SCHEMA_EXPORT/DEFAULT_ROLE
Processing object type SCHEMA_EXPORT/PRE_SCHEMA/PROCACT_SCHEMA
Processing object type SCHEMA_EXPORT/SEQUENCE/SEQUENCE
Processing object type SCHEMA_EXPORT/TABLE/TABLE
Processing object type SCHEMA_EXPORT/TABLE/TABLE_DATA
. . imported "MOVE_IT"."MY_TABLE"                         10 KB       100 rows
Processing object type SCHEMA_EXPORT/TABLE/STATISTICS/TABLE_STATISTICS
Job "SYSTEM"."SYS_IMPORT_SCHEMA_01" successfully completed at Sun Apr 8 23:36:08
2018 elapsed 0 00:00:06
```

Now we can log into the HRPDB to see if the user exists with their objects:

```
[oracle@exacs-node1 ~]$ sqlplus move_it/move_it@HRPDB
SQL*Plus: Release 12.2.0.1.0 Production on Sun Apr 8 23:37:53 2018
Copyright (c) 1982, 2016, Oracle.  All rights reserved.
Connected to:
Oracle Database 12c EE Extreme Perf Release 12.2.0.1.0 - 64bit Production
SQL> select object_name from all_objects where owner = 'MOVE_IT';
```

```
OBJECT_NAME
----------------------------------------------------------------
MY_SEQUENCE
MY_TABLE
```

This is a simple example, but it shows how we can easily move schemas around. We can also use Data Pump to move tables. The following command would export my_table:

```
expdp move_it/move_it@SRCPDB tables=my_table directory=dp_export_dir dumpfile=move_
it.dmp logfile=expdp.log
```

To export more than one table at a time, list multiple tables separated by a comma:

```
tables=my_table,your_table,their_table)
```

Full Transportable Export and Import

Now let's use Data Pump to move an existing version 11gR2 database into a version 12.2 PDB. For this, we need to do a full Data Pump export. We'll migrate a version 11gR2 (11.2.0.4) database into a PDB on our ExaCS. We'll turn it up to overdrive here and use a TDE-enabled version 11gR2 instance. Why? As stated, all databases are created with TDE automatically on the ExaCS, and with this in mind, we can use the TDE-enabled version 11gR2 database for an extreme case of moving TDE-enabled tablespaces from one instance to another TDE-enabled instance. As you use TDE more and more, this scenario will soon become the norm.

The first step is to create a PDB in the version 12.2 database we will use as the destination. To create a new PDB in the HRCDB database, we run the following SQL in the CDB. The WALLET_PASSWORD is the password of your TDE wallet you used on database creation:

```
SQL> create pluggable database pdb11 admin user pdb_adm identified by PASSWORD;
Pluggable database created.
SQL> alter pluggable database pdb11 open read write instances=all;
Pluggable database altered.
SQL> alter session set container = pdb11;
Session altered.
SQL> administer key management set key using tag 'tag' force keystore identified
by WALLET_PASSWORD with backup using 'backup';
keystore altered.
```

With the PDB created, we need to copy this new wallet over to the rest of the nodes in the service if we're using a local TDE wallet. Here we have a quarter rack, so we just need to copy the wallets over to the second node:

```
[oracle@exacs-node1 ~]$ scp /u02/app/oracle/admin/HRCDB/tde_wallet/cwallet.sso
oracle@exacs-node2:/u02/app/oracle/admin/HRCDB/tde_wallet/
[oracle@exacs-node1 ~]$ scp /u02/app/oracle/admin/HRCDB/tde_wallet/ewallet.p12
oracle@exacs-node2:/u02/app/oracle/admin/HRCDB/tde_wallet/
```

Finally, we bounce the database (or ensure that the wallet is open on all nodes in our new PDB):

```
[oracle@exacs-node1 ~]$ srvctl stop database -db HRCDB -stopoption abort
[oracle@exacs-node1 ~]$ srvctl start database -db HRCDB
```

Now we are ready to continue the process.

In the version 11gR2 database, we have application tablespaces and data we want to move. A quick look into this version 11gR2 database shows an inventory table and some data:

```
SQL> select * from user11.inventory;
ID    PRODUCT
----  --------------------
1     Toothpaste
2     Dog Food
3     Shoes
4     Butterflies
5     Plants
5 rows selected.
```

Along with this table, we want to move the tablespace it lives in, as well as the other application/data tablespaces. We log into the version 11gR2 database as sysdba and create an export directory:

```
SQL> create or replace directory dp_export_dir as '/home/oracle/';
Directory created.
```

Next, we put all the application/data tablespaces into read-only mode. To check the status, we can run the following SQL:

```
SQL> select tablespace_name, status from dba_tablespaces;

TABLESPACE_NAME          STATUS
----------------------   ---------
SYSTEM                   ONLINE
SYSAUX                   ONLINE
UNDOTBS1                 ONLINE
TEMP                     ONLINE
UNDOTBS2                 ONLINE
USERS                    ONLINE
WAFFLES                  ONLINE
THRAWN                   ONLINE
```

We will take the application data tablespaces WAFFLES, USERS, and THRAWN, so we set them to read-only mode. The other tablespaces are not application data tablespaces but system tablespaces, so they will be omitted from the export:

```
SQL> alter tablespace waffles read only;
Tablespace altered.
SQL> alter tablespace users read only;
Tablespace altered.
SQL> alter tablespace thrawn read only;
Tablespace altered.
SQL> select tablespace_name, status from dba_tablespaces;
TABLESPACE_NAME          STATUS
----------------------   ---------
SYSTEM                   ONLINE
SYSAUX                   ONLINE
UNDOTBS1                 ONLINE
```

```
TEMP                    ONLINE
UNDOTBS2                ONLINE
USERS                   READ ONLY
WAFFLES                 READ ONLY
THRAWN                  READ ONLY
8 rows selected.
```

Next, we can do a full export:

```
[oracle@on-prem-server ~]$ expdp system/password transportable=always full=y
directory=dp_export_dir  dumpfile=full_export.dmp logfile=full_export.log
VERSION=12 encryption_password=wallet_password encryption_mode=dual
.......
Master table "SYSTEM"."SYS_EXPORT_FULL_01" successfully loaded/unloaded
******************************************************************************
Dump file set for SYSTEM.SYS_EXPORT_FULL_01 is:
  /home/oracle/full_export.dmp
******************************************************************************
Datafiles required for transportable tablespace THRAWN:
  +DATAC1/db11/datafile/thrawn.dbf
Datafiles required for transportable tablespace USERS:
  +DATAC1/db11/datafile/users.dbf
Datafiles required for transportable tablespace WAFFLES:
  +DATAC1/db11/datafile/waffles.dbf
Job "SYSTEM"."SYS_EXPORT_FULL_01" successfully completed at Mon Apr 9 00:35:57
2018 elapsed 0 00:02:01
```

When the export is done, we copy the data files over into the location where the PDB will be, ensuring that we do not only copy over the database files and .dmp file, but the wallet files as well if TDE is enabled with this source database. For this example, we create a directory tde_ wallet in /tmp for the remote wallet files, then scp them over. Of course, your source wallet location will be different from the one used here:

```
[oracle@on-prem-server ~]$ scp -i keyfile.ppk /u01/tde_wallet/cwallet.sso
oracle@exacs-node1:/tmp/tde_wallet
[oracle@on-prem-server ~]$ scp -i keyfile.ppk /u01/tde_wallet/ewallet.p12
oracle@exacs-node1:/tmp/tde_wallet
```

We are using the brand-new empty PDB in the HRCDB database we named PDB11. Before we can import, we must copy the data files into the PDB11 data files home. In this example, we use ADMCMD to copy the data files after they are staged in /tmp from the source system:

```
ASMCMD> cp /tmp/thrawn.dbf +DATAC1/HRCDB/PDB11/DATAFILE/thrawn.dbf
ASMCMD> cp /tmp/users.dbf +DATAC1/HRCDB/PDB11/DATAFILE/users.dbf
ASMCMD> cp /tmp/waffles.dbf +DATAC1/HRCDB/PDB11/DATAFILE/waffles.dbf
```

When that's done, we need to ensure that an import directory exists in the PDB we are going to import into. Remember to alter your session to be in the PDB before running the following:

```
SQL> alter session set container = pdb11;
Session altered.

SQL> create or replace directory dp_import_dir as '/home/oracle/';
Directory created.
```

This next step will merge the version 11g keystore with the version 12.2 keystore so that we can use the data files we copied over if TDE was enabled on the source database. Run the following in the CDB. Check the location of the keystore before running this command. For a local wallet, use the following:

```
SQL> administer key management merge keystore '/tmp/tde_wallet' identified by
source_wallet_password into existing keystore
'/u02/app/oracle/admin/HRCDB/tde_wallet' identified by target_wallet_password with
backup;
```

And for a shared storage wallet, use this:

```
SQL> administer key management merge keystore '/tmp/tde_wallet' identified by
source_wallet_password into existing keystore
'/var/opt/oracle/dbaas_acfs/HRCDB/tde_wallet' identified by target_wallet_password
with backup;
```

Once we've altered the keystore, we copy the cwallet.sso and ewallet.p12 to all the nodes if not using shared storage so that they have the updated files with the merged keystores. Again, if you're using shared storage, this is not needed:

```
[oracle@exacs-node1 ~]$ cd /u02/app/oracle/admin/HRCDB/tde_wallet/
[oracle@exacs-node1 tde_wallet]$ scp ewallet.p12 oracle@exacs-
node2:/u02/app/oracle/admin/HRCDB/tde_wallet/
[oracle@exacs-node1 tde_wallet]$ scp cwallet.sso oracle@exacs-
node2:/u02/app/oracle/admin/HRCDB/tde_wallet/
```

Now we can run the import:

```
impdp system/password@PDB11 dumpfile=full_export.dmp
TRANSPORT_DATAFILES='+DATAC1/HRCDB/PDB11/DATAFILE/thrawn.dbf','+DATAC1/HRCDB/PDB11
/DATAFILE/users.dbf','+DATAC1/HRCDB/PDB11/DATAFILE/waffles.dbf' FULL=Y
DIRECTORY=dp_import_dir encryption_password=wallet_password
REMAP_TABLESPACE=TEMP:PDB_TEMP
```

Next, we log into the PDB with a user from the version 11gR2 database and look at the inventory table again in one of the migrated tablespaces in our new PDB, PDB11:

```
SQL> alter session set container = PDB11;
Session altered.
SQL> select * from user11.inventory;
ID      PRODUCT
----    --------------------
1       Toothpaste
2       Dog Food
3       Shoes
4       Butterflies
5       Plants
5 rows selected.
```

The last step is to set the tablespaces from read-only to read-write in the new PDB:

```
SQL> alter tablespace waffles read write;
Tablespace altered.
SQL> alter tablespace users read write;
```

```
Tablespace altered.
SQL> alter tablespace thrawn read write;
Tablespace altered.
SQL> select tablespace_name, status from dba_tablespaces;
TABLESPACE_NAME          STATUS
----------------------   ---------
SYSTEM                   ONLINE
SYSAUX                   ONLINE
UNDOTBS1                 ONLINE
PDB_TEMP                 ONLINE
USERS                    ONLINE
WAFFLES                  ONLINE
THRAWN                   ONLINE
```

RMAN

RMAN, or Recovery Manager, is the tool you'll use to perform backup and recovery tasks on the database. It was introduced in Oracle Database 8 and has grown in popularity and features ever since. In this section, we'll perform a few common scenarios for moving a database from on-premises into the Oracle ExaCS.

We start with a traditional backup/restore of an Oracle database. In this scenario, we take a full backup of a database, move it to a staging area on the ExaCS, and then recover it into a database on the service. We'll take a copy of a version 12.1 database using multitenancy on-premises and recover it into a version 12.1 database on the ExaCS. The database on-premises and in the cloud are both named NEWCDB (more on why in a minute).

To start, we obviously need to make a full backup of the version 12.1 on-premises database. We can do that with the following commands. First, we shut down the database:

```
[oracle@on-prem-server ~]$ srvctl stop database -db NEWCDB
```

Then we bring it back up, but only mounted using RMAN (on node 1 if using RAC):

```
[oracle@on-prem-server ~]$ rman target=/
Recovery Manager: Release 12.1.0.2.0 - Production on Sat Apr 14 17:52:41 2018
Copyright (c) 1982, 2014, Oracle and/or its affiliates.  All rights reserved.
connected to target database (not started)
RMAN>
```

Now we create a backup. First we start up the database but only mount it:

```
RMAN> startup mount;
Oracle instance started
database mounted
Total System Global Area     5872025600 bytes
Fixed Size                      8805528 bytes
Variable Size                2197816168 bytes
Database Buffers             2415919104 bytes
Redo Buffers                   75079680 byte
In-Memory Area               1174405120 bytes
RMAN>
```

Next, we get the database ID, or DBID. We will need it later when recovering:

```
RMAN> select dbid from v$database;
     DBID
----------
 385244854
```

Now we perform the backup:

```
RMAN> backup database plus archivelog;
```

After this is done, we need to get the backup onto the ExaCS. Depending on the size of the database, we can use the Oracle Cloud Infrastructure Data Transfer Service to save to a hard drive or just scp it to the cloud. For this example, we will scp it to a stage directory.

Creating a Stage Directory

On the Exadata Cloud Service, we can use /u02 as a stage directory if the database is a smaller one—if we need a very large stage area, we can create one with ASM Cluster File System (ACFS). In this case, we will temporarily borrow some space from the RECO (Recovery Area) on the storage servers and mount it as a file system.

To create this ACFS mount point, we first need to be the grid user. As root, we issue the following command:

```
[root@exacs-node1 ~]# su grid
```

Now as grid, we run asmcmd, a command line utility that lets us manage Oracle ASM instances, disk groups, access control, and volumes:

```
[grid@ exacs-node1~]$ asmcmd
```

We can quickly list the disk groups we have using ls, just as we would do on a Linux OS:

```
ASMCMD> ls
ACFSC3_DG1/
ACFSC3_DG2/
DATAC3/
DBFSC3/
RECOC3/
SPRC3/
```

TIP
Using lsdg is another option that will show how much space is available as well.

We use the following command to create a volume from RECOC3 that is 1 terabyte in size:

```
ASMCMD> volcreate -G RECOC3 -s 1T stage_vol
```

Once complete, we need to view the details:

```
ASMCMD> volinfo -G RECOC3 stage_vol
Diskgroup Name: RECOC3

        Volume Name: STAGE_VOL

        Volume Device: /dev/asm/stage_vol-82
        State: ENABLED
        Size (MB): 1048576
        Resize Unit (MB): 512
        Redundancy: HIGH
        Stripe Columns: 8
        Stripe Width (K): 1024
        Usage:
        Mountpath:
```

We now exit ASMCMD:

```
ASMCMD> exit
```

And exit the grid user back to root:

```
[grid@ exacs-node1~]$ exit
```

From the details of our ASM disk, we locate the Volume Device parameter. For our system it is shown here:

```
Volume Device: /dev/asm/stage_vol-82
```

We'll need this in the next step. To mount and format this volume, we issue the following command as root on the ExaCS:

```
[root@exacs-node1 ~]# /sbin/mkfs -t acfs /dev/asm/stage_vol-82
mkfs.acfs: version              = 12.2.0.1.0
mkfs.acfs: on-disk version      = 46.0
mkfs.acfs: volume              = /dev/asm/stage_vol-82
mkfs.acfs: volume size         = 1099511627776  (1.00 TB )
mkfs.acfs: Format complete.
```

NOTE
The path of your volume device will probably not match what I have here, so remember this step and substitute /dev/asm/stage_vol-82 with the path of your volume.

If we take a quick look in the /dev/asm directory, we can see the file system we just created:

```
[root@exacs-node1 ~]# cd /dev/asm
[root@exacs-node1 asm]# ls
c3_dg11v-397  c3_dg12v-397  c3_dg2v-348  stage_vol-82
```

We now need to add the file system via srvctl.

NOTE
*In the upcoming command, we reference the file system that we just
looked at in /dev/asm. Structure your command with that in mind.*

In the command we need to structure, we start with a reference to srvctl, but we need to use the srvctl used by the Grid Infrastructure in the correct directory. In my example, I have a version 12.2.0.1 grid, so I start the command as /u01/app/12.2.0.1/grid/bin/srvctl. (If you have another version, such as version 12.1.0.2, the command would start as /u01/app/12.1.0.2/grid/bin/srvctl, and for 18c, it would be /u01/app/18.1.0.0/grid/bin/srvctl.) The next parameter in the command is a reference to the mount point we saw in /dev/asm. In my example here, it was /dev/asm/stage_vol-82.

Next, we reference where the disk group that was created. For my system it was RECOC3. (It may be different in your service.)

Now, we name the directory we are mounting. Here we'll use stage_vol. And finally, where we want it mounted. In our ExaCS, we already have a volume called scratch, and we can use that to mount the new file system. With all those variables taken into consideration, here's the command:

```
[root@exacs-node1 /]# /u01/app/12.2.0.1/grid/bin/srvctl add filesystem -d
/dev/asm/stage_vol-82 -g RECOC3 -v stage_vol -m /scratch/stage_vol -u grid
```

The last step is to start the file system. Again, reference the Grid Infrastructure srvctl as we did in the last command and the mount point from /dev/asm. With those values, we run the following:

```
[root@exacs-node1 /]# /u01/app/12.2.0.1/grid/bin/srvctl start filesystem -d
/dev/asm/stage_vol-82
```

That's it! We have a new stage directory that is 1TB in size. We can check it with the following:

```
[root@exacs-node1 ~]# df -h | grep stage
/dev/asm/stage_vol-82   1.0T  2.6G 1022G  1% /scratch/stage_vol
```

We create a backup directory and grant the oracle user the ownership:

```
[root@exacs-node1 /]# cd /scratch/stage_vol
[root@exacs-node1 /]# mkdir backups
[root@exacs-node1 /]# chown oracle:oinstall backups
```

Now that we have the stage directory ready, we can copy our RMAN backup to it. Using scp, we can find the backup location and move all files within that directory (in this example, we will be using the 2018_4_19 directory for our backups and BACKUP_FILES represent all the backup files you will be moving):

```
[oracle@on-prem-server ~]$ scp -i keyfile.ppk BACKUP_FILES oracle@exacs-
node1:/scratch/stage_vol/backups/2018_4_19
```

NOTE
*In this example, I've referenced exacs-node1 as the location where I
was moving the files. This assumes that I have set up my local DNS
to know where exacs-node1 is located. You may need to use the IP
address of node 1 of your ExaCS when using scp to copy the local files.*

Recovering the Database

Now that we have staged the backups, we'll recover this database into a new database we created on our ExaCS. For this following example, we are going to make it as simple as possible. The database on the ExaCS has the same name as the database we'll bring over from on-premises. The name for both databases is NEWCDB.

NOTE
I am not going deep into RMAN here. You can consult many other resources to take a close look at the many options it offers.

Time to recover. We source the environment file on the ExaCS for the database we are recovering into. The file for the environment is NEWCDB.env, so as the oracle user, we issue the following:

```
[oracle@exacs-node1 ~]$ . NEWCDB.env
```

Then we shut down all nodes:

```
[oracle@exacs-node1 ~]$ srvctl stop database -db NEWCDB
```

And then start RMAN:

```
[oracle@exacs-node1 ~]$ rman target=/
```

We set the DBID to the one from the source database:

```
RMAN> set dbid 385244854
executing command: SET DBID
```

And then start the database but do not mount it:

```
RMAN> startup nomount
Oracle instance started
Total System Global Area    5872025600 bytes
Fixed Size                     2937152 bytes
Variable Size               1577062080 bytes
Database Buffers            3036676096 bytes
Redo Buffers                  80945152 bytes
In-Memory Area              1174405120 bytes
```

Using the files in our stage directory, we first need to recover the control file. The command shown here is for my system, so remember that your backup control filename will be different. In this example, the control files are on the RECOC1 disk group. We can use ASMCMD as we did before on the ExaCS to see the exact location:

```
RMAN> restore controlfile to '+RECOC1/NEWCDB/CONTROLFILE/control.ctl' from
'/scratch/stage_vol/backups/2018_4_19/controlNEWCDB_DB_36t0pec9_102_1';
Starting restore at 20-APR-18
using target database control file instead of recovery catalog
allocated channel: ORA_DISK_1
channel ORA_DISK_1: SID=1578 instance=NEWCDB1 device type=DISK
```

```
channel ORA_DISK_1: restoring control file
channel ORA_DISK_1: restore complete, elapsed time: 00:00:01
output file name=+RECOC1/NEWCDB/CONTROLFILE/control.ctl
Finished restore at 20-APR-18
```

NOTE
*If the database on-premises had a different name from the database
we are moving to the ExaCS, we could rename the database with the
following command:*

```
RMAN> ALTER SYSTEM SET DB_NAME=ONPREMDB SCOPE=spfile;
Statement processed
```

*Again, I made this simple and the database name on-premises is the
same as the name on the ExaCS. I include this command for your
reference.*

Continuing on, to reflect these changes, we bounce the database:

```
RMAN> shutdown immediate;
Oracle instance shut down
RMAN> startup mount;
connected to target database (not started)
Oracle instance started
database mounted
Total System Global Area      5872025600 bytes
Fixed Size                       8805528 bytes
Variable Size                 2080375656 bytes
Database Buffers              2533359616 bytes
Redo Buffers                    75079680 bytes
In-Memory Area                1174405120 bytes
```

Then we use the `catalog` command to add our backup pieces and image copies from our
stage location to the RMAN repository:

```
RMAN> catalog start with '/scratch/stage_vol/backups/2018_4_19/' noprompt;
Starting implicit crosscheck backup at 20-APR-18
allocated channel: ORA_DISK_1
Crosschecked 17 objects
Finished implicit crosscheck backup at 20-APR-18
Starting implicit crosscheck copy at 20-APR-18
using channel ORA_DISK_1
Finished implicit crosscheck copy at 20-APR-18
searching for all files in the recovery area
cataloging files...
cataloging done
List of Cataloged Files
=======================
File Name: +RECOC1/NEWCDB/ARCHIVELOG/2018_04_20/thread_1_seq_1.398.973913597
File Name: +RECOC1/NEWCDB/ARCHIVELOG/2018_04_20/thread_1_seq_2.402.973913697
File Name: +RECOC1/NEWCDB/ARCHIVELOG/2018_04_20/thread_1_seq_3.404.973913771
...........
searching for all files that match the pattern /scratch/stage_vol/backups/2018_4_19/
```

```
List of Files Unknown to the Database
======================================
File Name: /scratch/stage_vol/backups/2018_4_19/controlNEWCDB_DB_36t0pec9_102_1
cataloging files...
cataloging done
```

The `report schema` command shows us where our files will be going upon recovery:

```
RMAN> report schema;
List of Permanent Datafiles
===========================
File Size(MB) Tablespace           RB segs Datafile Name
---- -------- -------------------- ------- ------------------------
1    2000     SYSTEM               ***     +DATAC1/NEWCDB/DATAFILE/system.dbf
2    600      PDB$SEED:SYSTEM      ***     +DATAC1/NEWCDB/PDBSEED/DATAFILE/system.dbf
3    2000     SYSAUX               ***     +DATAC1/NEWCDB/DATAFILE/sysaux.dbf
4    600      PDB$SEED:SYSAUX      ***     +DATAC1/NEWCDB/PDBSEED/DATAFILE/sysaux.dbf
5    2000     UNDOTBS1             ***     +DATAC1/NEWCDB/DATAFILE/undotbs1.dbf
6    600      PDB$SEED:UNDOTBS1    ***     +DATAC1/NEWCDB/PDBSEED/DATAFILE/undotbs1.dbf
7    2000     UNDOTBS2             ***     +DATAC1/NEWCDB/DATAFILE/undotbs2.dbf
8    1024     USERS                ***     +DATAC1/NEWCDB/DATAFILE/users.dbf
........
```

Now we can recover the database. We run the following code block to recover our database into this new Exadata Cloud Database home:

```
RMAN>   run {
set newname for database to new;
restore database;
switch datafile all;
}
```

And then the temp files:

```
RMAN> run  {
set newname for database to new;
switch tempfile all;
}
```

Now that the database is restored, we recover it:

```
RMAN> recover database;
```

Note that during this process, you may see an error such as the following:

```
RMAN> recover database;
Starting recover at 20-APR-18
using channel ORA_DISK_1
datafile 29 not processed because file is read-only
starting media recovery
unable to find archived log
archived log thread=2 sequence=14
RMAN-00571: ============================================================
```

```
RMAN-00569: =============== ERROR MESSAGE STACK FOLLOWS ===============
RMAN-00571: ================================================================
RMAN-03002: failure of recover command at 04/20/2018 06:07:39
RMAN-06054: media recovery requesting unknown archived log for thread 2 with sequence
14 and starting SCN of 7834674
```

If this happens, recover to the SCN (system change number):

```
RMAN> recover database until scn 7834674;
Starting recover at 20-APR-18
using channel ORA_DISK_1
datafile 29 not processed because file is read-only
starting media recovery
media recovery complete, elapsed time: 00:00:04
Finished recover at 20-APR-18
```

Then open the database and reset the logs:

```
RMAN> alter database open resetlogs;
```

You may get the following error when running this command:

```
RMAN-00571: ================================================================
RMAN-00569: =============== ERROR MESSAGE STACK FOLLOWS ===============
RMAN-00571: ================================================================
RMAN-03002: failure of sql statement command at 04/20/2018 06:10:08
ORA-19751: could not create the change tracking file
ORA-19750: change tracking file: '+DATAC1/NEWCDB/CHANGETRACKING/ctf.314.972939713'
ORA-17502: ksfdcre:4 Failed to create file
+DATAC1/NEWCDB/CHANGETRACKING/ctf.314.972939713
ORA-15046: ASM file name '+DATAC1/NEWCDB/CHANGETRACKING/ctf.314.972939713' is not
in single-file creation form
ORA-17503: ksfdopn:2 Failed to open file
+DATAC1/NEWCDB/CHANGETRACKING/ctf.314.972939713
ORA-15012: ASM file '+DATAC1/NEWCDB/CHANGETRACKING/ctf.314.972939713' does not exist
```

Simply disable change block tracking:

```
RMAN> alter database disable block change tracking;
Statement processed
```

Then open the database:

```
RMAN> alter database open;
Statement processed
```

You can now SQL*Plus into the database and see the PDBs open and running that were previously on-premises:

```
SQL> show pdbs;
CON_ID    CON_NAME                OPEN MODE   RESTRICTED
--------- ----------------------- ----------- ----------
    2     PDB$SEED                READ ONLY   NO
    3     PDB121                  READ WRITE  NO
    4     COOLPDB                 READ WRITE  NO
```

The database is running only on the node we have been working on. We need to start it up on all nodes:

```
[oracle@exacs-56cmm1 ~]$ srvctl start database -db NEWCDB
```

We have just recovered an on-premises database into the Oracle Cloud, more specifically the ExaCS. If the source database had been TDE-enabled, we could have moved the wallet files over and placed them into the appropriate TDE directory indicated in the sqlnet.ora file.

Transportable Tablespaces

Transportable tablespaces are popular for moving data around, and they work especially well when moving to the Exadata Cloud. With transportable tablespaces, not only can we move select tablespaces from on-premises to the cloud, but we can go across character sets and across endianness.

Note, however, that there is a limitation with time zones and transportable tablespaces: You cannot move tables with `TIMESTAMP WITH TIMEZONE` data across platforms with different time zone file versions. You will need to use another method to move this data. You also should not move the SYSTEM or SYSAUX tablespaces.

Lastly, when working with encrypted tablespaces, you need to merge the wallets into the target database's wallet, as we did earlier in this chapter. In the following sections, we will work with transportable tablespaces to move subsets of data into the ExaCS, including various scenarios you may face.

Moving a Single Tablespace

For this example, we have an on-premises database with a tablespace called hr_data. This tablespace, having sensitive information in it, is encrypted with TDE. Our task is to use transportable tablespaces and move this from on-premises to the cloud. The database on-premises is

Endianness

Different platforms of servers and OSs store data in slightly different ways. More specifically, they arrange bytes in two methods, called big-endian and little-endian formats. In big-endian format, the most significant byte (the biggest byte) of the data is placed at the byte with the lowest address. The rest of the data is placed in order in the next 3 bytes in memory. In little-endian format, the last byte of a binary representation of the multibyte data type is stored first.

So, for example, when storing multibyte data types in memory, such as the value 12345678, in big-endian format, it will be stored as 12 34 56 78. In little-endian format, it will be stored in memory as 87 65 43 21.

IBM AIX, Solaris SPARC, and HP-UX all store their data in big-endian format. Windows (x86/ x86_64) and Linux (x86/ x86_64) store the data in little-endian format. This issue is important to know when you're moving data and files between two different OSs.

a version 12.2 database, with the hr_data tablespace being in a PDB called HRDATA. We'll use our popular HRPDB on the ExaCS. The data we are going to move is super-secret HR data:

```
SQL> select * from employees;
ID        NAME
--------- --------------------
1         Owen
2         Jennifer
3         Scott
```

We start on the source database. To be able to move a tablespace, it must be self-contained and must not have any dependencies on other objects in other tablespaces. We can use the `DBMS_TTS.TRANSPORT_SET_CHECK` procedure to see if we have any issues. The format takes in the tablespace for the `ts_list` parameter (we are in the container as sys to run this):

```
SQL> exec dbms_tts.transport_set_check( ts_list => 'hr_data', incl_constraints =>
true);
PL/SQL procedure successfully completed.
```

Next, we can take a look at the violations table:

```
SQL> select * from transport_set_violations;
no rows selected
```

No issues were found, so we can continue on to exporting the tablespace. As we did previously, we need to make the tablespace read-only:

```
SQL> alter tablespace hr_data read only;
Tablespace altered.
```

Also, as we did previously, we need to ensure that we have an export directory in the database/PDB we are using. We can reuse the code we used previously to create the directory in the PDB:

```
SQL> create or replace directory dp_export_dir as '/home/oracle/';
Directory created.
```

Now we can run the first part of moving a tablespace: the Data Pump export. To run this, we can use system or a user with the `DATAPUMP_EXP_FULL_DATABASE` role, and when importing, the `DATAPUMP_IMP_FULL_DATABASE` role. At the Linux OS command prompt, we run the following. (Note that we are exporting from a PDB, so we explicitly need to add that in the connection. Here we are going against the HRDATA PDB, thus the @HRDATA connection identifier. Also, remember to supply the wallet password, seeing that TDE is enabled on this tablespace.)

```
[oracle@on-prem-server ~]$ expdp userid=system/password@HRDATA directory=
dp_export_dir transport_tablespaces=hr_data dumpfile=hr_data.dmp
 logfile=hr_data_export.log encryption_password=wallet_password

Export: Release 12.2.0.1.0 - Production on Mon Apr 16 00:46:16 2018
Copyright (c) 1982, 2017, Oracle and/or its affiliates.  All rights reserved.
Connected to: Oracle Database 12c EE Extreme Perf Release 12.2.0.1.0 - 64bit
Production
```

```
Starting "SYSTEM"."SYS_EXPORT_TRANSPORTABLE_01":  userid=system/*******@HRDATA
directory=dp_export_dir transport_tablespaces=hr_data dumpfile=hr_data.dmp
logfile=hr_data_export.log encryption_password=*******
Processing object type TRANSPORTABLE_EXPORT/TABLE_STATISTICS
Processing object type TRANSPORTABLE_EXPORT/STATISTICS/MARKER
Processing object type TRANSPORTABLE_EXPORT/PLUGTS_BLK
Processing object type TRANSPORTABLE_EXPORT/POST_INSTANCE/PLUGTS_BLK
Processing object type TRANSPORTABLE_EXPORT/TABLE
Master table "SYSTEM"."SYS_EXPORT_TRANSPORTABLE_01" successfully loaded/unloaded
******************************************************************
Dump file set for SYSTEM.SYS_EXPORT_TRANSPORTABLE_01 is:
  /home/oracle/hr_data.dmp
******************************************************************
Datafiles required for transportable tablespace HR_DATA:
+DATAC1/SRCCDB/HRDATA/DATAFILE/hr_data.dbf
Job "SYSTEM"."SYS_EXPORT_TRANSPORTABLE_01" successfully completed at Mon Apr 16
00:46:54 2018 elapsed 0 00:00:37
```

Now it's time to scp the .dmp file, the tablespace, and the zipped wallet directory over to our ExaCS.

TIP
Use shared storage to reduce the number of steps here.

Copy the .dmp to all nodes:

```
[oracle@on-prem-server ~]$ scp -i keyfile.ppk hr_data.dmp oracle@exacs-
node1:/home/oracle
[oracle@on-prem-server ~]$ scp -i keyfile.ppk hr_data.dmp oracle@exacs-
node2:/home/oracle
```

Now scp the tablespace file (going to tmp so the grid user can access it):

```
[oracle@on-prem-server ~]$ scp -i keyfile.ppk hr_data.dbf oracle@exacs-node1:/tmp
[oracle@on-prem-server ~]$ scp -i keyfile.ppk hr_data.dbf oracle@exacs-node2:/tmp
```

And then scp the wallet.zip file (just on node 1):

```
[oracle@on-prem-server ~]$ scp -i keyfile.ppk wallet.zip oracle@exacs-
node1:/home/oracle
```

Next, on the ExaCS, we have all the files we need in /home/oracle and /tmp. First we need to unzip the wallet:

```
[oracle@exacs-node1 ~]$ unzip wallet.zip
```

This will create a tde_wallet directory.

Next, we copy the tablespace file from the file system into the PDB data file directory in ASM. As the grid user, we start ASMCMD and copy the file into our PDB data file directory:

```
ASMCMD> cp /tmp/hr_data.dbf +DATAC3/HRCDB/HRPDB/DATAFILE
```

Do we still have an import directory in this PDB? If not, we run the following as sys in the HRPDB (remembering that we must source the environment file for the database we are working with):

```
SQL> create or replace directory dp_import_dir as '/home/oracle/';
Directory created.
```

While connected as sys, we need to create the user that owns the data in the tablespace. Still in the PDB as sys, we run the following SQL to create the user hr_user:

```
SQL> create user hr_user identified by hr_user;
User created.
SQL> grant create session, resource, dba to hr_user;
Grant succeeded.
```

To merge the wallets, we need to be in the CDB as sys. We use the following to merge the wallet from the source database with the ExaCS database. We check to determine whether we are using shared or local storage for the TDE wallet. If we're using shared or local, we use that keystore location in the following command.

For local storage:

```
SQL> alter session set container = CDB$ROOT;
Session altered
SQL> administer key management merge keystore '/home/oracle/tde_wallet' identified
by on_prem_wallet_password into existing keystore
'/u02/app/oracle/admin/HRCDB/tde_wallet' identified by hrcdb_wallet_password with
backup;
```

And here it is for shared storage:

```
SQL> alter session set container = CDB$ROOT;
Session altered
SQL> administer key management merge keystore '/home/oracle/tde_wallet' identified
by on_prem_wallet_password into existing keystore
'/var/opt/oracle/dbaas_acfs/HRCDB/tde_wallet' identified by hrcdb_wallet_password
with backup;
```

As before, we need to copy the new wallet files to all the nodes in our Exadata Cloud cluster. If we're using a shared location for the TDE wallet, this is not needed:

```
[oracle@exacs-node1 ~]$ cd /u02/app/oracle/admin/HRCDB/tde_wallet/
[oracle@exacs-node1 tde_wallet]$ scp ewallet.p12 oracle@exacs-
node2:/u02/app/oracle/admin/HRCDB/tde_wallet/
[oracle@exacs-node1 tde_wallet]$ scp cwallet.sso oracle@exacs-
node2:/u02/app/oracle/admin/HRCDB/tde_wallet/
```

For the wallet to uptake the changes, we bounce the database:

```
[oracle@exacs-node1 ~]$ srvctl stop database -db HRCDB
[oracle@exacs-node1 ~]$ srvctl start database -db HRCDB
```

Now we are ready to import the .dmp and attach the tablespace to our PDB. Again, as we did with the export, we need to import into the HRPDB, thus the @HRPDB, and remember the wallet password we used for the export:

```
[oracle@exacs-node1 ~]$ impdp userid=system/password@HRPDB directory=dp_import_dir
dumpfile=hr_data.dmp logfile=hr_data_import.log transport_datafiles=
'+DATAC1/HRCDB/HRPDB/DATAFILE/hr_data.dbf' encryption_password=wallet_password

Import: Release 12.2.0.1.0 - Production on Mon Apr 16 00:47:34 2018
Copyright (c) 1982, 2017, Oracle and/or its affiliates. All rights reserved.
Connected to: Oracle Database 12c EE Extreme Perf Release 12.2.0.1.0 - 64bit
Production
Master table "SYSTEM"."SYS_IMPORT_TRANSPORTABLE_01" successfully loaded/unloaded
Starting "SYSTEM"."SYS_IMPORT_TRANSPORTABLE_01": userid=system/********@HRPDB
directory=dp_import_dir dumpfile=hr_data.dmp logfile=hr_data_import.log
transport_datafiles=+DATAC1/HRCDB/HRPDB/DATAFILE/hr_data.dbf
encryption_password=********
Processing object type TRANSPORTABLE_EXPORT/PLUGTS_BLK
Processing object type TRANSPORTABLE_EXPORT/TABLE
Processing object type TRANSPORTABLE_EXPORT/TABLE_STATISTICS
Processing object type TRANSPORTABLE_EXPORT/STATISTICS/MARKER
Processing object type TRANSPORTABLE_EXPORT/POST_INSTANCE/PLUGTS_BLK
Job "SYSTEM"."SYS_IMPORT_TRANSPORTABLE_01" successfully completed at Mon Apr 16
00:47:58 2018 elapsed 0 00:00:21
```

Now we log into the database and see the status of the tablespace:

```
[oracle@exacs-node1 ~]$ sqlplus hr_user/hr_user@HRPDB
SQL*Plus: Release 12.2.0.1.0 Production on Mon Apr 16 00:50:03 2018
Copyright (c) 1982, 2016, Oracle.  All rights reserved.
Connected to:
Oracle Database 12c EE Extreme Perf Release 12.2.0.1.0 - 64bit Production
SQL> select tablespace_name, status from dba_tablespaces;
TABLESPACE_NAME                    STATUS
---------------------------------  ---------
SYSTEM                             ONLINE
SYSAUX                             ONLINE
UNDOTBS1                           ONLINE
PDB_TEMP                           ONLINE
UNDO_2                             ONLINE
USERS                              ONLINE
HR_DATA                            READ ONLY
```

It's there, but read-only; here's a simple fix:

```
SQL> alter tablespace hr_data read write;
tablespace altered.
```

Finally, we make sure our secret HR data is still there:

```
SQL> select * from employees;
ID        NAME
--------- ----------------
1         Owen
2         Jennifer
3         Scott
```

Cross-Platform Transportable Tablespaces Using Backup Sets

You may face a situation in which your source or on-premises database has a different endianness from that of the ExaCS. Maybe you have a Solaris- or AIX-based system and want to move to the cloud. This is where cross-platform transportable tablespaces can help. You can convert the tablespace you want to move to the ExaCS to the correct endianness before you copy and restore it on the cloud. This enables us to move data from on-premises to the cloud between systems with different endianness.

In the following example, we'll move a tablespace from a Solaris SPARC system to the ExaCS. This tablespace is not encrypted on-premises and is accessed by only a single user, rman_admin, for simplicity.

As we did previously, we need to check for tablespace dependencies. We use the DBMS_TTS .TRANSPORT_SET_CHECK PL/SQL for this. We need to perform this SQL as sys in the PDB where the tablespace is located. Our tablespace is named xtts:

```
SQL> exec dbms_tts.transport_set_check( ts_list => 'xtts', incl_constraints =>
true);
```

Now we check for violations:

```
SQL> select * from transport_set_violations;
no rows selected
```

On the Solaris SPARC database, we need to connect to the database via RMAN and put the tablespace we want to transfer into read-only mode. We will be using a version 12.2 database for both source and target, so we will have to connect directly to a PDB with RMAN as SYSBACKUP. The user will need to have sysdba or the sysbackup privilege to connect and use RMAN. The user in this example, rman_admin, has both privileges:

```
[oracle@exacs-node1 ~]$ rman
Recovery Manager: Release 12.2.0.1.0 - Production on Sat Apr 21 17:56:50 2018
Copyright (c) 1982, 2017, Oracle and/or its affiliates.  All rights reserved.

RMAN> CONNECT TARGET "rman_admin/password@SPRCPDB AS SYSBACKUP"
connected to target database: SPRCCDB:SPRCPDB (DBID=112076)

RMAN> alter tablespace xtts read only;
Statement processed
```

Now we'll use RMAN to export the tablespace. Before we do the export, we need to query the V$TRANSPORTABLE_PLATFORM table to get the correct name of the destination platform:

```
RMAN> select platform_name, endian_format from v$transportable_platform;

PLATFORM_NAME                           ENDIAN_FORMAT
--------------------------------------- --------------
Solaris[tm] OE (32-bit)                 Big
Solaris[tm] OE (64-bit)                 Big
Microsoft Windows IA (32-bit)           Little
Linux IA (32-bit)                       Little
AIX-Based Systems (64-bit)              Big
HP-UX (64-bit)                          Big
```

```
HP Tru64 UNIX                        Little
HP-UX IA (64-bit)                    Big
Linux IA (64-bit)                    Little
HP Open VMS                          Little
Microsoft Windows IA (64-bit)        Little
IBM zSeries Based Linux              Big
Linux x86 64-bit                     Little
Apple Mac OS                         Big
Microsoft Windows x86 64-bit         Little
Solaris Operating System (x86)       Little
IBM Power Based Linux                Big
HP IA Open VMS                       Little
Solaris Operating System (x86-64)    Little
Apple Mac OS (x86-64)                Little
20 rows selected.
```

We're going to the ExaCS, which is Linux on x86_64, so we use Linux x86 64-bit. We can now structure our export statement. We have two choices on how this works: using the BACKUP FOR TRANSPORT or the BACKUP TO PLATFORM statement. Using these statements in our export produces two very different effects: The BACKUP FOR TRANSPORT statement prepares the export for transport but does not do the conversion, which would be done on the target system. The BACKUP TO PLATFORM statement does the conversion right on the source system, so the conversion is already done when we move the files to the ExaCS. In this example, we will be using BACKUP TO PLATFORM. Consequently, there are two statements for importing the tablespace on the target system, which we will cover shortly.

The following statement will export the tablespace and do the platform conversion on the source system:

```
RMAN> backup
to platform 'Linux x86 64-bit'
format '/tmp/xtts.bck'
datapump format '/tmp/xtts_dmp.bck'
tablespace xtts;

Starting backup at 21-APR-18
using target database control file instead of recovery catalog
allocated channel: ORA_DISK_1
channel ORA_DISK_1: SID=876 instance=SPRCCDB device type=DISK
Running TRANSPORT_SET_CHECK on specified tablespaces
TRANSPORT_SET_CHECK completed successfully
.........
channel ORA_DISK_1: starting piece 1 at 21-APR-18
channel ORA_DISK_1: finished piece 1 at 21-APR-18
piece handle=/tmp/xtts_dmp.bck tag=TAG20180421T181835 comment=NONE
channel ORA_DISK_1: backup set complete, elapsed time: 00:00:01
Finished backup at 21-APR-18
```

Now we can move the files to the ExaCS via scp to a shared storage location under the /scratch directory. This ACFS mount is an excellent place for moderately sized exports. For this example, the directory is /scratch/acfsc3_dg1. (On your system, the directory name under /scratch may be a bit different.)

```
[oracle@on-prem-server ~]$ scp -i keyfile.ppk xtts_dmp.bck oracle@exacs-node1:/
scratch/acfsc3_dg1
[oracle@on-prem-server ~]$ scp -i keyfile.ppk xtts.bck oracle@exacs-node1:/scratch/
acfsc3_dg1
```

Now it's time to restore the tablespace. On our ExaCS, we'll restore into our favorite HRPDB. First we use RMAN to connect to the PDB as someone with SYSBACKUP privileges. For this example, we can create the rman_admin user in the HRPDB and grant the user sysbackup access. As we did on the source database, we connect to RMAN:

```
[oracle@exacs-node1 ~]$ rman
Recovery Manager: Release 12.2.0.1.0 - Production on Sat Apr 21 17:56:50 2018
Copyright (c) 1982, 2017, Oracle and/or its affiliates.  All rights reserved.

RMAN> CONNECT TARGET "rman_admin/rman@HRPDB AS SYSBACKUP"
connected to target database: HRCDB:HRPDB (DBID=999933986)
```

It is now possible to restore the tablespace into this new database, which is also a different platform. Just as we did with the backup, we need to use the RESTORE or the RESTORE FROM PLATFORM statement. If we specified the BACKUP TO PLATFORM statement on the backup, we would use the RESTORE statement. If we used BACKUP FOR TRANSPORT, we would use the RESTORE FROM PLATFORM statement. The RESTORE FROM PLATFORM statement does the platform conversion here rather than on the source database. Regardless of the statement used or the conversion location, in our RESTORE statement, we need to use the FOREIGN TABLESPACE clause, because this tablespace does not belong to the source database yet. We reference the shared storage location (/scratch/acfsc3_dg1) where our exports are located:

```
RMAN> restore
foreign tablespace xtts to new
from backupset '/scratch/acfsc3_dg1/xtts.bck'
dump file from backupset '/scratch/acfsc3_dg1/xtts_dmp.bck';

Starting restore at 21-APR-18
using target database control file instead of recovery catalog
allocated channel: ORA_DISK_1
channel ORA_DISK_1: SID=344 instance=HRCDB1 device type=DISK
channel ORA_DISK_1: starting datafile backup set restore
channel ORA_DISK_1: specifying datafile(s) to restore from backup set
channel ORA_DISK_1: restoring all files in foreign tablespace XTTS
channel ORA_DISK_1: reading from backup piece /scratch/acfsc3_dg1/xtts.bck
channel ORA_DISK_1: restoring foreign file 41 to
+DATAC1/HRCDB/6960D633BE68C7C4E0530201000A14C5/DATAFILE/xtts.372.974055185
channel ORA_DISK_1: foreign piece handle=/scratch/acfsc3_dg1/xtts.bck
.........
IMPDP> Processing object type TRANSPORTABLE_EXPORT/POST_INSTANCE/PLUGTS_BLK
    IMPDP> Job "SYSBACKUP"."TSPITR_IMP_HRCDB_Fakd" successfully completed at
Sat
Apr 21 18:53:23 2018 elapsed 0 00:00:05
Import completed
Finished restore at 21-APR-18
```

The tablespace is restored.

If this tablespace had additional users with objects and we did not create them before the import, we would see errors similar to the following:

```
IMPDP> ORA-39123: Data Pump transportable tablespace job aborted
ORA-29342: user THE_JEFFREY does not exist in the database
```

Be sure to create any users who are using the tablespace you are moving before the import.

Next, as sys, let's look at the tablespace in the HRPDB:

```
SQL> select tablespace_name, status from dba_tablespaces;

TABLESPACE_NAME              STATUS
-----------------------      ---------
SYSTEM                       ONLINE
SYSAUX                       ONLINE
UNDOTBS1                     ONLINE
PDB_TEMP                     ONLINE
UNDO_2                       ONLINE
USERS                        ONLINE
HR_DATA                      ONLINE
XTTS                         READ ONLY
```

All we need to do is set it to READ WRITE and we can use the tablespace in the ExaCS database:

```
SQL> alter tablespace xtts read write;
Tablespace altered.
```

Pluggable Databases

We have been working with PDBs throughout the book for various tasks—from resource manager to connecting and running SQL. Now we need to see how we can use PDBs for migration to the cloud. In this section, we will look at how to move existing PDBs from one system to another, how to create PDBs from our non-CDB version 12.1 databases, and remote cloning.

PDB Unplug/Plug in

To start, we will look at one of the simplest methods of moving a PDB: PDB unplug/plug in, with both databases being on the same patch level. We'll take an on-premises PDB on a similar platform (Linux x86 64) and move it to the ExaCS. At a high level, the PDB will be unplugged, its files transferred to the ExaCS, and it then will be plugged into an existing CDB. Both databases in this example are version 12.2 databases.

Let's start with the on-premises PDB. This example includes a few "curve balls"—we'll have the on-premises PDB use TDE. Also, we'll move from a traditional file system to ASM.

Let's start on the source database. We log into the CDB as sys and export the keys for the PDB (if TDE is enabled), and then close the PDB we want to move.

NOTE
*In the exporting of keys, the password is the password of the local
wallet and the "secret password" can be anything.*

```
[oracle@on-prem-server ~]$ sqlplus
SQL*Plus: Release 12.2.0.1.0 Production on Sun Apr 22 18:02:44 2018
Copyright (c) 1982, 2016, Oracle.  All rights reserved.
Enter user-name: / as sysdba
Connected to:
Oracle Database 12c EE Extreme Perf Release 12.2.0.1.0 - 64bit Production
SQL> alter session set container = HOMEPDB;
Session altered.
SQL> administer key management export encryption keys with secret
"secret_password" to '/home/oracle/export.p12' force keystore identified by
"wallet_password";
keystore altered.
SQL> alter session set container = CDB$ROOT;
SQL> alter pluggable database HOMEPDB close instances=all;
Pluggable database altered.
```

Next, we unplug the PDB into a .pdb archive or export the description to an XML file and
manually move the data files. The .pdb archive contains the data files as well as the descriptive
XML and any wallet files. In this example, we'll create the XML and move the files manually. First,
we create the .xml export file:

```
SQL> alter pluggable database HOMEPDB unplug into '/home/oracle/homepdb.xml';
Pluggable database altered.
SQL> drop pluggable database HOMEPDB keep datafiles;
Pluggable database dropped.
```

Now that we have the database unplugged, we can scp the XML, wallet export, and data files
to the ExaCS:

```
[oracle@on-prem-server ~]$ scp -i keyfile.ppk homepdb.xml oracle@exacs-
node1:/home/oracle
[oracle@on-prem-server ~]$ scp -i keyfile.ppk export.p12 oracle@exacs-
node1:/home/oracle
[oracle@on-prem-server ~]$ scp -i keyfile.ppk
/u01/HOMEPDB/datafiles/homepdb_datafiles.dbf oracle@exacs-node1:/tmp
```

There will be multiple data files for the HOMEPDB move, but we provide this format that you
may use. We will be using the /tmp directory for the stage.

Now that we have the database in the cloud, we can plug it into our HRCDB database.
Remember that our PDB on-premises used a regular file system, where on the ExaCS, we have
ASM. Upon plugging in our PDB, we need to tell the database where to put the files. The next
code example is doing a few things:

1. We reference the homepdb XML file we created on the source system.

2. Then we have to tell the database where to get the files. This is the source_file_name_
   convert section of the code. Seeing we have staged the files in /tmp, we need to tell the
   database to look there, rather than where the files were. On our source system, the files were

in /u01/HOMEPDB, and we staged them in /tmp, so by using the command `source_file_name_convert = ('/u01/HOMEPDB/, '/tmp/')`, we do exactly that. (Look in /tmp rather than in /u01/HOMEPDB.)

3. We need to copy the files into AMS, thus the `copy` command.

4. The `path_prefix` tells the database to put the files in the HRCDB directory in ASM.

5. Lastly, if we have a temp file, we use it; otherwise, we create one with the `reuse tempfile` command.

Putting it all together, we have the following command to be run in the CDB on our ExaCS:

```
SQL> create pluggable database homepdb using '/home/oracle/homepdb.xml'
source_file_name_convert = ('/u01/HOMEPDB/, '/tmp/')
copy
path_prefix = '/+DATAC1/HRCDB/HOMEPDB/'
tempfile reuse;
pluggable database created.
```

Now that the PDB is plugged in, we can open it:

```
SQL> alter pluggable database HOMEPDB open read write instances=all;
Warning: PDB altered with errors.
```

What? Errors? We can see the PDB has opened in RESTRICTED mode:

```
SQL> show pdbs
CON_ID    CON_NAME      OPEN MODE    RESTRICTED
--------- ------------- ------------ ----------
2         PDB$SEED      READ ONLY    NO
3         HRPDB         READ WRITE   NO
7         HOMEPDB       READ WRITE   YES
```

We need to import the keys! So we run the following after logging into the CDB:

```
SQL> alter session set container = HOMEPDB;
Session altered.
SQL> administer key management import encryption keys with secret
"secret_password" from '/home/oracle/export.p12' force keystore identified by
"wallet_password" with backup;
keystore altered.
```

We'll move the new wallet with the imported keys to the other nodes if using local storage—but, first, we close the PDB:

```
SQL> alter session set container = CDB$ROOT;
Session altered.
SQL> alter pluggable database HOMEPDB close instances=all;
Pluggable database altered.
```

We scp the new wallet to all the nodes because we're not using shared storage. If we were using shared storage, we skip this scp step:

```
[oracle@exacs-node1 ~]$ scp /u02/app/oracle/admin/HOMECDB/tde_wallet/cwallet.sso
oracle@exacs-node2:/u02/app/oracle/admin/HOMECDB/tde_wallet/
[oracle@exacs-node1 ~]$ scp /u02/app/oracle/admin/HOMECDB/tde_wallet/ewallet.p12
oracle@exacs-node2:/u02/app/oracle/admin/HOMECDB/tde_wallet/
```

Finally, back in the CDB, we start up the HOMEPDB and check the status:

```
SQL> alter pluggable database homepdb open read write instances=all;
Pluggable database altered.
SQL> show pdbs
CON_ID    CON_NAME     OPEN MODE   RESTRICTED
--------- ----------- ----------- ----------
2         PDB$SEED     READ ONLY   NO
3         HRPDB        READ WRITE  NO
7         HOMEPDB      READ WRITE  NO
```

Non-CDB to a PDB

The next use case is a very popular one. Because all databases created on the ExaCS are multitenant (CDB/PDB), we need a way to move existing non-CDB version 12.1 databases into the cloud. In this section, we'll move a version 12.1 non-CDB database from on-premises onto the ExaCS; in the process, we'll make it a PDB in an existing CDB.

NOTE
Ensure that the two databases you are using are at the same patch set level.

Exporting the Key

This non-CDB database is on-premises, and we must move it to the cloud. If this database is using TDE, the keys need to be exported before we can go any further. We can export the keys using the following method.

If you're using version 12.1 with the October 2017 Bundle Patch or a later version, you can use the FORCE KEYSTORE clause in the import, eliminating the change of wallet type. You may also have to apply patch 28266679:

```
[oracle@on-prem-server ~]$ sqlplus
SQL*Plus: Release 12.1.0.2.0 Production on Sun Jun 24 01:24:47 2018
Copyright (c) 1982, 2014, Oracle.  All rights reserved.
Enter user-name: / as sysdba
Connected to:
Oracle Database 12c EE Extreme Perf Release 12.1.0.2.0 - 64bit Production
With the Partitioning, Real Application Clusters, Automatic Storage Management,
OLAP,
Advanced Analytics and Real Application Testing options

SQL> administer key management export encryption keys with secret
"secret_password" to '/home/oracle/export.p12' force keystore identified by
"wallet_password";
```

You can now skip to the next section, "Extracting the Key ID from the Database."

If you're not using the October 2017 or later Bundle Patch, use the following:

```
[oracle@on-prem-server ~]$ sqlplus
SQL*Plus: Release 12.1.0.2.0 Production on Sun Jun 24 01:24:47 2018
Copyright (c) 1982, 2014, Oracle.  All rights reserved.
Enter user-name: / as sysdba
Connected to:
Oracle Database 12c EE Extreme Perf Release 12.1.0.2.0 - 64bit Production
With the Partitioning, Real Application Clusters, Automatic Storage Management,
OLAP,
Advanced Analytics and Real Application Testing options
SQL>
```

To avoid encountering a bug when you're moving a non-CDB to a PDB, purge the recycle bin:

```
SQL> purge recyclebin;
Recyclebin purged.
```

Now, let's continue:

```
SQL> administer key management set keystore close;
keystore altered.
SQL> administer key management set keystore open identified by "wallet_password";
keystore altered.
SQL> administer key management export encryption keys with secret
"secret_password" to '/home/oracle/export.p12' identified by "wallet_password";
keystore altered.
```

Extracting the Key ID from the Database

Before we move on, we need to get the key ID from the non-CDB database:

```
SQL> select key_id from v$encryption_keys;
KEY_ID
----------------------------------------------------------------
Ab9sSB8/nU+7v0wVb5zbdjwAAAAAAAAAAAAAAAAAAAAAAAAAA
```

We keep this ID handy, because we may need it when we import the keys into the new PDB.

Moving the Non-CDB to the PDB

To prepare the non-CDB database for the description export, we must put it into read-only mode. First, we shut it down on all nodes:

```
[oracle@on-prem-server ~]$ srvctl stop database -db NONCDB
```

Then we start it up in read-only mode on the node we are using, but using SQL*Plus and connecting as sys on node 1 (if a RAC database):

```
[oracle@on-prem-server ~]$ sqlplus
SQL*Plus: Release 12.1.0.2.0 Production on Sun Jun 24 01:29:23 2018
Copyright (c) 1982, 2014, Oracle.  All rights reserved.
Enter user-name: / as sysdba
Connected to an idle instance.
SQL> startup mount
```

```
ORACLE instance started.
Total System Global Area 2.2924E+11 bytes
Fixed Size                    7659448 bytes
Variable Size              3.0602E+10 bytes
Database Buffers           1.9811E+11 bytes
Redo Buffers                529211392 bytes
Database mounted.
SQL> alter database open read only;
Database altered.
```

Once the database is in read-only mode, we must use DBMS_PDB.DESCRIBE to create an XML file we will use to plug this database into a CDB on the cloud:

```
SQL> BEGIN
  DBMS_PDB.DESCRIBE(
    pdb_descr_file => '/home/oracle/noncdb.xml');
END;
/
```

Before we start the move, we should check the compatibility of this non-CDB database. We start by using SCP to move the newly created XML file to the ExaCS:

```
[oracle@on-prem-server ~]$ scp -i keyfile.ppk noncdb.xml oracle@exacs-
node1:/home/oracle
```

Once there, we can run the following SQL to check the compatibility in the CDB we want to move to. As before, we are moving into our HRCDB, so we run the following SQL in the CDB of our HRCDB database:

```
SQL> set serveroutput on;
SQL> DECLARE
  compatible CONSTANT VARCHAR2(35) :=
    CASE DBMS_PDB.CHECK_PLUG_COMPATIBILITY(
          pdb_descr_file => '/home/oracle/noncdb.xml',
          pdb_name       => 'NONCDB')
    WHEN TRUE THEN 'Yes, it is Compatible'
    ELSE 'No, it is not Compatible'
END;
BEGIN
  DBMS_OUTPUT.PUT_LINE(compatible);
END;
/
Yes, it is Compatible
PL/SQL procedure successfully completed.
```

We can proceed.

NOTE
If the message were "No, it is not Compatible", we would need to look at the PDB_PLUG_IN_VIOLATIONS table for errors.

Now, back on-premises, we shut down the non-CDB database in preparation to move the database files:

```
[oracle@on-prem-server ~]$ srvctl stop database -db NONCDB
```

We copy the data files for this non-CDB to the /tmp directory of node 1 of our ExaCS so we can reference them when creating the PDB. Once the files have been moved into the /tmp directory, we can create the PDB.

We want to create the PDB in our HRCDB database. We need to source the HRCDB.env file to set the environment and SQL*Plus as sys into the CDB of the HRCDB database. Once there, we use the following SQL to create the PDB:

```
SQL> create pluggable database NONCDB using '/home/oracle/noncdb.xml'
SOURCE_FILE_DIRECTORY = '/tmp'
COPY
tempfile reuse;
Pluggable database created.
SQL> show pdbs;
CON_ID     CON_NAME                OPEN MODE   RESTRICTED
---------  --------------------    ----------  ----------
2          PDB$SEED                READ ONLY   NO
3          HRPDB                   READ WRITE  NO
4          NONCDB                  MOUNTED
```

Next, we run the ORACLE_HOME/rdbms/admin/noncdb_to_pdb.sql script. This script must be run before we can open the PDB. The script opens the PDB, performs changes needed to convert the non-CDB to a PDB, and closes the PDB when done:

```
SQL> alter session set container = NONCDB;
Session altered.
SQL> @$ORACLE_HOME/rdbms/admin/noncdb_to_pdb.sql
```

TIP
You may encounter Bug 26434999 "noncdb_to_pdb.sql fails when dbms_stats.set_global_prefs('concurrent','true') is set" when running this script. To ensure that you do not encounter the bug, disable the concurrent stats gathering before running the following script:

```
SQL> exec dbms_stats.set_global_prefs('CONCURRENT', 'OFF');
```

Bug 26434999 has been addressed in the January 2018 and later patch sets.
You may also encounter Bug 20978259 "Running noncdb_to_pdb .sql fails with ORA-600 [kspgsp2] . . . [recyclebin]." To fix this, purge the recycle bin on the source database (the non-CDB) or apply patch 20978259 to the target database.

After the script is finished, we can open the new PDB in read-write if it's not already open:

```
SQL> alter pluggable database NONCDB open read write instances=all;
Pluggable database altered.
```

NOTE
If the non-CDB has TDE enabled, you'll have to import the keys due to a PDB violation:

```
SQL> alter pluggable database NONCDB open read write instances=all;
Warning: PDB altered with errors
```

Importing the Keys into the New PDB

If you're using version 12.1 with the October 2017 Bundle Patch or a later version, you can use the FORCE KEYSTORE clause in the import, eliminating the change of wallet type. You may also have to apply patch 28266679. In the CDB of our HRCDB database, we can import the keys via SQL*Plus. The wallet password is the one we used upon the HRCDB database creation:

```
[oracle@exacs-node1 ~]$ sqlplus
SQL*Plus: Release 12.1.0.2.0 Production on Sun Jun 24 01:24:47 2018
Copyright (c) 1982, 2014, Oracle.  All rights reserved.
Enter user-name: / as sysdba
Connected to:
Oracle Database 12c EE Extreme Perf Release 12.1.0.2.0 - 64bit Production
With the Partitioning, Real Application Clusters, Automatic Storage Management,
OLAP,
Advanced Analytics and Real Application Testing options

SQL> alter session set container = NONCDB;
Session altered.

SQL> administer key management import encryption keys with secret
"secret_password" from '/home/oracle/export.p12' force keystore identified by
"wallet_password" with backup;
```

In this case, you can skip to the next section, "Post Import Steps."

If you're not using the October 2017 or later Bundle Patch, you need to import the non-CDB keys into the wallet of the new CDB. To do this, we start by removing the cwallet.sso file in the TDE directory of the node you are on. We check our sqlnet.ora file for the TDE wallet location:

```
[oracle@exacs-node1 ~]$ cd /u02/app/oracle/admin/HRCDB/tde_wallet/
```

Or, for shared storage, we use the following:

```
[oracle@exacs-node1 ~]$ cd /var/opt/oracle/dbaas_acfs/HRCDB/tde_wallet
```

Now we remove the file or rename it:

```
[oracle@exacs-node1 ~]$ mv cwallet.sso cwallet.sso.old
```

Once the wallet file is renamed, we can alter the wallet of the CDB. We SQL*Plus into the CDB of the HRCDB database as sysdba. Then we close the wallet:

```
SQL> administer key management set keystore close;
keystore altered.
```

Next, we open the wallet using the wallet password so that it no longer is an auto-login wallet. This password is the one we set for the database instance upon creation:

```
SQL> administer key management set keystore open identified by "wallet_password";
keystore altered.
```

After we open the wallet, we move to our new PDB:

```
SQL> alter session set container = NONCDB;
Session altered.
```

Then we open the wallet with the same password we used previously in the same SQL statement:

```
SQL> administer key management set keystore open identified by "wallet_password";
keystore altered.
```

We can now import the keys from the non-CDB database. We use the same password we just used for opening the keystore:

```
SQL> administer key management import encryption keys with secret
"secret_password" from '/home/oracle/export.p12' identified by "wallet_password"
with backup;
keystore altered.
```

Back in the CDB, we need to create a new auto-login wallet, again with the same password. We check our TDE wallet location so that we set the correct directory—shared or local storage. For local storage, we use the following:

```
SQL> alter session set container = CDB$ROOT;
Session altered.
SQL> administer key management create auto_login keystore from keystore
'/u02/app/oracle/admin/HRCDB/tde_wallet' identified by "wallet_password";
```

And for shared storage, we use this:

```
SQL> alter session set container = CDB$ROOT;
Session altered.
SQL> administer key management create auto_login keystore from keystore
'/var/opt/oracle/dbaas_acfs/HRCDB/tde_wallet' identified by "wallet_password";
```

Post Import Steps

We stop the database:

```
[oracle@exacs-node1 ~]$ srvctl stop database -db HRCDB
```

Before we restart it, we need to scp the new wallet file to the other nodes in the service. If we are using shared storage, we skip this step. If we are using local storage, we scp the files to all other nodes:

```
[oracle@exacs-node1 ~]$ cd /u02/app/oracle/admin/HRCDB/tde_wallet/
[oracle@exacs-node1 tde_wallet]$ scp ewallet.p12 oracle@exacs-
node2:/u02/app/oracle/admin/HRCDB/tde_wallet/
[oracle@exacs-node1 tde_wallet]$ scp cwallet.sso oracle@exacs-
node2:/u02/app/oracle/admin/HRCDB/tde_wallet/
```

Now we restart the database:

```
[oracle@exacs-node1 ~]$ srvctl start database -db HRCDB
```

Once the database is up, we can log in and see the status of the new PDB we created from a non-CDB:

```
SQL> show pdbs;
CON_ID    CON_NAME              OPEN MODE   RESTRICTED


--------- --------------------- ----------- ----------
2         PDB$SEED              READ ONLY   NO
3         HRPDB                READ WRITE  NO
4         NONCDB               MOUNTED
```

If the PDB is mounted and not open, we open it with the following command:

```
SQL> alter pluggable database NONCDB open read write instances=all;
```

Next, we switch to the PDB:

```
SQL> alter session set container = NONCDB;
Session altered.
```

Then check the wallet status in the PDB. It will also indicate if the location is shared or local storage. This next SQL shows local storage:

```
SQL> select wrl_parameter, status, wallet_type from gv$encryption_wallet;
WRL_PARAMETER
--------------------------------------------------------------------------------
STATUS                          WALLET_TYPE
------------------------------- --------------------
/u02/app/oracle/admin/HRCDB/tde_wallet/
OPEN                            AUTOLOGIN

/u02/app/oracle/admin/HRCDB/tde_wallet/
OPEN                            AUTOLOGIN
```

You may still have errors or PDB violations, indicated with the RESTRICTED column being YES for the PDB:

```
SQL> show PDBS;
CON_ID    CON_NAME              OPEN MODE   RESTRICTED
--------- --------------------- ----------- ----------
2         PDB$SEED              READ ONLY   NO
3         HRPDB                READ WRITE  NO
4         NONCDB               READ WRITE  YES
```

Check the PDB_PLUG_IN_VIOLATIONS table in the CDB for issues. Usually, datapatch needs to be run so that the PDB gets all the patches and options of the CDB:

```
[oracle@exacs-node1 ~]$ datapatch
SQL Patching tool version 12.1.0.2.0 Production on Sun Apr 29 01:22:50 2018
Copyright (c) 2012, 2017, Oracle.  All rights reserved.
Connecting to database...OK
Bootstrapping registry and package to current versions...done
Determining current state...done
Adding patches to installation queue and performing prereq checks...done
```

```
Installation queue:
For the following PDBs: NONCDB
    Nothing to roll back
    The following patches will be applied:
        25437695 (Database PSU 12.1.0.2.170418, Oracle JavaVM Component (APR2017))
        25397136 (DATABASE BUNDLE PATCH 12.1.0.2.170418)
        23026585 ()
        25859910 ()
Installing patches...
Patch installation complete.  Total patches installed: 4
Validating logfiles...done
SQL Patching tool complete on Sun Apr 29 01:28:14 2018
```

The last task is to add a TNS entry in the tnsnames.ora file for the new PDB. Using the $ORACLE_HOME/network/admin directory for the HRCDB database, we add a new reference to the new PDB. We must add this in the tnsnames.ora file on *all* nodes:

```
[oracle@exacs-node1 admin]$ vi tnsnames.ora
NONCDB =
  (DESCRIPTION =
    (ADDRESS = (PROTOCOL = TCP)(HOST = exacs-node-scan.clientsubnet.exacsvcn.
oraclevcn.com)(PORT = 1521))
    (CONNECT_DATA =
      (SERVER = DEDICATED)
      (SERVICE_NAME = NONCDB.clientsubnet.exacsvcn.oraclevcn.com)
      (FAILOVER_MODE =
        (TYPE = select)
        (METHOD = basic)
      )
    )
  )
```

We clear the violations by closing and opening the PDB:

```
SQL> alter pluggable database NONCDB close instances=all;
Pluggable database altered.
SQL> alter pluggable database NONCDB open instances=all;
Pluggable database altered.
SQL> show PDBs;
CON_ID     CON_NAME                    OPEN MODE   RESTRICTED
---------- --------------------------- ----------- -----------
2          PDB$SEED                    READ ONLY   NO
3          HRPDB                       READ WRITE  NO
4          NONCDB                      READ WRITE  NO
```

Now, if necessary, we need to activate the key in the PDB. First, we ensure that the keys are in the wallet:

```
SQL> alter session set container = NONCDB;
Session altered.
SQL> select key_id from v$encryption_keys;
```

And then we activate the key (use the key ID we pulled from the CDB previously):

```
SQL> administer key management use key
'Ab9sSB8/nU+7v0wVb5zbdjwAAAAAAAAAAAAAAAAAAAAAAAAAAAAA' identified by
"wallet_password" with backup;
```

Remote Clone a PDB or Non-CDB

A very easy and simple way of moving a non-CDB to a PDB is to remote clone it. This process needs a database link from the CDB to the non-CDB database, so depending on your company's security rules, this may work best with two databases already on the ExaCS—for example, if you have a non-CDB database you cloned over temporarily as a stepping stone into the cloud and now want to make it a PDB. This would also work if you are doing this fully on-premises in preparation to move to the ExaCS.

NOTE
In this example, both the non-CDB and the CDB will be version 12.1 and will be at the same patch level.

We need to create a user to connect with the database link in the source non-CDB database and give the user the correct permissions to clone the database. The user we will create will be named captain_rex and will be given the CREATE SESSION and CREATE PLUGGABLE DATABASE grants:

```
SQL> create user captain_rex identified by wolf;
User created.
SQL> grant create session, create pluggable database to captain_rex;
Grant succeeded.
```

Exporting the Key

If using version 12.1 with the October 2017 Bundle Patch or later, you can use the FORCE KEYSTORE clause in the import, eliminating the change of wallet type. You may also have to apply patch 28266679. Use the following SQL to export the keys from the non-CDB:

```
[oracle@exacs-node1 ~]$ sqlplus
SQL*Plus: Release 12.1.0.2.0 Production on Sun Jun 24 01:24:47 2018
Copyright (c) 1982, 2014, Oracle.  All rights reserved.
Enter user-name: / as sysdba
Connected to:
Oracle Database 12c EE Extreme Perf Release 12.1.0.2.0 - 64bit Production
With the Partitioning, Real Application Clusters, Automatic Storage Management,
OLAP,
Advanced Analytics and Real Application Testing options

SQL> administer key management export encryption keys with secret "secret_password" to
'/home/oracle/export.p12' force keystore identified by "wallet_password";
```

You can now skip to the next section, "Extracting the Key ID from the Database."
If you're not using the October 2017 or later Bundle Patch, here is the code to export the keys:

```
[oracle@exacs-node1 ~]$ sqlplus
SQL*Plus: Release 12.1.0.2.0 Production on Sun Jun 24 01:24:47 2018
Copyright (c) 1982, 2014, Oracle.  All rights reserved.
Enter user-name: / as sysdba
```

```
Connected to:
Oracle Database 12c EE Extreme Perf Release 12.1.0.2.0 - 64bit Production
With the Partitioning, Real Application Clusters, Automatic Storage Management, OLAP,
Advanced Analytics and Real Application Testing options
SQL>
```

To avoid encountering a bug when moving a non-CDB to a PDB, purge the recycle bin:

```
SQL> purge recyclebin;
Recyclebin purged.
```

Now you can continue:

```
SQL> administer key management set keystore close;
keystore altered.
SQL> administer key management set keystore open identified by  "wallet_password";
keystore altered.
SQL> administer key management export encryption keys with secret
"secret_password" to '/home/oracle/export.p12' identified by "wallet_password";
keystore altered.
```

Extracting the Key ID from the Database
As we did previously, we need to get the key ID from the non-CDB database:

```
SQL> select key_id from v$encryption_keys;
KEY_ID
---------------------------------------------------------------
Ab9sSB8/nU+7v0wVb5zbdjwAAAAAAAAAAAAAAAAAAAAAAAAAAAAAA
```

NOTE
Again, we need to keep this ID handy. We may need it when we import the keys into the new PDB.

Moving the non-CDB to the PDB
With the user created and the keys exported, we can put the database into read-only mode. But before we do this, let's work with only one node. We'll shut down the database across all nodes and then start it up in read-only mode on this node:

```
[oracle@exacs-node1 ~]$ srvctl stop database -db NONCDB
```

On node 1 (if a RAC-enabled database), we SQL*Plus as sys and start the database up, but mounted only, then read only:

```
SQL> startup mount
ORACLE instance started.
Total System Global Area 2.2924E+11 bytes
Fixed Size                   7659448 bytes
Variable Size             3.0602E+10 bytes
Database Buffers          1.9811E+11 bytes
Redo Buffers               529211392 bytes
Database mounted.
SQL> alter database open read only;
Database altered.
```

Before we can create a database link, we may need to add a TNS entry to our tnsnames.ora file for the non-CDB database—we must add this in the tnsnames.ora file on *all* nodes. The file is located at $ORACLE_HOME/network/admin for the target (HRCDB) database. The format is similar to the following:

```
NONCDB =
  (DESCRIPTION =
    (ADDRESS = (PROTOCOL = TCP)(HOST = exacs-node-scan.clientsubnet.exacsvcn.
oraclevcn.com)(PORT = 1521))
    (CONNECT_DATA =
      (SERVER = DEDICATED)
      (SERVICE_NAME = NONCDB.clientsubnet.exacsvcn.oraclevcn.com)
      (FAILOVER_MODE =
        (TYPE = select)
        (METHOD = basic)
      )
    )
  )
```

Once we have the entry into our tnsnames.ora file, we can SQL*Plus as sys and create the database link in the HRCDB database:

```
SQL> create database link NONCDB connect to captain_rex identified by wolf using
'NONCDB';
```

Let's test this link:

```
SQL> select 1 from dual@NONCDB;
 1
----------
 1
```

We have the link, so now let's create the clone, still as sys in the HRCDB:

```
SQL> create pluggable database YESPDB from NON$CDB@NONCDB;
Pluggable database created.
SQL> show pdbs;
CON_ID    CON_NAME                 OPEN MODE  RESTRICTED
--------- ---------------------    ---------- ----------
2         PDB$SEED                 READ ONLY  NO
3         HRPDB                    READ WRITE NO
4         YESPDB                   MOUNTED
```

We now need to run the non-CDB–to–PDB SQL script. We start by changing to the PDB and then run the script:

```
SQL> alter session set container = YESPDB;
Session altered.
SQL>@$ORACLE_HOME/rdbms/admin/noncdb_to_pdb.sql
```

NOTE
You may encounter Bug 26434999 "noncdb_to_pdb.sql fails when dbms_stats.set_global_prefs('concurrent','true') is set" when running this script. To ensure that you do not, disable the concurrent stats gathering before running the following script:

```
SQL> exec dbms_stats.set_global_prefs('CONCURRENT', 'OFF');
```

Bug 26434999 has been addressed in the January 2018 and later patchsets.
You may also encounter Bug 20978259 "Running noncdb_to_pdb .sql fails with ORA-600 [kspgsp2] . . . [recyclebin]." To fix this, purge the recycle bin on the source database (the non-CDB) or apply patch 20978259.

Once the script completes, we can open the PDB:

```
SQL> alter session set container = CDB$ROOT;
Session altered
SQL> alter pluggable database YESPDB open read write instances=all;
Pluggable database altered.
```

If we were using TDE, the message would be "Warning: PDB altered with errors" upon opening the PDB.

```
SQL> alter pluggable database YESPDB open read write instances=all;
Warning: PDB altered with errors.
```

We need to import the keys, just as we did before.

Importing the Keys into the New PDB

If you're using version 12.1 with the October 2017 Bundle Patch or later, you can use the FORCE KEYSTORE clause in the import, eliminating the change of wallet type. You may also have to apply patch 28266679. Use the following SQL to import the keys, with the wallet password being the password you used on database creation:

```
[oracle@exacs-node1 ~]$ sqlplus
SQL*Plus: Release 12.1.0.2.0 Production on Sun Jun 24 01:24:47 2018
Copyright (c) 1982, 2014, Oracle.  All rights reserved.
Enter user-name: / as sysdba
Connected to:
Oracle Database 12c EE Extreme Perf Release 12.1.0.2.0 - 64bit Production
With the Partitioning, Real Application Clusters, Automatic Storage Management,
OLAP,
Advanced Analytics and Real Application Testing options

SQL> alter session set container = YESPDB;
Session altered.

SQL> administer key management import encryption keys with secret
"secret_password" from '/home/oracle/export.p12' force keystore identified by
"wallet_password" with backup;
```

You can now skip to the next section, "Post Import Steps."

If you're not using the October 2017 or later Bundle Patch, check your sqlnet.ora file for the TDE wallet location, as we mentioned in the beginning of this chapter:

```
[oracle@exacs-node1 ~]$ cd /u02/app/oracle/admin/HRCDB/tde_wallet/
```

Or, for shared storage, use the following:

```
[oracle@exacs-node1 ~]$ cd /var/opt/oracle/dbaas_acfs/HRCDB/tde_wallet
```

Now remove the file or rename it:

```
[oracle@exacs-node1 ~]$ mv cwallet.sso cwallet.sso.old
```

Once the file is renamed, we can alter the wallet of the CDB. SQL*Plus into the CDB of the HRCDB database. Then we close the wallet:

```
SQL> administer key management set keystore close;
keystore altered.
```

Next, we open the wallet using the wallet password so that it no longer is an auto-login wallet. This password is the one you set for the database instance upon creation:

```
SQL> administer key management set keystore open identified by "wallet_password";
keystore altered.
```

After we set the password, we move to our new PDB:

```
SQL> alter session set container = YESPDB;
Session altered.
```

Here we open the wallet with the same password we used previously in the same SQL statement:

```
SQL> administer key management set keystore open identified by "wallet_password";
keystore altered.
```

We can now import the keys from the non-CDB database. Use the same password we just used for opening the keystore:

```
SQL> administer key management import encryption keys with secret "secret_password"
from '/home/oracle/export.p12' identified by "wallet_password" with backup;
keystore altered.
```

Back in the CDB, we need to create a new auto-login wallet—again, with the same password.

NOTE
Check your TDE wallet location so that you set the correct directory—shared or local storage.

We can create the wallet with local storage:

```
SQL> alter session set container = CDB$ROOT;
Session altered.
SQL> administer key management create auto_login keystore from keystore
'/u02/app/oracle/admin/HRCDB/tde_wallet' identified by "wallet_password";
```

Or if the database is using shared storage:

```
SQL> alter session set container = CDB$ROOT;
Session altered.
SQL> administer key management create auto_login keystore from keystore
'/var/opt/oracle/dbaas_acfs/HRCDB/tde_wallet' identified by "wallet_password";
```

Post Import Steps

Now we stop the database:

```
[oracle@exacs-node1 ~]$ srvctl stop database -db HRCDB
```

Before we restart it, we need to scp the new wallet file to the other nodes in the service.

NOTE
If you are using shared storage, you can skip this step.

If using local storage, scp the files to all other nodes:

```
[oracle@exacs-node1 ~]$ cd /u02/app/oracle/admin/HRCDB/tde_wallet/
[oracle@exacs-node1 tde_wallet]$ scp ewallet.p12 oracle@exas-
node2:/u02/app/oracle/admin/HRCDB/tde_wallet/
[oracle@exacs-node1 tde_wallet]$ scp cwallet.sso oracle@exacs-
node2:/u02/app/oracle/admin/HRCDB/tde_wallet/
```

Then restart the database:

```
[oracle@exacs-node1 ~]$ srvctl start database -db HRCDB
```

Once the database is up, log in and see the status of the new PDB we created from a non-CDB:

```
SQL> show pdbs;
CON_ID    CON_NAME               OPEN MODE   RESTRICTED
--------- ---------------------- ----------- -----------
2         PDB$SEED               READ ONLY   NO
3         HRPDB                  READ WRITE  NO
4         YESPDB                 MOUNTED
```

If the PDB is mounted and not open, we open it with the following command:

```
SQL> alter pluggable database YESPDB open read write instances=all;
```

Then we switch to the PDB:

```
SQL> alter session set container = YESPDB;
Session altered.
```

We can also check the wallet status in the PDB. This SQL is showing a wallet location on local storage:

```
SQL> select wrl_parameter, status, wallet_type from gv$encryption_wallet;
WRL_PARAMETER
--------------------------------------------------------------------
STATUS                      WALLET_TYPE
--------------------------- --------------------
/u02/app/oracle/admin/HRCDB/tde_wallet/
OPEN                        AUTOLOGIN

/u02/app/oracle/admin/HRCDB/tde_wallet/
OPEN                        AUTOLOGIN
```

You may still have errors or PDB violations, indicated with the RESTRICTED column being YES for the PDB:

```
SQL> show PDBS;
CON_ID    CON_NAME              OPEN MODE   RESTRICTED
--------- --------------------- ----------- -----------
2         PDB$SEED              READ ONLY   NO
3         HRPDB                 READ WRITE  NO
4         YESPDB                READ WRITE  YES
```

Check the PDB_PLUG_IN_VIOLATIONS table in the CDB for issues. Usually datapatch needs to be run so that the PDB gets all the patches and options of the CDB:

```
[oracle@exacs-node1 ~]$ datapatch
SQL Patching tool version 12.1.0.2.0 Production on Sun Apr 29 01:22:50 2018
Copyright (c) 2012, 2017, Oracle.  All rights reserved.
Connecting to database...OK
Bootstrapping registry and package to current versions...done
Determining current state...done
Adding patches to installation queue and performing prereq checks...done
Installation queue:
For the following PDBs: YESPDB
    Nothing to roll back
    The following patches will be applied:
        25437695 (Database PSU 12.1.0.2.170418, Oracle JavaVM Component (APR2017))
        25397136 (DATABASE BUNDLE PATCH 12.1.0.2.170418)
        23026585 ()
        25859910 ()
Installing patches...
Patch installation complete.  Total patches installed: 4
Validating logfiles...done
SQL Patching tool complete on Sun Apr 29 01:28:14 2018
```

The last task is to add a TNS entry in the tnsnames.ora file for the new PDB. Again, using the $ORACLE_HOME/network/admin directory for the HRCDB database, we add a new reference to the new PDB, remembering to add this in the tnsnames.ora file on *all* nodes:

```
[oracle@exacs-node1 admin]$ vi tnsnames.ora
YESPDB =
  (DESCRIPTION =
    (ADDRESS = (PROTOCOL = TCP)(HOST = exacs-node-scan.clientsubnet.exacsvcn.
```

```
oraclevcn.com)(PORT = 1521))
    (CONNECT_DATA =
      (SERVER = DEDICATED)
      (SERVICE_NAME = YESPDB.clientsubnet.exacsvcn.oraclevcn.com)
      (FAILOVER_MODE =
        (TYPE = select)
        (METHOD = basic)
      )
    )
  )
```

And we clear the violations by closing and opening the PDB:

```
SQL> alter pluggable database YESPDB close instances=all;
Pluggable database altered.
SQL> alter pluggable database YESPDB open instances=all;
Pluggable database altered.
```

Now, if necessary, we need to activate the key in the PDB. First, we ensure that the keys are in the wallet:

```
SQL> alter session set container = YESPDB;
Session altered.
SQL> select key_id from v$encryption_keys;
```

And then we activate the key (using the key ID we pulled from the CDB previously):

```
SQL> administer key management use key 'Ab9sSB8/nU+7v0wVb5zbdjwAAAAAAAAAAAAAA
AAAAAAAAAAAAA' identified by "wallet_password" with backup;
```

Remote Clone a PDB

We can remote clone a PDB to the cloud if a database link from the cloud to on-premises is available. In this example, we are using two version 12.2 instances that are at the same patch level.

To start, on the source database, we SQL*Plus as sys into the CDB so that we can create a PDB cloning user. Ensure that you are in the PDB:

```
SQL> alter session set container = PREMPDB;
Session Altered
SQL> create user captain_rex identified by wolf;
User created.
SQL> grant create session, create pluggable database to captain_rex;
Grant succeeded.
```

If we were using TDE in this PDB, we'd need to export the keys while still in the PDB:

```
SQL> administer key management export encryption keys with secret
"secret_password" to '/home/oracle/export.p12' force keystore identified by
"wallet_password";
```

Next, we put the source database into read-only mode. We will work only with node one while shutting down the database on the other nodes:

```
[oracle@on-prem-server ~]$ srvctl stop database -db PREMCDB
```

Then we SQL*Plus into the database as sys and start up, but only mounted, then read-only:

```
SQL> startup mount
ORACLE instance started.
Total System Global Area 2.2924E+11 bytes
Fixed Size                   7659448 bytes
Variable Size             3.0602E+10 bytes
Database Buffers          1.9811E+11 bytes
Redo Buffers               529211392 bytes
Database mounted.
SQL> alter database open read only;
Database altered.
```

Now we open the PDB in read-only mode (if it's not already open in read-only):

```
SQL> alter pluggable database PREMPDB open read only;
Pluggable database altered.
```

We are done with the source system. On to the target system.

On the target system, we need to add an entry into the tnsnames.ora file located at $ORACLE_HOME/network/admin for the source database. The format is similar to the following:

```
PREMPDB =
  (DESCRIPTION =
    (ADDRESS = (PROTOCOL = TCP)(HOST = exacs-node-scan.on-premises-server.com)(PORT =
1521))
    (CONNECT_DATA =
      (SERVER = DEDICATED)
      (SERVICE_NAME = PREMPDB.on-premises-server.com)
      (FAILOVER_MODE =
        (TYPE = select)
        (METHOD = basic)
      )
    )
  )
```

Similar to before, we create the database link in the CDB of the target database's PDB:

```
SQL> create database link PREMPDB connect to captain_rex identified by wolf using
'PREMPDB';
```

Let's test this link:

```
SQL> select 1 from dual@PREMPDB;
 1
----------
 1
```

Once we have verified connectivity, we can create the new PDB using the database link:

```
SQL> create pluggable database RCPDB from PREMPDB@PREMCDB;
Pluggable database created.
```

That's all! Now we need to check on the status of the PDB:

```
SQL> show pdbs;
CON_ID     CON_NAME                  OPEN MODE   RESTRICTED
---------  --------------------      ----------  ----------
2          PDB$SEED                  READ ONLY   NO
3          YESPDB                    READ WRITE NO
4          RCPDB                     MOUNTED
```

The database is mounted but not opened. We can open it with the following:

```
SQL> alter pluggable database RCPDB open instances=all;
Pluggable Database Altered
```

If we were using TDE, we'd need to import the keys after we used SCP to move them into /home/oracle. If you are using the ExaCS for both the source and target, then the file would have already been exported to /home/oracle. If you are remote cloning from an on-premises database, you need to SCP the export:

```
[oracle@on-prem-server ~]$ scp -i keyfile.ppk export.p12 oracle@exacs-
node1:/home/oracle
```

Now import the keys into the PDB:

```
[oracle@exacs-node1 ~]$ sqlplus
SQL*Plus: Release 12.1.0.2.0 Production on Sun Jun 24 01:24:47 2018
Copyright (c) 1982, 2014, Oracle.  All rights reserved.
Enter user-name: / as sysdba
Connected to:
Oracle Database 12c EE Extreme Perf Release 12.1.0.2.0 - 64bit Production
With the Partitioning, Real Application Clusters, Automatic Storage Management,
OLAP,
Advanced Analytics and Real Application Testing options

SQL> alter session set container = RCPDB;
Session altered.

SQL> administer key management import encryption keys with secret
"secret_password" from '/home/oracle/export.p12' force keystore identified by
"wallet_password" with backup;
keystore altered.
```

As before, we'll move the new wallet with the imported keys to the other nodes if not on shared storage—but first, we close the PDB:

```
SQL> alter session set container = CDB$ROOT;
Session altered.
SQL> alter pluggable database RCPDB close instances=all;
Pluggable database altered.
```

We then SCP the new wallet to all the nodes:

```
[oracle@exacs-node1 ~]$ scp /u02/app/oracle/admin/HRCDB/tde_wallet/cwallet.sso
oracle@exacs-node2:/u02/app/oracle/admin/HRCDB/tde_wallet/
[oracle@exacs-node1 ~]$ scp /u02/app/oracle/admin/ HRCDB /tde_wallet/ewallet.p12
oracle@exacs-node2:/u02/app/oracle/admin/HRCDB/tde_wallet/
```

Finally, back in the CDB, we start up the RCPDB and check the status:

```
SQL> alter pluggable database RCPDB open read write instances=all;
SQL> show pdbs;
CON_ID    CON_NAME                 OPEN MODE   RESTRICTED
--------- ----------------------   ----------  ----------
2         PDB$SEED                 READ ONLY   NO
3         YESPDB                   READ WRITE  NO
4         RCPDB                    READ WRITE  NO
```

You may still have errors or PDB violations, indicated with the RESTRICTED column being YES for the PDB:

```
SQL> show PDBS;
CON_ID    CON_NAME                 OPEN MODE   RESTRICTED
--------- ----------------------   ----------  ----------
2         PDB$SEED                 READ ONLY   NO
3         YESPDB                   READ WRITE  NO
4         RCPDB                    READ WRITE  YES
```

Check the PDB_PLUG_IN_VIOLATIONS table in the CDB for issues. Usually datapatch needs to be run so that the PDB gets all the patches and options of the CDB:

```
[oracle@exacs-node1 ~]$ datapatch
```

We add a TNS entry in the tnsnames.ora file for the new PDB. Again, using the $ORACLE_HOME/network/admin directory for the HRCDB database, we add a new reference to the new PDB, remembering to add this in the tnsnames.ora file on *all* nodes:

```
RCPDB =
  (DESCRIPTION =
    (ADDRESS = (PROTOCOL = TCP)(HOST = exacs-node-scan.clientsubnet.exacsvcn.
oraclevcn.com)(PORT = 1521))
    (CONNECT_DATA =
      (SERVER = DEDICATED)
      (SERVICE_NAME = RCPDB.clientsubnet.exacsvcn.oraclevcn.com)
      (FAILOVER_MODE =
        (TYPE = select)
        (METHOD = basic)
      )
    )
  )
```

If we did need to run datapatch, we'd clear the violations by closing and opening the PDB:

```
SQL> alter pluggable database RCPDB close instances=all;
Pluggable database altered.
SQL> alter pluggable database RCPDB open instances=all;
Pluggable database altered.
```

TDE, 18c, and PDBs

In version 18c, we have two modes for creating the TDE keystore: United and Isolated. The process for creating a keystore in the United mode is similar to how we have been doing it in versions 12.1 and 12.2. One keystore at the CDB level is shared by the CDB and all PDBs. As you saw in the previous examples, this sometimes creates issues.

In Isolated mode, each PDB can have its own keystore. This simplifies the moving of PDBs and lets us manage the keystore from within the PDB. In summary, note the following:

■ The United mode keystore settings and changes in the CDB root will apply to all PDBs. For example, the keystore that you create in the CDB root will be used by the root's associated United mode PDBs.

■ The PDBs that are configured in Isolated mode are allowed to create and manage their own keystores independently. An Isolated mode PDB has its own keystore, independent of the keystore of the CDB root and of other PDBs.

Isolated Mode

Let's see this in practice. To configure a PDB in Isolated mode, we first have to alter the SPFILE or set database parameters.

Changing the SPFILE
For an ExaCS service, the SPFILE is on ASM, so we need to pull it out, alter it, and put it back. In this example, we will use the HRCDB database again, but it is a version 18c database now. We start by shutting the database down:

```
[oracle@exacs-node1 ~]$ srvctl stop database -db HRCDB
```

For backup, I went in as the grid user and created a copy of the SPFILE on ASM. You can do the same if you wish:

```
[root@exacs-node1 ~]# su grid
[grid@exacs-node1 ~]$ asmcmd
ASMCMD> ls
ACFSC4_DG1/
ACFSC4_DG2/
DATAC4/
RECOC4/
SPRC4/
ASMCMD> cd DATAC4
ASMCMD> cd HRCDB
ASMCMD> cp spfileHRCDB.ora spfileHRCDB.ora.backup
copying +DATAC4/HRCDB/spfileHRCDB.ora -> +DATAC4/HRCDB/spfileHRCDB.ora.backup
```

Now, SQL*Plus as sysdba and create a PFILE from a SPFILE:

```
[oracle@exacs-node1 ~]$ sqlplus
SQL*Plus: Release 18.0.0.0.0 Production on Mon Jul 23 19:04:27 2018
Version 18.1.0.0.0
Copyright (c) 1982, 2017, Oracle.  All rights reserved.
Enter user-name: / as sysdba
Connected to an idle instance.
SQL> create pfile='/home/oracle/pfileHRCDB.ora' from
spfile='+DATAC4/HRCDB/spfileHRCDB.ora';
File created.
```

Edit the PFILE and add the following two entries. Ensure that DB_NAME in the wallet root path is the name of your database:

```
*.wallet_root=/var/opt/oracle/dbaas_acfs/DB_NAME/tde_wallet
*.tde_configuration="keystore_configuration=file"
```

For my service using the HRCDB, I would use this:

```
*.wallet_root=/var/opt/oracle/dbaas_acfs/HRCDB/tde_wallet
*.tde_configuration="keystore_configuration=file"
```

Next, we save the PFILE. We now have to re-create the SPFILE from this PFILE. We SQL*Plus again into the database:

```
[oracle@exacs-node1 ~]$ sqlplus
SQL*Plus: Release 18.0.0.0.0 Production on Mon Jul 23 18:49:06 2018
Version 18.1.0.0.0
Copyright (c) 1982, 2017, Oracle.  All rights reserved.
Enter user-name: / as sysdba
Connected to an idle instance.
SQL> create spfile='+DATAC4/HRCDB/spfileHRCDB.ora' from
 pfile='/home/oracle/pfileHRCDB.ora';
File created.
```

Setting Database Parameters

If you don't want to change the SPFILE, you can do this via parameter changes. Start by using SQL*Plus as sysdba:

```
[oracle@ exacs-node1 ~]$ sqlplus
SQL*Plus: Release 18.0.0.0.0 Production on Mon Aug 13 15:26:29 2018
Version 18.1.0.0.0
Copyright (c) 1982, 2017, Oracle.  All rights reserved.
Enter user-name: / as sysdba
Connected to:
Oracle Database 18c EE Extreme Perf Release 18.0.0.0.0 - Production
Version 18.1.0.0.0
SQL>
```

Now, set the wallet_root parameter (remember to use your database name):

```
SQL> alter system set wallet_root='/var/opt/oracle/dbaas_acfs/DATABASE_NAME/
tde_wallet' scope=spfile;
System altered.
```

Next, we need to exit and bounce the database:

```
SQL> exit
Disconnected from Oracle Database 18c EE Extreme Perf Release 18.0.0.0.0 -
Production
Version 18.1.0.0.0
[oracle@exacs-node1 ~]$ srvctl stop database -db HRCDB
[oracle@exacs-node1 ~]$ srvctl start database -db HRCDB
```

Now, back into SQL*Plus to set the `TDE_CONFIGURATION` parameter:

```
[oracle@ exacs-node1 ~]$ sqlplus
SQL*Plus: Release 18.0.0.0.0 Production on Mon Aug 13 15:26:29 2018
Version 18.1.0.0.0
Copyright (c) 1982, 2017, Oracle.  All rights reserved.
Enter user-name: / as sysdba
Connected to:
Oracle Database 18c EE Extreme Perf Release 18.0.0.0.0 - Production
Version 18.1.0.0.0
SQL> alter system set tde_configuration="keystore_configuration=file" scope=spfile;
System altered.
```

Again, we need to exit and stop the database:

```
SQL> exit
Disconnected from Oracle Database 18c EE Extreme Perf Release 18.0.0.0.0 -
Production
Version 18.1.0.0.0
[oracle@exacs-node1 ~]$ srvctl stop database -db HRCDB
```

Creating the New Wallet Homes

Now we need to move the existing wallet to a new location. We change the directory to the shared wallet location:

```
[oracle@exacs-node1 dbs]$ cd /var/opt/oracle/dbaas_acfs/DATABASE_NAME/tde_wallet
```

Here I'm going to use HRCDB as my database name—remember to substitute your database name:

```
[oracle@exacs-node1 ~]$ cd /var/opt/oracle/dbaas_acfs/HRCDB/tde_wallet
```

And we need to create a new directory:

```
[oracle@exacs-node1 tde_wallet]$ mkdir tde
```

Then we move the wallet files into that directory:

```
[oracle@exacs-node1 tde_wallet]$ mv cwallet.sso tde
[oracle@exacs-node1 tde_wallet]$ mv ewallet.p12 tde
```

Next, we start up the database:

```
[oracle@exacs-node1 ~]$ srvctl start database -db HRCDB
```

Database started, we log back in as sysdba and check the parameter:

```
SQL> show parameter wallet
NAME            TYPE         VALUE
--------------- ------------ -------------------------------
wallet_root     string       /var/opt/oracle/dbaas_acfs/HRCDB/tde_wallet
```

Change to the PDB:

```
SQL> alter session set container = HRPDB;
Session altered.
```

And now we create the isolated wallet:

```
SQL> administer key management isolate keystore identified by
"pdb_wallet_password" from root keystore force keystore identified by
"cdb_wallet_password" with backup;
keystore altered.
```

Now we open the wallet if it's closed:

```
SQL> administer key management set keystore open identified by "pdb_wallet_password";
keystore altered.
```

NOTE
More than likely, the wallet will already be opened, so you can ignore the error: "ORA-28354: Encryption wallet, auto login wallet, or HSM is already open."

And that's it. We now have an isolated wallet in the PDB:

```
SQL> select wrl_parameter, status, wallet_type from gv$encryption_wallet;
WRL_PARAMETER
------------------------------------------------------------------------------
STATUS                           WALLET_TYPE
-------------------------------  --------------------
/var/opt/oracle/dbaas_acfs/HRCDB/tde_wallet/725C06D793E8D281E05302001414B9E5/tde/
OPEN                             PASSWORD

/var/opt/oracle/dbaas_acfs/HRCDB/tde_wallet/725C06D793E8D281E05302001414B9E5/tde/
OPEN                             PASSWORD
```

It's a password-based wallet, but we can easily create an auto-login wallet independent of the CDB wallet:

```
SQL> administer key management create auto_login keystore from keystore
'/var/opt/oracle/dbaas_acfs/HRCDB/tde_wallet/725C06D793E8D281E05302001414B9E5/tde/
' identified by "pdb_wallet_password";
keystore altered.
```

Close and open the PDB so that the auto-login wallet is used:

```
SQL> alter pluggable database HRPDB close instances=all;
Pluggable database altered.
SQL> alter pluggable database HRPDB open instances=all;
Pluggable database altered.
SQL> select wrl_parameter, status, wallet_type from gv$encryption_wallet;
WRL_PARAMETER
------------------------------------------------------------------------------
STATUS                           WALLET_TYPE
-------------------------------  --------------------
/var/opt/oracle/dbaas_acfs/HRCDB/tde_wallet/725C06D793E8D281E05302001414B9E5/tde/
OPEN                             AUTOLOGIN

/var/opt/oracle/dbaas_acfs/HRCDB/tde_wallet/725C06D793E8D281E05302001414B9E5/tde/
OPEN                             AUTOLOGIN
```

Moving a PDB from One CDB to Another in Isolated Mode

Moving PDBs with 18c and Isolated mode is quite easy with a new system parameter, ONE_STEP_PLUGIN_FOR_PDB_WITH_TDE. Set this parameter to true:

```
SQL> alter system set one_step_plugin_for_pdb_with_tde = true;
```

We can move PDBs around without manually having to provide a keystore password when we import the TDE keys into the PDB after it has moved to a different CDB. For example, if we wanted to move this HRPDB to another CDB, we could close it:

```
SQL> alter pluggable database HRPDB close instances=all;
Pluggable database altered.
```

Then we take a PDB archive:

```
SQL> alter pluggable database HRPDB unplug into '/home/oracle/hrpdb.pdb';
Pluggable database altered.
```

We can then go to our other 18c database that has been prepped for an Isolated keystore. Now we create the new PDB in the other CDB:

```
SQL> create pluggable database HRPDB2 using '/home/oracle/hrpdb.pdb';
Pluggable database created.
```

And we open it:

```
SQL> alter pluggable database HRPDB2 open instances=all;
Pluggable database altered.
```

Next, we just need to open the wallet and create an auto-login wallet:

```
SQL> administer key management set keystore open identified by "wallet_password";
keystore altered.
```

The path used here is for the CDB we are moving the PDB into, which is INVCDB in this example. The wallet for a PDB in Isolated mode will be in the PDB GUID named directory under the CDB_NAME/tde_wallet directory:

```
SQL> administer key management create auto_login keystore from keystore
'/var/opt/oracle/dbaas_acfs/INVCDB/tde_wallet/BODYELECTRIC1001001SOS/tde/'
identified by "wallet_password";
keystore altered.
```

Close and open the PDB so that the auto-login wallet is used:

```
SQL> alter pluggable database HRPDB2 close instances=all;
Pluggable database altered.
SQL> alter pluggable database HRPDB2 open instances=all;
Pluggable database altered.
```

It's so easy!

Summary

As you can see in this very exhaustive chapter, there are many ways to move databases on to the Exadata Cloud Service. From RMAN to remote cloning, we can get our data onto the service without too much effort. Just remember that this is only a sample of what we can do. We can use other services in the cloud such as the GoldenGate Cloud Service, the Data Integration Service Platform, and a Data Move service, where we can physically ship encrypted drives to the data center.

Index

A

Access Control Lists (ACLs), 67
ACFS (ASM Cluster File System), 85, 151, 278, 291
ACLs (Access Control Lists), 67
Active Data Guard, 8
Activity log, 79, 80
addcronjob command, 133
ADMINISTER_ RESOURCE_MANAGER, 207
administrators
    details about, 17, 24
    password, 29–30, 54
    privileges, 207–208
Advanced Row Compression option, 179–182, 196
API keys, 113, 114
APIs
    CLI. *See* CLIs
    REST. *See* REST services
application type, 31
archive compression, 185, 186–188
ASM (Automatic Storage Management), 150
ASM Cluster File System (ACFS), 85, 151, 278, 291
ASM disks, 150, 151
auth tokens, 142–143, 144
authentication, 202

Automatic Storage Management (ASM), 150
availability domains, 47, 50, 65–69, 92

B

backup command, 133
backup network, 13, 21, 25, 45
backup sets, 290–293
backupDestination parameter, 108
backups. *See also* database recovery
    Activity log, 79, 80
    Backup Now option, 80, 81
    bkup CLI, 137–146
    in cloud container, 78
    configuration file for, 137
    configuring, 82
    decryption method, 33, 78
    deleting, 75, 145–146
    in ExaCS UI (OCI), 93–95
    in ExaCS UI (OCI-C), 77–82
    full, 80
    ibkup parameter, 108–109
    incremental, 80
    initializing data from, 32–33
    Keep Forever, 146
    listing, 133
    on-demand, 144
    on-premises, 78

backups (*cont.*)
    options, 25, 32, 145
    password, 139, 142, 143
    permissions, 144
    point-in-time, 80
    replacing database with, 77–79
    with REST services, 103, 108–109
    with RMAN, 277–278
    service gateways and, 139
    status, 144
    storage container access and, 138–139
    subnets, 48–49, 52
    VCNs and, 138
begin command, 134
big-endian format, 285
binary LOBs (BLOBs), 176, 196
bkup (database backup) CLI, 137–146
BLOBs (binary LOBs), 176, 196
block header, 173
bounce command, 130, 132
buffer cache, 230
Burst slider, 60–61

C

CA certificate bundle, 102
cache. *See also* memory
    CELL_FLASH_CACHE clause, 236–237
    Columnar Flash Caching, 236
    in-memory, 236
    RAM, 236
    Smart Flash. *See* Exadata Smart Flash Cache
Cache Fusion, 229
catalog command, 282
CDBs (container databases)
    creating new PDB in, 273–277
    creating resource plans, 208–214
    Instance Caging, 224–226
    limiting CPUs for, 216, 217, 224–226
    merging wallets, 288–289
    moving PDBs between, 319

    multitenancy and, 206–207
    plugging PDBs into, 293–296
    prerequisites for using Resource Manager with, 207–208
    recovering, 281–285
    remote cloning PDBs/non-CDBs, 304–311
    removing resource plans, 210–211
    resource plans, 207, 209–214
Cell Command Line Interface (CellCLI), 232–235, 259
cell disks, 233
cell IP address, 262
CellCLI (Cell Command Line Interface), 232–235, 259
CELL_FLASH_CACHE clause, 236–237
certificates, self-signed, 243, 245, 263
change block tracking, 284
changepassword command, 130
character LOBs (CLOBs), 176, 196
character sets, 31
CIDR blocks
    IP networks, 21
    OCI networks, 45–47, 49
Client for URLs (cURL), 102, 105–111
client subnets, 47, 52
CLIENT_ID, 220
CLIENT_MACHINE, 220
CLIENT_OS_USER, 220
CLIENT_PROGRAM, 220
CLIs (command line interfaces), 121–146
    bkup, 137–146
    configuring OCI CLI, 111–115
    connecting to ExaCS, 121–123
    dbaasapi, 123–129
    dbaascli, 129–134
    ExaCS. *See* ExaCLI; ExaCS CLIs
    exadbcpatchmulti, 135–137
    OCI. *See* OCI CLI
CLOBs (character LOBs), 176, 196
cloning
    instances, 86–87
    remote cloning PDBs/non-CDBs, 304–311
    sparse cloning feature, 83–87

cloud account, 15–17, 24
cloud containers, 78
Cloud Data Centers, 15
cloud service instances
    creating in OCI, 50–55
    creating in OCI-C, 22–25
cloud technology, 2
Cloud Tenant ID, 35–36
cloud.oracle.com, 15
cluster name, 52
clusters, 13, 14. *See also* VM clusters
Column Projection, 152
Columnar Flash Caching, 236
columnar format, 183, 184
command line interfaces. *See* CLIs
common header, 173
compartments, 38, 40–43, 45, 50
compression, 171–196
    Advanced Row Compression,
        179–182, 196
    archive, 185, 186–188
    considerations, 196
    data blocks, 172, 173–176, 177
    DBMS_COMPRESSION, 193–196
    extents, 172, 176, 177
    Hybrid Columnar Compression,
        182–193
    issues, 196
    segments, 172, 176–179
    types of, 193
    warehouse, 184, 185–186
compression units (CUs), 183, 184
compute nodes, 149
consumer groups, 204–206, 221, 222
container databases. *See* CDBs
cookies, 262–263
core count, 52
CPU core count, 92
CPU utilization, 216, 217, 224–226
CREATE USER privilege, 272
credentials, 36
CRON jobs, 133
crontab file, 145
Crypto Erase feature, 59

cURL (Client for URLs), 102, 105–111
cURL servers, 102
CUs (compression units), 183, 184

D

data
    moving. *See* migration
    relational, 196
    undo, 179
    unstructured, 196
data blocks, 172, 173–176, 177
data centers, 3–4
Data Guard, 96, 97
Data Pump, 270–277, 293
data storage percentage, 52
data warehouses, 184
Database as a Service console (DBCS),
    26, 29, 35
database backup (bkup) CLI, 137–146
database commands, 130–131
Database Control, 240–245
database creation
    with CLI, 117–118
    with dbaasapi tooling, 126–128
    pluggable databases, 273–277
    with REST services, 108
    starter database, 25–35
database deletion
    with CLI, 118
    with dbaasapi tooling, 128–129
    Delete Service modal, 75
database deployment, 34, 35, 73–87, 103
database ID, 33, 78
Database In-Memory option, 229
database instances. *See* cloud service
  instances
database operations
    ExaCS UI (OCI), 93–97
    ExaCS UI (OCI-C), 75–87
database recovery. *See also* restore
  operations
    with bkup CLI, 146
    container databases, 281–285

database recovery (*cont.*)
    ExaCS UI (OCI), 93–94
    ExaCS UI (OCI-C), 81–82
    latest command, 133
    in OCI-C, 81–82
    orec commands, 129, 133
    with REST services, 106–107
    restoring database (OCI), 93–94
    with RMAN, 281–285
    status of, 146
Database Resource Manager. *See* DBRM
Database Service Activity log, 79, 80
database type, 29
database workload, 54
Database-as-a-Service (DBaaS)
    instance, 247
databases
    bouncing, 130, 132, 282,
        288, 316
    cloning. *See* cloning
    connecting to via SQL Developer,
        240–246
    container. *See* CDBs
    creating. *See* database creation
    deleting. *See* database deletion
    features, 73–87
    lifecycle, 118
    managing with DBA panel, 250–251
    managing with EM Express, 240–246
    modifying with dbaasapi tooling,
        126–129
    modifying with dbaascli tooling,
        130–132
    moving. *See* migration
    name, 29, 50, 52, 144
    non-CDB, 296–311
    NoSQL, 183
    patching. *See* patches/patching
    pluggable. *See* PDBs
    recovering. *See* database recovery
    registering, 134
    replacing with backup, 77–79
    restoring. *See* restore operations
    snapshots of, 83–87

    standby, 33–34
    starting/stopping, 130
    status, 130
    system details, 50–52, 53, 55
    version, 29, 54
DBA panel, 250–251
DBaaS (Database-as-a-Service)
    instance, 247
dbaasapi tooling, 123–129
dbaascli tooling, 129–134
DBCS (Database as a Service console),
    26, 29, 35
dbhome commands, 129, 132
DBMCLI, 259
DBMS_COMPRESSION, 193–196
DBMS_SCHEDULER, 223
dbname, 134
DBRM (Database Resource Manager),
    203–224
    components, 203–204
    configuring, 207–214
    consumer groups, 204–206, 221, 222
    DBMS_SCHEDULER, 223
    demo, 214–218
    example, 204–206
    Intra-Database Resource Manager,
        218–223
    multitenancy and, 206–207
    overview, 203
    PDB resource plans, 207, 209–214
    prerequisites, 207–208
    resource plan directives, 204
    resource plans, 204, 207, 209–214
    setting limits on users/groups,
        218–222
    switching groups, 222–223
decryption method, 78
DELETE operation, 103
DHCP servers, 48
diagnostics, 265–268
digital cameras, 228
disk groups, 25, 235–236
disk redundancy, 52
disks, flash, 228–229

DMBS_COMPRESSION package, 193–196
DNS hostnames, 43
DNS label, 44–45, 48
DNS name, 92, 96
DNS resolution, 43, 48
DRAM cache, 230, 236
drives, flash, 228–229
DSS_CRITICAL_GROUP, 204
DSS_GROUP, 204
DSS_PLAN, 204

E

EF (Extreme Flash) Storage Servers, 149
egress rules, 45–46, 49, 139, 141
elastic command, 130–131
EM Console, 73
EM Express. *See* Enterprise Manager
    Express
email notifications, 28
endianness, 285
endpoint URI, 104, 105
endpoint-path, 104
Enterprise Manager Cloud Control, 251–259
    configuring hybrid gateway, 251–259
    considerations, 251
    ExaCLI, 259–268
    listing object/service details, 259–261
    managing/monitoring Exadata CS
        with, 261–263
Enterprise Manager Express (EM Express)
    considerations, 243, 245
    Database Control, 240–245
    managing monitoring Exadata CS
        with, 240–246
    overview, 243
    using with CDBs, 214–215
ETL_CRITICAL_PLAN, 204
ETL_GROUP, 204
ExaCLI, 259–268
ExaCLI examples, 263–268
ExaCS (Exadata Cloud Service)
    account details, 17–19
    activating account, 15, 16
    advantages, 2, 3, 7
    billing metrics, 17, 18
    CLIs. *See* CLI
    cloud account, 15–17, 24
    connecting to, 121–123
    connecting to via SQL Developer,
        246–250
    considerations, 2–3, 8
    creating in OCI, 35–55
    creating in OCI-C, 15–35
    Customize Dashboard, 16–17
    deleting service, 59, 90
    IP networks, 19–22
    local environment setup, 102
    logging in to, 15, 16
    managing/monitoring with DBA
        panel, 250–251
    managing/monitoring with EM Cloud
        Control, 261–263
    managing/monitoring with EM
        Express, 240–246
    migrating data/databases to. *See*
        migration
    overview, 1–8, 2–3
    query offloading, 152–154
    resource management. *See* resource
        management
    REST services, 102–120
    shapes, 4–6, 51
    Smart Scans, 154–165
    storage indexes, 153–154, 165–170
    user interface. *See* *ExaCS UI entries*
    versions, 4–6
    virtualization and, 6
ExaCS CLIs, 121–146
    connecting to ExaCS, 121–123
    dbaasapi tooling, 123–129
    dbaascli tooling, 129–134
ExaCS UI (OCI), 87–98
    backup operations, 93–95
    buttons, 88–90
    Data Guard associations, 96, 97
    database details/operations, 93–97
    database patching, 95, 98

ExaCS UI (OCI) (*cont.*)
  deleting service, 90
  managing tags, 90, 91
  node details/operations, 96–97
  overview, 87–88
  resources, 92–98
  restoring database, 93–94
  service details, 88–98
ExaCS UI (OCI-C), 58–87
  adding/removing OCPUs, 59–62
  Administration tab, 79, 80
  backup operations, 77–82
  console operations, 73–75
  database operations, 75–87
  database patching, 82–83
  deleting service, 59
  deploying database features, 73–87
  managing tags, 77, 78
  managing VM clusters, 70–72
  modifying, 58–72
  modifying firewalls, 62–69
  network details, 77
  overview, 58–87
  recovery operations, 81–82
  resources, 66, 76
  service details, 75–83
  sparse cloning/snapshots, 83–87
  viewing deployed databases, 73
Exadata Cloud at Customer model, 8
Exadata Cloud Service. *See* ExaCS
Exadata Database Machine
  architecture, 148–152
  configuring, 12–13
  considerations, 3
  database consolidation, 8
  hardware components, 149–150
  models/options, 10
  on-premises setup, 10–15
  options, 7–8
  pricing, 10
  query path on, 230
  securing, 13–15
  software components, 150–152
  software setup, 12–13

Exadata I/O Resource Manager (IORM), 74–75
Exadata Smart Flash Cache, 227–237
  CELL_FLASH_CACHE clause, 236–237
  Columnar Flash Caching, 236
  considerations, 236
  described, 229
  flash storage and, 228–229
  redo logs, 232
Exadata software, 152
Exadata Storage Server software, 152
Exadata Storage Servers, 149, 236
Exadata X2, 229
Exadata X5, 229
exadbcpatchmulti API, 135–137
exporting
  keys, 294, 296–297, 304–305
  schemas, 270–273
  tables, 270–273
  tablespaces, 290–291
extents, 172, 176, 177
external table feature, 156–159
Extreme Flash option, 229
Extreme Flash (EF) Storage Servers, 149

F

firewalls
  Database control and, 242
  modifying, 62–69
  ports, 122, 214, 242, 243
flash cache, 233, 234
flash cards, 228
flash disks/drives, 228–229, 234
flash log, 233
Flash Logging, 228, 231–232
flash storage, 228–229
flash volumes, 234, 235
floating IP address, 247
FORCE KEYSTORE clause, 296, 300, 304, 307
free space, 173, 174, 176

G

GET operation, 103
global cache, 229
GoldenGate service, 31
grid disk groups, 234
grid disks, 235
Grid Infrastructure, 29, 98, 150
groups
    adding users to, 42
    creating, 38, 39
    disk, 25, 235–236
    policies, 40–41
    security, 62–65

H

HC (High Capacity) Storage Servers, 149
HCC (Hybrid Columnar Compression),
    182–193
    considerations, 196
    long data types and, 196
    partitioned tables and, 188–189
    performance, 189–193
HCC compressed tables, 236
HCC tables, 185–186
High Capacity (HC) Storage Servers, 149
hostnames, 28, 34, 52
HTML files, 13
HTTP services, 103
HTTPS services, 103
Hybrid Columnar Compression. See HCC
hybrid gateway, 251–259

I

IaaS (Infrastructure as a Service), 207
ibkup parameter, 108–109
iDB (Intelligent Database protocol), 149
IDCS-based accounts, 104–110, 202
IDCS-based authentication, 202
IDM-based accounts, 104, 105
importing
    keys, 295, 300–301, 307–309
    schemas, 270–273

indexes
    segment creation with, 178
    storage, 153–154, 165–170
InfiniBand network, 149, 151
info command, 132
Infrastructure as a Service (IaaS), 207
ingress rules, 45–46, 49
in-memory cache, 236
Instance Caging, 224–226
instances. See also cloud service instances
    cloning, 86–87
    details about, 75, 76
Intelligent Database protocol (iDB), 149
interdatabase resource plan, 199
Intra-Database Resource Manager,
    218–223
I/O Resource Manager. See IORM
I/O resources, 74–75
IORM (I/O Resource Manager), 198–203
    options, 74–75
    REST APIs for, 103, 110
IP address prefix sets, 69
IP addresses
    cell, 262
    considerations, 122
    floating, 96, 247
    private, 96, 241, 243
    public, 96
    SCAN, 92
    viewing, 76
IP networks, 19–22, 241
IP subnet, 64
Isolated mode, 315–319

J

JSON payload, 108

K

key file name, 30
key ID, 297, 305
key value, 30

keys
API, 113, 114
creating, 30–31
exporting, 294, 296–297, 304–305
importing, 295, 300–301, 307–309
master, 134
passphrase, 31, 112
private, 31
public, 31, 73–74, 113

L

large objects (LOBs), 176
latest command, 133
LGWR (Log Writer), 232
license type, 52
list command, 133
LIST command, 259–261
listener commands, 129, 132–133
little-endian format, 285
LOBs (large objects), 176
Log Writer (LGWR), 232
logging/log files
Activity log, 79, 80
redo logs, 232
resetting, 284
Smart Flash Logging, 228, 231–232
long data types, 196

M

master key, 134
memory. *See also* cache
considerations, 25, 70
nodes, 25, 149
options for, 4, 5, 6, 10
metadata, 174
metrics, 265–268
migration, 269–320
with Data Pump, 270–277
move command, 130
moving non-CDB to PDB, 296–311
overview, 270
with pluggable databases. *See* PDBs

remote cloning PDBs/non-CDBs,
304–311
with RMAN, 277–285
TDE and, 270, 314–319
with transportable tablespaces,
285–293
using PDBs, 293–319
MODULE_NAME, 221
MODULE_NAME_ACTION, 221
move command, 130
multitenancy, 206–207

N

networks
backup, 13, 21, 25, 45
details about, 52, 54, 77
InfiniBand network, 149, 151
IP, 19–22, 241
OCI, 43–50
VCNs. *See* VCNs
virtual cloud network, 88, 92, 96
node clusters, 13, 14
node count, 51
node details/operations, 96–97
node operations, 104
nodes, 25, 149
non-CDB databases, 296–311
NoSQL databases, 183
NVM Express (NVMe) flash, 228
NVMe (NVM Express) flash, 228

O

OCI (Oracle Cloud Infrastructure)
creating ExaCS in, 35–55
creating ExaCS instances, 50–55
described, 2
ExaCS UI in. *See* ExaCS UI (OCI)
policy statements, 41–42
REST services in, 110–111
setting IORM in, 203
OCI CLI
configuring, 111–115
installing, 111

SDKs, 120
using, 115–120
OCI data centers, 3–4
OCI home page, 36–37
OCI networking, 43–50
OCI SDKs, 120
OCI-C (Oracle Cloud Infrastructure Classic)
creating ExaCS in, 15–35
creating ExaCS instances, 22–25
creating IP networks, 19–22
creating starter database, 25–35
ExaCS UI in. *See* ExaCS UI (OCI-C)
REST services in, 104–110
setting IORM in, 199–203
OCIDs (Oracle Cloud IDs), 111–112, 115–120
OCPUs (cores)
adding/removing, 59–62
bursting, 60–61
considerations, 24, 25
described, 59
scaling, 61, 89, 90, 120
OEDA (Oracle Exadata Deployment Assistant), 12–13, 15
OLTP (online transaction processing), 230, 232
OLTP workloads, 232
online transaction processing (OLTP), 230, 232
OPC (Oracle Public Cloud), 3
Oracle Advanced Compression, 179
Oracle cloud account, 15–17, 24
Oracle Cloud IDs (OCIDs), 111–112, 115–120
Oracle Cloud Infrastructure. *See* OCI
Oracle Cloud Infrastructure Classic. *See* OCI-C
Oracle Clusterware, 150
Oracle Database Server instances, 150
Oracle Database Server software, 150
Oracle E-Business Suite, 8
Oracle Exadata Deployment Assistant (OEDA), 12–13, 15
Oracle Grid Infrastructure, 150
Oracle home, 30, 85

Oracle Public Cloud (OPC), 3
Oracle recovery (orec) commands, 129, 133
Oracle Scheduler, 224
oracleHomeName parameter, 108
ORACLE_USER, 220
orec commands, 133
orec (Oracle recovery) commands, 129, 133
OTHER_GROUPS, 204
--OUTPUT TABLE PARAMETER, 115

P

partitioned tables, 181–182, 188–189
passphrase, 31, 112
passwords
administrators, 29–30, 54
backups, 139, 142, 143
changing, 130
considerations, 82
container owner, 32, 33
key export and, 294
Oracle Cloud account, 15
precautions, 157
requirements for, 30
"secret," 294
updating, 82
patches/patching
exadbcpatchmulti API, 135–137
with OCI CLI, 119–120
REST APIs for, 103, 109–110
patching databases, 82–83, 95, 98
PCI (Peripheral Component Interconnect), 228
PCI Express (PCIe), 228, 229
PCIe (PCI Express), 228, 229
PCTFREE parameter, 174, 175, 176
PDB unplug/plug in method, 293–296
PDBs (pluggable databases)
bouncing, 316
creating in CDBs, 273–277
importing keys into, 300–301, 307–309

PDBs (pluggable databases) (*cont.*)
    Instance Caging, 224–226
    Isolated mode, 315–319
    limiting CPUs for, 216, 217, 224–226
    migrating to cloud with, 293–319
    moving from one CDB to another, 319
    moving non-CDB to, 296–311
    multitenancy and, 206–207
    name, 29, 54
    performance profiles, 206, 211–214
    remote cloning, 304–311
    setting limits on users/groups,
       218–222
    setting parameters, 316–317
    showing status of, 284, 309, 313, 314
    United mode, 314, 315
    violations, 302, 303, 310, 311, 314
performance
    HCC, 189–193
    system resources and, 206, 211–214
Peripheral Component
   Interconnect (PCI), 228
permissions, 144
PFILE, 315–316
pitr command, 130
pluggable databases. *See* PDBs
policies, 40–41
policy statements, 41–42
ports
    Database Control and, 240–241
    ExaCS SCAN listener, 92
    firewall, 122, 214, 242, 243
    forwarding, 242, 243
    SSH tunneling and, 241–242
POST operation, 103
Predicate Filtering, 152–153
prereqs command, 134
private keys, 31
privileges, 207–208, 272
public keys, 31, 73–74, 113
purge command, 132
PUT operation, 103
PuTTY interface, 241–242
Python language, 120

Q

query offloading, 152–154
query optimization, 152–153
query predicates, 152–153

R

RACs (Real Application Clusters), 150
RAM cache, 236
RDS v3 (Reliable Datagram Sockets)
   protocol, 149
Real Application Clusters (RACs), 150
recovery. *See* database recovery
Recovery Manager (RMAN), 277–285
recycle bin, 297, 299, 305, 307
redo logs, 232
redo records, 232
regdb commands, 129, 134
regions, 37, 38
    selecting with Site selector, 66, 67
relational data, 196
Reliable Datagram Sockets (RDS v3)
   protocol, 149
remote cloning PDBs/non-CDBs, 304–311
report schema command, 283
reports, 17, 18
Representational State Transfer. *See* REST
resource consumer groups, 204–206,
   221, 222
resource management, 197–226
    Database Resource Manager. *See*
      DBRM
    Instance Caging, 224–226
    interdatabase resource plan, 199
    I/O Resource Manager, 198–203
resource plan directives, 204
resource plans
    CDB, 207, 211–214
    changing, 210–211, 224
    considerations, 225
    creating, 207–210
    examples of, 205–206
    interdatabase, 207

overview, 204
PDB, 207
pre-created, 204
using PDB performance profiles,
211–214
resources
details about, 66, 76
ExaCS UI (OCI), 92–98
ExaCS UI (OCI-C), 66, 76
managing. *See* resource management
performance profiles, 206, 211–214
restrictions, 42
types of, 42
REST APIs, 102, 103–104, 202, 203
REST servers, 102
REST services, 102–120
IORM, 200–203
in OCI, 110–111
in OCI-C, 104–110
REST (Representational State Transfer)
services, 102–120
restore operations. *See also* database
recovery
ExaCS UI (OCI), 93–94
ExaCS UI (OCI-C), 81–82
pitr command, 133
tables/tablespaces, 292
RMAN (Recovery Manager)
creating database backup, 277–278
database recovery, 281–285
exporting tablespaces with, 290–291
moving databases with, 277–285
restoring tablespaces with, 292
rotate masterkey command, 134
route tables, 47, 49, 138, 140
row chaining, 174
row data, 175, 177
row directory, 173, 174
row format, 175, 177
row header, 175
row migration, 174, 175
ROWID structure, 175
rows, 174
rules, security, 63–69

S

SATA (Serial AT Attachment), 228
SATA flash, 228
scaling OCPUs, 61, 89, 90, 120
SCAN DNS name, 92
SCAN IP addresses, 92
SCAN VIP, 96
schema import/export, 270–273
SCN (system change number), 133, 146,
232, 284
SCN command, 133
scp command, 270
SCSI/SAS interface, 228
security
Exadata Database Machine, 13–15
firewalls. *See* firewalls
passwords. *See* passwords
protocols, 67
security groups, 62–65
security lists, 45–49
security rules, 63–69
segments, 172, 176–179
Serial AT Attachment (SATA), 228
servers
cURL, 102
DHCP, 48
EF, 149
REST, 102
Service dashboard, 25, 35
service gateway, 138, 139, 141
service level, 29
SERVICE_MODULE, 221
SERVICE_MODULE_ACTION, 221
SERVICE_NAME, 220
SGA (System Global Area), 152, 232
single-level cell (SLC) flash, 229
Site selector, 66, 67
SLC (single-level cell) flash, 229
Smart Flash Cache. *See* Exadata Smart
Flash Cache
Smart Flash Logging, 228, 231–232
Smart Scans, 154–165
setting up, 154–159
using, 159–165

snapshots, 83–87, 104
software edition, 29, in 51
software keystore, 134
software release, 29
solid-state drives (SSDs), 228
sparse cloning, 83–87
sparse disk feature, 83–87
SPFILE, 315–316
SQL Developer, 246–251
    connecting to Exadata Cloud Service
      with, 246–250
    managing database with DBA panel,
      250–251
SQL*Plus, 150, 155
SSDs (solid-state drives), 228
SSH access, 73–74, 103
SSH connections, 241–242
SSH host, 247–248
SSH keys, 89, 90
SSH public key, 30, 52
SSH tunnels, 241–242, 246
sshkey parameter, 134
stage directory, 278–280
standby database, 33–34
start command
    database, 130
    listener, 133
status command
    database, 130
    listener, 130
    software keystore, 134
stop command
    database, 130
    listener, 132
storage cells, 149, 203, 259–268
storage containers, 32, 138–139
storage indexes, 153–154, 165–170
subnets, 47, 48–49, 52
Subscription slider, 60
Sun Flash Accelerator F20, 229
SwingBench tool, 207, 214, 216–218
SWITCH_CONSUMER_GROUP_FOR_
    SESS, 223
SWITCH_CONSUMER_GROUP_FOR_
    USER, 223

SWITCH_CURRENT_CONSUMER_
    GROUP, 223
SYS_GROUP, 204
system administrators. See administrators
system change number. See SCN
System Global Area (SGA), 152, 232

T

table directory, 173, 174
tables
    external, 156–159
    HCC, 185–186
    moving with Data Pump, 270–273
    partitioned, 181–182, 188–189
    restoring with RMAN, 292
tablespaces
    considerations, 176
    dependencies, 286, 290
    moving a single tablespace, 285–289
    moving to another platform, 290–293
    moving with backup sets, 290–293
    restoring with RMAN, 292
    transportable, 285–293
    violations, 286, 290
tags
    adding, 90, 91
    considerations, 28, 146
    managing, 77, 78
TDE (Transparent Data Encryption),
    270, 314–319
TDE commands, 129, 133–134
TDE keystore, 314–319
TDE wallet, 133, 270, 273, 288
TDE wallet location, 270, 300, 301, 308,
    317–318
temporary segments, 179
Tenant ID, 35–36
time zones, 146, 285
TNS entry, 303, 306, 310, 312, 314
tnsnames.ora file, 303, 306, 310, 312, 314
Transparent Data Encryption. See TDE
transportable tablespaces, 285–293
tunneling over SSH, 241–242

U

UI (user interface). *See ExaCS UI entries*
undo data/segments, 179
United mode, 314, 315
universal credits, 59, 61–62
Update Exadata IORM option, 74–75
URLs, 241, 242
user interface. *See ExaCS UI entries*
users
    adding to groups, 42
    creating, 38, 39
    details about, 38
UTC timestamp, 146

V

variable header, 173
VCNs (virtual cloud networks)
    backups and, 138
    considerations, 207
    modifying, 92
    OCI networking and, 43–49
virtual cloud networks. *See* VCNs
virtual machines. *See VM entries*
virtualization, 6
virtualized Network Interface Card (vNIC), 67

VM clusters
    details about, 24–25
    managing, 70–72
VM Subsetting feature, 71
VMs (virtual machines), 207
vNIC (virtualized Network Interface Card), 67

W

warehouse compression, 184, 185–186
WriteBack mode, 230–231
WriteThrough mode, 230–231

X

X5 Exadata Cloud Service, 4–5
X6 Exadata Cloud Service, 5
X7 Exadata Cloud Service, 6
XML files, 13, 294

Z

ZDLRA (Zero Data Loss Recovery Appliance), 12, 72
Zero Data Loss Recovery Appliance (ZDLRA), 12, 72
ZFS Storage Appliances, 196

Beta Test Oracle Software

Get a first look at our newest products and features—and help perfect them.

You must meet the following criteria:

✔ Licensed Oracle customer or
   Oracle PartnerNetwork member

✔ Oracle software expert

✔ Early adopter of Oracle products

Apply at: oracle.com/goto/beta

Join the World's Largest Developer Community

 Download the latest software, tools, and developer templates

 Get exclusive access to hands-on trainings and workshops

 Grow your network with the Developer Champion and Oracle ACE Programs

 Publish your technical articles—and get paid to share your expertise

ORACLE DEVELOPER COMMUNITY developer.oracle.com
Membership Is Free | Follow Us on Social:

🐦 **@OracleDevs**   📘 **facebook.com/OracleDevs**

Certification
MATTERS

72% Experienced a Greater Demand for Their Skills[1]

67% Said Certification was a Key Factor in Recent Raise[1]

64% Received Positive Impact on Professional Image[2]

Oracle University
Differentiate Yourself to Attract Employers

certification.oracle.com

Push a Button
Move Your Java Apps to the Oracle Cloud

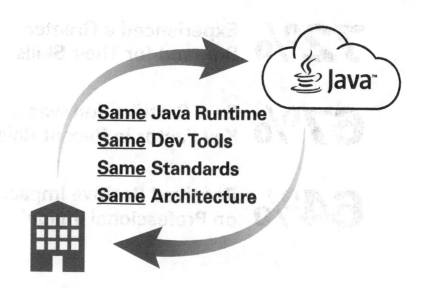

Same Java Runtime
Same Dev Tools
Same Standards
Same Architecture

... or Back to Your Data Center

Oracle Learning Library

Created by Oracle Experts
FREE for Oracle Users

- ✓ Vast array of learning aids
- ✓ Intuitive & powerful search
- ✓ Share content, events & saved searches
- ✓ Personalize your learning dashboard
- ✓ Find & register for training events

ORACLE®

oracle.com/oll

Don't Miss Out

ENGAGE WITH YOUR PEERS ON
THE PLATFORM OF YOUR CHOICE

ORACLE
MAGAZINE

Subscribers:
320,000+

Audience:
IT Managers, DBAs,
Programmers, and
Developers

PROFIT

Subscribers:
66,000+

Audience:
Top Executives and
Line of Business
Managers

Subscribers:
254,000+

Audience:
Developers,
Programmers,
and Architects

ORACLE®

For more information or to sign up for a FREE subscription:
Scan the QR code to visit Oracle Publishing online.